CATHOLICS OF CON

For as far back as school registers can take us
available to any Irish child was to be found outsic
traces, for the first time, the transnational education, careers, and lives of more
than two thousand Irish boys and girls who attended Catholic schools in England,
France, Belgium, and elsewhere in the second half of the nineteenth century. There
was a long tradition of Irish Anglicans, Protestants, and Catholics sending their
children abroad for the majority of their formative years. However, as the cultural
nationalism of the Irish revival took root at the end of the nineteenth century,
Irish Catholics who sent their children to school in Britain were accused of a pro-
Britishness that crystallized into still recognisable terms of insult such as West
Briton, Castle Catholic, Squireen, and Seoinín.

This concept has an enduring resonance in Ireland, but very few publications
have ever interrogated it. *Catholics of Consequence* endeavours to analyse the education and subsequent lives of the Irish children that received this type of transnational education. It also tells the story of elite education in Ireland, where schools
such as Clongowes Wood College and Castleknock College were rooted in the
continental Catholic tradition, but also looked to public schools in England as
exemplars. Taken together the book tells the story of an Irish Catholic elite at once
integrated and segregated within what was then the most powerful state in the
world.

Ciaran O'Neill is Ussher Lecturer in Nineteenth-Century History at Trinity
College Dublin. His interests are particularly focused on transnational and social
history, with a particular emphasis on connections shared between Ireland, Britain,
and both Imperial and European networks.

Catholics of Consequence

Transnational Education, Social Mobility, and the Irish Catholic Elite 1850–1900

CIARAN O'NEILL

OXFORD

UNIVERSITY PRESS

OXFORD
UNIVERSITY PRESS

Great Clarendon Street, Oxford, OX2 6DP,
United Kingdom

Oxford University Press is a department of the University of Oxford.
It furthers the University's objective of excellence in research, scholarship,
and education by publishing worldwide. Oxford is a registered trade mark of
Oxford University Press in the UK and in certain other countries

First published 2014
First published in paperback 2016

Published in the United States of America by Oxford University Press
198 Madison Avenue, New York, NY 10016, United States of America

British Library Cataloguing in Publication Data
Data available

Library of Congress Cataloging in Publication Data
Data available

ISBN 978–0–19–870771–4 (Hbk.)
ISBN 978–0–19–878373–2 (Pbk.)

Acknowledgements

This book has emerged slowly, from research conducted within three institutions, and was finally finished in a fourth. Along the way I have been lucky to have met some wonderful scholars, colleagues, and friends. In Galway, Mary Harris, Pete Morriss, and Mark Haugaard were all wonderful teachers. At Liverpool the staff and postgraduate community at the Institute of Irish Studies created a relaxed, supportive, and positive atmosphere in which to work. I am immensely grateful to Frank Shovlin, Diane Urquhart, the late Ian McKeane, Pat Nugent, Kevin Bean, Linda Christiansen, Dorothy Lynch, Viola Segeroth, Carmen Tunney-Harper, Cathy Davies, and Angela Duffy for their part in sustaining that. Niall Carson and Whitney Standlee read the manuscript in its entirety prior to publication and made many useful suggestions. My fellow postgraduate travellers, Jimmy Fennessy, Kati Nurmi, Paddy Hoey, and Anna Pilz were all major influences on this book as well as valued friends—as are John O'Shea, Serena Iervolino, and Roland Enmarch. At Oxford I gained much from conversations with Tim Wilson, Senia Pašeta, Gabriel Glickman, Mike Griffin, David O'Shaughnessy, Toby Barnard, James Golden, Mark Williams, Gemma Clark, Richard Ansell, and Marc Mulholland. In Dublin, my new colleagues and students at TCD have provided me with a platform to write, think, and teach, and I consider it a privilege to be able do so. There are three people to whom I owe more than mere thanks. Marianne Elliott was a source of unwavering support and encouragement as my PhD supervisor. Roy Foster had faith in my work at a vital moment, and James H. Murphy has questioned, cajoled, and inspired many aspects of this work—even its title.

My PhD research on the English schools was funded primarily by the 2007 award of a Travelling Studentship by the National University of Ireland, and I am pleased to have any opportunity to acknowledge its support. The British Association of Irish Studies has supported me (and many others) at early-career stage with postgraduate bursaries and I am happy to thank them. I will also take the opportunity to thank the many archives and libraries I have visited and, more particularly, the people I have met there. I thank the National Library of Ireland for their constant support of scholars. Elsewhere in Dublin I am grateful to the librarians and archivists of UCD, TCD, the Dublin Diocesan Archives, the Irish Jesuit Archives, and the Central Catholic Library of Ireland. During the course of this research project I impinged on many a school archivist. In Ireland, I thank the archivists of Clongowes Wood College, Blackrock College, Belvedere College, Loreto (St Stephen's Green), Castleknock College, and the Irish Jesuit Archives in Leeson St. In England, the English Benedictine Congregation facilitated research visits at three of their monasteries. At Downside Abbey I was ably assisted by Abbot Aidan Bellenger and Simon Johnson, at Ampleforth by Dom Anselm Cramer, and Douai by Abbot Geoffrey Scott. For the work on the English Jesuit schools I thank Anna Edwards and Fr Tom McCoog for access to the Archives of the British Province at Farm Street in Mayfair. At Stonyhurst I was made welcome by their excellent archivist David Knight. Sister Helen Forshaw was a pleasure to work with at the Archives of the Society of the Holy Child Jesus at Oxford. For help with particular aspects of the book I am grateful to Maurice Whitehead. At Oxford University Press, Cathryn Steele, Jeremy Langworthy, and Stephanie Ireland guided the MS to completion and were professional every step of the way. The manuscript benefited much from suggestions made by OUP's anonymous reviewers and I thank them for engaging so fully with my work. Finally, I take this opportunity to acknowledge the extraordinary generosity of Liam Chambers in sharing his work in progress on the Irish College, Paris. For their open-door policy in Dublin and London I thank Kieran Gordon, Colin Syron, and the Houstons, Brenda, David and Paul. For allowing me to write up parts of this book in beautiful Kuhmalahti I thank my Finnish family, Erkki, Merja, Kirsi, Lauri, Juho, and Helli.

My greatest debt is to my family, Liam, Áine, Caoimhe, and Cliodhna, who have been a constant source of encouragement and support, both individually and collectively. The book is dedicated, with much love, to Maija.

Contents

List of Figures, Tables, and Maps

FIGURES

TABLES

MAPS

List of Abbreviations

ABPSJ	Archives of the British Province of the Society of Jesus
ACA	Ampleforth College Archive
BCA	Blackrock College Archives
BL	British Library
BM	British Museum
DAA	Downside Abbey Archives
DIB	*Dictionary of Irish Biography*
DPhil	Doctoral Degree
EBC	English Benedictine Congregation
EHR	*English Historical Review*
HC	House of Commons sessional papers
HL	House of Lords sessional papers
IHS	Irish Historical Studies
IJA	Irish Jesuit Archives
NAI	National Archives of Ireland
NLI	National Library of Ireland
NHI	*New History of Ireland*
NUI	National University of Ireland
OSA	Oratory School Archives
PhD	Doctoral Degree
RIA	Royal Irish Academy
SCA	Stonyhurst College Archives
SHCJ	Society of the Holy Child Jesus
TCD	Trinity College Dublin
TNA	The National Archives of the UK
UCC	University College Cork
UCD	University College Dublin
UCDA	University College Dublin Archives

1

Introduction

The problem of where to school a child is one seldom based on simple criteria such as curriculum, teaching quality, or the door-to-door commute. Instead, a concerned parent dwells on a host of quantifiable and unquantifiable factors—from university progression rates to gender balance, sports facilities, school ethos, and reputation. Education is part of a calculated gamble parents take on the future of their children and as such is one of the most revealing social processes that a historian can analyse. This book will concern itself with just one aspect of this process as experienced by Irish children in the nineteenth century—Catholic elite education—but the conundrum of school selection is one that resonates elsewhere across space and time and its central concerns are universal wherever people have a choice presented to them.

One of the most divisive educational issues in modern societies is the link between private education and social class. There is a strong culture of elite education across most of central and Western Europe and there can be no real question as to its continued effectiveness in those areas: several recent reports both in the UK and Ireland have proven beyond even unreasonable doubt that an elite education continues to enhance the career trajectory and life-chances of those who avail of it.[1] In Ireland the existence of an upper tier in education is obscured somewhat by the fact that top-performing fee-charging schools are to a great degree subsidized by the state in the form of teacher salaries. Under British rule in the nineteenth century, provision of secondary or intermediate education had developed organically and with little or no state intervention. Post-independence an economically impoverished Irish state enabled a system of public–private partnership to develop in the south by simply awarding capitation grants to each school regardless of their entrance fee, a system that is still largely intact today, and one that means that Irish parents opting for a more exclusive education will usually opt for a school based in Ireland. State subsidy of elite education happens in some other EU states, Denmark for example, but it is still rather exceptional. An elite or high-status

---

[1] See Alan Milburn, *Fair Access to Professional Careers: A Progress Report* (London, 2012). For equality in Irish education see Vincent Greaney and Thomas Kellaghan, *Equality of Opportunity in Irish Schools: A Longitudinal Study of 500 Students* (Dublin, 1984); Christopher T. Whelan and Damian F. Hannan, 'Class Inequalities in Educational Attainment among the Adult Population in the Republic of Ireland', *The Economic and Social Review*, 30/3 (Jul. 1999), 302–3; Department of Education and Science, *DEIS (Delivering Equality of Opportunity for Irish Schools): An Action Plan for Educational Inclusion* (May, 2005).

education is as a consequence more affordable in Ireland than elsewhere, meaning that a greater spread of the middle class have access to top-performing schools if they so wish. To parents this might seem a particular boon; to the historian of education it is a peculiar anomaly.

R. V. Comerford has argued that the 'great constant' of history is the 'manoeuvring for survival and advancement of self and family through access to material resources and socio-political advantage'.[2] One of the most effective methods of doing this across most modern societies has been the provision of an education that is exclusive, expansive, and expensive. The decision to send one's child along this route is today sometimes considered ideologically problematic, depending as it does one's income level and ability to fund such an education. In the nineteenth century such a sensibility was very rare indeed, with an elite education seen to be a desirable goal for the aspiring middle class and a rite of passage for the wealthy. For most Irish parents, accessing a truly elite education in the nineteenth century required them to send their children away from home for most of their formative adolescent years, and at great expense. Hundreds of the wealthiest Irish families—Catholic and Protestant—opted for a transnational education for their children. This book is about why they chose to do so.

I ELITES AND TRANSNATIONAL EDUCATION

The potential effect of receiving an education 'elsewhere' is difficult to measure. In the study of contemporary elites and power relations the school as an institution has long transfixed social scientists as a mechanism for the reproduction of social values and social status within an existing (or aspirant) ruling caste.[3] Though much of the scholarship on the education of elites has thus far concentrated on the production or reproduction of elites within certain nation-states, recent studies have begun to see the need to expand beyond the boundaries of the nation and to take account of international or globalized forms of elite education. This has mostly applied to studies of the twentieth century but a very good case can be made for the global nature of nineteenth-century education, and this will be one of the central ideas throughout this book.[4] From the Irish perspective if we can take the history of elite education and further complicate it within a historical British–Irish colonial relationship, and still further by concentrating on the Catholic population in an acknowledged period of upward social mobility, then the potential for confusion is greatly increased.

This book will examine the provision and reception of elite education for Irish Catholics over a fifty-year span between 1850 and 1900. It will begin with a section on Irish elite education at home before exploring transnational aspects of

---

[2] R. V. Comerford, *Ireland* (London, 2003), 266.
[3] Pierre Bourdieu, *The State Nobility: Elite Schools in the Field of Power* (Stanford, 1996).
[4] See e.g. Julia Resnik (ed.), *The Production of Educational Knowledge in the Global Era* (Rotterdam, 2008).

Irish education in sections two and three. In looking elsewhere for education the Irish ought to be considered part of a much wider transnational phenomenon of strategic educational migration. Christina de Bellaigue has noted that English girls were often sent to boarding schools in France in the nineteenth century, but very few travelled in the other direction. Wealthy Spanish merchants were happy to send their children to London schools in the nineteenth century, and the nouveaux riches of the New World proved equally willing to lavish their money on elite schools across Northern and Central Europe in order to add much-needed cultural capital to their new-found riches.[5] Finnish and Norwegian elites availed of schools and universities in Copenhagen and Stockholm for much the same reason. Swedish medical students flocked to Paris, as did Serbian intellectuals.[6] The motivation behind such investment was not always academic. Rather it was about acquiring an international education of high quality and high status, as well as gaining valuable experience of the core in order to position oneself in the periphery.

Traditional European forms of intermediate education involved the provision of a classical humanistic schooling that would effectively control a narrow gateway to higher social and occupational categories. In practice this meant that access to institutions that could provide such an education was restricted to the narrow social group that could afford it. The work of Fritz K. Ringer and others has shown that the training of national elites was a concern across many European societies in the nineteenth century.[7] More recently Robert Anderson has shown how from the 1840s the major European polities began to seek ways to separate and expand publicly funded schools from the classical models which preceded them. The result was a great deal of intercultural borrowing and the remodelling of education to cater for an expanding bourgeoisie and rapid industrialization and urbanization.[8] Almost all of these reforms were aimed at the middle to lower segments of society, meaning that many elite schools—from gymnasium, lycée, to public school—were unaffected by such modernizing forces for much of the century. The cultural pay-off of attending any such elite school remained the same despite the apparent democratization of access to secondary education. Furthermore, and almost as a badge of pride, the curriculum at elite schools remained rooted in classical humanist subject matter, thus differentiating it still further from the modern

---

[5] Christina de Bellaigue, *Educating Women: Schooling and Identity in England and France 1800–1867* (Oxford, 2007); Bernardo Rodriguez Capparrini, 'Alumnos Españoles en el Internado Jesuita de Beaumont (Old Windsor, Inglaterra), 1861–1868', *Archivum Historicum Societatis Iesu*, 76/151 (Jan.–Jun. 2007), 3–38.

[6] Stephan Curtis, 'Swedish in Name Only: The International Education of Nineteenth-century Swedish Medical Students and Practitioners', *History Of Science*, 50/3 (Sep. 2012), 257–88; Ljubinka Trgovčević-Mitrović, 'Les Boursiers serbes en France de 1878–1914', *Revue d'Europe Centrale*, 7/1 (1999), 45–57. See also Agnes Bernard et al., *L'Enseignement des elites en Europe centrale: 19–20e siècles* (Krakow, 1999).

[7] Fritz K. Ringer, 'The Education of Elites in Modern Europe', *History of Education Quarterly*, 18/2 (Summer, 1978), 159–72; Lenore O'Boyle, 'The Problem of an Excess of Educated Men in Western Europe, 1800–1850', *The Journal of Modern History*, 42/4 (Dec. 1970), 471–95.

[8] R. D. Anderson, 'The Idea of the Secondary School in Nineteenth-century Europe', *Paedagogica Historica*, 40/1–2 (2004), 93–106.

secular model. For Irish families a nineteenth-century boarding school education in Britain or on the Continent remained an important signifier of elite status and in fact provided something equivalent to the eighteenth-century 'Grand Tour' experience. It involved immersion in a foreign culture, fluency in other languages, and the sort of expensively procured exoticism that now sends wealthy children away on gap-year adventures.

The structure of this book will itself reflect a transnational approach, matching the directional flow of Irish children in their late childhood or early teens from Irish schools to English, French, or Belgian alternatives and then (usually) back to Ireland in adulthood. This horseshoe pattern of adolescent movement can hardly be said to constitute a long-term migration, but it is likely to have made a signifi-cant impact on children who were very often as young as ten or eleven years old when sent a considerable distance from home, and placed in a boarding school that may have had as many as ten or twelve different nationalities in the student body. Utilizing a transnational approach allows the historian to 'track more mobile seg-ments of the population to differently governed locales' and therefore is cognizant of the importance of national boundaries while showing the same indifference to them as borders of containment as did the migrants being studied. The possibili-ties of such an approach are particularly exciting for Irish historiography, which has tended to take the nation as its focus for much of its professional period. Transnational history, by shifting the emphasis from 'national histories or a chroni-cle of inter-state affairs', to one of 'transnational connections and circulations, by people, goods, capital, ideas and tastes', promises to take those interested in Irish history beyond what Enda Delaney has recently characterized as an 'island story'.[9]

Such an approach has limitations, both in a general sense and in an Irish con-text, but the most pressing one for those enthused by it is that the transnational field has become self-referential and too heavily theorized.[10] It is hoped to avoid the worst excesses of this by rooting the analysis of this strategic migration in straightforward archival research. To facilitate this process a prosopographical methodology has been used in this study—essentially a historical approach which involves the compilation of multiple biographies in order to establish some pat-terns within that particular group. In this case, the prosopography is composed of a database of 2,739 Irish boys and girls at school outside Ireland in the second half of the nineteenth century. Of that total figure a central body of 1,303 were Irish boys attending four of the most prestigious Catholic schools in England. This core group is further complemented by a prosopography of 203 Irish girls at an English convent boarding school near Hastings on the south coast of England, also derived from archival research. To this original research will be added an analysis

---

[9] Akira Iriye and Pierre-Yves Saunier (eds), *The Palgrave Dictionary of Transnational History* (Basingstoke, 2009); Enda Delaney, 'Our Island Story? Towards a Transnational History of Late Modern Ireland', *Irish Historical Studies*, 37/148 (Nov. 2011), 599–621.

[10] For more on the limits of transnational history see C. A. Bayly et al., 'AHR Conversation: On Transnational History', *The American Historical Review*, 111/5 (Dec. 2006), 1441–64; Ian Tyrell, 'Making Nations/Making States: American Historians in the Context of Empire', *The Journal of American History*, 86/3 (Dec. 1999), 1015–44.

of the 1,233 boys attending the Irish College in Paris in the same period. This last addition is made possible by the extraordinary database generated by Dr Liam Chambers from the registers of the college, now housed at the Centre Culturel Irlandais in Paris. It is hoped that the information we have on this cohort of 2,739 Irish boys and girls will give us, for the first time, a greater insight into the lives of those availing of superior education outside Ireland in the second half of the century as well as a rare glimpse at the Irish Catholic elite in gestation and during a half-century of relative calm in Irish society.

The work of scholars such as Pierre Bourdieu and Michel Foucault on the relationship between knowledge, institutions, and power has naturally affected this work, as has the practical application of sociological techniques affected the structure of the book without directing it. It takes for granted that concepts such as habitus, social capital, and cultural capital are widely accepted and in regular use in relation to education, becoming a dominant theoretical foundation and analytical tool to study the 'manifestation of social inequality in educational processes and outcomes'.[11] Present-day debates on the relationship of elites to education often centre on the precise meaning and value of an international education to circulating elite groups with a high level of mobility. Anne-Catherine Wagner has argued for the concept of 'international capital' as a way to understand the transactional gain of a global education for modern elites, but this idea may certainly be applied to historical elites as well.[12] An international education displayed an identification with something larger than what was merely local, as well as proving a certain level of economic capacity beyond the reach of the vast majority of the general population. The methodology pursued in this book may be primarily based on an empirical and prosopographical approach, but it is squarely rooted in theories of power and elites, and related concepts such as cultural capital, international capital, and cosmopolitanism.

Defining an Irish elite, and then an Irish Catholic elite, has proven somewhat problematic. The term is commonly used but has never been adequately defined, partly because so many of those we could include in it were so well integrated into a pan-British and Irish elite in the nineteenth century. Most restrictions on Catholic social mobility had been removed in a strictly legal sense by Reform Acts in the late eighteenth century and again by the passing of Catholic Emancipation measures in 1829. This meant that the only significant restrictions on Catholic social mobility from 1829 onwards were social and cultural, but these were nonetheless powerful ones and demonstrably effective. Because of this, Catholic-blocked mobility was evident in the Irish establishment throughout the nineteenth century,

---

[11] Rachelle Winkle-Wagner, 'Foundations of Educational Inequality: Cultural Capital and Social Reproduction', *ASHE Higher Education Report*, 36/1 (May, 2010), 1–21 at 2; See also Mads Meier Jæger, 'Equal Access but Unequal Outcomes: Cultural Capital and Educational Choice in a Meritocratic Society', *Social Forces*, 87/4 (2009), 1943–71.

[12] Anne-Catherine Wagner, 'L'Internationalisation de la formation des élites: vers une recomposition des classes dirigeantes?', in Mihai Dinu Gheorghiu (ed.), *La Mobilité des élites: reconversions et circulation internationale. Bilans et réflexions sur les possibilités de recherches comparatives Nord – Sud et Est – Ouest* (Iasi, 2011), 79–96.

and as a result Irish historians have generally conceived of the Catholic elite as a middle-class rival elite which came to prominence in the closing decades of the century.[13] This is the picture given to us by Senia Pašeta, Tom Garvin, and John Hutchinson over the past thirty years, and recently reinforced by Fergus Campbell in *The Irish Establishment* (2009). This book certainly aims to revise that picture by identifying a Catholic elite composed of people who were highly integrated into the governing structure of Ireland at all levels—local and national—as landlords, professionals, businessmen, county officers, civil servants, or member of religious orders. The reason for separating them out from the British elite is attractive precisely because they were something of an aberration in a Protestant state and along with the Presbyterian elites of Scotland and the north-east of Ireland the only identifiable group operating within the British state with clearly defined alternative goals and loyalties. Members of these elites could and did mingle, but each retained a distinctive culture which betrayed that in the nineteenth century religion and religious freedom mattered just as much and often more than any republican ideal of a pluralist nation.[14]

Scholars of elites in Britain, France, and America have long accepted the importance of higher education to both the reproduction of existing elite groups, and its role in facilitating the infiltration of the middle classes to positions of power in the second half of the nineteenth century. This took different forms in different nations and polities. In France, Christophe Charle has recently argued that the percolation of a legal elite or a *noblesse de robe* in nineteenth-century France was greatly facilitated by a legal training which operated as an effective cartel.[15] In the Grande-Écoles and the law faculties of Paris the presence of a few non-representative students and *professeurs* from a lower middle-class background did not effectively threaten the stability of elite groups. In a more 'traditional' society such as England, the public school system has long been accepted as a mechanism by which elite groups retain power down to the present day. This is accomplished rather simply—by controlling entry by either charging prohibitive fees and/or utilizing an interview process—thus restricting access into what has been the favoured recruiting ground for the most prestigious legal, academic, political, and military institutions for several centuries. The question in the Irish case is not then one of exceptional development but rather one of particular manifestation. Should we see the willingness of Irish Catholic and Protestant families to pursue overseas education as typical core–periphery colonial dynamics or were they simply acting rationally by utilizing available and rather obvious resources to improve the life-chances of their children?

A further complication is that Ireland was not straightforwardly separate from the educational market in Britain, or more particularly that of England. When

---

[13] See Ciaran O'Neill, 'Introduction', *Irish Elites in the Nineteenth Century* (Dublin, 2013).

[14] David W. Miller discusses this in an eighteenth-century context in 'Irish Christianity and Revolution', in Jim Smyth (ed.), *Revolution, Counter-revolution and Union: Ireland in the 1790s* (Cambridge, 2000).

[15] Christophe Charle, 'Elite Formation in Late Nineteenth Century: France Compared to Britain and Germany', *Historical Social Research*, 33/2 (2008), 249–61.

an Irish boy or girl was educated in an English school they were not travelling to a radically different jurisdiction in a political or legal sense, but there is plenty of evidence to support the idea that they entered an environment where they were considered different to their peers, and that in most cases they proudly declared themselves to be so. The only point at which this educational migration pattern became strictly transnational in a technical sense was therefore in the minority of cases where Irish children attended schools on the Continent or further afield. Choosing to use the term transnational in preference to the somewhat fussier 'transregional' is therefore a conscious decision. By doing so I aim to recognize the idea that the union of Great Britain and Ireland may be considered to have comprised at least three or four imagined 'nations' that were recognized as distinct from each other by the majority of those inhabiting them in the period examined.

This strategic migration to England was divided along denominational lines, reflecting the division of Protestant and Catholic on both islands. Catholic boys and girls were unlikely to endanger their faith or reputation by attending one of the 'great' English public schools such as Harrow or Eton, or any of the relatively small Anglican schools for girls. Instead they went to the nearest acceptable alternative, an expensive and remote Catholic school in England, or on the Continent. This religious divide was evident across all social strata in Ireland but was particularly pronounced at the highest levels, where the various strands of the Protestant and Catholic gentry, intelligentsia, and the rising business elite appeared to form homogenous and opposing blocs as the nineteenth century progressed. This divergence was particularly marked in the south of Ireland, where Catholics enjoyed at least some of the distribution of resources and wealth. This competition was less marked in the northern half of the island, as Catholic wealth simply did not develop on the same scale or at the same rate as in the south in the nineteenth century. Although these denominational 'blocs' competed directly, it was arguably that very competition that defined and legitimated their high positions in society. Today, in much the same way, graduates of elite universities like Oxford and Cambridge or Harvard and Yale might affect or project inter-institutional rivalry and competition without seeming, to the outside world, to have experienced a very different educational experience. Taken this way the fact that both Protestant and Catholic Irish elites appear at English public schools in the nineteenth century is further evidence of a semi-conscious reciprocity. This dynamic was evident in the development of parallel education systems at home. Despite repeated attempts to encourage non-denominational education the system that emerged in Ireland of the nineteenth century was, as F. S. L. Lyons so memorably put it, 'inexorably denominational'.[16]

In most respects the education of both Catholic and Protestant elites in Ireland was identical, in that it involved travelling considerable distance and paying restrictive fees to receive a very similar education to that they might have received at home for much less trouble. Take, for example, General Sir Hubert Gough,

---

[16] F. S. L. Lyons, *Ireland Since the Famine*, 11th edn (London, 1989), 91.

an Irish Protestant born in 1870 and educated first at Eton before graduating to Sandhurst and eventually commanding the British Fifth Army in World War I. Sir Hubert (full name Hubert de la Poer Gough) later wrote an autobiography that was defensive for several reasons, not least his many alleged deficiencies as a military commander in Flanders.[17] His autobiography is really a study of his con-flicted loyalties in a time when Irish identity was being redefined. 'In upbringing', Sir Hubert wrote, 'I am an example of so many other people brought up in one country and taught to love it and be proud of it, but educated in another country and taught to love that, and to be proud of it as well.' Gough's experience fur-ther illuminates our complicated subject when he reveals that his mother, Harriett Anastasia de la Poer, was a Protestant daughter of a (mostly) Catholic family in Waterford.[18] His first cousins, therefore, were all Catholic by custom and though that altered much about their relationship it did not preclude a near-identical transnational schooling. His Catholic de la Poer cousins had also attended a pub-lic school in England—the exclusive Catholic Oratory School in Birmingham, run under the management of John Henry Newman—which had been set up to cater for those who wished to have a Catholic version of the Eton experience. 'I have always thought that the patriotism which at one time was universally held in these islands', Gough continued, 'is only strengthened here by various minor allegiances... I am, for one thing, a firm supporter of the Old School Tie.'[19] Gough reveals himself as a conflicted memoirist of the type we have become accustomed to in Irish history and letters—comfortable and successful in both England and Ireland, but uncomfortable and defensive when trying to explain to others how that was so.

II THE IRISH EDUCATION SYSTEM(S)

Not only was Irish education in the nineteenth century characterized by religious division, it was also typically a truncated, unsatisfying experience for many of those who went through it. The largest provider of education from the 1740s onward was always the hedge school, a pre-industrial form of community-based education provided by a transient and insecure class of teachers who were usually recruited and loosely line-managed by the parish priest.[20] Some valuable work has been done on these schools, which were not always salubrious establishments. One inspector in 1824 noted that a school he had reviewed in the diocese of Kildare and Leighlin

---

[17] The main source for those interested in Protestant educational migration in the nineteenth cen-tury is Kieran Flanagan, 'The Rise and Fall of the Celtic Ineligible: Competitive Examinations for the Irish and Indian Civil Services in Relation to the Educational and Occupational Structure of Ireland, 1853–1921', 2 vols. (DPhil, University of Sussex, 1977).

[18] Harriet's mother was Frances Power, also a Protestant, a daughter of Sir John Power of Kilfane. Religion was very often divided by gender in mixed marriages in this period.

[19] General Sir Hubert Gough, *Soldiering On* (London, 1954), 15.

[20] Louis M. Cullen, 'Merriman in a World of Schoolmasters', *Eighteenth-century Ireland*, 26 (2011), 80–94.

was covered by a roof that 'was neither thatched nor slated but covered with bog sods and clay'. The students sat on seats of stone in this school that stood on the 'droop of a hill' and when rain fell it passed 'copiously through the roof'.[21] In rural areas such structures were erected by the local farmers for the rudimentary education required by children soon to be distracted from lessons by a full quotient of manual labour. In towns, this form of free-market school was pervasive across Ireland and varied in quality from excellent to awful. The National Schools gradually replaced these hedge schools across much of rural Leinster, Munster, and Ulster, though education in Connacht was somewhat retarded by a combination of episcopal resistance to the state system and a demonstrable regional bias in state funding for building schools in Ulster and north Leinster between 1835 and 1850.[22] Nonetheless by the mid 1840s the Commissioners of National Education had managed to create or refurbish over 2,000 schools, catering for more than a quarter of a million children however variable their attendance.[23] This state-funded primary-level education delivered a more structured system to Irish children from 1831, improving literacy from an already relatively impressive base. The state system was an experimental one, recently characterized by one historian as having been designed to elevate the masses in Ireland, without quite raising them up 'above their station'.[24] This system resulted in a bottom-heavy education system, where the numbers recorded at primary level dwarfed those receiving an intermediate education throughout the century.

Formal education typically cut off for most Irish children between ten and fourteen years of age. This pattern was common across all modernizing societies and in Ireland the number of children engaged in full-time secondary or intermediate level education was miniscule at less than 1 per cent of the population. At intermediate level the 'free-market' approach was to last much longer, with widespread partial state funding appearing in 1878, and free secondary education much later in 1967–8.

In 1861 there were just over 22,000 children in some form of secondary education in Ireland with the number rising to 35,000 by 1901 (Table 1.1), the increase being almost exclusively the result of increasing numbers of Catholics entering the system after the regularization of partial state funding in 1878. The Intermediate Act resulted in an overall rise of almost 40 per cent in numbers attending intermediate schools nationwide, a figure that compared well with other European nations such as France and Belgium—which both experienced an increase of 43 and 53 per cent respectively in the same period.[25] For a more complete picture of Irish

---

[21] Quoted in Martin Brenan, *Schools of Kildare and Leighlin A.D. 1775–1835* (Dublin, 1935), 475.

[22] See Kevin Lougheed, 'National Education and Empire: Ireland and the Geography of the National Education System', in David Dickson, Justyna Pyz, and Christopher Shepard (eds), *Irish Classrooms and the British Empire: Imperial Contexts in the Origins of Modern Education* (Dublin, 2012), 5–17.

[23] John Coolahan, 'The Daring First Decade of the National Board of Education 1831–1841', *Irish Journal of Education*, 17/1 (Summer, 1983), 33–54 at 51.

[24] Michael C. Coleman, *American Indians, the Irish, and Government Schooling* (Nebraska, 2007), 267.

[25] Brian Redmond Mitchell, *European Historical Statistics 1750–1975*, 2nd edn (London, 1981), 786–806.

Table 1.1 Total number of 'superior' (intermediate) schools, and students in Ireland by denomination, 1861–1901*

	Total Schools	RC (Total)	COI (Total)	Presbyterian (Total)	Methodist (Total)	All other (Total)	Total
1861	729	10,679 (49%)	7,677 (35%)	3,300** (15%)	–	–	21,674
1871	574	10,968 (52%)	6,563 (31%)	3,694** (17%)	–	–	21,225
1881	488	10,145 (50%)	6,490 (32%)	2,357 (12%)	589 (3%)	824 (4%)	20,405
1891	475	13,772 (57%)	6,234 (26%)	2,737 (11%)	701 (3%)	827 (3%)	24,271
1901	490	23,897 (68%)	6,433 (18%)	3,187 (9%)	923 (3%)	866 (2%)	35,306

* This table was compiled by Kieran Flanagan, 'The Rise and Fall of the Celtic Ineligible', p. 61. Some caution ought to be taken with the census description of 'Superior Schools', which amounted to a category including any school where a foreign language was taught. With this in mind it is likely that the true number receiving anything like a five-year intermediate education was significantly lower.

** For 1861 and 1871 minority denominations were grouped with Presbyterians.

education we ought to add the 1,500 to 2,000 Irish boys being educated outside Ireland, plus an unknown but likely smaller number of girls also being educated outside Ireland. This figure was split unevenly between Protestant and Catholic elite families, but was drawn from the wealthiest and most influential of both sects.

Throughout the nineteenth century up to three times as many Protestants as Catholics pursued an elite education outside Ireland. The more prestigious Protestant schools clustered in the north-east of Ireland and in Dublin, but Protestant elite schooling as a whole was somewhat underdeveloped.[26] Despite the existence of a network of endowed schools, some dating back to the sixteenth century and nominally under the control of the Commissioners of Education from 1813, Protestant middle- and upper-class education had foundered amidst rampant corruption and bad governance since the late eighteenth century.[27] Low numbers and the perception of poor management considerably hampered the reputation of these endowed schools. The most recognizably elite school for Protestants in Ireland was St Columba's College in Dublin—a Protestant patriot project set up under William Sewell in the 1840s with the intention of creating 'something more than a Winchester or Eton' in Ireland.[28] The school amassed enormous debts and was on the verge of folding before Sewell left to set up Radley

[26] For work on Protestant elite schooling see Flanagan, 'The Rise and Fall of the Celtic Ineligible'; 'The Shaping of Irish Anglican Secondary Schools, 1854–1878', *History of Education*, 13/1 (1984), 27–43.

[27] These endowed schools included the Erasmus Smith schools, the Diocesan Free schools, and the Royal Grammar schools. See Christopher F. McCormack, 'The Endowed Schools Commissions 1791–1894, as Mediators of Superior Schooling in Ireland' (PhD, UCD, 2010)

[28] Christopher Hibbert, *No Ordinary Place: Radley College and the Public School System* (London, 1997), 18; Justyna Pyz, 'St Columba's College: An Irish School in the Age of Empire', in David

College in 1847, just outside the city of Oxford. Contemporary critics estimated the figure of Irish Protestants being schooled in England at in excess of 1,300 per annum in the 1880s.[29] This was a continuation of a much longer tradition of elite landed families sending their sons to English public schools. R. B. McDowell noted that in the second half of the eighteenth century over 250 Protestant Irish boys had attended Eton and Harrow alone, and other established schools show a similar pattern stretching back to their foundation in the sixteenth and seventeenth century.[30] Ian D'Alton has shown how debilitating this was felt to be on a local level in Protestant Cork earlier in the century. A sense of outrage and affront at this privileging of English education prompted several middle-class Protestants to set up Cork Grammar School to try to reverse the pattern, though that goal was never fully realized.[31] With the majority of wealthy Protestant families sending their children to England for their education in the nineteenth century, St Columba's remained the only Irish Protestant public school in what was a stagnant domestic market made to seem provincial and undesirable by the global reputation of English public schools.

Catholic intermediate education also developed slowly in Ireland. Large numbers of Catholic families had been sending their sons and daughters to the Continent since the 1590s, though of course monastic links between both islands and Europe long predated this period.[32] Restrictive penal legislation meant that from the early eighteenth century the education of the majority Catholic population in boarding schools in Ireland was prohibited. This meant that many Catholic gentry families sent their children to a network of schools across the Spanish Netherlands, France, and Spain where they were educated alongside the sons and daughters of English and Scottish families suffering under the same legislation. This Continental tradition of Catholic education disintegrated around the time of the French 'Terror' 1793–5, just as the penal laws were relaxed in Britain and Ireland, and the bulk of the exiled English and Scottish Catholic communities relocated to new foundations in England, retaining their three-kingdom clientele for the rest of the nineteenth century. From this point onwards the bulk of Irish Catholic boys who left the country for their education were schooled in England at the successor institutions of these same Continental colleges in what was effectively an unbroken

---

Dickson, Justyna Pyz, and Christopher Shepard (eds), *Irish Classrooms and British Empire: Imperial Contexts in the Origins of Modern Education* (Dublin, 2012).

[29] Maurice C. Hime, 'Home Education, or Irish Versus English Grammar Schools for Irish Boys' (London, 1887), 2–3; *'Intermediate Schools in Ireland'* (London, 1887); Frederick R. Falkiner, 'The Irish Schoolboy Exodus and the Educational Endowments Act', Dublin University Review, 1/11 (Dec. 1885).

[30] R. B. McDowell, *Ireland in the Age of Imperialism and Revolution, 1760–1801* (London, 1979), 147. I am grateful to Mary Hatfield for pointing out an unpublished overview of Irish schooling in England in M. C. M. Davis, 'The Upbringing of Children in Ireland 1700–1831 from Visual and Historical Sources', 2 vols. (MLitt, TCD, 1992), 137–80.

[31] See Ian D'Alton, 'Educating for Ireland? The Urban Protestant Elite and the Early Years of Cork Grammar School, 1880–1914', *Éire-Ireland*, 46/3–4 (Fall/Winter, 2011), 201–66.

[32] See Jane Ohlmeyer, *Making Ireland English: The Irish Aristocracy in the Seventeenth Century* (New Haven, CT, 2012), 433–5; R. Po-Chia Hsia, *The World of Catholic Renewal, 1540–1770*, 2nd edn (Cambridge, 2005), 89.

tradition. For girls the pattern was different, and the lure of a Continental education proved a stronger draw for a variety of reasons—not least of which was how fashionable it was among English girls throughout the century. The education received by these children differed little in content from that available at home. This strategic educational migration pattern continued in Ireland in reduced form long after independence into the 1950s and 1960s when the disparity in fees charged for private education in England and at home became unbearable for all but the wealthiest families. Cormac O'Malley, son of the republican rebel Ernie O'Malley, attended Ampleforth College in York in the 1950s, and John Harrison remembered being called a 'bog-man' by his contemporaries at Stonyhurst at about the same time.[33] Back in the nineteenth century the aspirational attitudes of those Catholics sending their children to English schools did not always endear them to their less wealthy co-religionists—who could count the majority of the secular clergy amongst their number. Most of the Catholic Bishops of Ireland were drawn from the rural middle-class, and thought little of the practice of sending a child to England for their schooling. Something of that disapproval can be seen in a letter sent by Paul Cullen (later Archbishop of Dublin) to his good friend Thomas Kirby in Rome. Cullen visited Oscott College in Birmingham in 1842 and found a student body that was 'mostly Irish'. Unimpressed by this, Cullen observed that 'the Irish are so long accustomed to stoop to Englishmen, that they look up to everything in England as superior to what they have at home. If the same establishment was in Ireland', he mused, 'it [would] be considered as nothing—certainly no John Bull [would] send his children over there for education.'[34]

The second half of the nineteenth century represented the high-water mark of school-based migration from Ireland to schools in England and across Western Europe. Back at home in Ireland the list of schools providing a similarly exclusive education was much smaller. For Catholic boys there were no more than four socially exclusive boarding schools. Two of these were run by the Jesuits, Clongowes Wood College in Co. Kildare and St Stanislaus College, Tullabeg, Co. Offaly. The third was run by the Vincentians, Castleknock College west of Dublin, and the fourth by the Holy Ghost Fathers, Blackrock College, which was situated by the coast south of Dublin city. For Protestant boys, there was only one: St Columba's in Rathfarnham. A wealthy Catholic girl would have had even less choice, but might have attended the Loreto Convent in Rathfarnham, the Sacred Heart Convent at Mount Anville, the Laurel Hill Convent in Limerick, or the various Ursuline, Loreto, or Sacred Heart convents which equalled it in reputation. A Protestant girl was as likely as her brothers to attend a school in England, but for those that remained there was a similarly limited choice outside some well-known day-schools in Dublin such as Alexandra College. For Irish schools deliberately

[33] 'John Harrison remembers his time as an Irish rebel at an English public school', *Irish Times*, 9 Apr. 1996.
[34] Archives of the Pontifical Irish College Rome, Kirby Papers, Cullen to Kirby, 4 Jul. 1842, #100. Formerly available at <http://www.cflr.beniculturali.it/Patrimonio/IstitutiCulturali/cpi_new/serie/index_serie.htm>.

targeting the children of the wealthy, the main rivals were overseas, in England and, to a lesser extent, France and the Low Countries. Elite education in Ireland in 1850 was therefore a transnational affair, but its capacity for personal and economic transfiguration was no less remarkable then than it is now. Wherever an Irish child learned their lessons in the nineteenth century it could be argued that they were receiving a transnational education. Even those unlucky enough to learn those lessons in the discomfort of a 'hedge school' early in the century were learning Latin, Hebrew, and Greek in places as far away from the metropole as rural Kerry.[35]

This book, however, is not concerned with lower middle-class or working-class access to secondary education, though it will happily acknowledge the need for more work to be done on it. Instead, it will concentrate on the provision of elite education and, to a lesser extent, the demand for replication of it at newer bourgeois institutions that characterized the second half of the nineteenth century, a moment in which it seemed it was the desire of most aspirational middle-class parents to send their children to boarding schools with a strong central ethos and even stronger capacity to socialize.[36] That this type of education has thus far escaped the attention of Irish historians is partly a product of the primacy of the nation-state as a conceptual lens, and partly because of the character of histories of Irish education more generally.

III THE EDUCATION QUESTION(S) AND THE MURDER MACHINE

Much of Irish educational history has dwelt on state commissions, legislation, and denominational funding to the exclusion of the social and cultural effects of schooling on children. The historian Joseph Lee bemoaned as early as 1973 the fact that education has long been relegated by Irish historians to nothing much more than 'a branch of the diplomatic history of church–state relations' in the long nineteenth century.[37] This contest was a protracted affair, a tussle between a state system that had a recognizable agenda of secular liberal reform and a Catholic clergy bent on extending and protecting their market share of the education of the majority. It is true that from 1850 onwards the Catholic hierarchy became more vocal on the issue of education and under Paul Cullen, the Archbishop of Dublin, they demanded as one of their primary goals for the second half of the nineteenth century 'separate, state-supported, education for Catholics as a right' across all levels of education.[38] The resolve of the Irish hierarchy in the matter of

---

[35] See Antonia McManus, *The Irish Hedge School and its Books, 1695–1831* (Dublin, 2002), 124–9.
[36] David Newsome, *Godliness and Good Learning: Four Studies on a Victorian Ideal* (London, 1961); J. R. de S. Honey, *Tom Brown's Universe: The Development of the Public School in the 19th Century* (London, 1977).
[37] Joseph Lee, *The Modernisation of Irish Society 1848–1918* (Dublin, 1973), preface.
[38] John Coolahan, *Irish Education: History and Structure*, 4th edn (Dublin, 1987), 18.

denominational education was consistent with papal priorities. In 1873 Pope Pius IX declared to the German Literary Society that it was a Catholic duty to 'teach all nations' and that their right to do so separate from state interference was absolute: 'Instruction', he repeated, 'belongs entirely to the Church.'[39] This remained the fundamental position of the Catholic Church on education throughout the nineteenth century, and was later almost fully realized at secondary level in Ireland in the twentieth century, leaving Catholic education in the Free State and beyond not only 'denominationally controlled, but clerically controlled'.[40] The after-effect of this clash of Church and State over educational issues has meant that little work has been done on the private provision of education in the nineteenth century and that too great an emphasis has been placed on the clash between militant Catholicism and the liberal state.[41]

Two education debates in particular have generated a literature—mostly referred to as the 'National School system' and the 'University Question'. The missing link, secondary education, has merited just one full-length analysis: T. J. McElligott's invaluable (but basic) survey *Secondary Education in Ireland 1870–1921* (1983). The national school system, founded in 1831 by Edward Stanley, is by contrast something of a *cause célèbre* in Irish educational history—implicated heavily in the colonial project and the loss of the Irish language. Over time the national school system came to be clerically controlled in most parts of rural Ireland. This meant that the Catholic Church was less concerned about it than it was about university education—which was for them the major educational issue of the second half of the century. What has seldom been acknowledged however is the extent to which the Church, that is to say the secular clergy, were excluded from many of the major providers of secondary education in Ireland—the bulk of which was done by foreign or domestic 'regular' orders over which the bishops exerted little control. Though the bishops had much control over primary education and quite limited control over third-level education through the Catholic University and later the Royal University, they were not large-scale providers of secondary education, even taking diocesan seminaries into account. In part, this was a choice on their behalf and one borne of a belief that secondary or intermediate education was a matter of private middle-class investment. Forced to rule on the matter in relation to a bitter territorial dispute between the English hierarchy and the Jesuits in 1877–81, the Vatican made a clear distinction in the encyclical *Romanes Pontifices* between the right of bishops to control parish schools and smaller orders, and the right of the regulars to control their own schools without Episcopal interference. In fact, the

---

[39] Pius IX was Pope between 1846 and 1878, quoted in J. M. Feheney, *Catholic Education in Trinidad in the Nineteenth Century* (Dublin, 2001), 17.

[40] J. H. Whyte, *Church & State in Modern Ireland 1923–1970* (Dublin, 1971), 17.

[41] Aidan Enright has recently pointed to this overemphasis in Aidan Enright, 'Catholic Elites and the Irish University Question, 1860–80: European Solutions for an Irish Dilemma', in Brian Heffernan (ed.), *Life on the Fringe: Ireland and Europe 1800–1922* (Dublin, 2012), 177–96. Another recent article reawakens the familiar debate. See Tom O'Donoghue and Judith Harford, 'A Comparative History of Church–State Relations in Irish Education', *Comparative Education Review*, 55/3 (Aug. 2011), 315–41.

bishops did not even have the courtesy right of visitation to such schools, though they were of course invited to visit at least annually. The only power granted to the bishops with respect to regular orders and the founding schools was nevertheless a considerable one. No new foundation could be opened by a regular order without the express consent of both the local bishop and the Holy See.[42]

The issue of the funding of intermediate education was eventually resolved in 1878, with a system of indirect endowment. A payment-by-results scheme was installed using the interest accruing from the sum recouped by the state from the disestablishment of the Church of Ireland in 1869. The million or so pounds freed up by disestablishment was then reinvested, yielding *c*.£30,000 per annum which would fund the administration of prize funds based on exam results. These prizes were issued directly to the students, and school administrators received a flat rate based on the examination performance of their students.[43] 'The intermediate education system' was, as one historian has noted, 'simplicity itself. It was the Victorian commercial code applied to education.'[44] By superimposing a payment-by-results scheme on top of an underdeveloped, flawed, and private secondary sector the state did not merely paper over cracks, but cemented the entire substructure. Its great selling-point was that it left the denominational aspect of intermediate education untouched, thereby pleasing the Catholic bishops and ensuring that Catholic boys and girls could now receive a state-funded Catholic education from the earliest age to adulthood, untroubled by any of the apparatus of state. The Catholic elite could continue to pursue a high-profile education unbesmirched by government interference, and the Catholic Church retained effective control over the primary sector as well as the bulk of the newer intermediate education providers. There was no standardization, no inspectorate and no direct state involvement—most schools could teach whatever they liked, and decided their own fees. Though it was a system that made no one actor very happy it in fact allowed the bishops to retain control over the schools they coveted, the Catholic elite the freedom to choose an education without bowing to the pressure of the bishops, and the state to fund Catholic education by proxy and without fear of losing political face in England. The payment-by-results system itself was eradicated early in the life-cycle of the Free State, but the denominational division it had cemented did not, and the reputation of the measure has never recovered.

Patrick Pearse's essay, *The Murder Machine* has informed many nationalist interpretations of the history of education in Ireland. Anybody studying the subject has

---

[42] Lest there be any doubt in the matter Pope Leo XIII declared: 'That it is unlawful for Religious Orders to create for themselves new establishments, by erecting new churches, or opening monasteries, colleges, or schools, without having first obtained the express licence of the local Ordinary, and of the Apostolic See.' Leo XIII, *Romanos Pontifices*, 1881.

[43] For two much-neglected papers on this financial aspect of education in Ireland see Áine Hyland, 'The Treasury and Irish Education: 1850–1922: The Myth and the Reality', *Irish Educational Studies*, 3/2 (1983), 57–82; Peter W. Airasian et al., 'Payment by Results: An Analysis of a Nineteenth Century Performance-Contracting Programme', *The Irish Journal of Education/Iris Eireannach an Oideachais*, 21/2 (Winter, 1987), 80–91.

[44] D. H. Akenson, *A Mirror to Kathleen's Face: Education in Independent Ireland 1922–1960* (London, 1975), 12.

come across this term—which has endured, one imagines, because it is so memorably named. The phrase itself, with its insinuation of sacrifice, of grinding demoralizing industrialization, has proved difficult to resist for later writers. Again and again it crops up in relation to education. Pearse's characterization of the system as the most 'grotesque and horrible of the English inventions for the debasement of Ireland' has informed much of the twentieth-century literature on the subject, but it is also overstated and unfair, as the Intermediate Education Act was neither grotesque nor an English invention. In the next section it will be argued that the 1878 Act was, in fact, an Irish Catholic invention—supported by the hierarchy but conceptualized by the elite Catholic schools of Ireland for the financial benefit of Irish Catholic education generally. The Intermediate Act provided partial funding for an unequal and essentially elitist system by remunerating the schools and candidates that performed best in individual subjects. The funding provided by the Act was minimal and its main effect was to stimulate female education and to dramatically increase access to an extended secondary education for lower middle-class Catholics, allowing religious orders such as the Patrician Brothers and the Christian Brothers to thrive. The Act made no financial difference to elite schools other than to increase the value of their brand. Instead it offered the opportunity to compete publicly with the endowed Protestant schools and for a public and impartial body to adjudicate on their respective merits.

Elite education in Ireland was not radically altered by legislation or the churches in the nineteenth century. Any funding that arrived served only to stimulate intermediate education at lower middle-class level and the wealthiest Irish children continued to attend the same five or six schools in Ireland or to travel abroad for their education. The obvious indicator of elite education in this period is that of an immersive boarding school experience. This immersion led to the type of deep bonds that are difficult to replicate, and that took place during adolescence—that most impressionable stage of the life cycle. It is not difficult then to imagine why the clubbing together of old boys and old girls was so prevalent in this era. Many of those who grew up with their school authorities as substitute parents and their fellow students as proxy families grew to cherish the memory of those support structures in later life.

IV CATHOLICS OF CONSEQUENCE

This is not a book about Irish nationalism or unionism. Nor is it a book about rebellion or coercion. It has little to say of triumph or of dissonance and is more about continuity than change. It is rather a book about people who thought of advancing their ambitions slowly and in generational terms. It is a book about relatively wealthy Catholics who considered themselves to be drawing alongside their Protestant rivals in the quest for social status and localized power as the nineteenth century came to an end. Within this social group there were families that saw themselves as 'Catholics of consequence', whether they were metropolitan new money or predestined for a life as a comfortable country squire, whether they held public office or made their money in commerce or banking. These are the fabled 'West Britons' of Ireland, baited at the *fin de siècle* by bully-boy journalists such as D. P. Moran and captured so well by James Joyce in his character, Gabriel Conroy, in *The Dead*. Shoneens, Squireens, and Tommy Atkins[45] were the insults hurled at them by the cultural revivalists—many of whom were educated in much the same way themselves. Part I of this book probes such cultural confusion in four Irish Catholic schools before we step off the island in Parts II and III in search of those schooled in the forgotten corridors and assemblies of Irish educational history.

---

[45] Tommy Atkins was a common slang term for a soldier in the British army. Shoneen (sometimes written Seanín, Seonín or Shawneen) derives from the diminution of the name 'John' (Sean) in the Irish language, as heard through an English accent and thus carrying with it unwelcome connotations of servility and obsequiousness. 'Squireen' is more easily explained as a term which mocks the pretensions of a parish gentry when compared to those considered the true landed elite. All three were slang terms in the later nineteenth century and both Shoneen and Squireen were pejorative terms, whereas 'Tommy Atkins' could be both celebratory and derogatory.

PART I

2

An 'English Education'
Irish Catholic Schools for Boys 1850–1900

Christian brothers be damned! said Mr. Dedalus. Is it with Paddy Stink and Mickey Mud? No, let him stick to the jesuits in God's name since he began with them. They'll be of service to him in after years. Those are the fellows who can get you a position.

James Joyce, *A Portrait of the Artist as a Young Man*
(Dublin, 1972), 71

Within the past fifteen years Clongowes has seen members of her past occupy, to take Ireland alone, the positions of Lord Chancellor, Lord Chief Justice and Lord Chief Baron; Chairman of the Irish Parliamentary Party, President of the Royal College of Physicians, Governor of the Bank Of Ireland, Resident Commissioner of National Education; Chairman of the Intermediate Education Board, of the Chambers of Commerce of Dublin and Cork, and of the Port and Docks Board of Dublin.

Rev. Timothy Corcoran, SJ, 'The Story of Clongowes Wood AD 1450–1900'
(Dublin, 1900), 35

That the most prestigious Irish schools were consciously modelled on English public schools is a charge that has often been levelled and deserves consideration. At first glance the accusation has some merit. Like Eton or Harrow, Irish schools such as Clongowes Wood and Castleknock are widely considered to be socially exclusive. Housed in impressive and antiquated estates, they charge prohibitive fees and enjoy an elevated status in the public consciousness, just like their English equivalents. The schools continue to stock the most lucrative professions and their students tend to come from the 'D4' area of affluent suburbs in south Co. Dublin.[1] With consistently high levels of academic excellence, these state-supported schools deserve the moniker of 'elite' schools. Yet it is difficult to cast off the impression that these schools are watered-down versions of the real thing, especially when compared to English public schools which are typically twice their size and charging fees

---

[1] That the schools are generally connected in the popular mind to the most lucrative professions can be seen in a recent speech in the Oireachtas by Labour TD Anne Ferris, who in a critique of the current judiciary in Ireland maintained, sarcastically, that the only variety evident in the judicial nominees in Ireland was between 'wealthy middle aged white man schooled in Clongowes...to the wealthy middle-aged white man schooled in Blackrock College'. *Dáil Eireann Debate* 734/2, 2 Jun. 2011, 263.

three times as much. About 10,000 Catholic boys attended this type of Irish school between 1850 and 1900. Some used them as preparatory schools before going on to an even more prestigious school in England, France, or Belgium, but the large majority remained in Ireland for the bulk of their teenage years. The assumption that these boys would do well in life can be seen in the quotation above, taken from Joyce's *A Portrait*. That assumption would seem to be legitimized by the 'positions' attained by old boys in the second passage, taken from Clongowes' earliest school history. Were such boys socialized and moulded into an 'establishment' group of Castle Catholics in the way that the two quotations suggest?

I AN IRISH ETON?

Describing a school as the 'Eton of Ireland' or an 'Irish Eton' has been common since the mid nineteenth century, indicating the considerable reputation of that school globally. It has been recently ascribed even to the relatively modest Cistercian College, Roscrea.[2] Other Irish schools which regularly receive or claim this label include Clongowes, Kilkenny College, Glenstal Abbey, Blackrock, Portora Royal School, and St Columba's.[3] Depending on who delivers it the label 'Irish Eton' can carry with it either a great deal of pride or an implied accusation of disloyalty and West-Britonism, of embedded elitism and a commitment to reproducing an unfair and hierarchical social structure.[4] Such schools have, therefore, over a long period of time become entwined in the public mind as the junior partner in a colonial elite—their reported nineteenth-century toasts of 'To the Queen and Pope' marrying two apparently irreconcilable and opposing monarchs. This image was partly reinforced by the enthusiastic response of the major Catholic schools to the visit of Queen Victoria in 1900—who was careful to visit three of Dublin's best-known Catholic schools without actually entering any of them.[5] The *Castleknock Chronicle* rhapsodized the first ever visit of an English sovereign to their school on 22 April of that year, noting how the Queen sported a black bonnet 'in which sparkle sprays of silver shamrock' and a parasol 'embroidered with the national emblem'.[6] Read backwards through the lens of independence such displays of loyalty have been seen as anachronistic, though perhaps the visit of Queen Elizabeth II to the

[2] David Sharrock, 'Brian Cowen Raises a Glass to Leadership of Fianna Fáil', *The Times*, 9 Apr. 2008.
[3] For references old and new see e.g. 'In praise of Glenstal', *Irish Times*, 5 Feb. 2008; 'The Fighting Beresfords', *The Pall Mall Gazette*, 11 Jan. 1898; 'The Eton of Ireland Moves into the Eighties', *Irish Times*, 17 Nov. 1983; 'St Columba's College', *Irish Times*, 11 Jun. 1866; 'Ireland's Eton', *The Irish Press*, 22 Apr. 1985. Some, such as Portora, claim it for themselves: see <http://www.portoraroyal.co.uk/History_of_School.aspx>.
[4] Much of the language here is borrowed from the widely used theories of the French sociologist Pierre Bourdieu (1930–2002)
[5] These were Castleknock College and two convent schools—Sacred Heart, Mount Anville and Loreto Convent, Rathfarnham. See James H. Murphy, *Abject Loyalty: Nationalism and Monarchy in Ireland during the Reign of Queen Victoria* (Cork, 2001).
[6] *The College Chronicle, Castleknock*, 1/15 (Jun. 1900), 5.

Republic in 2011 will have helped to contextualize a regard for the person of the monarch that runs deceptively deep in Irish culture.[7]

The comparison to English public schools is nonetheless an inadequate one. For one thing, the Irish buildings are nowhere near as impressive as those of an Eton or Harrow. The numbers attending Irish schools are quite low in comparison, and their foundation dates relatively modern.[8] Their modernity is, of course, the result of penal restrictions on Catholic education in the eighteenth century, and the oldest of these schools in continuous operation is Clongowes Wood, founded in 1814, which took over from Carlow College as the most important and socially exclusive Catholic school in Ireland. By contrast, Eton was founded in 1440, Harrow in 1572. Yet these schools continue to rank as among the most expensive and prestigious schools in Ireland, and their impact on Irish society has been too significant for them to be dismissed as imitation public schools. The real reason why the schools became and remained popular is a rather simple one: they facilitated upward social mobility for Catholics without sacrificing religious principles. Their reputation as 'West British' schools, slavish in their devotion to English standards and practices, has endured, though this is a reflexive accusation and one that has been thoroughly undermined by their continuous popularity since independence in 1922. The market share for the schools has, in fact, increased throughout the twentieth century, with numbers hitting new heights from the 1960s onwards as the flow of Irish children to English and French schools subsided. The schools themselves have not always been savvy in their self-defence, however—in 2000 Clongowes Wood joined the standard-bearing lobbying group of unashamedly elitist British public schools, the Headmasters and Headmistresses Conference (HMC) and by doing so they have themselves invited comparison with schools such as Eton and Harrow.

The idea of an 'Irish Eton' is further compromised by the fact that, whatever the denomination, at no point during the nineteenth century can any Irish school have been considered to have offered the most prestigious education available to an Irish child. In this sense we can never really truly regard the Irish schools as elite in the strictest sense, but rather aiming for that status. Thousands of Irish children travelled overseas in search of a better-regarded educational product in what became known as a 'schoolboy exodus'. Nevertheless, the domestic schools have also had a major impact on Irish society, especially when the question of volume comes into question. An English Catholic school such as Stonyhurst College in Lancashire educated almost 500 Irish boys between 1850 and 1900. Offering substantially the same education and curriculum, Clongowes Wood in Ireland schooled closer

---

[7] For more on this relationship see Murphy, *Abject Loyalty*; James Loughlin, *The British Monarchy and Ireland, 1800 to the Present* (Cambridge, 2007).

[8] Harrow School was founded in 1572, charges £10,310 per term basic fees (£30,930 per annum) and has an enrollment of *c*.830 pupils. See the most recent inspection report, <http://www.isc.co.uk/schools/england/london-area/harrow/harrow-school>.

to 3,000, allowing us to make the assumption that its impact on Irish society, and that of its closest rivals, is worth analysing.

Previous scholarship on Ireland's most prestigious boarding schools has tended to accentuate the influence of the Intermediate Education Act (1878) in shaping a revolutionary and competitive middle class.[9] Institutional or school histories have mostly tended to cloud the central issues by focusing on school leaders, architectural history, and worst of all, the fortunes of successive rugby and cricket teams. What is of most importance in an account of any school, of course, is its effect upon its students. Plucking out the most prominent 'pastmen' of the schools will not aid us in our attempt to reckon the impact of an education at schools such as Clongowes or Castleknock. Historians of the schools have typically argued that their Anglocentrism was merely a reflection of a wider trend in the Irish upper-middle class. In his history of Castleknock College, James H. Murphy argues that whatever British or English elements were visible at the school were the result of the general cultural climate in Ireland and had little or nothing to do with any supposed influence from English public schools.[10] To this might be added the fact that the Anglicization of education in Ireland was part of a much wider proliferation of Anglophone culture in the second half of the nineteenth century. Jerome Karabel has identified similar phenomena in the US in the late nineteenth century, in particular at the New England elite schools which continue to dominate the entrance rolls at Ivy League universities. New England schools such as Lawrenceville, Groton, and Middlesex, exhibit similar Anglicization to Clongowes or Castleknock—in fact the buildings at Groton (1884) were deliberately modelled on those at Charterhouse and Trinity College, Cambridge.[11] Similar imitation emerged even in countries with no historical or contemporary colonial connections to modern England or Britain. For example, Swedish schools such as Lundsberg Skola (1896) and Solbacka Läroverk (1903) deliberately imitated schools such as Harrow and Eton and saw themselves as potential 'sister schools'.[12] Anglicization was as advanced at elite level elsewhere, and the deeply embedded nature of Irish Anglicization is complicated still further by the role played by its people in the colonization of other territories, not least those emerging from the schools such as those discussed in this chapter.[13]

---

[9] See Senia Pašeta, *Before the Revolution: Nationalism, Social Change and Ireland's Catholic Elite 1879–1922* (Cork, 1999), ch. 2.

[10] James H. Murphy (ed.), *Nos Autem: Castleknock College and its Contribution* (Dublin, 1996).

[11] Jerome Karabel, *The Chosen: The Hidden History of Admission and Exclusion at Harvard, Yale and Princeton* (New York, 2006). For recent analyses of elite education in the US see Daniel Golden, *The Price of Admission: How America's Ruling Class Buys its Way into Elite Colleges—and Who Gets Left Outside the Gates* (New York, 2006); Mitchell L. Stevens, *Creating a Class: College Admissions and the Education of Elites* (Cambridge, MA, 2007).

[12] See Petter Sandgren, 'The Etons of the Swedish Welfare State: The Transnational Spread of the British "Elite-Boarding School" Ideology', paper read before the Fifth Annual Graduate Conference in European History (GRACEH 2011)—Transfers and Demarcations (Florence, 2011).

[13] For a recent exploration of this see Barry Crosbie, *Irish Imperial Networks: Migration, Social Communication and Exchange in Nineteenth-century India* (Cambridge, 2012), ch. 1.

II ELITE IRISH CATHOLIC SCHOOLS AND IRISH SOCIETY

The Irish schools educated a more socially diverse demographic than elite schools in England, Sweden, or America. When James Joyce attended the Jesuit college at Clongowes Wood, near Clane, between 1888 and 1891 there was little in his family background to suggest that he would become the school's most famous alumnus. Clongowes had just amalgamated with its former prep school at Tullabeg and was on its way to regaining its place as the most prestigious Catholic school in Ireland, having underperformed in the state-funded intermediate examinations since their appearance in 1878. Clongowes was the most prestigious of a group of four relatively small Catholic schools that could legitimately boast of the consistent success of their past pupils in later life. Two of these schools were run by the Jesuits (Clongowes and Tullabeg), one by the Vincentian congregation (Castleknock), and one by the Holy Ghost Fathers (Blackrock College). Those attending the schools represented a mix of both the established landed elite and the rising middle and merchant classes, whose sights were trained on elite status or some degree of upward social mobility. This desire for equality within the union motivated a gradual but systematic reduction of obvious difference between an education received at English elite schools and at the Irish schools that sought to emulate them. This reduction of difference, which can also be read as imitative or emulative behaviour, depended mostly upon superficial factors such as the acquisition of a particular accent, sense of fashion, and an ability to compete in specific high-status sports. It was a successful formula, and by 1900 the list of prominent past pupils was difficult to ignore, not least because the schools themselves were so keen to advertise it.

Such obvious emulation was resented by many cultural nationalists, and reviled by the more advanced. First among those who publicly denounced the schools for their imitation of English models was the journalist D. P. Moran in his nationalist weekly, *The Leader*, where he referred to the school he had attended, Castleknock College, as 'that cricket and ping-pong College', and a 'brake on the Irish wheel'.[14] Nevertheless, the education provided at these schools produced tangible results and won for them a national reputation for excellence. Future Taoiseach and President of Ireland, Éamon De Valera, received his primary education at Bruree National School and later at the Christian Brothers school in Charleville. He won a scholarship to attend the prestigious Blackrock College, in south Dublin, from 1898 to 1901, and remembered in later life that he could not understand that other boys cried on their first night at the school:

> From the time I heard that I was to go to Blackrock I was really walking on air...I remember well how happy I was on that night—my first night in the College.

---

[14] Murphy (ed.), *Nos Autem*, 101–2.

I could not understand why boys coming to such a place should be weeping. I heard some sobbing; but for me this coming was really the entry into heaven.[15]

De Valera had grown up in relatively modest circumstances in Co. Limerick. For a boy like him an education at Blackrock was a privilege, not a right. The opportunity to excel brought attendant pressures. Another prominent nationalist—Michael Joseph Rahilly (seated to the right in Figure 2.1) later to earn enduring fame as the self-declared 'the O'Rahilly' in the Easter Rising of 1916—was bombarded with letters from home during his time at Clongowes Wood (1890–2). 'Don't allow me to be disappointed', his father warned.[16] The pressure placed on Rahilly by his middle-class father reveals much about the demographics of Irish elite education, as does De Valera's first-night elation. The stakes were high for a boy from a modest background, even though Irish elite schools were not nearly as socially exclusive as their British counterparts, despite the presence of boys from a gentry background.

This social mixture had ramifications. For more established elite Catholics the accommodation of boys like De Valera who were not from a gentrified background threatened to dilute social caste. The most obvious way to avoid this was to send

Figure 2.1 The O'Rahilly (seated, right) beside Nancy Brown and his sons, Mac (seated), Niall (front left), and Aodogán (front right)

[15] UCDA, 'Typed Manuscript of Dictobelt made 24 Apr. 1956, Éamon's Office', De Valera Papers, P150/22.
[16] UCDA, Richard Rahilly to Michael J. Rahilly, 17 Sep. 1890, The O'Rahilly Papers, P102/44

one's child overseas for their education and a great many did. A correspondent of Lady Bellew admonished her for her choice of an Irish school over an English one in the 1840s. By choosing to send her sons to Clongowes Wood she faced the prospect of their associating 'with a class of boys... far beneath them in station, in deportment, in domestic training, in habits of early education'. This was an important consideration, her correspondent protested, as 'delicacy of mind and delicacy of manner are much more nearly allied than is generally supposed'.[17] The powerful socializing force of a school was a prime concern for mothers and fathers sending adolescents away during their most impressionable years and the fear of social degradation or compromise was a significant one. In this concern the Irish elite experienced the same fear of *déclassement* as had the French elite when they sought to divert the expanding middle class from the traditionally elite *lycées* in the 1830s.[18] This greater democratization of education meant that the Irish schools' affordability counted against them when the richest of their potential clientele chose a school for their children and few among the rich thought that a greater diversity of background was a desirable quality in their social circle. Such naked exclusivity was rarely disguised and was in fact tacitly supported by a succession of Victorian governments. When the idea of greater government funding for intermediate education was suggested to the Powis Commission on education in Ireland in 1870 the general report noted that parents wishing to prolong the education of their offspring should be doing so on their own initiative. 'They have no claim upon the public for assistance' the commission argued, and to do any more for them 'would be to demoralize the middle classes into recipients of public charity'.[19]

Intermediate education in Ireland was a private-sector phenomenon in the nineteenth century. Even after the provision of limited state funding to all schools in 1878, the purchase of a school, its maintenance, and the tuition provided there were all considered outside the remit of the government. It was natural, therefore, that aspects of the education provided at the four most prestigious Catholic schools in Ireland in the period were dictated by the demands of their target market—the wealthy Irish Catholic laity—and their desire to succeed in an increasingly credentialist professional and bureaucratic society.

Any person receiving an extensive and holistic intermediate education in the first half of the nineteenth century in Ireland was likely to have been either sponsored by the clergy or relatively wealthy in their own right. At Clongowes (Figure 2.2) the early prospectuses dictated that age of admission was generally between the age of seven and fourteen and that children younger than twelve years of age were to be charged £50, those older than twelve to be charged 50 guineas. The lower-status diocesan colleges, such as St Kieran's College in Kilkenny,

---

[17] National Library of Ireland (NLI), Henrietta Beaumont to Lady Bellew (undated, but probably early 1840s), Mount Bellew Papers, MS 27,276.
[18] R. D. Anderson argues that Francois Guizot's educational reforms in 1833 was largely a response to such fears. R. D. Anderson, 'Secondary Education in Mid Nineteenth-century France: Some Social Aspects', *Past & Present*, 53/1 (1971), 126.
[19] Royal Commission of Inquiry into Primary Education (Ireland), Vol. I, HC 1870 [c.6], XXVIII Pt. I, 505

Figure 2.2 Clongowes Wood College, *c.*1901

were charging £20 (per boy) a year for equivalent education and board, catering for a more rural middle-class of strong farmers and shopkeepers.[20] In 1838 St Malachy's diocesan college in Belfast charged just £14, with an additional charge of £4 for optional tuition in mathematics, and a further £4 for tuition in English, French, and music, suggesting there was no compulsion to study even quite basic subjects.[21]

At Clongowes the education offered was of an altogether different nature to that available at diocesan colleges. The composition of the early staff at Clongowes reflected the cosmopolitan and transnational nature of the Jesuit order, even at a time of low ebb. Many of the early Jesuits had trained in Sicily and Stonyhurst between 1809 and 1814, prior to the setting up of the Irish mission under Fr Peter Kenny, SJ, and most had spent several years training outside Ireland.[22] In addition to a full classical course, pupils were expected to pay extra for fencing, drawing, dancing, and music, and the flat rate was 50 guineas per annum without optional

---

[20] The diocesan colleges were educational institutions where both lay boys and future priests were educated together. As many as 50% of these boys carried on to major seminaries and became priests. See John Kearney, 'The Diocesan Colleges', *The Furrow*, 3/11 (Nov. 1952), 580–7.

[21] *The Collegian*, Centenary Number (Belfast, 1933), 20.

[22] 'The Irish Jesuits since 1800', *The Irish Monthly*, 18/199 (Jan. 1890); Thomas J. Morrissey, *As One Sent: Peter Kenney S.J. 1779–1841* (Dublin, 1996); Kevin A. Laheen, 'Further Letters of Robert Haly, S. J., 1810–29, in the Irish Jesuit Archives', *Collectanea Hibernica*, 44/45 (2002/2003), 173–213; 'To Palermo and Back, Seventy Years Ago', *The Irish Monthly*, 9/98 (Aug. 1881), 441–6.

extras.[23] Joel Mokyr estimates that the average per capita income in Ireland was under £16 as late as 1841. The majority of the population survived at a high risk of starvation on farms of 15 acres, and less than 3 per cent of the population could be considered well-off.[24] An education at Clongowes Wood, at 50 guineas per child, was therefore deliberately restricted to a tiny minority of the Irish Catholic population, and to label the school 'middle-class', using any modern conception of the term, would be incorrect. Indeed the Jesuits admitted a two-tier hierarchy within their own network of schools by setting up day-schools in the 1840s, such as Belvedere College in Dublin and St Francis Xavier's in Liverpool. These schools provided a good deal: a comparable curriculum and standard of teaching as at the Jesuit boarding schools for as little as 2 guineas per term.[25] It is to be assumed that parents paying up to five times that much for an education at Clongowes or Tullabeg were not doing so for purely academic reasons.

The Jesuits also founded St Stanislaus College (referred to generally as Tullabeg) in 1818 near Rahan, Co. Offaly. The college was originally intended to serve as a noviciate for the order but instead became a preparatory college or 'feeder' for Clongowes.[26] It was considered customary for boys to progress from Tullabeg to Clongowes between the ages of thirteen and fifteen. The tradition continued uncontested until the 1860s. In fact, the numbers rarely rose above forty or fifty, finally expanding to a respectable figure of ninety or so during the Rectorate of John Ffrench (1850–5).[27] A prospectus from this period reveals a blend of classical European and Anglocentric education, as well as the increasingly professional and middle-class tone of the education provided there:

> The course of instruction, besides Reading, Writing, Arithmetic, Bookkeeping, Mathematics, the elements of Surveying etc with the usual adjuncts of an English mercantile education, comprises the French, Latin and Greek Languages with Italian if required. Annual pension 25 guineas.[28]

A charge of 25 guineas was prohibitive to the majority, but also masked a host of 'extras' that added to the already considerable cost. The newly built non-denominational model schools were charging (at the higher rate) between

---

[23] First Prospectus of Clongowes Wood College (Jun. 1814), reprinted in William A. Menton, *The Clongowes Union Centenary Chronicle* (Clongowes Wood, 1997), 26.
[24] Joel Mokyr, *Why Ireland Starved: A Quantitative and Analytical History of the Irish Economy 1800–1850* (London, 1983), 18–19.
[25] McRedmond notes that St Ignatius himself had strictly forbidden that fees should be charged for anything but the cost of boarding. Clongowes and Tullabeg had special permission to charge such high fees via a dispensation of the Jesuit Superior General in 1833. See Louis McRedmond, *To the Greater Glory: A History of the Irish Jesuits* (Dublin, 1991), 158–60.
[26] For the basic history of Tullabeg see Kevin Laheen, *The Jesuits in Tullabeg: The Early Years from Mission 1810 to Province 1860* (Limerick, 2007); *The Jesuits in Tullabeg: A Century of Service, 1814–1914* (Limerick, 2009); *The Jesuits in Tullabeg, 1817–1991: The Final Curtain 1991* (Limerick, 2010)
[27] John Ffrench was the second son of Lord Ffrench, of Castle French, Roscommon. The Athy family was descended from Humphrey de Freyne, who accompanied Strongbow on the first Norman invasion in 1172. John later held the title of Baron de Freyne of Coolavin, succeeding his brother Arthur. His nephew, Arthur, attended Clongowes and later Beaumont College (1871–4).
[28] IJA, Tullabeg Papers, FM/TULL/31. This prospectus is substantially the same as one printed during Fr Bracken's tenure as Rector in the late 1840s.

10 shillings and £1 per term, targeting the expanding middle-class.[29] For their 25 guineas at Tullabeg, students could expect an introduction to the Continental Jesuit system of education along with more practical elements of education such as book-keeping and surveying.[30] The inclusion of the latter two clearly indicates the shift away from traditional Jesuit educational philosophy to a hybrid form of education incorporating skills required by both the modernizing economy and state structure and the expanding British Empire. This shift is referred to explicitly in the prospectus with the advertisement of an 'English mercantile' education, showing that the school was already outward-looking, and cognizant of the opportunities presented by the union and the Empire, while also appealing to broader range of social backgrounds than an Eton or Winchester. In this period Tullabeg educated several high-profile Irishmen, a fact the school exploited to considerable commercial effect later in the century. Sir Nicholas O'Connor (Tullabeg: 1852–6) had a spectacular diplomatic career, culminating in his appointment as British Ambassador to the Ottoman Empire in 1897. Sir William Francis Butler (Tullabeg: 1847–9) was a successful soldier and was temporarily Commander-in-Chief of the British Forces in South Africa during the Boer War in 1898, although what memories he had of his schooldays at Tullabeg 'were not happy ones'.[31] By the 1870s, and up until its dramatic closure in 1886, Tullabeg was arguably the top-performing school in Ireland, and certainly the best academically.

The primary reason for the expansion of Tullabeg was the energy and drive shown by William Delany, SJ—a forgotten Victorian headmaster whose charisma and drive are easily comparable to figures such as Edward Thring at Uppingham— reminding us that schools are mostly the sum of their staff.[32] At Tullabeg, Delany was as positive a force for his students and their parents as he was a worry to his superiors. Born the son of a baker in Leighlinbridge, Co. Carlow, Delany was educated first in Carlow College and then in Maynooth. Having decided to join the Society of Jesus, Delany was sent to the novitiate in St Acheul in Amiens, France.[33] A precocious sense of propriety accompanied Delany into adulthood, it seems that from an early age he had given much attention to his accent and pronunciation and 'attached great importance to the manners and conventialities he studied in the "nicer people" he met'.[34] Delany took his vows in February of 1858 and subsequently taught elementary arithmetic at Clongowes for two and a half years. Transferred to Tullabeg in 1860, he took charge of a third-year class and took them

---

[29] Earl Powis, *Royal Commission of Inquiry into Primary Education (Ireland)* (Powis Commission), Vol. 7. Containing the report of the commissioners 1870 [C.6], 92.

[30] The teaching philosophy of the Society of Jesus is derived from the *Ratio Studiorum* (1599). This system was influenced by the humanistic traditions of the Renaissance period, and places a heavy emphasis on philosophy and the classics. See R. Schwickerath. 'Ratio Studiorum', in *The Catholic Encyclopedia* (New York, 1911).

[31] Sir William Francis Butler, *Sir William Butler: An Autobiography* (London, 1911), 4.

[32] Edward Thring (1821–77) was headmaster of Uppingham School in Leicestershire and one of the most influential public school educationalists on the nineteenth century.

[33] IJA, Lambert McKenna, SJ, 'Fr William Delany and his Work for Irish Education', unpublished MS in Lambert McKenna Papers, 24

[34] McKenna, SJ, 'Fr William Delany', 18.

to 'Rhetoric' or sixth year in 1863–4. The following year he was made Assistant Prefect of Studies before departing to Rome for three years to study theology.[35] On his return he was made Prefect of Studies and immediately began work on what was to be a decade of structural, educational, and social improvement at Tullabeg.

Fr Delany was made Rector in 1870 and in his first two years he rebuilt the boys chapel, converted another chapel into a study hall, remodelled the east wing of the house and had part of the River Silver deepened and enclosed to provide better bathing facilities for his boys. Such expansion came at a cost and his first year alone the figure in the accounts for 'extraordinary' expenditure had reached £957.[36] To put his expenditure in perspective, a glance at the accounts for the academic year 1868–9 shows that, before Delany began building, Tullabeg was running at a profit of about £1,660. One hundred and twenty scholars at £30 each equalled £3,600 which, added to profits from the sale of butter and fees charged for mending clothes for the boys, made an income of £3,960. Expenditure for that year totalled £2292 15s 6d.[37] By 1873–4 the costs had risen considerably, as had the anxiety of his superiors. At this point St Stanislaus was running with current debts of about £2,671. Unperturbed, Delany had a hydraulic ram constructed in the river to supply the house with water, built new quarters for the servants, and, after an outbreak of scarlatina in 1874, he rebuilt the infirmary to cater for any recurrence. Delany was intent on constructing a state-of-the-art educational facility, and was untroubled by any financial repercussions. His profligacy earned him a stern rebuke from his General in Rome. In September of 1875, he wrote

> When I knew you at Rome, I saw you to be well disposed and full of love of religious discipline. For the good of the province, I hoped for much from you, but sadly events did not correspond with the expectations. I named you Rector, and I don't know what special fruit to yourself and the college that office brought. Many quarrels are referred to me... and I ask you to examine yourself before the crucifix if you proceed according to the spirit of St Ignatius, if you always keep before you the rules of your office"[38]

Father Delany's perceived extravagance drew much criticism from within the order. His reputation for poor financial control was to precede him for the rest of his life.[39] His ability to radically change the status quo extended far beyond merely the physical structure of Tullabeg; in his time he was to apply his considerable abilities to every facet of life at the school. Tullabeg was a radically different school by the time he left it in 1880.[40]

---

[35] Thomas J. Morrissey, *Towards a National University: William Delany, S.J. (1835–1924): An Era of Initiative in Irish Education* (Dublin, 1983), 18.

[36] IJA, Statements of Accounts, Tullabeg Papers.

[37] IJA, Statements of Accounts, Tullabeg Papers.

[38] Quoted in Morrissey, *Towards a National University*, 24.

[39] When he was appointed as Prefect of Studies to the planned university at Temple Street, he was told that he would be subject to the Vice-Rector and have no control over expenditure, accounts, discipline, or housekeeping, to which he replied acerbically that it was therefore of 'comparatively little importance' who the Prefect was. Morrissey, *Towards a National University*, 65.

[40] For a general account of the school see Laheen, *The Jesuits in Tullabeg: The Early Years; The Jesuits in Tullabeg: A Century of Service; The Jesuits in Tullabeg: The Final Curtain 1991*.

Figure 2.3 Castleknock College, *c*.1880–1900

St Vincent's College or Seminary, Castleknock (referred to as Castleknock College, see Figure 2.3) was founded in 1835.[41] In later years, one of the Vincentian community inferred, during an unveiling of a portrait of Daniel O'Connell, that Castleknock enjoyed a unique status in Ireland as the only superior school in Ireland to have had purely Irish roots. Castleknock was set up to ease the pressure on Maynooth, then catering for 250 clerical students. It continued to provide a quality education to both lay and clerical students until the foundation of the ecclesiastical seminary at Clonliffe College in 1859.[42] With the pressure to produce priests for the diocese somewhat diminished, Castleknock thrived as an increasingly lay establishment.[43] Initially fees were set at a competitive rate of 25 guineas, but rose to £45 by 1838.[44] Castleknock was more connected to the Catholic hierarchy than Clongowes or Tullabeg and this was partly to do with their provision of priests to the Dublin diocese. Despite this essentially Irish

[41] It was a continuation of a day-school in Dublin that had been founded in 1833 by a group of progressive Irish priests that had been ordained together at Maynooth College. Fr Campbell, 'Castleknock: The College and the Castle', *The College Chronicle, Castleknock*, 54 (Jun. 1939), 1.

[42] Murphy also asserts that while Castleknock is sometimes regarded as an almost exclusively ecclesiastical establishment in this period, in reality only 23% of the intake entered Maynooth between 1836 and 1861. The bulk of the pupils were from moderately wealthy rural backgrounds, or the sons of Dublin merchants. Murphy, *Nos Autem*, 99.

[43] *The College Chronicle, Castleknock*, 1/15 (Jun. 1900), 5.

[44] *St Vincent's Castleknock Centenary Record 1835–1935* (Dublin, 1935), 77–85.

Figure 2.4 Blackrock College, *c.*1901

character, the school continued to attract students from all over the world, and its reputation was such that it was second only to Clongowes for much of the nineteenth century.

The French College, Blackrock (now Blackrock College, see Figure 2.4) was founded in south Dublin by a group of French priests in 1860 at the invitation of Cardinal Paul Cullen, Archbishop of Dublin, and their connection to the hierarchy remained a strong one. So too did their French inheritance—to the extent that their pupils were known locally as 'Boney boys' (after Napoleon) in the early years of the school.[45] The first prospectus was quite definite in outline and aim. It boasted that the education provided had 'all the advantages of a Continental combined with a sound English education'. Fees were charged at 30 guineas per boy, or 40 guineas including extras such as drawing, gymnastics, German and Italian.[46] By the end of the decade the number of pupils attending the French College had reached 200, and the school was charging as much as £73 for boys taking advantage of the extensive extras on offer.[47] In addition to Père Leman, the French priest Fr Edward Reffé is remembered as the dynamic force in

[45] Sean Farragher and Annraoi Wyer, *Blackrock College 1860–1995* (Dublin, 1995), 9.

[46] First Prospectus of French College, Blackrock, reprinted in Farragher and Wyer, *Blackrock College 1860–1995*, 8.

[47] BCA, Entry 42, Ledger of Student Accounts 1867–74. Paul Coutin D'Arcy of East India Road, Poplar, London ran up a bill of £73 6d in 1870–1.

the school's first half-century. French was a working language in the school, and the staff composition was international and cosmopolitan. Blackrock had entered Irish elite education offering an education that blended Continental and English principles and it proved a successful formula. In terms of prizes won, the school was the most successful in Ireland at end of the nineteenth century, although its status as a relative newcomer meant that Clongowes and Castleknock were always considered above it in social status.

III ELITE IRISH CATHOLIC SCHOOLS AND IRISH SOCIETY

Too often school histories concentrate entirely on architectural or pedagogical history, so that the hapless enthusiast ends up with a comprehensive knowledge of school leaders, school characters, and school cloisters—but only an impressionistic account of the students. It is only when we attempt to quantify the influence of a school on wider society that we are confronted with the question of 'product'. Between 1850 and 1900 Clongowes Wood College educated 2,778 boys, the vast majority of whom were Irish-born. Tullabeg educated 1,820 boys from 1850 until its closure in 1886, with even fewer foreign-born boys in the cohort. Similarly precise figures are unavailable for Blackrock College, which only began enrolling in 1861, but Castleknock educated 2,489 boys between 1850 and 1900. At a time when less than 5 per cent of Irish boys or girls attended school, this represented a large percentage of those exposed to a superior education in Ireland. Table 2.1 indicates the number of boys entering the colleges by decade:

Table 2.2 indicates that numbers at the schools grew as the century wore on, showing that a greater proportion of Irish Catholic families could afford a relatively expensive education, and that the ranks of the professional and merchant classes were expanding. At Clongowes alone the numbers attending had almost doubled between 1850 and 1900, though this was partly down to its assimilation of Tullabeg in 1886. Tullabeg had done much to harm the prestige of Clongowes through the 1870s at a time when it was the best-performing school in Ireland under the watch of its Rector, William Delany, SJ.

Table 2.1 Total number of boys attending Clongowes, Tullabeg, and Castleknock, 1850–1900

	1850–9	1860–9	1870–9	1880–9	1890–9
Clongowes Wood	478	398	425	651	826
Tullabeg	335	498	594	393*	–
Castleknock	342	392	467	552	736

* Tullabeg closed in 1886.

Table 2.2 Total number of boys attending Clongowes, Tullabeg, and Castleknock (graphed), 1850–1900

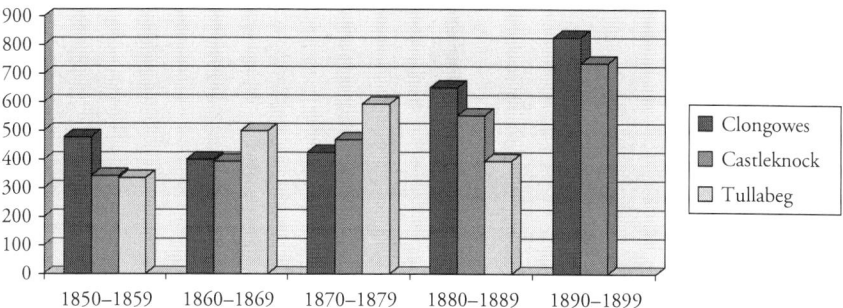

Geographical Origins

The register of students attending Clongowes Wood between 1850 and 1900 provides addresses for 96 per cent of the group. Irish historians have in the past presumed that schools such as Clongowes and Castleknock catered for 'comfortable' Catholics in Kildare and Meath, but this is not the case.[48] The county that contributed the most students to Clongowes was Dublin, with 27 per cent, perhaps unsurprisingly given its population and proximity to the school. This pattern is replicated at both Tullabeg and Castleknock, and indeed at the English Catholic colleges considered in the next chapter. Co. Kildare, the county in which Clongowes was located, accounts for just 3 per cent of enrolments at the school, a statistic which emphasizes the elite and non-local nature of the student body. In fact the surrounding counties of Laois, Offaly, Carlow, Wicklow, and Meath combined account for a mere 6 per cent of the total, although much larger percentages of students hailed from more populous and affluent counties such as Cork (12 per cent). The nine counties of Ulster accounted for just over 5 per cent of enrolments, almost equalled by those travelling from abroad (4 per cent). Of the latter group the highest number travelled from England (34), with America and Australia equally well represented (17 each). Students travelled from such diverse locations as Ceylon, Newfoundland, Trinidad, Canada and India to study at Clongowes—a fact that emphasized the international reputation of the school, as well as the trade and Empire connections abundant in the Irish Catholic world.

The Tullabeg register provides an address for 1,637 boys (90 per cent) who attended the school between 1850 and the year of its closure in 1886. The geographical distribution of the pupils reveals a distinct Munster and Leinster majority, with 75 per cent coming from these provinces—32 per cent and 43 per cent

---

[48] Louis M. Cullen, 'Catholic Social Classes under the Penal Laws', in T. P. Power and Kevin Whelan (eds), *Endurance and Emergence: Catholics in Ireland in the Eighteenth Century* (Dublin, 1990), 71.

respectively. Connacht accounted for just 13 per cent of the cohort, with Ulster counties faring even worse at 10 per cent. A further 2 per cent of boys came from abroad, from as far away as Canada, Newfoundland, Argentina, America and the South American sugar colony at Demerara.[49] The city and county of Dublin accounted for 22 per cent of the intake at the school. At Blackrock the foreign cohort was also noticeable. Writing home at Christmas in 1877 Maurice John Nunan complained that it was 'very lonesome at Christmas, no one stays here but those from India and America'.[50]

As part of the school history published in 1996, Castleknock College provided a county-by-county breakdown of students who attended the school. Between 1860 and 1890 some 1,328 boys were educated at Castleknock, with a considerable majority (56 per cent) from the Leinster counties, and 28 per cent of this group from Dublin. Munster accounted for 26 per cent of Castleknock's intake, with Ulster next in line with 9 per cent, though the majority of these came from just one county, Monaghan—a trend peculiar to this school only. In Castleknock's case it was Connacht that was the most badly represented province, with just 5 per cent of boys at the school coming from the western counties. Three per cent of boys came from abroad.[51]

All three schools have a near-identical geographical demographic, as can be further emphasized by a full county-by-county breakdown in Maps 2.1–2.3. Tullabeg, in a more accessible location for those in Connacht and the south midlands, could reasonably have been expected to draw most of their cohort from the south and west of the country—especially with the school moving away from its prep-school past and offering a viable alternative to Clongowes Wood from the 1850s. That almost 400 boys came to Tullabeg from Dublin is indicative of its success in this respect. Offaly, the county in which the school itself was located, accounted for a mere 3 per cent of enrolments, an indication perhaps of the exclusivity of the school, and also the socio-economic status of Catholics in the local area. Equally, the absence of any significant proportion of students from Ulster at either Castleknock or Tullabeg points to the lack of Catholic wealth in the province, references by both Marianne Elliott and Oliver P. Rafferty in their histories of Catholic Ulster. Rafferty notes that though there was a slow development of a Catholic middle class in the nineteenth century they were not at any stage encouraged to partake in civic life and were often excluded from it. In 1880 there was only one magistrate out of a total seventy-four in Co. Fermanagh, and in 1886 only five of ninety-five officers of Belfast Corporation were Catholic, which gives some indication of how limited their social capital was in both town and county throughout the nineteenth century.[52]

---

[49] Published school lists are available for all three schools. These totals were compiled from the lists of both Tullabeg and Clongowes Wood contained in Timothy Corcoran, SJ, *The Clongowes Record 1814–1932* (Dublin, 1932), 165–251; for Castleknock see *St Vincent's Castleknock Centenary Record 1835–1935* for the full list. Totals for Castleknock 1860–90 were taken from Michael Johnston, Donal MacNiocla and Ronan MacNioclais, Appendix E, in Murphy (ed.), *Nos Autem*, 311.

[50] BCA, Maurice John Nunan to James Nunan, Mallow, 17 Oct. 1877.

[51] Murphy (ed.), *Nos Autem*, 311.

[52] Oliver P. Rafferty, *Catholicism in Ulster 1603–1983: An Interpretative History* (London, 1994), 157: Marianne Elliott, *The Catholics of Ulster: A History* (London, 2000), 324.

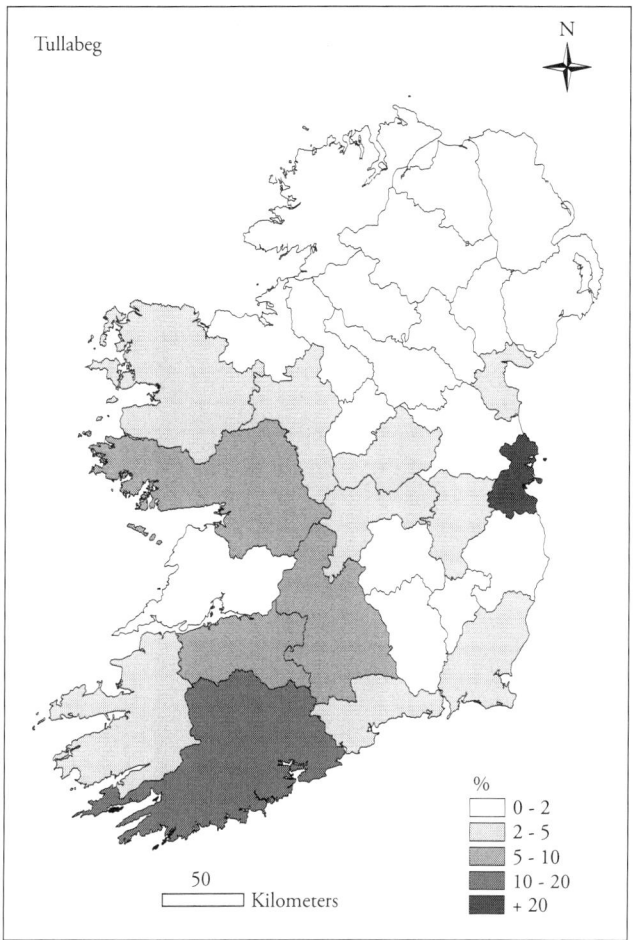

Tullabeg

N

%
0 - 2
2 - 5
5 - 10
10 - 20
+ 20

50
Kilometers

Map 2.1 Tullabeg boys by county of origin, 1850–86

The picture emerging is therefore one of a southern elite, corresponding with what Kevin Whelan has called the 'Catholic core' of rich families in the south and south-west of Ireland, with limited representation in Connacht and almost none in Ulster.[53] It is likely that the predominance of south Munster addresses at such schools was linked to a gradual increase in prosperity in the region, stemming from transatlantic trade in the preceding century. David Dickson notes in his study of the region that, although Catholic landowning in the region was decimated following the Nine Years' War (1594–1603), transatlantic trade boosted the regional economy. Land value increased by a factor of five or six between 1690 and 1830, the

[53] Kevin Whelan, 'Catholic Mobilisation 1750–1850', in Louis Bergeron and L. M. Cullen (eds), *Culture et pratiques politiques en France et en Irlande XVIe–XVIIIe siècle* (Paris, 1991), 235–58.

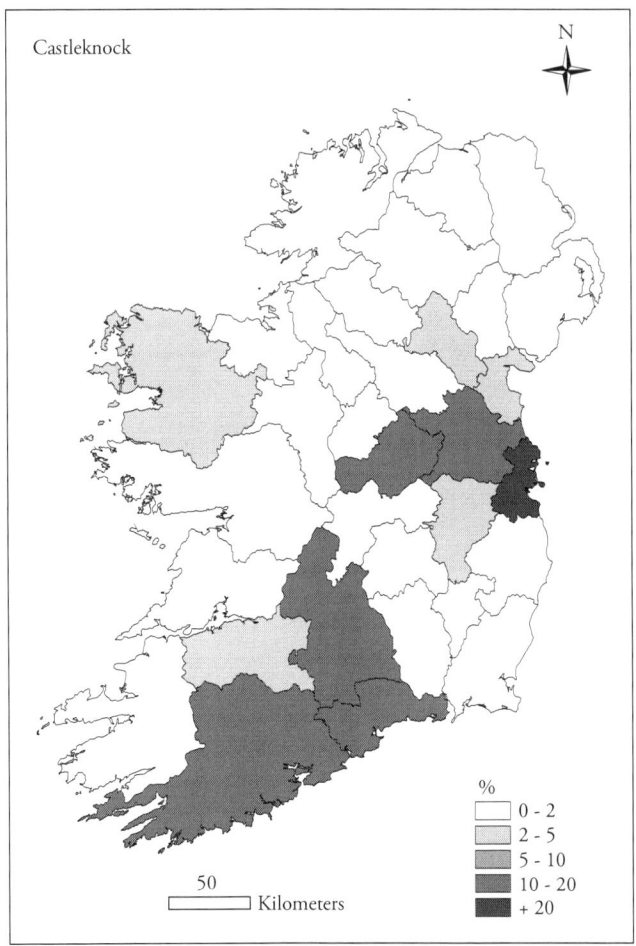

Map 2.2 Castleknock boys by county of origin, 1860–90

population trebled and there was a corresponding increase in social stratification.[54] Rural and urban areas are equally represented in the south Munster area. Three generations of the Egan family of jewellers at Cork can be found at Clongowes in the nineteenth century—as were the descendants of the major Catholic merchant family, the Ronaynes of Youghal, and one of very few Catholic families that had held on to their land through the penal period, the various branches of the Coppinger family.[55]

---

[54] David Dickson, *Old World Colony: Cork and South Munster, 1630–1830* (Madison, US, 2005), 83 and 496.
[55] Patrick Maume, 'Barry M. Egan (1879–1954)', *DIB*.

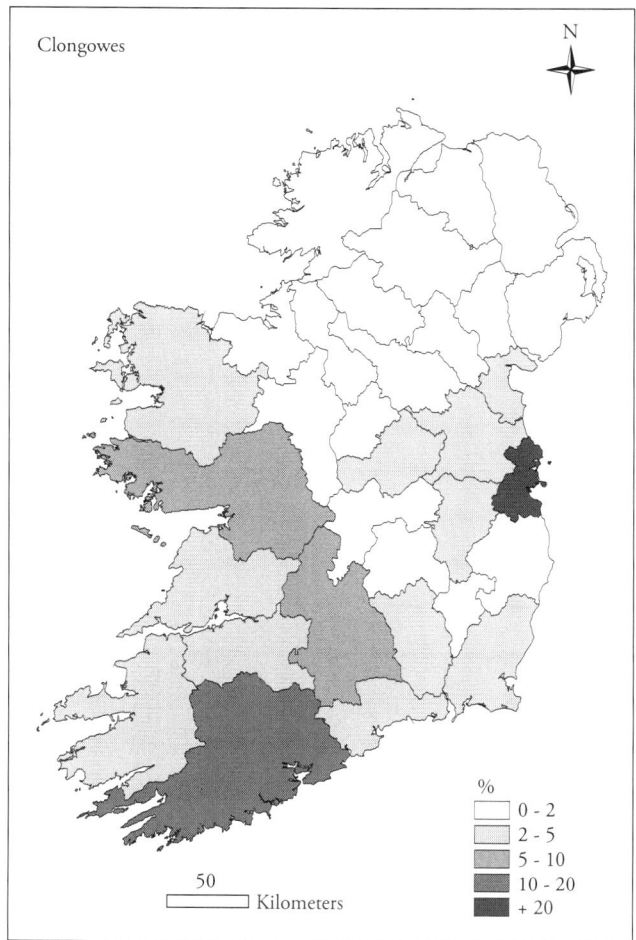

Clongowes

N

%
☐ 0 - 2
☐ 2 - 5
▨ 5 - 10
▨ 10 - 20
■ + 20

50
Kilometers

Map 2.3 Clongowes boys by county of origin, 1850–1900

The other major regional representation is the city and county of Dublin. The Dublin cohort at Clongowes and Tullabeg are almost all based either in fashionable city-centre addresses such as Merrion Square or Rutland Square, or in the southern suburbs of the city (Map 2.4). Of those Dublin boys attending Clongowes 1850–1900 the address provided most often was the Kingstown–Glenageary area (now Dun Laoghaire) which accounted for 19 per cent of the addresses given by Dublin boys. Altogether, the wealthier south of Dublin was   home to 83 per cent of those with a known address.[56] The majority of the Dublin cohort resided in a small cluster of suburbs just south of the city that were renowned for their affluence—Kingstown, Rathmines, Monkstown, Rathgar, Dalkey and Blackrock.

---

[56] The number of specific and recorded Dublin addresses is 295, with 244 of them in the southern suburbs. Corcoran, SJ, *The Clongowes Record*, 165–221.

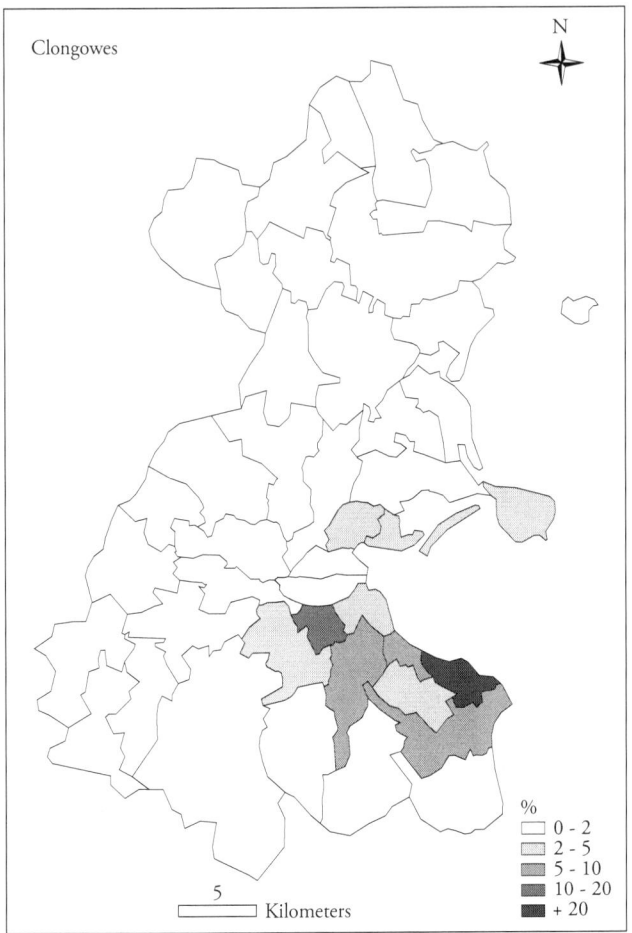

Map 2.4 Clongowes boys by electoral district, Co. Dublin, 1850–1900

This suggests a clear cultural and economic divide in Catholic Dublin. Even where an address is provided in the north of the city, it is generally in one of the few affluent suburbs such as Clontarf or Howth. This pattern is replicated at smaller urban centres such as Cork city or Waterford city, and further reinforces the idea that choice of school was simply one of many criteria by which a Catholic family's social position or upward mobility might be measured.

The picture for Cork is similar, with a greater distribution of students coming from outlying towns (Map 2.5).

Those attending the Irish Catholic elite schools were a mix of the landed Catholic gentry, the 'informal gentry', and the newer urban elites that had made their money in the world of commerce or trade.[57] Once a financial threshold was

---

[57] David Dickson has used this term in relation to the mixture of Catholic stakeholders, merchants, and major landowners in south Munster that coexisted and prospered in the late eighteenth century.

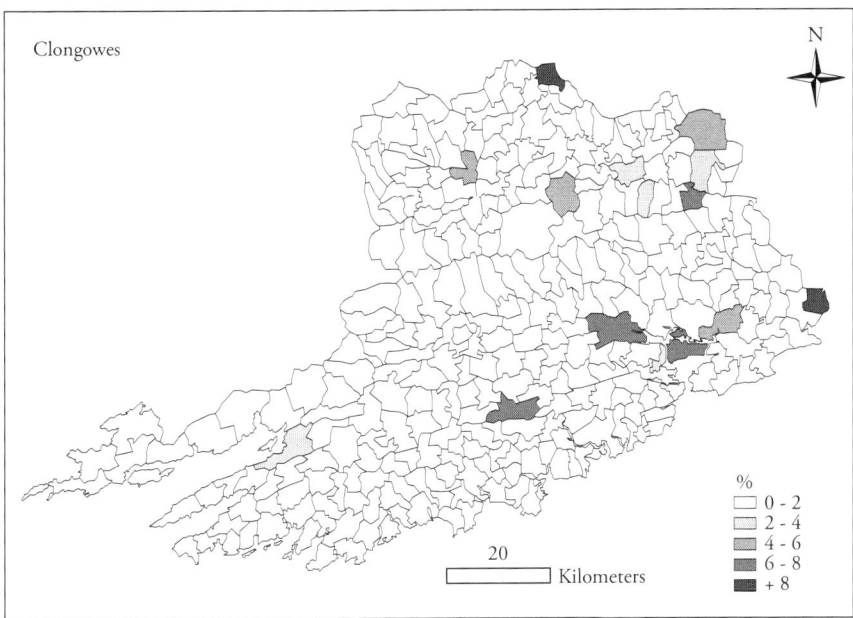

Clongowes

Map 2.5 Clongowes boys by electoral district, Co. Cork, 1850–1900

crossed, elite education was available and easily procured. Lawrence Stone has noted in his analysis of the landed gentry of England that the aspirant 'middling sort' were anxious to imitate their social superiors and eagerly copied their education, manners, and behaviour. By doing so he argued that they effectively solidified the class structure by supporting a homogenized culture of gentility but left 'elite hegemony unaffected'. In this way England was developing an aristocratic bourgeoisie, rather than a bourgeois aristocracy in the nineteenth century.[58] Entry to the very highest levels of the English power structure proved difficult for the English 'middling sort', but social mobility remained relatively fluid below the highest tier. In Ireland, as in England, it was an air of gentility that could set a boy apart—and this was most easily achieved at a boarding school.

IV ELITE IRISH CATHOLIC SCHOOLS AND IRISH SOCIETY: CURRICULUM AND CATHOLICITY

[T]he pupils trained in this College aspire to respectable positions in society. Therefore they should be found among the leading merchants, barristers,

David Dickson, 'Jacobitism in Eighteenth-century Ireland: A Munster Perspective', *Eire-Ireland*, 39 (Fall/Winter, 2004), 77.

[58] Lawrence Stone and Jeanne C. Fawtier Stone, *An Open Elite? England 1540–1880* (Oxford, 1986), 292–7.

doctors, landowners etc. in Ireland. How important then that they should be
well-trained and grounded in piety?[59]

Thomas Morrissey on Castleknock *c.*1894

The education on offer at Irish Catholic elite schools was European and therefore
transnational in origin, but was nonetheless comparable to that on offer at English
public schools—which was itself also European and transnational in origin. Both
systems were heavily reliant on teaching a thorough grounding in the ancient
Greco-Roman world. At Clongowes, the oldest of the schools, the curriculum
remained largely untouched in the early decades. In 1841 the pattern was much
the same as it might have been in 1814. The custom book of the Prefect of Studies
shows that in 1841 the senior class (Rhetoric) and the middle classes (Grammar
I and II) were taught with a heavy emphasis on the classics:

> **Rhetoric**—Horace, Homer, Virgil, Cicero, Racine, Livy, Testament Greek
> grammar, geography, catechism, geology, history, astrology, globes (celestial),
> declamation, Anacreon
> **Grammar I**—Lucian, Ovid, Cicero, Latin, French, prosody, catechism,
> French dialogues, Xenophon, Telemaque, Greek grammar, history, botany,
> geography, declamation, terrestrial globes.[60]

Though the *Ratio Studiorum* was European in origin the prescribed scholastic
workload did not differ a great deal from that offered at the major English schools,
and by offering Greek the school could align itself with what was soon to become
a prerequisite for a recognizably elite education state-wide.[61] A devout Catholicism
was emphasized at Clongowes above all other considerations, and sometimes to
the detriment of other academic disciplines. It was this system that Thomas Francis
Meagher, the famous separatist, Young Irelander, and orator, decried in public.
Meagher was highly critical of the Jesuit system of education which he experienced first at Clongowes Wood (1834–40) and afterwards at Stonyhurst (1841–3).
Speaking of his time at Clongowes he sought to reconcile his love of the school
with his disdain of its curriculum:

> That's the fault I find with Clongowes. They talked to us about Mount Olympus and
> the Vale of Tempe: they birched us into a flippant acquaintance with the disreputable
> gods and goddesses of the golden and heroic ages; they entangled us in Euclid; turned
> our brains with the terrestrial globe...but, as far as Ireland was concerned, they left
> us, like blind and crippled children, in the dark. They never spoke of Ireland. Never
> gave us, even what is left of it, her history to read...In that beautiful grand castle

[59] Murphy (ed.), *Nos Autem*, 47
[60] IJA, Custom Book of the Prefect of Studies 1841, Papers of Clongowes Wood College, SC/
CLON/31.
[61] Sheldon Rothblatt has argued that the study of Greek became prevalent in the eighteenth
century, and built up to a crescendo in the nineteenth century when the importance of Greek history, political thought, and philosophy became a cornerstone of elite education in Britain. Sheldon
Rothblatt, *Tradition and Change in English Liberal Education: An Essay in History and Culture* (London,
1976), 46.

of theirs, circled by their fruitful gardens and grain-fields, walled in by their stately dense woods of beech-trees, walnut and firs, they lived and taught—so it seems to me now—rather as hostages and aliens, than freemen and citizens. But I can't bear to say anything against Clongowes, it is to me a dear old spot. Long may that old tree, on which I've carved my name, put forth its fragrant blossoms, multiply its fruit, lift its aged head to Heaven, and receive thereon the dews which fertilize, and the golden beams that propagate.[62]

The other schools experienced a similar emphasis on the abstract and the politically neutral. We have already seen that the role of Tullabeg was merely preparatory at this stage, and Blackrock was a more modern institution owing to its late entry into the market in 1860. Castleknock has left us little record of its early years, but we know that it was a school with a considerable number of ecclesiastical students and followed a course broadly similar to that employed at the main Irish seminary, Maynooth. Placed in context this political reticence or conservatism was not all that difficult to justify: Catholic Emancipation was not yet a generation old and within living memory it had been forbidden for a school such as Clongowes to even exist.

In many respects the curriculum pursued at the Catholic schools can be seen as progressive. It has sometimes been argued that Catholic schools in the nineteenth century were anti-science.[63] Such assumptions are undermined by the development of science at schools such as Castleknock, which had a telephone installed in 1885, and constructed an electric model train railway in the same year.[64] In 1875 Blackrock students were studying electricity and magnetism from Atkinson and Ganot's, *Natural Philosophy for General Readers and Young Persons* (1872).[65] This scientific curiosity was tempered by an attachment to the study of the classics that reflected the wider belief in British and Irish society in their intrinsic value as a complete aesthetic and historical frame of reference.[66] The resulting emphasis on the classics lasted well into the twentieth century and, as Christopher Stray has argued, a shared knowledge of the ancient Mediterranean world played a significant role in 'maintaining the solidarity of elite social groups and the exclusion of their inferiors' through schooling.[67] The classical bias in Irish education was

---

[62] Arthur Griffith (ed.), *Meagher of the Sword: Speeches of Thomas Francis Meagher in Ireland 1846–1848* (Dublin, 1916), 271.

[63] For a recent articulation of this belief that the Catholic Church was anti-Enlightenment see John Wilson Foster, 'Natural History in Modern Irish Culture', in Peter J. Bowler and Nicholas Whyte (eds), *Science and Society in Ireland: The Social Context of Science and Technology, 1800–1950* (Belfast, 1997), 125. See also Justin Wallace, 'Science Teaching in Irish Schools 1860–70', *The Irish Journal of Education*, 6/1 (Summer, 1972), 50–64.

[64] James H. Murphy, 'The Irish Catholics in Science Debate: John Tyndall, Cardinal Cullen and the Uses of Science at Castleknock College in the Nineteenth Century', in Juliana Adelman and Eadaoin Agnew (eds), *Science and Technology in Nineteenth Century Ireland* (Dublin, 2011).

[65] Sean Farragher, 'The French College Inspected, 1860–1880', in *Blackrock College Annual* (1955). For a more thorough investigation of this issue see Don O'Leary, *Catholics and Science: From 'Godless Colleges' to the Celtic Tiger* (Cork, 2012).

[66] See David Newsome, *Godliness and Good Learning* (London, 1961), 64; John R. de S. Honey, *Tom Brown's Universe: The Development of the Victorian Public School* (London: Millington, 1977), 130–2.

[67] Christopher Stray, *Classics Transformed: Schools, Universities, and Society in England 1830–1960* (Oxford, 1998), 11.

revealed when in 1880 the Royal University of Ireland set as its highest award a studentship in Ancient Classics, valued at £500. An unpublished student journal at Blackrock in the 1860s reveals a high standard had been achieved in the composition of classics, the quality of which was comparable to any rival school in Ireland or Britain.[68]

Catholic doctrine and devotion was a central and pervasive element in the education delivered at these schools. The effect of this on the boys attending may only be guessed at, though at all four schools the exposure was high and participation was encouraged. Upon entering Castleknock College, a boy was automatically enrolled as a member of the Sacred Heart Sodality—effectively an out-of-hours prayer group incentivized by the school authorities, who gave preferential treatment for those boys who proved themselves sufficiently enthusiastic in their devotion. The Sacred Heart 'cult' was essentially a Jesuit one which was ultramontane in character and symbolized a Catholic 'vision of the nation'.[69] It was particularly strong in France, where it came to signify the contempt with which the revolution of 1789 was held by the royalist Catholic right. By the 1880s the society of the Sacred Heart was widespread in Ireland across all social classes, with active sodalities in thirty-five of Dublin's fifty-three parishes.[70] Devotion to the Sacred Heart was itself admirably transnational, with the President of Ecuador, Garcia Moreno, going so far as to consecrate his entire country to it in the 1870s.[71]

All new entrants to Clongowes signed a pledge to conform to the prayers and good works of the Arch-Confraternity of Paris.[72] One such signatory was James Joyce, a sodalist at both Clongowes Wood and the Jesuit day-school, Belvedere College, where he was sent when the family could no longer afford to keep him at Clongowes. Indeed a scene in *A Portrait of the Artist as a Young Man* (1916) describes a fictional conversation between Fr Conmee, SJ and Stephen Dedalus where the priest extols the virtues of a vocation:

> – In a college like this, he said at length, there is perhaps one boy or two or three boys whom God calls to the religious life. Such a boy is marked off from his companions by his piety, by the good example he shows to others. He is looked up to by them; he is chosen perhaps as prefect by his fellow sodalists. And you Stephen, have been such a boy in this college, prefect of Our Blessed Lady's sodality. Perhaps you are the boy in this college whom God designs to call upon himself.

---

[68] See BCA, *The French College Literary Journal*, II (Jun.–Dec. 1869).

[69] The power and scope of the cult has perhaps its most impressive realization in the neo-Byzantine cathedral which dominates the Paris skyline, the *Sacré-Cœur* at Montmartre. James McMillan, ' "Priest Hits Girl": on the Front Line in the "War of the Two Frances" ', in Christopher Clark and Wolfram Kaiser (eds), *Culture Wars: Secular–Catholic Conflict in Nineteenth-century Europe* (Cambridge, 2003), 83–4.

[70] Colm Lennon and Robin Kavanagh, 'The Flowering of the Confraternities and Sodalities in Ireland, *c.*1860–*c.*1960', in Colm Lennon (ed.), *Confraternities and Sodalities in Ireland: Charity, Devotion, and Sociability* (Blackrock, 2012), 76–96 at 80.

[71] Raymond Jonas, *France and the Cult of the Sacred Heart: An Epic Tale for Modern Times* (Berkeley, CA, 2000), 235.

[72] IJA, Papers of Clongowes Wood College, SC/CLON/77.

A strong note of pride reinforcing the gravity of the priest's voice made Stephen's heart quicken in response.[73]

In this way devotional Catholicism was represented by the priests as the pinnacle of a boy's education at the school. This emphasis was partly motivated by the need for more vocations from within the student body, but was mostly the natural effect of Catholic doctrine. Sodalities were far from rare in Ireland, and certainly not the preserve of Catholic elite colleges. By 1954 (the Marian year) there were 450 of them in Ireland.[74] Religious instruction was a marked feature of English public schools, but the prevalence of sodalities and the frequent spiritual 'retreats' given to boys, made for a different if comparable experience. Spirituality suffused throughout the schools and was invoked whenever possible. When a student fell gravely ill at Blackrock in 1871 Fr Ebrenecht noted wearily 'One of our students—down with rheumatic fever—was given up by two doctors. We made a novena to Our Lady of Lourdes. He is doing well at the moment...To be Bursar here is *une charge terrible.*'[75] Every aspect of the school was affected by such religious devotion—the famous blue-and-white strip sported by the Blackock College rugby team is in fact a reference to the colours of the Virgin Mary. At the Irish schools discussed here, no separation of Catholicism and education was thought possible. Therefore a politically neutral and essentially conservative Catholic education was on offer at the elite schools, with a distinct emphasis on the study of the classics. Beyond these central tenets, the influence of external events and the demands of a secular and increasingly credentialist society were paramount to the educational policies adopted by the schools.

The school journals of Clongowes Wood and Castleknock provide evidence of the influence and demands of the labour market. The school journal began in 1885 at Castleknock and a decade later at Clongowes. Aimed at a wider readership than just past and present pupils, these journals were produced at a loss for advertising purposes and were often noted in the national press for their 'beautiful production' and articles of 'literary merit and great historical interest'.[76] They offer the reader a fascinating fusion of nationalism and imperialism, as well as an invaluable source for anyone interested in the day-to-day running of the schools. The *College Chronicle, Castleknock* of 1895 included a story entitled 'From Darkest Africa—A Pastman's Story of the Cape', written by Alfred J. McNally and detailing his time in South Africa. It is written with avid readers of *The Boy's Own* in mind:

Who ever heard of anybody going to Africa of his own free will? The impression I had of Africa was that it must be a very greyish-brown sort of country—at least, all the maps said so...Gorillas, black men, lions, elephants and alligators, were my idea of its population...I find life in many ways pretty much the same as it is everywhere else. The same bustle of business man; the everlasting chase after "power and pelf";

---

[73] Joyce, *A Portrait of the Artist as a Young Man*, 120.
[74] Gregory Ffrench, 'The Sodality of Our Lady', *The Furrow*, 5/9 (Sep. 1954), 542.
[75] Sean Farragher, 'Blackrock College One Hundred Years Ago', in *Blackrock College Annual* (1971)
[76] 'The Clongownian for June', *Irish Times*, 21 Jun. 1898; 'The Clongownian', *Freeman's Journal*, 26 Jun. 1897.

the same social amenities; the dinners, the dances, the tennis and croquet parties; the scandals; the same religious controversies (but not so bitter as in Ireland); the same loves and the same hates.[77]

Very often the journals provided contributions on desirable occupations that revealed the underlying ambitions of those receiving an elite education. An article by H. C. Kane, a past pupil of Castleknock, was entitled 'My Career as a Midshipman'. Kane described a naval career spanning Malta, Beirut, and Bermuda. *The Clongownian* offered as a lead article in its first issue an article by 'J.C.', a Tullabeg pastman, on his career in the Indian Civil Service. Past pupils of these schools had achieved prominent positions in the army and the authorities were enthusiastic in their acclaim. Any promotion was noted in the journals and the careers of old-boys such as Major General Francis Clery (Clongowes: 1854), chief of staff in occupied Egypt 1886–8, were lauded.[78]

The other great theme of the journals was a strain of patriotism and moderate nationalism. The leaders of 1798 were regularly lionized in the *The Clongownian* as were the old Gaelic clans. In 1895 the subject of the prize-winning student essay was Owen Roe O'Neill, written by a young Thomas Kettle, later a significant Home Rule MP and nationalist thinker. References to a local leader of the United Irishmen, Hamilton Rowan, also abounded in the early issues of the Clongowes journal, and an article on Lord Edward FitzGerald won the prize essay competition on the eve of the 1798 centenary year in Christmas 1897.[79] This patriotism depended a great deal on the antiquity of the event celebrated and the social class of the patriot celebrated. No mention was made of more controversial or proletarian forms of nationalism, such as land agitation or Fenianism. In fact, even the topic of Home Rule was avoided in the school journals.

Despite the inclusion of both imperial and patriotic references in the school journals, nationalist commentators such as D. P. Moran frequently derided the major Catholic schools for their journal content in wounding editorials such as this one in 1901: 'We have before us a copy of the *Castleknock Chronicle*. Castleknock College is a West British institution on the borders of Phoenix Park'; and in 1902: 'The spirit of the Seoínín is much in evidence in the *Clongownian*, the official publication of the eminent Tommy Atkins College, Clongowes.'[80] It is therefore relatively difficult to pin down the self-proclaimed identity of the schools. No distinction or clear preference was shown in the pages of the school journal between those individuals who supported the idea of a free Ireland and rebellion against the British, and those that took full advantage of the fruits of Empire, but there was a preponderance of the latter among the alumni, and hardly any mention of the former.

[77] Alfred J. McNally, 'A Pastman's Story of the Cape', *The College Chronicle, Castleknock*, 1/10 (Jun. 1895), 21–2.

[78] Francis Clery was the fourth son of a Cork wine merchant, James Clery. See Richard Hawkins, 'Sir Cornelius Francis Clery 1838–1926', *DIB*.

[79] See *The Clongownian* 1/1 (Jun. 1895); *The Clongownian*, 1/2 (Jun. 1896); *The Clongownian*, 1/4 (Jun. 1897).

[80] D. P. Moran, 'Current Affairs', *The Leader*, 29 Jun. 1901; D. P. Moran, 'Current Affairs', *The Leader*, 12 Jul. 1902.

Figure 2.5 Former pupil John Redmond with Dr Nicholas Donnelly, Clongowes, 31 May 1914

The Irish elite schools had a complex relationship with the political convictions of former pupils, and this was also true in the reverse. Former pupils such as John Redmond (Clongowes: 1858) preferred to accentuate the 'tone' of the school rather than any political influence. Speaking on the occasion of the Clongowes centenary on 31 May 1914, Redmond (Figures 2.5 and 2.6) maintained it was improper to speak of his political convictions but was content to say that at Clongowes he been taught 'by precept and by example the lessons of truth, of chivalry, and of manliness...I was taught here that the highest duty of a gentleman was in every circumstance of life to play the game.'[81]

Redmond's allusion to 'playing the game' was no accident, and it hinted at the dual function of elite schools as leaders in sport but also in the provision of raw material for the war effort which was then looming. The phrase itself may have been popularized as a result of Henry Newbolt's poem *Vitae Lampada* (1892) with its celebratory lines, 'The river of death has brimmed his banks/And England's far, and Honour a name/But the voice of a schoolboy rallies the ranks:/"Play up! play up! and play the game!" ', but the connection of military competence with sporting prowess was of course much older.[82]

---

[81] 'Clongowes Centenary', *Irish Independent*, 1 Jun. 1914.
[82] Many thanks to Whitney Standlee for referring me to the supposed origins of the phrase. For more see J. A. Mangan, *The Games Ethic and Imperialism: Aspects of the Diffusion of an Ideal* (London, 1985).

Figure 2.6 John Redmond addressing Clongowes Wood College, May 1914

The over-representation of Clongowes and other Catholic elite schools in the war dead was indicative of this.

Quite apart from this slow march toward mass-militarization, the second half of the nineteenth century witnessed the explosion of popularized field games. Elite schools were at the vanguard of this development, and in particular English public schools. Games were only one noticeable part of what Bourdieu would later characterize as the cult of 'taste'—the idea that conspicuous consumption of certain commodities and experiences become a 'social weapon' by which the highest in society can mark itself off from the low, and indeed the other way around. Thus, at vital junctures games such as rugby football were promoted at the schools, and others, such as association football, were restricted. A particular speaking style was encouraged and boys were at all times urged to behave in a gentlemanly and noble fashion. Shaping behaviour by the inculcation of rule-based sports and social codes was all the more achievable in the solitude and isolation of a secluded boarding school.

V PLAYING THE GAME: CIVILIZATION, MANNERS, AND THE CULT OF 'EXTRAS'

In 1983 a letter appeared in the *Irish Times* problem column from a concerned mother seeking advice on choosing a school for her second son. The family lived in one of the richest parts of Ireland, Killiney in south Co. Dublin, and therefore had a wide array of schools to choose from:

> I sent my first son to the Christian Brothers, and he has got pretty good results all round, but he has a frightful Dublin accent. Also they play no games at the school, there is no music, no debating, no 'extras' at all...Now I have to decide where to send my next son. I would prefer to send him somewhere with a bit more polish and more extras. Among those suggested have been Blackrock, Gonzaga...I have heard that the Jesuits are the tops in education. Is this true?[83]

The letter, but for the mention of the Jesuit day-school Gonzaga, founded in 1950 in Ranelagh, might have been written a hundred years before. The concerned mother was echoing social concerns related to 'frightful' accents that were, in fact, much older than that. In their 1798 collaboration *Practical Education*, Richard Lovell Edgeworth and his daughter Maria claimed that a public school education could remove a potentially debilitating lack of social graces or 'rusticity':

> Persons of narrow fortune, or persons who have acquired wealth in business, are often desirous of breeding up their sons to the liberal professions; and they are conscious that the company, the language, and the style of life, which their children would be accustomed to at home, are beneath what would be suited to their future professions. Public schools efface this rusticity, and correct the faults of provincial dialect: in this point of view they are highly advantageous.[84]

It was this 'polish' that was desired. It is, of course, next to impossible to prove that schools such as Clongowes and Blackrock intended to cultivate a certain style of speech or accent, although it is certainly true that speech-making and correct enunciation were prized assets in Victorian society as a mark of respectability. Writing in 1921, a former Clongowes student and prominent Dublin writer Arthur E. Clery maintained that '[i]n the "spot-diagnosis" of social position, clothes hold the first place; accent comes second. Manners are a very bad third. In all countries there is an accent that is thought to equate with spats, another with corduroys.'[85] Seemingly intangible accomplishments such as a fine accent and deportment, in addition to games, debating, and all the other 'extras' are the clearest indicators of an elite education, and always have been. As both Maria Edgeworth and the author of the 1983 letter indicate, the curriculum pursued at an elite school was only important in relation to the national standard; it was the 'extras' that set a school apart and removed any provincialism or 'rusticity'.

'Refinement' in one's conduct and manners became one of the central themes of Victorian society, and was a continuation of what scholars such as Oliver Goldsmith had often referred to as 'taste' and 'civilization' a hundred years previously. The word 'politeness', William Godwin noted in 1823, descended to

---

[83] 'Question? Time', *Irish Times*, 5 Apr. 1983.

[84] Quoted in Linda Mugglestone, *Talking Proper: The Rise of Accent as Social Symbol* (Oxford, 2002), 226.

[85] Corduroys, now so beloved of academics and other professionals, were considered distinctly working-class at the time this was written. Arthur E. Clery, 'Accents: Dublin and Otherwise', in *Studies: An Irish Quarterly Review*, 10/40 (Dec. 1921), 545.

us from both Latin and Greek and meant to polish or to make smooth.[86] Thus ideas and concepts such as urbanity, politesse, and civility were inherited by the Victorians at a moment when the position of the aristocracy in the social order was for the first time under real threat. This had a profound effect across the various classes. For the majority the result was an ever increasing expectation of cleanliness and 'respectability' amongst the lower orders. For those with greater aspirations the ability to conform to accepted signals of civility, manners, and taste were increasingly seen as a basic requirement for the socially ambitious. May Laffan's novel *Hogan M.P.* (1874) lacerated such aspirants, describing in full colour the vagaries and petty jealousies of Irish middle-class culture, as did the later work of Katherine Cecil Thurston in novels such as *The Fly on the Wheel* (1908). A cultured accent and refined taste in art are rarely native to a provincial thirteen-year-old, and Irish youth was no different to any other in that respect. A concerted effort was necessary if the sons and daughters of Irish Catholic families were to adopt them. A boarding school education, with its immersive, socializing qualities, was the preferred remedy.

Elocution featured at all four schools, as did a vigorous tradition of debating. In 1883 Blackrock College spent over £18 hiring Professor Motler to practise correct speech with the boys. The same Professor Motler, 'a charming old-world type', appeared at Clongowes also in this period, which implies he had cornered this particular market.[87] These were accepted elements of a 'refined' education. This refinement is difficult to quantify, but was well articulated by J. S. Sheehy in the *College Chronicle, Castleknock* in 1907. 'The "spirit" or "tone" of Castleknock is its most marked characteristic', he wrote, 'there is in the first place the religion of the Castleknock...in the next place the great refinement, the real culture of the College. Castleknock men are gentlemen to their finger-tips.'[88] This preoccupation with civilized behaviour can also be found at the other schools. At Tullabeg William Delany imported copies of Roman paintings and hung them in a gallery so that his boys who often came from 'utterly artless homes, towns and wilds could gain a tolerable idea of what a Raphael or Titian looked like'.[89] Such accessories created not only a spirit of appreciation amongst the boys, but added lustre when visitors arrived. In nationalist circles such apparent artifice was considered intolerable and base. 'There is no word in the English language we have come to detest so much as the word "respectable"', complained the editor of *The United Irishman* in 1901, '[r]espectability in Ireland means shoneenism, sleveenism and cringing, debasing soullessness'.[90] For the school authorities at Clongowes and the other

---

[86] Oliver Goldsmith, 'On the Cultivation of Taste', in Peter Cunningham (ed.), *The Works of Oliver Goldsmith*, 12 vols. (New York, 1900), VII, 51; William Godwin, 'Of Politeness', in *Reflections on Education, Manners and Literature* (Edinburgh, 1823), 296.

[87] BCA, Grande Livre, Section Professeures, 23; John B. Kelly, 'Some Clongowes Memories 1879–1885', *The Clongownian*, 11/1 (Jun. 1926), 38.

[88] J. S. Sheehy, 'The Soul of a Great School', *The College Chronicle, Castleknock*, 2/22 (Jun. 1907), 19.

[89] Fr George O'Neill, 'The Story of a Hundred Years (Tullabeg 1818–1918)', *The Clongownian*, 8/3 (Jun. 1919), 252.

[90] *The United Irishman*, 31 Aug. 1901, 4.

schools, to have neglected this aspect of the education of their charges would have been as unworthy as to have neglected arithmetic.

The visit of Queen Victoria to Ireland, in April of 1900, was the occasion of much excitement in Ireland. It also helped to radicalize a generation of national-ists that would become more famous over the next twenty years as the leaders of the revolutionary generation. Maud Gonne, for example, helped to organize a Patriotic Children's Treat Day as a sort of juvenile protest at the estimated 50,000 children that had turned out for the Queen's Day in the Phoenix Park, organized by Lady Arnott.[91] As if to accentuate the ideological struggle for the youth of Ireland, the Queen spent much of her private three-week visit with children of all backgrounds. One aspect of this was relevant to the elite schools; for the first time ever an English monarch visited Irish Catholic boarding schools. The three chosen for the honour were all schools with a high social status, and two were convent schools for girls. The Loreto and the Sacred Heart Convents were both located in the south Co. Dublin suburbs of Rathfarnham and Dundrum respectively.

The only boys' school visited by the Queen was Castleknock College. Her choice of school may have been influenced by the fact that the current Lord Chief Justice of England, Charles Russell, Baron Russell of Killowen had been educated at the school in the 1840s, albeit just for one academic year. Castleknock had made Russell first president of the old-boys union, a masterstroke D. P. Moran later regarded as 'about the most barefaced piece of advertising' he had ever seen.[92] The Queen's visit to the school was reported widely in the national press and nowhere more enthusiastically than in the Castleknock school journal:

> Sunday, April 22nd, 1900 marks a memorable day in the annals of Castleknock. On that day Queen Victoria visited the College. The event is historic, as being the first occasion that an English sovereign visited an Irish Catholic College...Three ringing cheers greeted the arrival of the royal carriage, and the aged Queen bowed her gracious acknowledgements.[93]

The piece highlights both the ecstatic reception of the monarch by the boys, and reveals the pride attached to such a visit by those running the school—who gave their boys a week off to celebrate. For a successful school such as Castleknock a royal visit confirmed a place at the summit of Irish education and Irish society. The Jesuits consoled themselves with the fact that at least Fr William Delany, SJ was a prominent member of the Citizen's Reception Committee, which had decorated the city in honour of the Queen.[94]

The development of sport in the Irish Catholic colleges mirrored that of the public schools in England and in some cases was directly imported.[95] In fact,

---

[91] Jeanette Condon, 'The Patriotic Children's Treat: Irish Nationalism and Children's Culture at the Twilight of Empire', *Irish Studies Review*, 8/2 (Aug. 2000), 167–78.

[92] Quoted in Murphy (ed.), *Nos Autem*, 98.

[93] *The College Chronicle, Castleknock*, 1/15 (Jun. 1900), 4.

[94] IJA, Citizens Reception Committee to Fr William Delany, SJ, 16 Mar. 1900, William Delany Papers, J456/354.

[95] Rugby football, for example, transferred to Blackrock College in the 1870s via Alexander Cruikshank, a former pupil at Rugby School. Farragher and Wyer, *Blackrock College 1860–1995*, 47.

almost all ties with sport in the four colleges are either directly or indirectly connected to England and played an important part in the creation of the public
image of the schools. Gaelic games, such as hurling, were not publicly endorsed
by the school authorities except in that insecure window after the transfer of
powers in 1922. In England the Clarendon Report noted the significant amount
of time devoted to organized sport in the early 1860s. This sporting ethos was
defended by schools such as Eton College as of 'the highest value in the formation of a character well-adapted for the duties of after-life'.[96] The importance of
sport was not questioned, just the balance between academic achievement and
recreation.

Sport played a comparable role in Irish schools at this time, and was valued
for its ability to instil discipline in the student body. The idea of organized sport
and public games between rivals was one that developed in English public schools
from 1860 onwards. The type of sport endorsed by the educators, however, was
dictated by its social status, and it is therefore a useful indicator to the historian
of education as it reveals much about any given school's self-image and ambition. Clongowes contested its first out-match in standard cricket in 1861, a game
of symbolic importance and against Trinity College, Dublin.[97] Blackrock had a
cricket team by 1865, but the game developed more slowly there owing to a lack
of playing space. The decision to purchase the neighbouring Williamstown Castle
and estate in 1875 allowed Blackrock to become 'a sport-oriented school almost
overnight'.[98] Castleknock, however, was an exception. Remembering his time at
the school John Ward (Castleknock: 1869–77) recalled that only two half-days
a week were devoted to games and that cricket 'had hardly counted' during his
time at the school.[99] The sport grew slowly in Ireland, mainly among those with
ample leisure and time, hence the patronage of the upper classes and, of course,
schoolboys.

It was at Tullabeg that the game of cricket reached a peak as a useful social tool.
William Delany, SJ had forcibly introduced cricket on his arrival at Tullabeg in
1860, successfully negotiating the initial unfavourable reaction from the boys,
who had 'cut balls with knives and smashed bats when Prefects were not looking'
in protest.[100] Tullabeg was the first school to 'entertain' established Dublin cricket
teams such as The Phoenix and Na Shuler as a matter of course, underlining the
importance of the social aspect of the game. The entertainment often involved
an overnight stay for prominent and influential men of the world, and the senior
boys were encouraged to mingle with them at the customary banquet held in their
honour. The policy of inviting influential socialites was a carefully considered one;
by showing them a school capable of producing boys to match England's finest,

[96] TNA, Rev. Stephen Hawney, 'Eton College', The Clarendon Commission Papers, H.O.73
58/1/21.
[97] Peter Costello, *The History of Clongowes Wood College, 1814–1989* (Dublin, 1989), 116.
[98] Farragher and Wyer, *Blackrock College 1860–1995*, 46.
[99] *St Vincent's Castleknock Centenary Record 1835–1935* (Dublin, 1935), 104.
[100] McKenna, SJ, 'Fr William Delany', 59.

both academically and in the 'games of social life', the Rector subtly introduced the idea of equality of position to both pupil and visiting dignitary. This social networking was also a marked aspect of elite education in England. Headmasters such as Vaughan at Harrow (1845), and Thring at Uppingham (1853) were pioneers in the introduction of organized games in the public school system.[101] It was these schools that popularized the idea of sport as both a disciplinary and morally regenerative tool, and it was these schools that Irish Catholic schools sought to emulate.

The game of rugby football became a social necessity in Irish schools towards the end of the period examined here, and by the early twentieth century had supplanted cricket as the sport of choice for the upper classes.[102] Schools such as Clongowes, Castleknock, and Blackrock became principally defined by their participation in the sport and are to this day often referred to informally as the 'rugby schools'.[103] Throughout the twentieth century rugby provided Irish schools with the kind of binary rivalries that are common between English public schools.[104] Such games reinforce the position of the school in the public eye, and every year the Leinster Schools Cup receives generous coverage in the Irish national press.

The rival code of association football, or soccer, appeared in Ireland in 1878 and became instantly popular.[105] By the early 1890s however, the association code had become a common pastime of the working classes in Ireland and England. This tarnished the image of the game at an elite level and was promptly downgraded at public schools across Britain. One student at Clongowes, Gerard More O'Ferrall complained in the school journal in 1895 that the Jesuit fathers had gone so far as to remove the association goalposts on the school grounds in an attempt to discourage a game that no longer had any social status.[106] O'Ferrall's letter makes it clear that a decision had been taken at management level to prioritize rugby at the expense of association football for social reasons. The same thing occurred at Castleknock several years later when rugby was enforced on the student body at the expense of the association code.[107] Such pragmatism was a marked feature of Catholic elite education. Games were effective accessories, but only if they were the right ones.

---

[101] See J. A. Mangan, *Athleticism in the Victorian and Edwardian Public School: The Emergence and Consolidation of an Educational Ideal*, 2nd edn (London, 2000), 13–21.

[102] To a certain extent this was due to the fact that cricket, being a summer game, became less suitable as the summer vacations gradually lengthened at boarding schools.

[103] This label was recently applied to them by a prominent sports journalist, see Tom Humphries, 'Ireland's Grand Illusion Fails to Fool Lost Generations', *The Times*, 21 Mar. 2009, 4–5.

[104] The Eton vs Harrow cricket match at Lord's drew 38,000 spectators at its peak in 1914, while Marlborough and Wellington only recently called a halt to their annual game of rugby, one that had run since 1870. Gareth A. Davies and Stephen Adams, 'Public School Fall Out Leads to Rugby Ban', *Daily Telegraph*, 13 Feb. 2008.

[105] Neal Garnham, *Association Football in Pre-partition Ireland* (Belfast, 2004), 29.

[106] *The Clongownian*, 1 (1895), 43.

[107] *Castleknock Centenary Record*, 267.

VI SOCIAL MOBILITY

The *Dictionary of Irish Biography* (*DIB*) provides a wealth of detail on social mobility and Irish education. Of the 595 Catholic males in the database born between 1835 and 1890, at least 99 of them were educated at Clongowes, Tullabeg, Castleknock, and Blackrock—almost one in every five. The majority of the boys attended Clongowes, where the rate of social mobility can be said to have been relatively stable. Studies of British social mobility show that the frequency with which boys moved within similar-grade occupations was quite high, but the rate of dramatic upward or downward social mobility tended to be quite low. Andrew Miles has seen that this trend is consistent across Europe, and that any real rise in the rate of mobility over the period 1839–1914 was primarily as a result of the decline of the primary productive sector and the concurrent growth of white-collar occupations. As such, intra-class mobility was much more frequent than inter-class mobility and the Victorian period was characterized more by class homogenization than was previously thought.[108] This is certainly the case with the sample of Irish boys taken from the *DIB*, even allowing for the fact that, by virtue of having an entry in the dictionary, their lives ought to exhibit an atypically high level of achievement than the majority of their peers. Table 2.3 illustrates the extent to which boys at the Irish schools remained within their father's occupational class or outside of it. Blackrock, with a more modest clientele, proved the best option for those seeking to dramatically improve the fortunes of the next generation.

Intergenerational mobility in the *DIB* sample proved to be reasonably high, as might be expected from a database of exceptional people. Upward mobility was steady and seldom dramatic; there were very few cases of 'rags to riches' stories in Irish life and advances tended to be gradual and incremental instead. The case

Table 2.3 Social mobility at all four schools relative to father's occupation

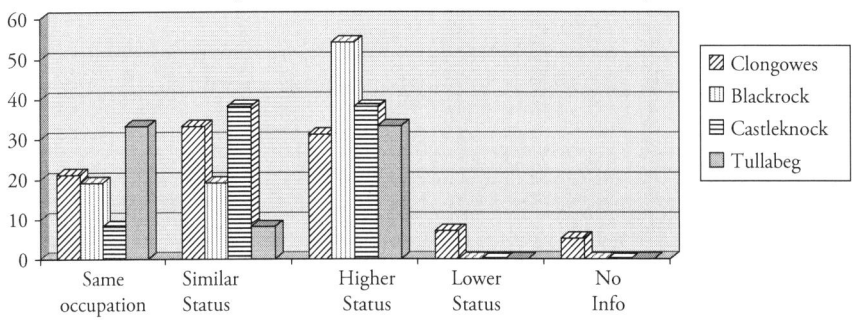

[108] Andrew Miles, *Social Mobility in Nineteenth and Early Twentieth-century England* (Basingstoke, 1999), 33, 177. See also similar results for Dutch social mobility in the same period, Marco H. D. van Leeuwen and Ineke Maas, 'Social Mobility in a Dutch Province, Utrecht 1850–1940', *Journal of Social History*, 30/3 (Spring, 1997), 619–44.

of the Rahilly family may again prove useful in illustrating this point. Michael Joseph Rahilly was born in 1875, the third son of Ellen and Richard Rahilly of Ballylongford, Co. Kerry. Richard, a merchant and magistrate, claimed indirect descent from the renowned poet Aodhagan Ó Rathaille and his wife Ellen claimed to be a relative of another famous Irish poet, James Clarence Mangan. After his time at a local school and Clongowes (1890–3) Michael trained (unsuccessfully) as a doctor at UCD before a brief spell in the family business ended with his premature retirement. His involvement in advanced nationalist circles and eventually his participation in 1916 ensured that Michael, by then calling himself 'the O'Rahilly', warranted a *DIB* entry. His death was recorded in a poem by W. B. Yeats and further enhanced his legend. His own sons rose to the top of Irish republican society in the twentieth century. The eldest surviving, 'Mac' O'Rahilly was a barrister, a founder member of the political party Clann na Poblachta and gave the oration at the burial of Maud Gonne in Glasnevin cemetery in 1953.[109] Aodogán was a co-director of the major semi-state company Bórd na Móna and later director of the revived Greenore port company near Carlingford Co. Louth. Richard became an engineer thus ensuring that the family status quo was not seriously threatened by the actions of one errant son.

Indeed, the lives led by several of the boys included in the *DIB* make categorization a challenge. For example, Alfred Aylward attended Tullabeg in the late 1850s, the son of a school inspector in Wexford. Over the course of his life he fought for Garibaldi in Italy, posed as a surgeon on the Union side of the American Civil War (1861–5), and was arrested for his Fenian links in Dublin in 1866–7 before leaving for South Africa where he worked as a digger in the diamond fields and edited a local paper. In addition to all this he claimed, somewhat dubiously, to have been a Russian spy in India, to have traded slaves in Africa, and to have been a reporter in the 'wild west'. He may have died in a train crash in America, in Sudan serving the Mahdi forces, or perhaps in Sweden.[110] Does Aylward represent a case of upward or downward social mobility? He certainly epitomizes physical mobility. Reviewing a short South African biography of Aylward in 1984 one scholar referred to him as one of a genre of 'feckless adventurers', which is about all one can say of him.[111]

Aylward left behind an account of his time in South Africa, *The Transvaal of Today* (1878), but autobiographical sources of this nature tend either to be scarce or equally dubious. A similar source descends to us from Sudan. Frank Power's *Letters from Khartoum* was published posthumously by his brother Arthur in 1885. Frank 'le Poer' Power, son of a Dublin bank manager, led a comparably colourful life to Aylward. At various times in his tragically short life Power served as a foreign correspondent, a soldier, an artist, and even a British Consul. He met a grisly end at the hands of the forces of the Mahdi in Khartoum (where he was acting consul)

---

[109] 'Funeral of Maud Gonne MacBride', *Irish Times*, 30 Apr. 1953.
[110] For more on Aylward see David Murphy, 'Alfred Aylward (1843–89)', *DIB*; Alfred Aylward, *The Transvaal of Today* (Edinburgh, 1878)
[111] Kevin Shillington, 'Review of Ken Smith, *Alfred Aylward: The Tireless Agitator* (Johannesburg, 1983)', *Journal of Southern African Studies* 11/1 (Oct. 1984), 182.

in August of 1884, from whence his reports of the siege to *The Times* in London had gained him an international reputation in the months following the death of the Governor General C. E. Gordon. Power was simultaneously regarded as an amusing charlatan in Ireland and a chivalrous hero in England. The journalist John Augustus O'Shea recalled that '[a] ripple of good-natured laughter used to run brightly across the faces of Irishmen in the [H]ouse of [C]ommons when his dispatches were gravely read from the government benches'.[112]

In contrast to Aylward and Power, the majority of the 10,000 or so boys that went through the schools led perfectly dull lives. Many remained in the family business, or took up an occupation similar to that of their father and with similar or slightly increased earning power. The most dramatic upward social mobility was seen at Blackrock, the least dramatic at Clongowes. This reflects the more mixed intake of Blackrock, which drew heavily from the urban merchant class and also from high-earning tradesman who were local to the school. Very often the most spectacular examples of upward social mobility were the result of emigration to countries where the class lines were not as clearly drawn, or more easily circumnavigated by an outsider. A Blackrock boy, William Mackay Laffan, provides a good example of such a trajectory. Born in 1848, he was the son of a clerk in the customs house in Dublin, and his sister May Laffan would later achieve prominence as a significant Irish novelist. Laffan entered his last days in 1909 with addresses in Lexington Avenue, NYC and Long Island. A personal friend of J. P. Morgan, Laffan had become a publishing tycoon and art collector who was widely (but falsely) believed by contemporaries to have descended from a Chief Justice of England and to have graduated from TCD—proof that even an address on Long Island is not always enough to quell the insecurity of those who achieve a high position in life.[113] Similarly, the son of a relatively modest Tipperary landowner, Sir Michael Francis O'Dwyer was a star pupil at Tullabeg in the 1870s. O'Dwyer had a stellar career in the Indian Civil Service, rising to the position of Lieutenant Governor of the Punjab, but is now remembered for his commendation of the conduct of General Reginald Dwyer at the massacre of Amritsar in 1919.[114]

Much more typical for a boy of relatively modest background was the career trajectory of Lucius O'Callaghan, who attended Blackrock in the 1890s. Lucius left school and trained with his father, the architect John Joseph O'Callaghan, a prominent Irish architect who oversaw the construction of the Union building in Oxford and was known for his Gothic style still visible at Chorley town hall and at many Catholic churches across Ireland. As Lucius approached maturity as an architect around 1905 the major Catholic commissions were drying up across

---

[112] Bridget Hourican, 'Frank le Poer Power (1858–84)', *DIB*; Arnold Power (ed.), *Letters from Khartoum: Written during the Siege by the Late F. Power* (London, 1885).

[113] In 1910 J. P. Morgan donated $100,000 to Yale to set up a William M. Laffan Professorship of Assyriology and Babylonian Literature. For more on Laffan see Helen Kahn, 'William Mackay Laffan (1848–1909)', *DIB*.

[114] Kevin Kenny, 'The Irish in Empire', in Kevin Kenny (ed.), *Ireland and the British Empire*, Oxford History of the British Empire Companion Series (Oxford, 2004), 90–2.

Table 2.4 Top five occupations of boys at all four schools

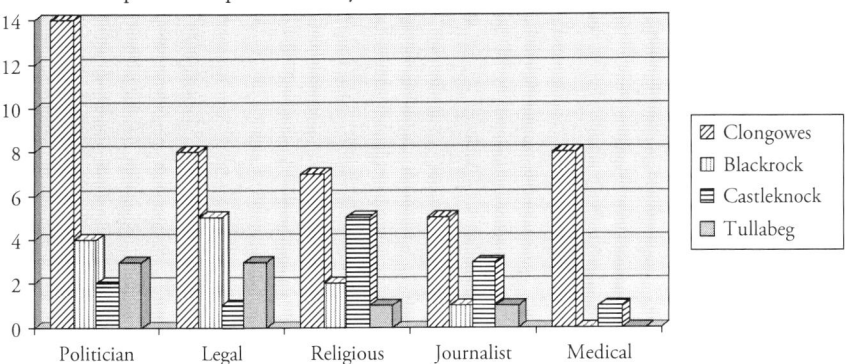

Ireland, and his main legacies are the Carenegie libraries at Tralee and Kingstown, and various banks in Ferbane, Edgeworthstown, and Kilcock.[115]

Exceptional cases aside, there are nonetheless distinct patterns that we can observe in the *DIB* sample (Table 2.4) and from an analysis of the school magazines. The most popular professions were typically in the religious life, or the professions which enjoyed the highest status: medical, military, and legal. Apart from the over-representation of political careers that might be expected of a biographical project such as the *DIB*, the sample is reasonably indicative of the careers pursued by the typical graduate of an elite Irish school. It can be supported by looking at a year-group at any one of the schools. For example, of the eighteen boys that left Blackrock in 1876 six joined the Holy Ghost Fathers, three more entered the secular priesthood—meaning that half the class entered the religious life. Another six entered the medical profession, one became a commissioned officer in the army, another a National School Inspector, and the last tried his hand at market gardening.[116] In the following year a similar breakdown was evident, though only four were ordained priests for the Holy Ghost Congregation. Other white-collar careers such as architect, engineer, and the various branches of the sciences came into vogue toward the end of the century. The schools had various specialisms—a great many Blackrock graduates entered the civil service or became medical professionals, whereas Clongowes enjoyed greater penetration in the legal and political sphere. The reasons for this were often institutional—Blackrock had a specialist civil service wing in the school for much of this period, and Clongowes could call on a 'tradition' of high legal representation. *The Clongownian* noted in 1908 that there were forty-eight old boys actively practising as barristers or judges.[117]

[115] Daniel Beaumont, 'Lucius O'Callaghan 1877–1945'; John Joseph O'Callaghan (1838–1905)', *DIB*.

[116] Farragher, 'Blackrock College 100 Years Ago', *Blackrock College Annual* (1976); Farragher, 'Blackrock College 100 Years Ago', *Blackrock College Annual* (1977).

[117] *The Clongownian*, 5/1 (Jun. 1908), 70–1.

Most boys that entered the religious life after attending one or other of the schools came from relatively modest backgrounds. The Jesuit Fr John Conmee, SJ, so prominent in the fiction of James Joyce, was the son of a prosperous farmer from Westmeath and attended both Castleknock and Clongowes. Nicholas Donnelly (Figure 2.5), a Castleknock graduate and later auxiliary Archbishop of Dublin, was the son of a Dublin merchant. John Francis D'Alton, at Blackrock in the 1890s, rose from being the son of a Mayo shopkeeper to become a cardinal and a classical scholar.[118] Many of the priests at Blackrock went out into the missions, a hazardous and often tragic undertaking. Fr Thomas Coyle died young in Sierra Leone, while Frs Michael Dunne and Edward Conyngham returned 'broken in health' from the West Indies in the 1880s. The difficulties with acclimatization worked both ways. The first-ever native African student to arrive at Blackrock, Joseph Fye, was sent back to his native Gambia via Liverpool after just two years because of ill-health.[119]

The imperial connections of the elite Irish schools are important, but ought not to be overstated.[120] Frequent mention was made of those boys who had done well in India and elsewhere but there is little to suggest that a greater proportion of Irish boys entered the Indian Civil Service (ICS) than did English boys from public schools such as Winchester. References to old boys in the Empire abound in the school journals, but it was natural that the schools should seek to use their careers as a way of reinforcing a successful and elite public image. Blackrock College were therefore keen to trumpet a career like that of Sir Michael Thomas Yarr of the Army Medical Service, an ophthalmologist who was medical attendant to the King of Siam 1895–1900 and had published several medical studies and handbooks. Born in Cloughjordan in Tipperary, Yarr was educated at Blackrock in the 1870s and joined the Army Medical Service in 1886, was promoted to the rank of Surgeon General by 1916, and knighted in 1917, and while his achievements were exemplary, for those at school they were a great exaggeration of the possibilities of Empire.[121]

The graduates of elite Irish schools were also very likely to become embroiled in military conflict, though this should not automatically be seen as a declaration of either political or emotional loyalty to the union. The elite schools of England suffered disproportionate losses across the board, especially in World War I and the Irish schools were no different. The total number on active service from Clongowes was 604, with an estimated 94 fatalities.[122] At Castleknock the figure was 256 volunteers,

---

[118] Diarmaid Ferriter, 'John Francis D'Alton (1882–1963)', *DIB*.

[119] Fye left the school in 1886–7. Farragher, 'Blackrock College 100 Years Ago', *Blackrock College Annual* (1982); *Blackrock College Annual* (1986).

[120] See Ciaran O'Neill, 'Education, Imperial Careers and the Irish Catholic Elite in the Nineteenth Century'; Timothy G. McMahon, 'Irish Jesuit Education and Imperial Ideals', in David Dickson, Justyna Pyz, and Christopher Shepard (eds), *Irish Classrooms and the British Empire: Imperial Contexts in the Origins of Modern Education* (Dublin, 2012).

[121] Yarr's most important contribution was probably a military handbook. See Sir Michael Thomas Yarr, *Manual of Military Ophthalmology for the Use of Medical Officers of the Home, Indian, and Colonial Services* (London, 1902); 'Sir Michael Thomas Yarr K.C.M.G., C.B.', *British Journal of Ophthalmology*, 21/3 (1937), 332–3.

[122] *The Clongownian*, 7/3 (Jun. 1919), 293.

with 93 either killed or wounded. The exceptional circumstances of 1914–1919 saw a great many boys engage in military service who otherwise might have avoided it. As a result the typical rank achieved by a graduate of Clongowes or Castleknock was much lower than in the relatively stable years prior to the Boer War, and any boy with rank was likelier to be a professional soldier.

The success of elite education—particularly if expensive—has always depended on academic reliability and a high performance of graduates in the labour market. The Irish schools could demonstrate a track record in both by the end of the nineteenth century. At a Clongowes old-boy dinner in 1896 one of its most successful products, Chief Baron of the Exchequer Christopher Palles, rose to toast his fellow Clongownians with a triumphant flourish. 'We are now upon equality with any other persons in the kingdom, and we are quite prepared to take our stand on that, and to prove it not only equality in name, but an equality that we are determined to maintain.'[123] We should not take for granted, of course, that Palles was including all Catholics in this assessment—but rather Catholics of his own ilk and education. His audience was receptive; all had bought into this idea and by raising a glass were helping to project it.

VII IRISH CATHOLIC SCHOOLS AND THE MAKING OF THE INTERMEDIATE

Historians of Irish education have thus far accepted the conclusion of Norman Atkinson in his 1969 history of Irish education, that after the Powis Commission on national education (1870): 'Successive British administrations were in no hurry to engage in a further tussle with the intricacies of Irish education. It was only after stern prodding by Irish members…that Disraeli's government were persuaded to take action.'[124] P. J. Dowling and John Mescal both agree that the impetus for the bill came from Irish members in the House of Commons.[125] Only John Coolahan's study of Irish education comes close to recognizing the influence of the Irish Catholic colleges when he notes a link between the staff at Blackrock College and that of St Mary's College, Port of Spain, Trinidad.[126]

Sir Patrick Keenan, the man most often credited for the creation of the Intermediate Act, had trialled a payment-by-results scheme at Trinidad in 1869, with much success. It was this system that was eventually adapted to the needs of Ireland. That the Holy Ghost Fathers at Blackrock had direct experience of this scheme was important to subsequent developments in Ireland. A campaign of letters beginning in 1872 from within Blackrock, ostensibly from the pen of

---

[123] Chief Baron Christopher Palles, 'Address to the Clongowes Union 1896', in Menton, *The Clongowes Union Centenary Chronicle*, 78.
[124] Norman Atkinson, *Irish Education: A History of Educational Institutions* (Dublin, 1969), 114.
[125] P. J. Dowling, *A History of Irish Education: A Study in Conflicting Loyalties* (Cork, 1971), 133; John Mescal, *Religion in the Irish System of Education* (Dublin, 1957), 104–5.
[126] John Coolahan, *Irish Education: History and Structure* (Dublin, 1981), 62.

the professor of English at the school, Edward Howley, contained many of the provisions that were to feature in the Act of 1878.[127] Thus Blackrock, it might be argued, brought the issue to public attention—copies of Howley's pamphlet were sent to Randolph Churchill, John Henry Newman, Matthew Arnold, and other luminaries. The payment-by-results scheme that Blackrock proposed did not meet with universal approval, but was successful in achieving the overarching and stated goal of the Catholic hierarchy to secure the continuation of denominational education at intermediate level.

Much more direct, however, was the intervention of Fr William Delany, SJ of Tullabeg, who is alleged to have drafted the majority of the bill that was read in the House of Commons in collaboration with one of his ex-pupils—a fact that has escaped all but Delany's biographer. The past pupil, Judge Mathias MacDonnell Bodkin made the claim originally in 1914 and then reiterated it in an article published in *The Clongownian* in 1924:

> My friendship with Father Delany begun in my school days, stretched out into my afterlife. I frequently visited my old college during the years of his pre-eminently successful rectorship, when it headed the schools of Ireland, Catholic and Protestant, under the Intermediate Education Act (an Act, by the way, which I helped him to draft into legal form, clause by clause, nearly fifty years ago, in one of the parlours of Tullabeg).[128]

Delany's correspondence corroborates the claim made by his biographer that he was involved in a consultative capacity as the bill passed through parliament, as letters to Sir Patrick Keenan and John Cassidy testify.[129] The Catholic colleges therefore initiated the bill, allegedly had a hand in its drafting, and promoted it with the help of such supporters as Lady Londonderry, Lord and Lady Portarlington, Lord Randolph Churchill and his father, the Duke of Marlborough, then Lord Lieutenant of Ireland—all personal acquaintances of Fr Delany.[130] Tullabeg was at that moment the leading light of the Irish elite colleges, politically well connected and, along with Blackrock, the root of the Intermediate Education Act of 1878. It should therefore be seen as no coincidence that the leading school in Ireland, according to the published results of the first year of the intermediate system (1879) was Blackrock College, or that Tullabeg carried off fifteen gold medals (a fifth of the total awarded) before its closure in 1886.[131] The game was, to some extent, already rigged in their favour.

---

[127] Howley was prompted to do so by Père Leman, president of Blackrock College, and it was Leman who maintained the correspondence with Patrick Keenan and others after its publication. Sean Farragher, 'Education Act 1878', *Blackrock College Annual* (Dublin, 1958).

[128] Mathias MacDonnell Bodkin, *Recollections of an Irish Judge* (London, 1914) 24–5; 'Father Delany as I Knew Him', *The Clongownian*, 10/2 (Jun. 1924), 17.

[129] John Cassidy was in constant communication with Gerald FitzGibbon, then Solicitor General of Ireland. See IJA, William Delany Papers, J465/221, J465/298, J465/299–304.

[130] Lord Randolph Churchill was forceful in his demand for an improvement in intermediate education for Ireland. See e.g. Motion for a Select Committee, HC Deb., 4 Jun. 1878, Vol. 240, cc. 1216–36.

[131] 'The Intermediate Examinations', *Freeman's Journal*, 19 Sep. 1879; IJA, Tullabeg Papers, Souvenir of St Stanislaus College, Tullabeg, Kings County (Dublin, 1910), FM/TULL/38.

The Irish Catholic hierarchy were content enough that the bill would go ahead, and that it would benefit less-wealthy Catholics. An important battle over property and jurisdiction had played out between the hierarchy and the largest teaching order in the country, the Christian Brothers, between 1875 and 1878, which had a significant effect on intermediate education. The Christian Brothers, through an appeal to the Holy See, had successfully prevented the hierarchy from claiming the right of ownership and inspection of their schools, which they had specifically asserted at the Synod of Maynooth in 1875. The resulting schism between the Brothers and their main source of funding meant that the congregation did not continue its impressive growth. Emmet Larkin has argued that class differences underpinned this clash, as the Brothers were generally drawn from more modest backgrounds than the bishops. In response to the congregation's plea for better remuneration for their teachers, Cardinal Cullen remarked that the Brothers did not belong to the 'better-off class of society' and 'had no reason to expect a costly maintenance'.[132] Removed from direct control of the Christian Brothers, the Irish hierarchy was relegated to a consultative role as the main moves in intermediate education were being made from within the teaching orders, and in this sense we can argue that the Intermediate Act was negotiated by those above the bishops in social status and sympathies, for the benefit of those below them.

The first examinations were held in the summer of 1879 and the results were published in the *Freeman's Journal* on 18 September. To widespread surprise three of the top five positions were occupied by Catholic schools. Blackrock occupied first place in Ireland, and Tullabeg and Castleknock followed closely behind with second and fourth place respectively. Two northern endowed schools, almost totally Protestant in composition, Royal School Belfast and Foyle College, took third and fifth place respectively. Perhaps the biggest surprise of the results was the poor performance of the most prestigious and socially exclusive of the Catholic Colleges, Clongowes Wood.[133] The only non-elite school to appear on the list was a provincial seminary in Co. Monaghan. The gamble taken by the Catholic schools had paid off spectacularly. In the following five years Blackrock and Tullabeg dominated the prize lists—with Castleknock and Clongowes a little further behind. When the 1881 prize lists were published the new Rector at Tullabeg, Aloysius Sturzo, revealed he would have been 'very much pleased but for the competition of the French College who got 30 prizes and 36 exhibitions...I wonder how [they] got so many clever boys and taught them so well.'[134] The Catholic schools emerged from the published list as the clear leaders in their field, and consolidated their position at the top of Irish education. Such high performance had come at considerable cost, however. The achievement of Tullabeg and Blackrock in topping the poll in 1879 was surprising to many, but seems obvious in retrospect. Delany was

---

[132] Quoted in Emmet Larkin, *The Roman Catholic Church and the Emergence of the Modern Irish Political System 1874–1878* (Dublin, 1996), 346.

[133] Clongowes was under enormous financial pressure at the time with debts of over £25,000. This was eventually alleviated by the amalgamation with Tullabeg in 1886. IJA, Tullabeg Papers, Draft letter Delany to Tuite, FM/TULL/33.

[134] IJA, William Delany Papers, Aloysius Sturzo to William Delany, 6 Oct. 1881, J456/387/15.

known to be an educationist of the highest repute, and spared no expense when it came to either the comfort of his boys, or the payment of his teachers. A principal advantage the Catholic schools had over their Protestant rivals was their access to relatively cheap labour, relying as they did on members of their own communities to do the bulk of the teaching at nominal cost. This system meant that high teaching standards were often dependent on the talent within the order at any one time. To make up the deficit, lay teachers or 'externs' were sometimes employed at Catholic schools, though this was not encouraged by superiors. Inspecting the school in 1880, John Pentland Mahaffy (later provost of Trinity College) noted that the average bill for a boy at Tullabeg was £55 per annum, and that the annual income of the school about £8,000. He estimated that only about half of that sum was necessary for the maintenance of the school, and noted:

> The rest goes to the support of the Jesuit teachers, the salaries of a few lay assistants, the large hospitalities of the establishment and in general improvement. Everything is richly and completely appointed, and there is constant entertaining of visitors...The boys are supplied with three good school libraries, besides a fourth reference library for the higher school and a master's library. They have a good cricket-ground and a large ball alley, and so carefully are sports encouraged that a yearly sum is charged in the accounts for subscription to them...But it was evident that the whole energies of the place were directed to passing various examinations, especially the Intermediate.

Mahaffy was incorrect on only one point; the income at Tullabeg was in fact, over £9,000 at a time when the extensive western estates of Lord Clanmorris, totalling some 18,111 acres was worth just £8,263.[135] The report ended with a remarkable aside, and one that to some extent confirms that Delany was the central character in the creation of the intermediate system in Ireland. Mahaffy noted that the university question 'constantly occupied' Delany and that the 'new University will probably be arranged (like the intermediate) in such a manner as to suit his views exactly'.[136]

Delany required teaching of the highest standard, and was prepared to pay for it. In 1880, when queried by his Provincial, he justified his offer of a £200 per annum salary to a lay (or extern) teacher of mathematics on the rather blunt basis that he was an exceptional teacher.[137] The sum of £200 was a great deal beyond the average teacher's salary in Ireland and Britain. A Christian Brother's salary at the time was somewhere in the region of £30 to £50 per annum, and indeed a small Christian Brothers school could be run for a year for less than the cost of one maths teacher at Tullabeg.[138] At Radley College in Oxford, where fees were set at one of the highest rates in England (£117 per child before compulsory extras were added on)

---

[135] IJA, William Delany Papers, Delany to Tuite (undated 1880), J456/23; Hussey de Burgh UH, *The Landowners of Ireland* (Dublin, 1874), 82.

[136] McKenna, SJ, 'Fr William Delany', 84

[137] Morrissey, *Towards a National University*, 26–7.

[138] Smaller foundations that aspired to elite status, such as the Carmelite Terenure College could not afford such exorbitant expenditure and consequently are absent from the intermediate prize lists in the early years. See Fergus A. D'Arcy, *Terenure College 1860–1910* (Dublin, 2009), 111–12.

teaching fellows were paid no more than £150 per annum in 1880.[139] Delany's argument with the Provincial (James Tuite) over staff costs reveals the conflicting pressures on the head of an elite college. When pressed, he railed on his superior:

> No doubt it is more desirable that in a Jesuit college the work should be done by Jesuits. But where are the Jesuits? If this college had depended solely on its Jesuit staff for the past five years its reputation and its numbers and its income would be very far indeed from what they are. In those five years the pension has been increased from 32 guineas to 45 and yet the numbers gone up from 100 to 170 and promise to go beyond that.

The pressure on Delany was serious, and he made it clear in the letter to his superior that he had a distinct idea of the beneficiaries, should his school close down: 'Shall we send them away, say we are not competent either to teach them or to get them taught, and hand them over to the French College [Blackrock]?'[140] This issue of external teachers was eventually what to lead to his demotion early in the academic year 1880–1.[141] Tuite had apparently heard enough of Delany's arguments, and following the discovery of several anomalies in the Tullabeg accounts by another Jesuit, Fr Maguire, it is reasonable to assume that Tuite grasped his chance to rid himself of a Rector whose attitude to finance was anathema to his own. Maguire reported back that Delany had been 'paying staff under the heading of Farm labour and College improvements costing a sum of more than £500'.[142] In any case, the most successful and dynamic Irish educationist of his generation was demoted, but only for a short time. His ability as an educational leader saw him become first president of University College Dublin, just as Mahaffy had predicted.

If Delany had bought success at Tullabeg, then it would be difficult to say otherwise of Castleknock. In preparation for the very public test, Rev. Peter Byrne incentivized his staff, offering financial bonuses if their pupils excelled. The boys were promised cash prizes up to £3 each for a performance that would do both themselves and the school credit, and an extern was employed solely to coach exam candidates at a salary of £130 per annum.[143] The results fees were therefore worth very little to the elite colleges. This is perhaps best exemplified by comparing the annual income of Tullabeg (roughly £9,000) to the total amount paid in results fees to all schools across Ireland by the Board of Intermediate Education for the same year (£7,462).[144] In 1886, the last year of its existence, Tullabeg earned £158 from the results fees, not even enough to cover the salary of Delany's maths teacher.[145] In the same year Castleknock earned £126 in prize money, which represented about 3 per cent of their annual income—their fees alone amounting to

---

[139] Christopher Hibbert, *No Ordinary Place: Radley College and the Public School System* (London, 1997), 128.

[140] IJA, William Delany Papers, Delany included a detailed account of the duties and payment of the staff with this letter, Delany to Tuite undated 1880, J456/23.

[141] IJA, William Delany Papers, Aloysius Sturzo to Delany, 8 Oct. 1881, J456/349.

[142] IJA, William Delany Papers, Matthew Maguire to James Tuite, 31 Aug. 1880, J456/Box 23.

[143] Murphy (ed.), *Nos Autem*, 71.

[144] *Report of the Intermediate Education Board for the Year 1880* (Dublin, 1881), 4.

[145] *Report of the Intermediate Education Board for the Year 1886* (Dublin, 1887), 30.

over £4,500 without the usual extras taken into account. Blackrock, for their part, paid Dr John Casey, a world-famous mathematician based at Trinity College, £100 a year for occasional lessons outside of his teaching commitments at the Catholic University in Stephen's Green—meaning that their boys were being tutored by a man generally regarded as the co-founder of modern geometry of the circle and triangle.[146]

It was public acclaim that motivated the elite colleges, not a financial reward that amounted to a tiny percentage of their annual income. Nevertheless, it was commonly perceived that Catholic schools depended on results fees to stay afloat. Certainly, the Christian Brothers benefited enormously from the intermediate fees, entering huge numbers for the examinations and carrying off significant sums.[147] Between 1881 and 1901 the number of Catholics recorded by the census as having received an intermediate education more than doubled from 10,145 to 23,897, while the number of those attending Anglican schools actually declined. In light of these numbers it must be admitted that the Intermediate Act benefited Catholic education enormously. The impact at the elite schools was less obvious, but no less revolutionary. Faced with an annual examination of their perceived worth, and finding themselves subject to public opinion for the first time, the elite colleges were forced to take account of the received image of their educational 'product' and spent their money accordingly.

VIII RULE ETONIA: IRISH CATHOLIC PUBLIC SCHOOLS?

If Irish Catholic schools could not quite compete with the structure, tradition, and influence of the established public schools of England, they could at least compete with the education provided there. The boys that graduated from Clongowes, Blackrock, Tullabeg, and Castleknock could expect to know just as much Latin and play cricket just as competently as any Eton or Winchester graduate. This, in turn allowed them parity of esteem and performance at open examinations and, provided the boy had enough financial backing, a shot at the high-status professions and the army. The highest levels of society remained difficult to access, something that also hindered their co-religionists in England. Considering this handicap, the elite Catholic schools of Ireland probably over-achieved in their quest to give their graduates the best chance at upward social mobility. The schools provided an atmosphere that was, at a surface level, very obviously Anglocentric. Schools such as Blackrock and Tullabeg naturally looked to the most famous and accomplished peers in Britain and Ireland for inspiration. In 1898 *The Clongownian* published a list that encapsulated this aim (Table 2.5). It made reference to the fact that

---

[146] BCA, Grand Livre, Section Professeurs, 23.

[147] Ten years after the introduction of the payment-by-results scheme, the Christian Brothers were able to generate over £1,071 from 425 successful candidates at nineteen schools nationwide. See *Report of the Intermediate Education Board for the Year 1889* (Dublin, 1890), 36–41.

Table 2.5 Entries in the Indian Civil Service lists, 1898*

St. Paul's	6
Dulwich	6
Eton	4
Charterhouse	4
Clifton	4
Clongowes	3
Rugby	3
Winchester	3
Manchester	3
Merchant-Taylors	3

*'Indian Civil Service', *The Clongownian*, 2/1 (Christmas, 1898), 16.

Clongowes men had enjoyed much success at the Indian Civil Service examinations: 'We can see that practically all the successful candidates come from great public schools; and it will be a matter of pride to Clongownians to find that their college ranks high in comparison with the best English schools. The lists show the following order, according to the number of successes.'

Presumably, it was indeed a matter of some pride to old Clongownians that their school was on a par with schools such as Rugby and Winchester. Such statistics proved that their project was in some ways a successful one. Christopher Palles spoke of Irish Catholics being 'upon equality' in his speech at the Clongowes Reunion in 1896. Such equality may have been unavailable to the majority of Irish Catholics, but it was demonstrably available to those in the room at the time. They had paid a little extra for the polish, and as with the public school boys of England, they expected a return for it. However, beneath the Eton suits and cricket creases lay schools that constantly strove to instil Catholic values in their students. The Anglocentrism was mostly then surface level, and tolerated for the sake of the target market. Within a generation of the Palles speech, hurling, rebellion, and Cúchulainn would briefly (though never entirely) replace cricket, loyalty, and Tom Brown in the pages of the school annual. In the background the Catholic elite schools simply got on with the work of advancing the careers of those boys that passed through.

By the early twentieth century Irish Catholic education had improved dramatically at third level and at primary level, but secondary education remained a luxury for most. As with the modern system, the unregulated nature of secondary education can be seen to have provided parents with an opportunity to send their children to a school which would provide a recognizably elite education. By providing such an education, schools such as Clongowes and Blackrock could argue that they moulded their boys into an influential body of young men with a firm commitment to Catholic values—a group that might have otherwise been lost to a non-Catholic school at home or abroad. These schools were outward-looking and students from Clongowes, Blackrock, Tullabeg, and Castleknock were typically based in the prosperous cities of Dublin and Cork, or from well-to-do rural back-grounds. The expansion of the Empire and the increase in civil service positions provided this group with the possibility to expand on their ambition and it was this availability of opportunity that incentivized a certain level of mimicry and imitation of English public schools—then the most successful and best-known model in the world.

No mention has been made in any history of Irish education of the direct impact of the elite schools upon state-wide intermediate education in the period 1878–1924. The system of education that was adopted has been widely accepted as a wholly negative system by twentieth-century historians of education without reference to its success as a compromise in 1878, and one that particularly benefited lower middle-class Catholic education while making no comparable difference to any other denomination. The elite Catholic schools emerged victorious from a system they had helped to design, thus reaffirming their place at the top of the domestic social hierarchy of education.

Despite their success and ambition, the Irish elite schools were consistently bypassed by many of the major Catholic elite families throughout the nineteenth century. Despite teaching a similar curriculum to an equivalent standard, at a cheaper tariff than that demanded by English Catholic colleges, the allure of a prestigious English education proved irresistible to sections of the Irish laity. Frederick Falkiner argued in 1885 that this section of the upper classes returned to Ireland 'with contempt for all Irish things and Irish people'.[148] The following two chapters will, for the first time, attempt to come to terms with why they felt it was a worthwhile investment.

---

[148] Frederick R. Falkiner, 'The Irish Schoolboy Exodus', in *The Dublin University Review*, 2 (Dec. 1885), 329.

PART II

3

'Surely Ireland Is not Ceylon or Burma?'
Irish Boys at English Catholic Public Schools 1850–1900

We congratulate the young Irishmen who have so well upheld the intellectual reputation of their native land among strangers, but we cannot help asking why so many of them should have been exiled to seek in another country the education which they could as easily procure at home? There is something extraordinarily unpatriotic and unnatural in this system. Surely, Ireland is not Ceylon or Burma, that in order to be counted civilised, our own young men must be sent across the seas to learn the manners of those who are, by the fortunes of war, our masters.

> 'Irish Talent in England', *The Irish Catholic*, 27 Jul. 1889, 4

Irish West Britons are made in Ireland and in England—the most finished specimen is not unnaturally turned out in England. Some boys are sent to Irish colleges, where they are taught to play cricket, rugby football, and mayhap, tennis. In the English Colleges such as Stonyhurst, Edgbaston, and Beaumont, they are taught pretty much the same things, no doubt. But in the latter places they are taught an "accent", and that consideration takes the hearts of the papas and mammas in the villages of Leinster, Munster and Connaught.

> D. P. Moran, 'General Remarks', *The Leader*, 10 Nov. 1900, 5

Throughout the nineteenth century and well into the twentieth some of the wealthiest Catholic families in Ireland chose to pursue an English education in preference to an Irish education. The most prestigious schools in England all had a significant percentage of Irish boarders throughout the nineteenth century. So prevalent was the Hibernian strain that some English schools were in danger of being comprehensively colonized. For example, the intake at the Benedictine school at Downside, near Bath, was more than 50 per cent Irish in some years, and averaged 36 per cent throughout the 1870s. At St Edmund's College in Ware the project of writing a triumphant history of that 'great English Catholic school' was compromised when it emerged that the majority of its early graduates were not, in fact, ethnically English.[1] The schools themselves were somewhat reluctant

---

[1] Paul Shrimpton, *A Catholic Eton? Newman's Oratory School* (Herefordshire, 2005), 210.

to admit to their reliance on the Irish for income, which partly explains the near total absence of any reference to it in school histories or the contemporary school prospectuses, advertisements, and journals.

The mere fact of substantial Irish attendance at English schools is of interest, and of course lends itself to accusations of colonial mimicry and a slavish devotion to English manners and mores. This was certainly the view of *The Irish Catholic*, which decried the practice in 1889—comparing Ireland to Ceylon or Burma in its acceptance of a minor role in the colonial exchange. This was unhelpfully simplistic. The tradition of overseas education extends much further back, and the majority of the schools attended by Irish-born boarders in the second half of the nineteenth century were originally Continental institutions which had migrated to the remote English countryside at that critical juncture between the relaxation of penal restrictions on Catholics in 1793 and the Napoleonic persecution in the first decades of the nineteenth century.

Education is something more than the provision and reception of knowledge; it depends on factors that cannot easily be measured. The weight of antiquity, of prestige, and of power attaches itself to some institutions more than others. Continental seminaries such as the Irish colleges in Paris, Douai, and Leuven are lauded in Irish Catholic history for having acted as incubators of religion, language, and culture in the seventeenth and eighteenth centuries. No such history exists of the strategic migration to England though the evidence available shows that the type of family sending children to England in the nineteenth century was similar to the families utilizing Continental education in the previous centuries.

The 'school experience' is peculiar to each institution and varies accordingly. The decision to send a son to a boarding school in England can neither have been taken lightly, nor without a level of strategic planning. The reception of Irish boys in this English context and among an international and diverse student body is worth considering in light of a global Catholic elite in the nineteenth century. After all, these boys were a very different type of Catholic in Britain to those who often feature in our Diaspora histories, where the emphasis has usually been on migrant pauperism and the hellish conditions endured by those who left Ireland in the nineteenth century.

I EDUCATION, THE IRISH, AND THE ENGLISH CATHOLIC ELITE

The presence of a significant number of wealthy Irish Catholics at English schools brings into sharp relief a fact known to historians of both groups for many years: that the accepted binary of a pompous English Catholic establishment and its gently paternalist accommodation of Irish migrant pauperism is an insufficient one if we are to understand the complexity of the Anglo-Irish Catholic relationship. The sociologist Mary Hickman has done valuable work on working-class Catholic migrants and their integration into the British education system at elementary level in the nineteenth century, but little has been written of the middle-class and wealthy Irish who were willing to pay a considerable price to educate their sons and daughters in England.[2] Irish Catholics were present at every level of British and Irish society, before, during, and after the penal era, and their power was considerable.[3]

The great majority of Irish Catholics in Britain were poor, especially those travelling over in the wake of the famine, but so too, by definition, were the majority of the faithful of any religion. In the eighteenth century the resident or 'native' English Catholic population had accounted for less than 1 per cent of the total population and was comprised of small pockets of practising Catholics, particularly in the north-east, north-west, and the midlands of England.[4] These communities were facilitated in their worship by strong landed magnates who had survived centuries of punitive taxation. Indeed, they often worshipped at a secluded chapel *inside* the house of such a landed family. The influx of Irish migrants in the nineteenth century entirely changed this social dynamic and ruptured this comfortable paternalist relationship forever. After the Napoleonic period the character of English Catholicism had changed from a predominantly rural and recusant Church to a predominantly urbanized one which was part Irish, industrialized, and working class.[5] This did little for the social claims of the recusant gentry. V. A. McClelland has put the number of Catholics in England at 600,000 persons in 1850, with the recusant or 'Old Catholics' accounting for just 25,000 of this figure. The remainder were of Irish origin, plus a few thousand scattered converts. Dismissive of their poverty-addled Irish co-religionists, alien to both the Establishment and to the alternative tradition of non-conformity, these few English Catholics were without obvious allies, though this did not necessarily reduce their clamour for political and social equality.

The stability of Catholicism in England was further rocked by the slow-burning 'Oxford movement', a prolonged theological argument which spilled over into a large-scale defection of intellectuals from the Episcopal Church to the Roman, starting with John Henry Newman in 1845—an act which probably made him the first household Catholic name in England since the Glorious Revolution. The 'convert' families had little in common with the recusant northern families, and this complicated relations between the hierarchy and the laity even further as the nineteenth century wore on, as the hierarchy proceeded to recruit heavily from the converts and, perhaps, to pander to the new recruits from Ireland to such

---

[2] See Mary J. Hickman, 'Integration or Separation? The Education of the Irish in Britain in Roman Catholic Voluntary-aided Schools', *British Journal of Sociology of Education*, 14/3 (1993), 285–300.

[3] Some work has been done on the development of an Irish Catholic network in metropolitan London in the long eighteenth century. See John Bergin, 'The Irish Catholic Interest at the London Inns of Court, 1674–1800', *Eighteenth-Century Ireland: Iris an dá chultúr*, 24 (2009), 36–61.

[4] For an overview of Catholics in England the two standard works of reference remain John Bossy, *The English Catholic Community 1570–1850* (Oxford, 1975) and M. D. R. Leys, *Catholics in England: A Social History* (London, 1961).

[5] Leopold Gooch, 'From Jacobite to Radical: The Catholics of North East England 1688–1850' (unpublished PhD, University of Durham, 1989), 1.

an extent that they alienated the landed class—some of whom remained loyal to socially selective regular orders such as the Society of Jesus. With such a sea-change in their fortunes it was small wonder that many of the English Catholic gentry washed their hands of any real involvement or membership of the secular clergy, where they would be forced to minister to a faithful they no longer recognized and take orders from a hierarchy they considered socially inferior. This antipathy was shared on both sides of the divide, with the Catholic bishops of England proving themselves much more openly hostile toward the regular orders, and in particular the Jesuits. This antipathy was laid bare most famously in the course of two disputes surrounding the opening of Jesuit schools in major urban centres. The first of these disputes centred on the opening of St Francis Xavier in Liverpool in the 1840s, and the second on the opening of another Jesuit college in Manchester in the mid 1870s.[6] During the course of the second dispute the leader of the secular hierarchy, Cardinal Manning, wrote to the Bishop of Salford and the man who would succeed him as Archbishop of Westminster to say that he had 'long felt' that the English province of Jesuits was 'altogether abnormal, dangerous to themselves, mischievous to the Church in England'.[7] If the seculars and regulars maintained a dignified and respectful distance in Ireland, the battle lines were explicit in England.

On a surface level those with the most in common within this complex Catholic union were the wealthiest English and Irish Catholic gentry, both of which had landowning and high Tory sensibilities in common.[8] This materialized—the Irish elite schooled alongside the English after all—but not in any structured way. As long as Fenianism and disloyalty were associated with Irish Catholicism in the British worldview the public espousal of Irish causes by English Catholics was unthinkable. The English Catholic gentry regarded themselves as rightful custodians of England and even had some reasonable grounds for doing so. After all, the premier peer of the kingdom, the Duke of Norfolk, was a Catholic. The nineteenth-century influx of Irish migrants sullied the image of self-regarding aristocrats who thought of themselves as altogether a different class of Catholic. As Sally Jordan has pointed out, wealthy English Catholics had a 'dual and paradoxical' position in the English class hierarchy as both 'members of the social elite and of a periodically persecuted and repressed religion, at whose head was a foreign power'.[9] This split loyalty lent itself to the accusation that the Catholic gentry were

---

[6] See Martin John Broadley (ed.), *Bishop Herbert Vaughan and the Jesuits: Education and Authority,* Catholic Records Society Series 82 (Woodbridge, 2010); Oliver P. Rafferty, 'The Jesuit College in Manchester, 1875', *Recusant History*, 20/2 (1990), 291–304; Maurice Whitehead, 'The Contribution of the Society of Jesus to Secondary Education in Liverpool: The History of the Development of St. Francis Xavier's College c.1840–1902' (PhD, University of Hull, 1984).

[7] Broadley (ed.), *Bishop Herbert Vaughan and the Jesuits*, 56.

[8] Though there were certainly Liberal Catholics as well, in politics at least. For the best work on Catholic high politics in the second half of the nineteenth century see Oliver P. Rafferty, *The Catholic Church in a Protestant State: Nineteenth-century Irish Realities* (Dublin, 2008); Dermot Quinn, *Patronage and Piety: The Politics of English Roman Catholicism* (Basingstoke, 1993).

[9] Sally Anne Jordan, 'Catholic Identity, Ideology and Culture: The Thames Valley Catholic Gentry, from the Restoration to the Relief Acts' (PhD, University of Reading, 2002), 11.

somehow less English than their Anglican counterpart, though this was a barb usually employed by politicians who knew the value of residual anti-Catholicism to their prospective vote in England. Far from being a threat to the Anglican establishment the English Catholic elite had a tendency to overreach in their conformity. The proof of this can be found not only in the behaviour of the most established Catholic families, but in the schools to which their children were sent. Dermot A. Quinn has pointed to the nineteenth-century imitation of Eton and Rugby at schools such as Stonyhurst and Downside, believing it to be 'beyond parody'. Was Latin verse 'the better construed', Quinn asked, 'for its being done *ad majorem Dei gloriam?*'[10] The question was reasonable in a nineteenth-century context, but becoming an archetypal English public school was merely the latest in a series of transformations undertaken by those schools in their many centuries of existence.

Since the Reformation, English Catholic education has been a story of transnational movement, of innovation and dogged survival. The majority of the oldest Catholic institutions in England are in fact originally Continental foundations, built with the purpose of prolonging the Catholic faith in Britain from a safe distance in innocuous French and Belgian towns such as Douai, Liège, and Leuven. The return of the suppressed Jesuit community to Britain in 1794, just after the passage of the Catholic Relief Acts, was necessarily low key. The school that eventually settled at Stonyhurst was founded by an Englishman at St Omer in the Spanish Netherlands in 1593. Surviving a turbulent period in the history of Catholicism, the school fled first in 1762 to Bruges, where it was suppressed along with the entire society in 1773, only to reappear at Liège and then finally at Stonyhurst, 13 miles from the town of Preston in north Lancashire.[11] In one form or another, it has been in business for over 400 years. The same is true of the famous seminaries at Ushaw and Ware, and of the Benedictine foundations at Downside and Ampleforth—which had been founded in France in the early seventeenth century at Douai and Dieulouard respectively. Many of these schools educated Irish boys also, and in many ways the nineteenth-century schooling of wealthy Irish Catholics at English Catholic schools is simply a continuation of this Continental recusant period—to the extent that we can trace families from generation to generation along with them. In the mid seventeenth century Irish lords such as Valentine Browne (Earl of Kenmare) and Jenico Preston (Viscount Gormanston) were all attending these same recusant English colleges that their descendants would attend on their return to England after 1794. This transnational aspect gave rise to some apparently inexplicable customs at the schools. For example, at Stonyhurst a 'Blandyke' was the commonly used term for a vacation day in the nineteenth and twentieth century. The term itself is actually derived from the name Blandeques, a tiny town 3 miles from the original site of the school at St Omer some 200 years previous, which the

[10] Dermot A. Quinn, 'English Roman Catholics and Politics in the Second Half of the Nineteenth Century' (DPhil, Oxford, 1986), 178.

[11] Maurice Whitehead, *English Jesuit Education: Expulsion, Suppression, Survival and Restoration, 1762–1803* (Surrey, 2013); Hubert Chadwick, *St Omers to Stonyhurst: A History of Two Centuries* (London, 1962).

Jesuits had used as a location for vacation days in the seventeenth century. Not all the English foundations returned from the Continent, but the ones that did not, such as the English College at Lisbon and the Benedictine college at Douai, were, as a rule, very minor establishments. As with all educational systems these schools formed a hierarchy of status through intense competition, and it was the Jesuit Stonyhurst College that sat at the top, along with Oscott, a secular diocesan establishment in Birmingham, until the middle of the nineteenth century. Together these colleges educated the bulk of the Catholic gentry of Ireland and Britain until a greater array of choice was provided by new foundations such as Beaumont or the Oratory, or the resurgent Benedictine schools at Downside and Ampleforth.

That Irish families were sending their children to such schools did not escape the notice of the Irish hierarchy. In 1872 a 'Committee of Irish Catholics' set up by

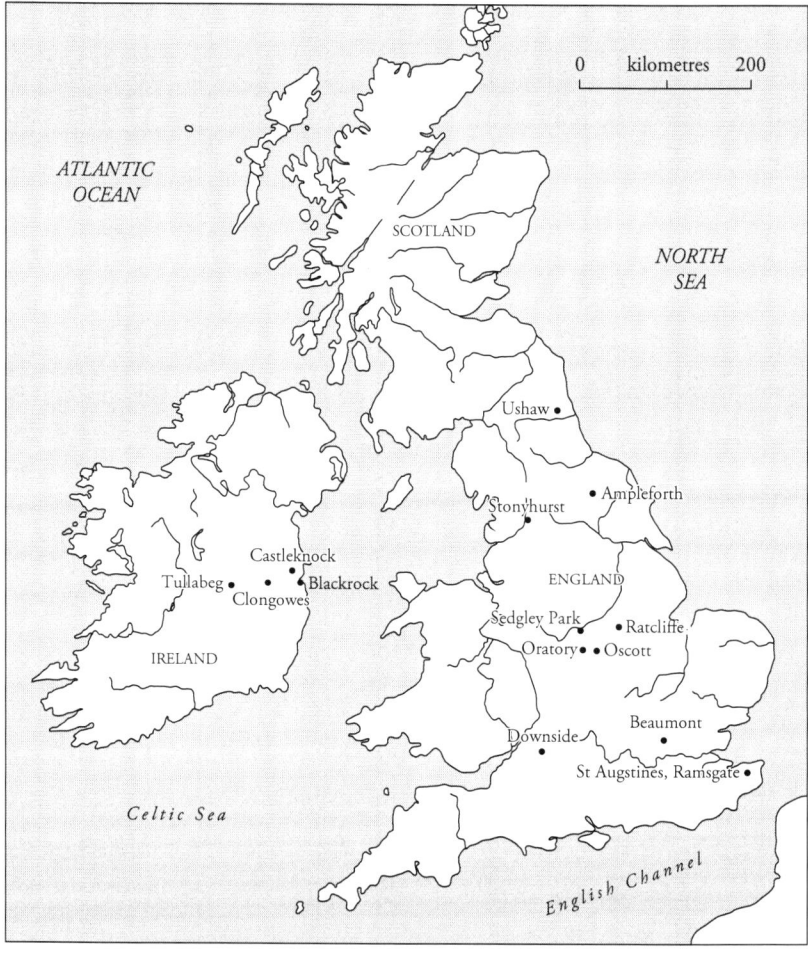

Map 3.1　Main Catholic elite colleges in England and Ireland, 1850–1900

Cardinal Cullen named a total of ten schools (shown in Map 3.1) in England that it had contacted in order to ascertain the number of Irish boys boarding with them. This commission put the figure at 250 Irish Catholics attending English boarding schools, and as many as fifty attending Continental establishments. The ten colleges cited in England were Oscott (1794), Stonyhurst (1794), Ushaw (1808), Ratcliffe (1845), Downside (1814), Sedgley Park (1763), Edgbaston (1859), Beaumont Lodge (1860), Ampleforth (1802), and St Augustine's, Ramsgate (1865). By 1872, these ten colleges represented the most important Catholic public schools for boys in Britain. However, they were far from equal on the social scale. Stonyhurst and Oscott were undoubtedly the most prestigious and socially exclusive of the Catholic schools for most of the nineteenth century, though they faced serious competition from fashionable rivals such as the Prior Park of Bishop Augustine Baines in the 1830s, John Henry Newman's Oratory School in Edgbaston in the 1860s, and the Benedictine schools from the 1890s.

Several of the schools identified turned out not to be suitable for analysis. Ratcliffe College was disregarded for a lack of archival resources, Ushaw College was primarily a seminary and therefore less attractive to the wealthiest Catholic laity, as was another prominent school (not mentioned by the committee), St Edmund's College, Old Ware. Sedgley Park and St Augustine's College in Ramsgate were further down the social ladder from a school such as Stonyhurst— and catered for the middle classes mainly, achieving roughly the same status as minor Jesuit schools like Mt St Mary's in Derbyshire (1842) or St Francis Xavier, Liverpool (1842). Nonetheless all of these establishments were educating significant numbers of Irish boys from foundation, and the Catholic committee was most likely under-estimating the numbers of Irish Catholic boys being educated abroad, though that figure would increase exponentially if we were to include those attending schools from families who had immigrated to England permanently.[12] Of the four colleges we focus on in this study all were taking in an average of 21 per cent Irish boys per year, so even at its lowest there were somewhere between thirty and forty Irish boys in the school at any one time. If we apply that just to the ten schools above we can say that there were at least 300 attending at any one time, and as many as 500 or so in many of those years.

From 1794, Stonyhurst (Figure 3.1) was the de facto headquarters of the Jesuits in England, and remained so until the establishment of the Farm Street church in Mayfair, London in 1849.[13] Stonyhurst was a site of European significance in the Catholic world and the school there was, along with Oscott, the most prestigious for Catholics in either Britain or Ireland for much of the nineteenth century. Despite this strong connection to the most influential Catholic laity, the English Catholic hierarchy strongly disapproved of the Jesuit presence in England, believing that its reputation for militancy endangered English Catholicism. This led to a rather curious situation whereby the Vicars Apostolic (the precursors to the

---

[12] Committee of Irish Catholics, *Intermediate and University Education in Ireland* (Dublin, 1872), 269.

[13] Tom Muir, *Stonyhurst* (Stonyhurst, 2006), 84–7.

Figure 3.1 Fr George Kelly, SJ teaching in a classroom in the New South Front of Stonyhurst College, *c.*1907–10[14]

reinstated hierarchy) refused to recognize that there was a Jesuit presence on the island at all until 1828 (and only when prompted to do so by the Pope) despite their educating the majority of the Catholic gentry.[15] It was from Stonyhurst that the decision was made to expand Jesuit teaching on the island after Catholic emancipation was won by O'Connell in 1829. The first such move was to establish a day-school in Liverpool in 1842, the same year as Belvedere College was founded in Dublin, and for precisely the same reason: to teach the sons of lower middle-class Catholics in an urban environment. The Jesuits therefore employed a class hierarchy even within their own educational structure. From the earliest years the intake at Stonyhurst was a mix of Irish, English, and Continental Catholic nobility, with the numbers attending rarely exceeding 200 in the first half-century of its existence. The reputation of the school was national, and an open hostility towards the work of the Society of Jesus was particularly evident in the public sphere even after emancipation. An opinion piece published

[14] ABPSJ, Beaumont College Archives 31/2/2/B. This photograph probably dates from 1907–10 and was probably originally taken by Br William McKeon. The photograph is of a classroom in the New South Front at Stonyhurst, and features prominent maps of Britain, Greece, and Italy alongside the Virgin Mary, capturing something of the essence of elite Jesuit education in the period. My thanks to Anna Edwards and David Knight for sourcing information on the photograph. For G. Kelly's obituary see *Chaplains' Weekly*, 15 Feb. 1948

[15] Bernard Basset, SJ, *The English Jesuits: From Campion to Martindale* (Sussex, 1967), 377.

in *The Times* in 1836 characterized the college at Stonyhurst as a subversive enemy within, of independent and glorious wealth, and bent on the 'conversion of Protestants' and the promulgation of 'downright rank Popery'.[16]

Oscott College had a large Irish contingent at the school from its foundation in 1792–3. The school, just outside Birmingham, was unusual in that the motivation for its foundation came from the Catholic gentry itself, particularly those with Cisalpine leanings, and the Catholic hierarchy were somewhat hostile to its liberal tendencies. The college was deliberately and explicitly designed to offer a public school education along the lines of an Eton or Winchester, with a more modern and therefore less violent approach to internal discipline. The government of the establishment was contested by the Catholic gentry who, in effect, wanted to keep it free of episcopal or secular influence as much as possible. They were thwarted in this objective and had to settle for joint management with the hierarchy, though their attempt to do it on their own shows an early example of the independence of mind in the wealthiest English Catholics, one that would later find expression in Newman's Oratory School in the same city some seventy years later.[17] Fees were expensive: Daniel Ryan of Inch House, Thurles attended Oscott in 1802 and his school bill amounted to £100 19s 10½d—a fee that could easily have kept three to four tenant-farmer families for an entire year. The school competed with Stonyhurst for both English and Irish boys and was so Irish in its sympathies by 1828 that Daniel O'Connell presented its Rector with a fine carved armchair, 'embroidered in Irish green', which can still be seen at a chapel at Oscott.[18] Between 1840 and 1847 the college was under the patronage of Nicholas Wiseman, a writer and philosopher with a European reputation, and later the first Archbishop of Westminster in the restored Catholic hierarchy 1850–65. After the departure of Wiseman the fortunes of the school waned a little and, as Oliver P. Rafferty has pointed out, the wooing of O'Connell by Wiseman had much to do with his fame in any case. Oscott remained right at the top of Catholic education until the closure of its lay college in 1889, and indeed had become something of a global draw by the 1870s, when it boasted a school list that included Alfonso Iturbide, heir presumptive to the Emperor of Mexico, Italian aristocrats such as the Borromeos and the Ghislieri, and a nephew of the President of Ecuador.[19] Their main competitor for the wealthiest Catholics in the union, while open, were not the Benedictines (who would assume that mantle in the twentieth century) but the Jesuits.

The lack of a Jesuit centre in the south of England was felt to be of disadvantage to the order as competition from other schools intensified throughout the first half of the nineteenth century. The pretensions of both Oscott and the ultimately

---

[16] 'Truro', 'To the Protestants of England', *The Times*, 11 Aug. 1836

[17] This point is well made by V. A. McClelland, 'School or Cloister? An Educational Dilemma 1794–1880', in *English Benedictine History Commission* (1997), 7.

[18] Unfortunately the green velvet has been dispensed with in a recent restoration. Judith Champ, 'Assimilation and Separation: The Catholic Revival in Birmingham *c.*1650–1850' (PhD, University of Birmingham, 1984), 166.

[19] McClelland, 'School or Cloister?', 4.

failed Roman Catholic university project of Bishop Peter Augustine Baines at Prior Park near Bath had signalled a threat to Stonyhurst in the 1830s and 1840s, and numbers declined as the competition encroached on their traditional clientele. This threat intensified further with the foundation of the Oratory School in Birmingham in 1859, under the direction of the celebrated educationist John Henry Newman, and by the twentieth century Jesuit education had been relegated below both Oratorian and Benedictine in terms of social prestige.

The early nineteenth century had seen the Catholic colleges emulate elite Anglican institutions, a fact that is especially obvious in terms of the grandeur of their architecture. Ushaw and Oscott had both modelled their buildings in the first half of the nineteenth century on buildings at Oxford, and the buildings at Downside were so ambitious that they even attracted comment in the House of Commons.[20] Newman's own part in this emulation saw him take charge of the Oratory School at Birmingham, a new foundation designed specifically to appeal to the Oxford converts and the more modern-minded gentry. The Oratory opened in 1859 and the style of education aimed at imitating the best that public schools such as Eton sought to provide. Some of the major Irish Catholic landowners sent sons to the Oratory, among them the 12th Earl of Westmeath, 14th Viscount Gormanston and the 7th Earl of Granard, no doubt encouraged by the patronage of the premier peer of England, the Duke of Norfolk.[21] A recent history of the Oratory has noted that Newman was keen to keep the school as *English* as possible, by limiting the number of Irish and other foreign-born boys. He was only partially successful in his attempt. Between 1859 and 1872, out of a total of 248 admissions, thirty-three (13 per cent) Irish boys attended the school and forty-two (17 per cent) 'foreigners'. It is clear that this decision was taken to retain its reputation as a school for the upper class only, and that too large an Irish middle-class contingent would prohibit this.[22] Nevertheless, the school remained a small one for most of the nineteenth century, roughly half the size of Stonyhurst.

This naked assertion of the need to provide a more professional education to the Catholic laity acted as an impetus to the old guard. As Fr Levi noted, 'the Oratory was founded because Oxford converts supposed Stonyhurst and the Jesuits to be ungentle, un-English and out of date'.[23] Stonyhurst, one of the most remote of the older institutions, was geographically disadvantaged by its northern location and a southern base and a new-look school for the elite was now deemed necessary if the Jesuits were to retain their dominance in the sector. The foundation of a second elite school, Beaumont College, was therefore a direct response by the

---

[20] Stonyhurst modelled its chapel on King's College, Cambridge. Shrimpton, *A Catholic Eton?*, 24–6.

[21] OSA, Oratory School Society: Members Name Book; OSA, The Oratory School Lists 1859–1919.

[22] Shrimpton, *A Catholic Eton?*, 210. The percentages used here are derived from figures provided in Shrimpton's thesis, see Paul Shrimpton, 'John Henry Newman and the Oratory School, 1857–72: The Establishment of an English Catholic Public School by Converts from the Oxford Movement' (PhD, Institute of Education, University of London, 2000), 232.

[23] Fr Peter Levi, SJ, *Beaumont 1861–1961* (London, 1961), 16.

society to the changing needs of both the Irish and English Catholic elites, and was a more modern and progressive institution as a result. Beaumont Lodge was situated in Old Windsor in Berkshire, near the Royal residence. The unfavourable climate in 1854, so soon after the hostile reaction to the re-establishment of the Catholic ecclesiastical hierarchy in 1850, made the purchase of a prominent house in Berkshire a daring one. The house served as a Jesuit novitiate for seven years, before the novices moved to Manresa House in Roehampton, London, to make way for a school that catered for between 100 and 200 boys annually for the rest of the nineteenth century. The records are imperfect for the early years, but show that the school intake rose dramatically from just four pupils in 1861 to well in excess of one hundred in 1866, and a much wider array of nationalities are evident in the student registers than at Stonyhurst.[24]

There were no Irish boys in the original party that arrived at Stonyhurst in 1794, though that would soon change. A link developed between Stonyhurst and Trinity College in Dublin (TCD), which had begun to accept Catholics in 1793. V. A. McClelland rightly identifies three early examples of this path to elite position in Ireland: Thomas Wyse, Richard Lalor Sheil, and Stephen Woulfe.[25] Sheil and Wyse were contemporaries at Stonyhurst, then at TCD in the early 1800s. Thomas Wyse (1791–1862) was a politician, educational reformer, diplomat, and the driving force behind the establishment of the 'Godless' Queen's Colleges in Ireland in 1845. Richard Lalor Sheil (1791–1851) graduated from TCD in 1811, became a leading figure in the movement for Catholic emancipation with Daniel O'Connell and enjoyed success both in the legal profession and later as a parliamentarian. Stephen Woulfe (1787–1840) was the first Catholic ever appointed to the Inner Bar in Ireland 1838. A Stonyhurst education, then, could go a long way in Ireland in the early nineteenth century.

The insularity of the Irish Catholic elite was apparent even by this early stage. The descendants of Stephen Woulfe and Richard Lalor Sheil, for instance, would later become classmates at the Oratory School in Birmingham in the 1890s. In a letter home to his father in 1893 John Woulfe Flanagan mentions having seen his cousin Denis Sheil 'a good many times' in his first weeks at the school.[26] Denis was a nephew of Richard Lalor Sheil, and related to Jack by virtue of his mother (Mary Woulfe, daughter of Stephen Woulfe). The pattern of success and access to a high-profile education in England was one that often transferred from generation to generation in this way, thereby ensuring the social status of the family.

The last school considered is Downside College (now School), in the village of Stratton-on-the-Fosse, nearly equidistant from Bristol and Bath. The rule of St Benedict is a widely popularized and published text, though there is some controversy as to the correct date of its creation, and indeed as to who might be

---

[24] ABPSJ, Beaumont College Archives, Register of Boys admitted to St Stanislaus College, London, 5/3/31/B.

[25] V. A. McClelland, *English Roman Catholics and Higher Education 1830–1903* (Oxford, 1973), 21.

[26] NAI, Woulfe Flanagan Papers, Jack Woulfe Flanagan in a letter to John Woulfe Flanagan, 20 Jun. 1893, 1189/6 (8).

the correct author.[27] It is widely acknowledged that the rule, whatever its provenance, came to be associated with the Italian saint, Benedict of Nursia, around AD 530. It became, and remains, the most common of Monastic rules. The English Benedictine Congregation (EBC) was first formed in 1216 as an umbrella group for the various foundations, but lapsed with the Dissolution of the Monasteries between 1535–40 and was revived officially in 1633 by Rome by the document *Plantata*. The EBC, like all Benedictine Congregations is simply a federation of independent institutions, and underwent major reforms under Pope Leo XIII towards the end of his pontificate at the turn of the nineteenth century. The main effect of these reforms was to return the EBC to a monastic tradition, rather than a missionary one, and to reconstitute the authority of the monasteries at Downside, Douai, and Ampleforth by abolishing the Provinces and 'ensuring the full subjugation of returning missioners to the monastic priors'.[28]

The main schools of the EBC were originally known as St Gregory's College, Downside; St Laurence's College, Ampleforth; and St Edmund's College, Douai. For the sake of clarity they will be referred to throughout the book as Downside, Ampleforth, and Douai. Ampleforth began life as St Edmund's, Dieulouard near the border of Luxembourg and France most likely in 1608. Downside School began a year earlier as St Gregory's College, Douai in 1607, and settled near Bath in 1914. Douai School has its roots in the foundation of St Edmund's, Paris in 1615, from where it migrated to Douai in 1820, and to its present site in Reading in 1903. The removal of two of the Benedictine communities to England in the late eighteenth century was an enforced one, and a direct result of the French Revolution. While on the Continent, both St Gregory's and St Laurence's had already educated Irish boys, much the same as the Jesuits had done through the same period. The locations eventually settled upon by these separate communities were of great practical importance to their Irish market. St Gregory's settled at Stratton-on-the-Fosse, some 18 miles from the port of Bristol, and therefore easily reachable for any southern Irish boy. St Laurence's, on the other hand, settled at Ampleforth, in Yorkshire, some 50 miles away from the port of Hull, which was at any rate the wrong side of the country for Irish boys. Predictably, Irish recruitment was much higher at Downside. Both Ampleforth and Downside, now famous for their popularity, achievement, and exclusivity, cannot be considered as direct competitors with the Jesuits through the nineteenth century. 'Stonyhurst and Beaumont', one historian has noted 'were both names known to the general public many years before those of the Benedictine schools became prominent. The rise of Downside and Ampleforth...dates from the early years of the present [twentieth] century.'[29]

---

[27] The controversy hinges on whether St Benedict adapted his rule from an earlier anonymous text *Regula Magistri*, an argument that has raged since the publication of an explosive article on the matter by Dom David Knowles, 'The Regula Magistri and the Rule of St Benedict', in David Knowles, *Great Historical Enterprises: Problems in Monastic History* (London, 1963), 135–95.

[28] Columba Cary Elwes and Abbot Justin McCann, *Ampleforth & its Origins* (London, 1952), 232.

[29] H. O. Evennett, *The Catholic Schools of England and Wales* (Cambridge, 1944), 65–6.

Between 1802 and 1895, recent estimates place the number of Irish at Ampleforth at roughly 5 per cent, with around 81 of the 1,634 boys Irish-born, and for this reason it is not as significant a school as the other four in relation to the Irish Catholic elite, though it certainly became much more important in the twentieth century.[30] A complete list of the boys published in the Ampleforth school magazine bears this out, with the addition of another fifteen boys in the last five years of the century putting the figure at a maximum of ninety-six, with as many as seventy of those educated between 1850 and 1900. Downside was a much more 'Irish' school, particularly from its foundation at its present site in 1814. The community actively marketed itself to the Irish gentry from foundation. Writing to Christopher Dillon Bellew of Mountbellew, Co. Galway in May of 1814, the year of the move to Downside, a member of the community urged him to 'recommend it to our common friends'.[31] This call for Irish boys at the foundation of the school seems anomalous when one considers the absence of any acknowledgement of the extent of the Irish contingent in the main history of Downside in the nineteenth century by Dom Henry Norbert Birt, a member of the community. The only direct reference made to the Irish cohort in Birt's history, written in 1902, is a quoted letter from one English parent to another on the subject of the school's reputation and suitability in 1838. The letter, written by a Dr Coombes, sought to appease the interested party by maintaining that as to the 'proportion of English to Irish students, the latter is comparatively small'.[32] That the doctor was careful to downplay the Irish connection reinforces the idea that the more balanced the ratio of Irish to English students at an elite Catholic school in England the more likely it was to have damaged its reputation with the native Catholic laity. The absence of the Irish in Birt's published history of Downside indicates that it was still seen as a negative as late as 1902.

A relatively recent history of the Benedictines in England does little to dispel the idea that the Irish contingent, if referred to at all, was considered a necessary evil. Dom Bernard Green maintained that prior to the second half of the nineteenth century the boys at Downside were 'mostly tradesmen's sons or else Irish'.[33] The proportion of Irish students at the college was certainly high. The 1841 census indicates that of the forty-one boys resident at Downside school, just three years later, fifteen were Irish-born, meaning that more than a third of the boys at the school were Irish.[34] Furthermore, all but two of the English boys were born in a different county, suggesting that the catchment was non-local and therefore unlikely to ever have been the sons of tradesmen.

---

[30] See Anthony Marrett-Crosby, *A School of the Lord's Service: A History of Ampleforth* (Ampleforth, 2002), 126–8. For the early history of Ampleforth see Peter Galliver, 'The Early Ampleforth College', *Recusant History*, 28/4 (Oct. 2007), 511–29; Cary-Elwes and McCann, *Ampleforth and its Origins*.

[31] Michael Lorymer OSB to Christopher D. Bellew, 21 May 1814, Mountbellew Papers, NLI, MS 27, 206.

[32] Henry Norman Birt, *Downside: The History of St. Gregory's School from its Commencement at Douay to the Present Time* (London, 1902), 218.

[33] Dom Bernard Green, *The English Benedictine Congregation: A Short History* (London, 1980), 8.

[34] The full breakdown of the 1841 census is available in J. A. M., 'An Old Census Return', *The Downside Review*, 11 (Mar.–Dec. 1892), 246–64.

II ENGLISH CATHOLIC SCHOOLS AND
THEIR IRISH PUPILS

The number of Irish-born boarders at all four of the premier English schools was remarkably constant. On average one in five boys were Irish residents, or in raw numbers 1,302 (21 per cent) out of 6,615 (Table 3.1). The registers of Stonyhurst College in Lancashire show that from the beginning of the calendar year 1850 to the end of 1899 a total of 2,691 students were recorded. Of these, at least 462 (17 per cent) can be proven to have been Irish-born. At Beaumont College 1,608 boys attended the school between 1861 and 1900, 294 (18 per cent) of those are known to have been Irish. The highest proportion of all was at Downside School, where at least 309 Irish boys boarded between 1850 and 1900, out of a total of 1,074 (29 per cent). At Oscott the total number at the school was 1,142, of which 238 (21 per cent) were Irish-born. These figures are far from absolute as there are large gaps in the registers, particularly at the Jesuit schools. At Stonyhurst, for example, record-keeping was lax in the period 1884–90, and at Downside we have much more reliable information from 1856–86 than during the periods either side of those years. The percentages given here are therefore conservative, and in all likelihood Irish representation was greater than 20 per cent in both Beaumont and Stonyhurst, and nearer to 33 per cent at Downside in real terms. This was also the case at Oscott, where the percentage of Irish known to have attended hovers at an average of 21 per cent, but the potential percentage may have been as high as 27–33 per cent most years.

The geographical distribution of the Irish boarders throws up some surprises (Maps 3.2–3.5). A clear pattern emerges from what is a reasonably complete list of addresses, with 440 (95 per cent) of the Stonyhurst cohort and 273 (93 per cent) of the Beaumont cohort traceable. At Downside the figure is comparably complete, where 291 of the boys have a known county of origin, or 94 per cent of the cohort. All three schools follow a distinct pattern, roughly comparable to that visible at the Irish schools. Dublin is again the area from which most of the

Table 3.1 Number of Irish boys attending Stonyhurst, Downside, and Beaumont, 1850–1900*

	1850–9	1860–9	1870–9	1880–9	1890–9
Stonyhurst (462)	62	98	137	70	95
Downside (309)	36	65	82	65	61
Beaumont (294)**	–	49	78	94	74
Oscott (238)**	71	53	72	42	–

* The main sources used for compiling these figures are as follows. For Stonyhurst: SCA, Stonyhurst College Register 1841–70; Stonyhurst College Register 1870–1927; SCA, Card file, 'Past pupils'. For Beaumont College see ABPSJ, Beaumont College Archives, Beaumont College Registers 5/3/31B; List of Boys at Beaumont College 1861–76, 5/2/20. For Downside see DAA, Register of Students at Downside, C/52/H; *List of Boys at St Gregory's* (Downside Abbey, 1972). For Oscott the student lists have been collected for 1794–1889 and published in the school magazine and online.

** Beaumont opened in 1861, Oscott closed in 1889 and records are consistent to 1885.

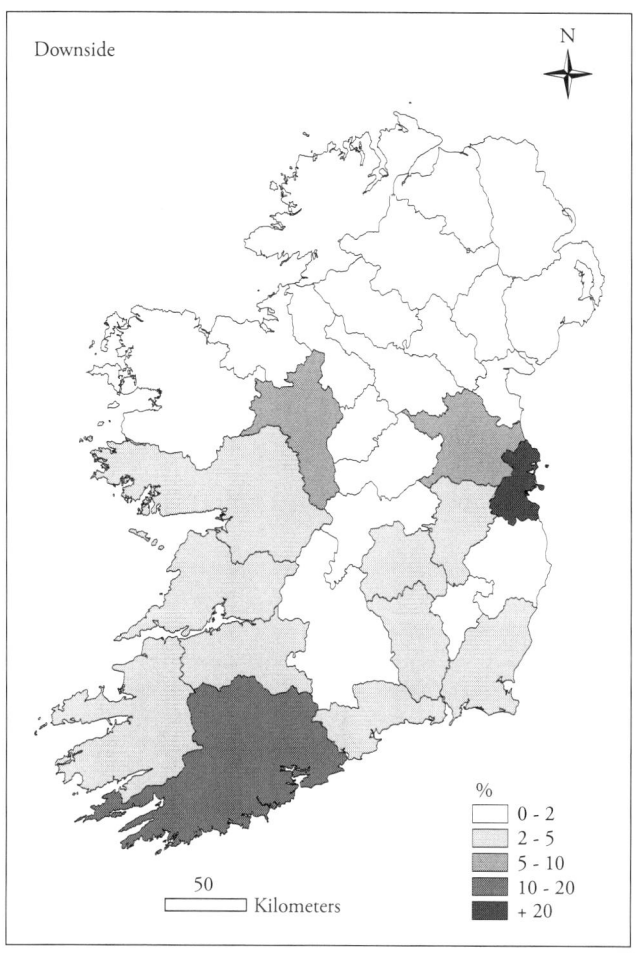

Map 3.2 Irish boys at Downside by county of origin, 1850–1900

boys are drawn, along with the south Munster nexus of counties Cork, Limerick, and Waterford, along with smaller concentrations in Connacht counties such as Galway and Roscommon—where Catholics retained large estates. Ulster is again absent from this picture, reinforcing the theory that if we are to speak of an Irish Catholic elite in the nineteenth century we must effectively think of Ireland as already partitioned—at least in educational terms. Beaumont College had only eight pupils from Ulster between 1861 and 1900, six from Belfast City. This absence of elite (or even middle-class) northern Catholics points to a difference in expectations and to a marked difference in the prescribed route to elite status. The north-east corner of Ireland was by far the most industrialized area on the island. Nevertheless, as late as 1861 Catholics supplied only 15 per cent of the professions and a paltry 22 per cent of the merchant classes in Ulster—this despite enjoying a

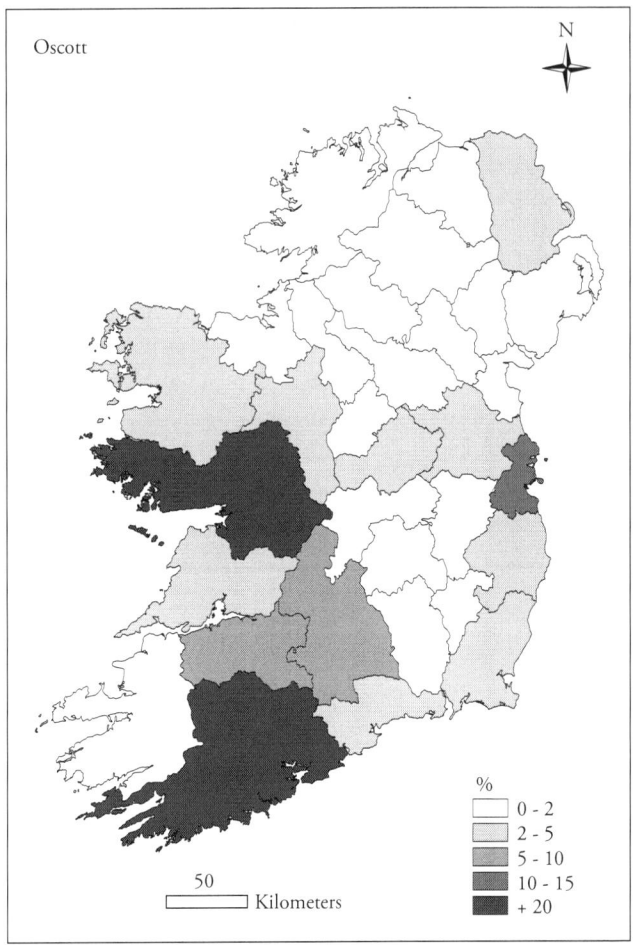

Map 3.3 Irish boys at Oscott by county of origin, 1850–1900

slight majority of the total population at 51 per cent.[35] It is somewhat understand-
able then that the pattern emerging from the south of the average pupil having
been plucked from either the landed gentry or the rising middle class was not replicated in the north. The major landed Catholic families of the north whose sons
attended the Jesuit schools in the period were the Montagus of Portstewart, Co.
Derry, and the Whytes of Loughbrickland, Co. Down. The Montagu family sent
six sons to Stonyhurst between 1891 and 1895, all of whom were the offspring of
Richard Acheson Cromie Montagu, JP, a convert to Roman Catholicism.[36]

---

[35] Marianne Elliott, *The Catholics of Ulster* (London, 2000), 305.
[36] The Montagu family was at the centre of an unfortunate court case at the end of which their bio-
logical mother was sentenced to twelve months' imprisonment, having been found guilty of the man-
slaughter of the boys' sister, and the prolonged physical abuse of the younger boys. Austin Montagu,

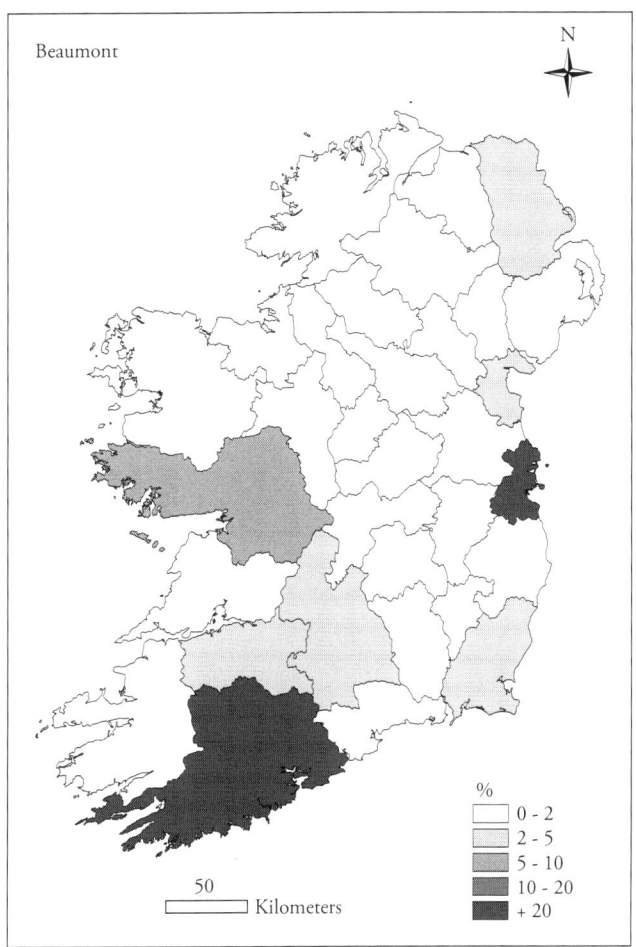

Map 3.4 Irish boys at Beaumont by county of origin, 1861–1900

The urban–rural divide is more difficult to decode, but the distribution of pupils in urban areas was straightforward. The more fashionable the address the more likely a family was to have a son at an English school. Thus, in Cork, rich Catholic families such as the Murphy brewers favoured fashionable addresses in Blackrock, Tivoli, and Montenotte, or closer to the city at Sunday's Well, Sidney Parade, or the South Mall. In Dublin, suburban areas such as Blackrock, Monkstown, Dundrum, and Glenageary were popular, as were the upmarket inner-city squares such as Fitzwilliam Square, Merrion Square, or even Rutland Square at a push. There was little variation in this. The only north Dublin address given by anyone

cited in the case, entered Stonyhurst at the early age of eight in 1893, presumably as a result of this. *The Belfast News-Letter*, Tuesday, 5 Apr. 1892.

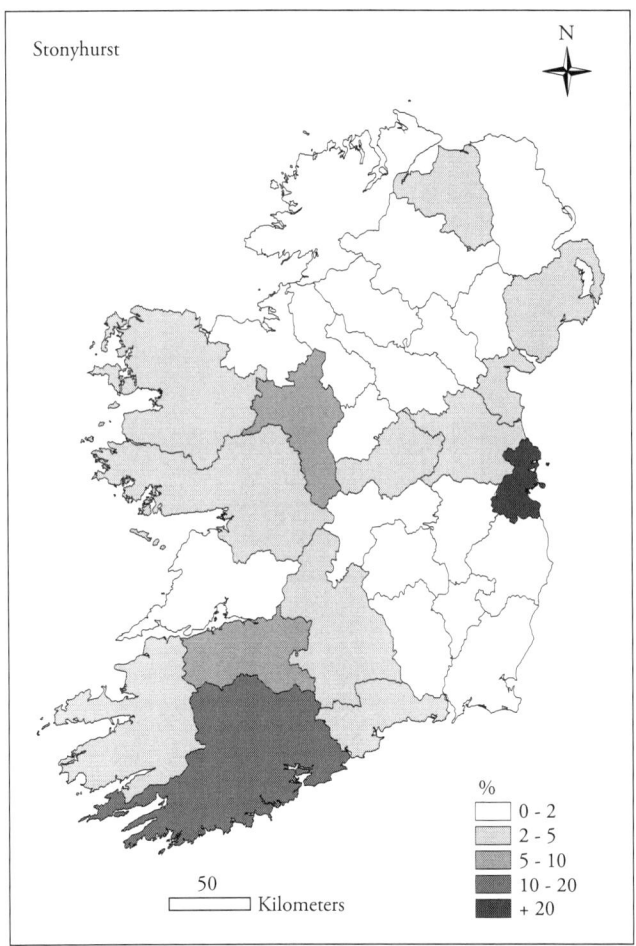

Map 3.5 Irish boys at Stonyhurst by county of origin, 1850–1900

attending Downside, for instance, was that of Martin E. Bourke, at 1 Victoria Buildings, Howth.[37]

In rural Ireland the picture is very different. Some of the cohort from rural Munster, for example, inherited more than 10,000 acres. The Oratory School graduate Rivallon de la Poer, son of the Papal Count Edmond James de Poher de la Poer, came into an estate of 13,460 acres in Waterford and Tipperary on his father's death in 1915. A more typical estate was that of the Taaffe family of Smarmore Castle in Co. Louth. Before his premature death aged just nineteen in 1890 George Robert Taaffe, at Stonyhurst in the 1870s, stood to inherit 5,147 acres spread across five counties from his father John Taaffe. In the end, his cousin

[37] DAA, Register of Students 1856–86, C/52/H.

(also called George, and also educated at Stonyhurst) took over the property. Such estates often encased a rather impressive 'big house', an example of which can be seen in Figure 3.2.

Most boys attending the four schools entered the schools quite young (Table 3.2). At Stonyhurst it was common for Irish boys to attend Hodder, the attached preparatory school, before entering Stonyhurst itself aged eleven to thirteen. The cost of attendance varied from year to year and from boy to boy. In all cases however, the fees paid at Catholic schools were much lower than those paid at Eton, Winchester, or any of the other established Anglican public schools, though still far beyond the reach of most Irish families. The reasons for this discount was obvious: the

Figure 3.2 The de la Poer residence, Gurteen Le Poer, Kilsheelan, Co. Waterford, *c.*1920

Table 3.2 Irish boys entering Oscott, 1860–1900, by age on entry

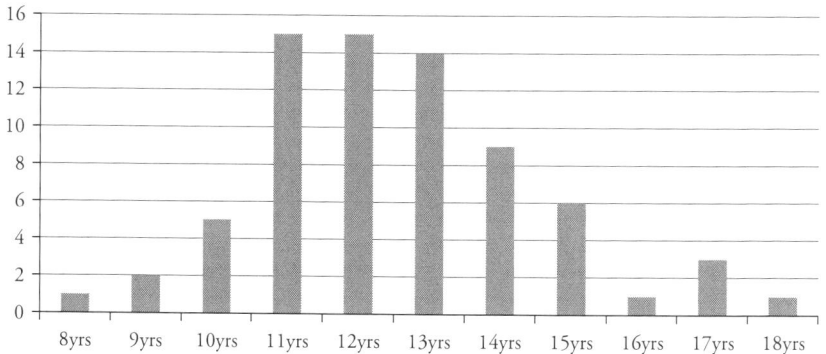

staff turnover at schools such as Eton was much higher and quite costly—even if it was live-in. Catholic schools did not incur the type of salary costs because the bulk of their teaching staff were members of the order running the school. This meant that a school such as Stonyhurst—one of the top twenty schools in Britain in terms of pupil numbers throughout the nineteenth century and offering a comparable curriculum to all of its rivals—was anything up to half as expensive at all times, coming in at a basic £60–£90 per annum when at Eton or Harrow tuition could cost £120–180.[38] In one reading then, the Catholic elite were, in terms of fees at least, competitively advantaged when compared to their Anglican counterpart. Despite this the money spent by wealthy Catholic families on education was considerable. Arthur French paid a total of £129 10s altogether at Beaumont in 1874. This consisted of £70 tuition fees, £26 travel expenses, extras such as music lessons (£10), and various other minor but cumulative costs.[39] Often a discount was applied where more than one sibling was in attendance at the same school and at the same time—as in the case of Arthur's class-mates William and Walter Morrogh, whose combined total came to £167 10s 2d. At around the same period the average salary for a constable in the Dublin Metropolitan Police would have been about £75 per annum, with a national school teacher surviving on £49 per annum plus a house of variable quality.[40] These were not average Irish boys, from average Irish Catholic families, and yet there is some evidence to suggest that although accepted at the schools discussed they were not treated in every case as equals.

III SCHOOL LIFE AND 'IRISHNESS' AT ENGLISH CATHOLIC PUBLIC SCHOOLS

> In spite of a large infusion of foreigners and some disaffected Irish, we were a patriotic crowd, and our little pulse beat time with the heart of the nation.[41]
>
> Arthur Conan Doyle (Stonyhurst: 1868–75)

John Breen left his home in Castlebridge, Co. Wexford in 1853 to make the four-day trip to Downside. He was just twelve years of age and had little ink-ling that he would later spend much of his life teaching at the school as Dom Dunstan Breen, and eventually die there, aged seventy, in 1911. The journey from Castlebridge to Downside involved overnight stays at Dublin, Chester, and Bristol. Accompanied by his father, young John travelled in style, staying in the best hotels and hiring a carriage and pair for the last leg. Having said

---

[38] These comparative figures are taken from T. W. Bamford, *Public School Data: A Compilation of Data on Public and Related Schools (Boys) Mainly from 1866*, Aids to Historical Research, 2 (Hull, 1974), 11, 43.

[39] Arthur French entry, ABPSJ, Beaumont College Archives, Beaumont College Accounts 1870–4, 5/2/9.

[40] Figures taken from Tony Farmar, *Privileged Lives: A Social History of Middle-class Ireland, 1882–1989* (Dublin, 2010), 10.

[41] Arthur Conan Doyle, *Memories and Adventures*, 4th edn (Oxford, 1989), 16.

his goodbyes his first night at the school was traumatic. 'Only those who have experienced it', Breen recalled many years after the event, 'can form any adequate idea of the feeling of utter abandonment and desertion that comes upon a somewhat spoiled lad at such a moment.' With no pony to ride and 'no servants to pet and flatter' him he felt alien, disconsolate, and cried himself to sleep.[42] Of course, as we have seen with Éamon DeValera at Blackrock, it was an exceptional boy who did not stifle tears on his first night at a new school. Presumably this was magnified for a boy such as Breen, who found himself in a foreign school full of strange accents and new reference points. What would his 'Irishness' mean at so dramatic a remove?

Old boys of the English schools in this period tended to agree on just one aspect of life there—that the food was awful. Oliver St John Gogarty hated Stonyhurst, referring to it as an 'alien English school' where he was made to feel like a criminal and treated with 'dislike, suspicion and distrust'.[43] The journalist Percy FitzGerald attended the school in the 1850s and had altogether more positive recollections, though he remembered an Irish versus English cricket match at Stonyhurst being stopped in the 1850s to facilitate a fight between a 'turbulent Paddy and an Englishman'.[44] Nonetheless, there is little in the school records and magazines to indicate that being Irish was in any way a negative label in the day-to-day operation of the schools. Figure 3.3 indicates just how numerous Irish boys were at Beaumont in any given class. The boys' home addresses were entered without comment alongside those of their English classmates and, so far as the school archives were concerned, they shed much of their Irish identity at the door. Incidental references to 'Hibernians' were not rare however, and a great deal can be gleaned from private diaries of priests and monks and from the memoirs of old boys that provide clues as to the conflict and cooperation between the various nationalities at the schools. On the death of O'Connell in 1847, for instance, a young Jesuit at Stonyhurst recorded his fears that there was 'a great stir among the Irish: probably O'Connell's death will produce a crisis'.[45] It was generally St Patrick's Day that provided an opportunity for the boys to flaunt their patriotic pride. At the Jesuit colleges of Stonyhurst and Beaumont it was common practice for the Irish to 'sport the green', on St Patrick's Day—much to the annoyance of the teaching staff. The extent to which the Irish boys were allowed to celebrate the day was variable. In 1868 the school journal at Beaumont reads 'St Patrick's Day—Opposed any concession to the Hibernians. They got nothing.' In 1887 the greatest concern

---

[42] Dom Dunstan Breen, 'A New Boy's Experiences, 1853', *The Downside Review*, 6 (1887), 37. For biographical info see 'Dom Dunstan Breen', *The Downside Review*, 30 (1911), 344; *The Belmont Clothing Book; English Benedictine Novices 1860–1920*, St Laurence Papers VI (Ampleforth Abbey, 2003), 1.

[43] Oliver St John Gogarty, *It Isn't this Time of Year at All: An Unpremeditated Autobiography* (New York, 1954), 40–1; 'Tom Kettle—A Talk by Oliver St John Gogarty', University College Dublin Archives, Tom Kettle Papers, LA 34/9, n.d.

[44] The Irish boys won, 100 to 99. Percy FitzGerald, *Stonyhurst Memories, or Six Years at School* (London, 1895), 142.

[45] SCA, Entry 24 May 1847, Private Diary of Tom Ullathorne, SJ, 1844–1852.

Figure 3.3 Irish boys in 'Grammar' class at Beaumont, 1891–2, circled.

was instead the heavy snowfall on St Patrick's which led to a 'regularly organised snow-fight' in the school, with much excitement and fatigue the result and only a few 'black eyes and bleeding faces'.[46]

Such displays of Irish identity might easily fit in with what Colin Kidd has labelled a 'sentimental' Scottish nationalism in the same period—one that sought to use the symbols and labels of Scottish difference as a means to establish a union of distinct but equal factions within British society.[47] Taken this way the sporting of shamrock on Patrick's Day, or an Irish versus English cricket match might be seen as nothing more than an obvious way for Irish boys to mark out some territory in a multinational student body by the display of relatively non-threatening symbols and gestures. In 1889, 32 boys out of the 141 students were sporting green on Patrick's Day, a significant visible bloc in any school. Sentimental patriotism may well have been characteristic of wealthy Irish families, but anecdotal evidence supports the view that being Irish meant a little more than that. Despite their education at an English public school with

[46] See ABPSJ, Entry 17 Mar. 1868, Prefect's Journal 1865–71, Beaumont College Archives, 5/1/2; Entry 17 Mar. Prefect's Journal 1883–9, Beaumont College Archives, 5/1/5

[47] Colin Kidd, 'Sentiment, Race, and Revival: Scottish Identities after the Enlightenment', in Brockliss and Eastwood (eds), *A Union of Multiple Identities: The British Isles, c.1750–c.1850* (Manchester, 1997), 110–26.

all the attendant establishment values in place (barring religious observance), Thomas Francis Meagher and, later, Joseph Mary Plunkett and Charles Gavan Duffy displayed a virulent and developing separatist nationalism which was not in any way quenched at schools such as Stonyhurst and was in some cases stoked by an English education. Stonyhurst produced as many nationalists as loyalists, the former constituting what Arthur Conan Doyle referred to as the rebellious 'disaffected Irish' in his account of his schooldays. Meagher was surely the most persecuted of all, if we are to believe his account of his time there. When the Jesuits attempted to rid him of his 'brogue' he rebelled, and cost himself the role of the Earl of Kent in a school production of *King Lear*. 'It wasn't the first time the brogue entailed the forfeiture of title and estate', Meagher noted. 'I felt I was a martyr to the peculiarities of my race.'[48] Meagher's gift for hyperbole aside, it is well to admit that he more than made up for his theatrical disappointment later in life, and that missing out on a school play was a tame excuse for martyrdom.

One of the most peculiar manifestations of a separate Irish identity was an 'Irish Garden' at Stonyhurst College (seen from the air in Figure 3.4). Edmund Waterton,

Figure 3.4 Stonyhurst College from the air, *c.*1930

[48] Quoted in Michael Cavanagh, *Memoirs of General Thomas Francis Meagher* (Massachussets, 1892), 30.

an English pupil at the school in the 1840s, dismissed the garden as a place where Irish boys 'amused themselves by talking of O'Connell and repeal and spouting blarney'.[49] This garden seems to have been set aside with the consent of the school authorities and to have acted as a rather unusual Irish-only space at the heart of an English public school. The orator Richard Lalor Sheil is believed to have been the instigator of the project, which was later carried on by Thomas Francis Meagher in his time at the school in the 1840s. According to an article handwritten by a student in 1861, the garden was set up by the Irish boys so as to have 'some token of union' with home as it was 'a frequent thing for an Irish boy to remain here [at Stonyhurst] for two or more years without interruption'. At various points the name bestowed on the garden changed in accordance with the major political movements, so that it was renamed 'The Repeal' at the height of O'Connell's power.[50] The garden itself seems to have become unfashionable by the 1870s, when the Home Rule and the Land Question debates began to change perceptions of the Irish in Britain. There are, however, examples of such territorial behaviour at other schools. At the Holy Child Convent School at St Leonards-on-Sea, near Hastings, a similar proportion of Irish girls in the student body hit on a novel and pragmatic way of acknowledging the dominant nationalities. On St George's Day the Irish girls would organize a themed party for their English classmates and the English girls returned the favour on what they called 'St Pat's'.[51] Pleasant and cordial interaction was general; no black eyes or bleeding faces were recorded there.

At the Benedictine school at Downside, Irishness was never accorded the same geographical or literal space as at Stonyhurst, although it was 'performed' at various points in the period. Downside had a strong culture of debating and amateur drama. In an article about the theatrical tradition at Downside an Irish old boy, William Tarpey, recalled one of the more amusing aspects of being Irish at the school. During the early 1870s, Tarpey maintained, it was customary for the Irish boys to be typecast as the murderers or villains in whatever play the school happened to stage. As a result 'the murderers in *Richard III* were unquestionably Irish...Irishmen mingled with the crowd that listened to Marc Anthony in the forum, and were loudest in their denunciation of Brutus.' According to Tarpey, even King Duncan in *Macbeth* had at least one son who was an Irishman.[52] This also occurred at Stonyhurst, where Oliver St John Gogarty was cast as a villain in the 1896 production of *Macbeth* (Figure 3.5). That the monks at Downside would assign murderous or criminal parts to Irish boys, though doubtless it was an unconscious act, nevertheless points to their existing status within the school as somehow different, a rogue element.

---

[49] Edmund Waterton was the son of the naturalist Charles Waterton, of Walton Hall, Yorkshire. He later married Josephine Ennis, daughter of an Irish MP who also attended the school. Rev. George Gruggen and Rev. Joseph Keating, SJ, *Stonyhurst: Its Past History and Life in the Present* (London, 1901), 86.

[50] SCA, 'An Irishman', *The Stonyhurst Examiner and Times*, 3/3 (Apr. 1861).

[51] 'St Pat's and St George's', *The St Leonards Chronicler* (Hastings, 1922), 31–32.

[52] William B. Tarpey, 'Reminiscences of the Theatre Royal, Downside', *The Downside Review*, 6 (1887), 110.

Although the criminal stereotype revealed a paternalist attitude towards the Irish at Downside there is ample evidence to suggest they gave as much in return. As the Home Rule crisis erupted in the mid 1880s it became a frequent topic of discussion in a student body which was almost a third Irish. A debate was held in 1885 on the proposition 'Home Rule would be beneficial to Ireland'. The record shows that an Irish boy, William FitzGerald, spoke emotively for the proposition, and was seconded by an English classmate, Anthony Kynaston. Speaking against the motion were two Irish boys, Richard Madden and George Nugent. The motion was defeated, seven votes to fourteen. Of the three Irish speakers, William FitzGerald died young and Richard Madden became a captain in the Royal Army Medical Corps. The most landed of the three, George Nugent, became a Benedictine monk, thus neatly removing himself from the wider debate on redistribution of property. His father, Walter Nugent, had an estate of 7,955 acres, mostly centred around their house at Donore, Co. Westmeath.[53] That there were political differences between Irish boys is something that is not generally evident from official school records, though it can be found elsewhere. Writing home to his mother in 1881, an Irish boy, Lucien Bonaparte-Wyse, noted the division caused in the Irish cohort by the death of Disraeli. 'I am also sorry that Lord Beaconsfield is dead', he wrote. 'In *The Graphic* there is a great mourning for him. All the pages are surrounded with black rims...all the boys seem to go against him, such as the FitzGeralds and nearly all the other boys.'[54] Contradictions, polarized opinion and simple political ignorance feature across the group—reminding us, perhaps, that teenagers do not change all that much from generation to generation.

As tempting as it is to dwell on an Irish–British binary at the English Catholic schools, it would nevertheless be a mistake. English Catholics constituted the single largest grouping, with the Irish boys the next significant bloc. Interspersed with this domestic group was usually a host of other nationalities. The ultimate effect was an education that was distinct from that available to most children in the period—a cosmopolitan and international mixture of old-world and new-world wealth. Writing home to his father, Lucien Bonaparte-Wyse indicated that he had struck up an intense friendship with a 'very rich' French boy named Boson de Périgord.[55] 'This boy has taken a great fancy to me', Lucien noted, 'and takes me to the Abbe's room and gives me coffee, sweets and all sorts of eatables. I like him myself too very much.'[56] There is no real indication as to whether the

---

[53] John Bateman, *The Great Landowners of Great Britain and Ireland* (Leicester: Leicester University Press, 1971), 339.

[54] This boy was a grandson of Sir Thomas Wyse, MP, the educationist and past pupil of Stonyhurst. Lucien Bonaparte-Wyse to his mother, Ellen Bonaparte-Wyse 29 May 1881, Bonaparte-Wyse Papers, NLI, MS 41,615/17.

[55] He was, in fact, very rich. This boy was Boson de Talleyrand-Périgord (1867–1951), later the 6th Duc de Tallyrand and the second son of a famous Parisian aristocratic family. He later inherited the vast German estates belonging to his family after much unfortunate acrimony. See 'Miss Helen Morton to Wed Count De Perigord', *New York Times*, 29 Mar. 1901.

[56] Lucien Bonaparte-Wyse to his father, Captain William Charles Bonaparte-Wyse, 26 Mar. 1882, Bonaparte-Wyse Papers, NLI, MS 41, 615/17.

relationship developed beyond this rather innocent point, although it was hardly unusual for intense homosocial or homosexual relationships to develop in such an enclosed world. The Jesuit system of constant supervision, even at night, aimed to eradicate such intense relationships between their pupils although every now and then a boy, such as Louis McKenna at Beaumont was sent home for an offence recorded without elaboration in the registers as *causa immor*. Towards the end of the century several careful references to the sexual purity of British and Irish boys are made by the school authorities at a time when the influx of students from South American backgrounds brought the issue of sexual maturity into sharp relief. The subject of the 'precocious' libido of foreign pupils was raised in a private circular by the Conference of Catholic Headmasters in 1898. Not only did they suffer from a 'great want of truthfulness', but a 'Latin American boy of twelve' was the equivalent in precocity of an English lad of 'sixteen or seventeen', a fact the Headmasters blamed squarely on the warmer climate of their upbringing. The circular to all Headmasters recommended that such boys should only be taken in if they were below the age of twelve, because if they were received at this 'tender age' they could be 'formed and moulded into boys of no less excellent—and in some instances, of more excellent—character and moral fibre than our own English boys'.[57]

It is difficult to gauge the likely effect of this international milieu on Irish boys, other than to say that it almost certainly broadened their horizons in much the same way that the Grand Tour broadened that of their forebears. At Oscott College in Birmingham we can find three sons of an unremarkable Irish landowner, Matthew D'Arcy of Kilcroney, Co. Wicklow, in the same class of 1870 as three sons of the President of Nicaragua, Pedro Joaquín Chamorro Alfaro. In the same class sat two scions of the Russian nobility, the Boutourlinns, and Robert Ashurst Gradwell, of Dowth Hall, Co. Meath. The Irish were simply one strand of an international Catholic elite looking to capitalize on the social status accorded to an English public school education in the nineteenth century.

When speculating on the likely socializing effect of this education on Irish boys it is tempting to overstate the importance of peculiar manifestations of separate identity and territory such as Stonyhurst's Irish Garden or Oscott's green-velvet chair. Instead we should take inclusive rituals to be rather more important. Such rituals would emphasize the collective nature of belonging to an international or transnational elite. We may take one such example of a practice from Downside which thrived in the period before improved transport links made it possible for the majority of the boys to travel home every Christmas. In a tradition which dated from the school's tenure in northern France, there was a 'Court' elected at Downside every Christmas. This involved a 'Choosing King' night early in the school year where all but the last two classes in the school would effectively elect a monarch from the student body. The king would then nominate officers of his court, including a Lord Chief Justice, Earl Marshal, Mayor of the Palace, and

---

[57] 'The Education of Catholic Foreign Pupils in England', Private Circular from the Conference of Catholic Headmasters May 1898, SCA.

so on. The name of the uncrowned king would remain a secret from the monks until his coronation at Christmas. The king, once crowned, was, it appears, the head of the school over Christmas—with a room made separate and designated a 'Palace', and allowed special privileges such as freedom of movement and separate dining arrangements during the holiday period. Two banquets would take place in his honour; Birt leaves us with a description of the first, 'the Officer's Feast':

> To do honour to the occasion, the king and his court were attired in their robes, and it was the etiquette for visitors to appear in evening dress. He was the chosen one of the school, and so could feel that he possessed the respect and love of his school fellows. He sat in the place of honour...On his right, dispensing the hospitality in his name, sat the prior; on his left, the bishop of the diocese, who rarely failed to be present...And it was wonderful how the boy-king and his officers rose to their position, and behaved with all the dignity and courtly mien befitting their exalted rank. It was in truth education in the highest sense of the word.[58]

No doubt this sham court depended a great deal on the patience of the community, who were nevertheless fully complicit in this monarch-making. The practice was discontinued after 1878, though the folk memory of the tradition remained important at the school. Many Irish boys filled the role of king, eleven between 1850 and 1878. One such Irish boy-king was Denis O'Conor, himself a member of a famous Irish sept and a future MP. His brother was Charles Owen O'Conor, who eventually inherited the title of Prince of Connacht in real life and bore the arms of Ireland at the coronation of Edward VII. Denis was made king in 1857 and remembered that 'theoretically the king was an absolute monarchy, ruling supreme over his court, and being superior to everyone for the time being; even the highest in the house paid him respect, and he was always addressed as "Your Majesty"'.[59] The role was one which depended on the honour of the boy selected, and his self-control was key to its survival at the school.

The tradition of the Court at Downside achieved several educational goals. First, it taught the boys that correct behaviour and the respect of one's peers could result in a reward that outshone all others at the school and afforded a universal respect, with temporary power of considerable proportions. Second, it established in all the young boys at Downside a deep and tangible respect for the idea of monarchy, giving them a micro-experience of how a court might function—complete with favouritism, politicking, and extravagant feasts. Last, it established that the authority of the monks was something that was not final, not even within the school itself, and that the boys should look to God and to their conscience for the correct manner in which to govern, and by extension, be governed. For Irish boys, it may have seemed incongruous to be subordinate under yet another crown, but considering the fact that it often happened that every other year they were to defer to an Irishman, the blow was undoubtedly softened.

---

[58] Birt, *Downside*, 259–60.
[59] Denis O'Conor, 'Ye Court of St Gregory, Downside', *The Downside Review*, 2 (1883), 115–16.

IV ENGLISH CATHOLIC ETONS? CURRICULUM AND ETHOS AT ENGLISH CATHOLIC SCHOOLS

In his work on John Henry Newman's Oratory School, Paul Shrimpton has argued persuasively that the school was set up in the 1860s as a deliberate imitation of the established public schools, and in particular Eton. This was influenced heavily by the upbringing of Newman's friends and backers in the venture, the Tractarian converts Edward Bellasis and James Hope Scott—the latter an Old Etonian. The nineteenth century saw the Catholic schools gradually resign themselves to the prevailing fashions of English public school education and by the early decades of the twentieth century the most successful English Catholic schools were the ones that had made the most overt concessions to them. Ampleforth adopted a House system and thrived, Stonyhurst hesitated and lost ground it never recovered.[60] 'Vain it is to hope to swim against the current', was the wry response of one Irish monk at Downside to changes in educational policy, as he lamented the slow decline of the educational values he had long treasured.[61]

As with Clongowes Wood and Tullabeg in Ireland, Stonyhurst and Beaumont both employed the Jesuit education blueprint *Ratio Studiorum* in the education of their boys. This was periodically tweaked to accommodate the changing trends, but the core reliance on the teaching of the classics remained a constant. David Newsome and John Honey have both argued that the British public school system was reliant on the teaching of classics as the core subjects throughout the nineteenth century. This was the result of a widespread belief in their intrinsic value as a complete aesthetic and historical frame of reference.[62] This implicit understanding that the classics provided an entire value-system for elite education may account for their longevity at Stonyhurst, though we might just as easily claim that the classics had traditionally been accentuated as at the core of the *Ratio Studiorum* and that it was rather that the two value systems simply sprang from the same source. Either way, a thorough background in the classics would prove a useful indication of the equivalent status of the elite education of Catholic students when compared with their Protestant peers in the outside world. In a society where an extensive knowledge of Tacitus and Thucydides marked out the graduates of Eton and Oxford so conspicuously, a similar education would establish Stonyhurst boys as their equals, in learning at least.

The school system at Stonyhurst was run under the familiar Jesuit system. The school had three main strands: a separate preparatory school (Hodder), the College proper, and a wing devoted to a higher course of study known as the philosophy

---

[60] For more on this see Peter Galliver, 'Development of Ampleforth College as an English Public School 1802–1954' (DEd, University of Leeds, 1999); Bernardo Rodriguez Capparini, 'A Catholic Public School in the Making: Beaumont College during the Rectorate of the Reverend Joseph M. Bampton, S.J. (1901–1908)', *Paedagogica Historica*, 39/6 (Dec. 2003), 737–57.

[61] E. C. Butler, 'The School Calendar Twenty Years Ago', *The Downside Review*, 12 (Mar.-Dec. 1893), 56.

[62] See David Newsome, *Godliness and Good Learning* (London, 1961), 64; John R. de S. Honey, *Tom Brown's Universe: The Development of the Victorian Public School* (London: Millington, 1977), 130–2.

course. The philosophy course at the school became something of a global *cause célèbre* in the 1870s, when an impostor claimed the estate of a Stonyhurst old boy in an inheritance scandal that was for many years the longest trial in history, usually referred to as the 'Tichborne case'.[63] The philosophers have been the subject of a major study and will not be discussed at length here, other than to remark that theirs was traditionally seen as a gentlemanly and leisured course, badly supervised and ineffective.[64]

In the college proper, boys were divided upon entry according to ability and placed in the most relevant class in a system that ran from Elements through Figures, Rudiments, Grammar, Syntax, Poetry and Rhetoric—a system that mirrored the public school equivalent of a primer year, followed by first to sixth form. Typically the Irish boys entered aged between eleven and thirteen and were placed in one of the bottom three classes according to their existing knowledge of the core subjects. Of the twelve Irish boys who entered Beaumont in 1876, for example, all but four were between ten and twelve years old at admission. The youngest was William Woodcock from Dublin (just eight years old) and the oldest was Thomas Prendergast, from Tipperary, who was sixteen on arrival. Prendergast had spent three and a half years at Blackrock College prior to his arrival, and so is representative of the minority Irish set that 'finished' in England.[65]

At Downside the school calendar remained remarkably consistent. In 1867 honours students had to contend with five Latin and Greek texts, a considerable French course, minor Shakespeare and Milton for English, in addition to mathematics and natural philosophy. The course finds some limited room for science in natural philosophy, but very little for geography.[66] The situation had not changed a great deal by 1882; a report sent to the Registrar of the University of London found that students were comparatively better at Greek than at Latin, and that the teaching of science was deficient, but improving.[67] The daily pattern of schoolwork remained more or less intact from the 1850s at Downside. In a school day that began at 5.40 a.m. and ended at 9.10 p.m., a typical schedule in the 1870s allowed

---

[63] The 'Tichborne affair' was 291-day nineteenth-century legal case in the United Kingdom involving Arthur Orton (1834–98), an imposter who claimed to be the missing heir Sir Roger Tichborne (1829–54). The case exposed much anti-Catholic sentiment in England, as well as many damaging misrepresentations of life at Stonyhurst College, where Roger Tichborne had been enrolled as a student in 1849. Tichborne had gone missing and was presumed lost at sea, having left for Chile in 1852. Orton was eventually exposed as a fraudulent imposter, but was nevertheless buried with 'Sir Roger Charles Doughty Tichborne' on his coffin in 1898, see 'Dead, but Still the Claimant: Arthur Orton to Be Buried as Sir Roger Tichborne—His Wife Keeps Her Title', *The New York Times*, 18 Apr. 1898. For perspective on the interesting colonial aspect to the trial see Carrie Dawson ' "The Slaughterman of Wagga Wagga": Imposture, National Identity, and the Tichborne Affair', *Australian Literary Studies*, 21/4 (Oct. 2004), 1–13.

[64] H. J. A. Sire, *Gentlemen-philosophers: Catholic Higher Education at Liège and Stonyhurst 1774–1916* (London, 1988).

[65] ABPSJ, Beaumont College Archives, Student Registers, 5/3/31B.

[66] DAA, Course of Studies 1867–68, St Gregory's College, Downside, *Downside Reports 1860–1883*, A/40/B.

[67] DAA, Philip Magnus to the Registrar of the University of London, 14 Sep. 1882, Courses of Study at Downside 1878–91, C/1412/vII.A.3.D (iv).

for two and a half hours recreation, four hours class-time, almost four hours independent study, and roughly an hour of religious practice between morning mass and prayers.

External state examiners invariably pointed to an over-reliance on the classics, though schools such as Eton and Harrow were equally guilty of this. The yardstick in all such inspections was the established public schools. Mr Bryce, visiting Stonyhurst in 1865 on behalf of the Taunton Commission, noted that the school excelled in providing a decent academic training to each boy enrolled but that it was at the expense of individual achievement. Bryce maintained that there were 'far fewer ignorant boys', but that there were also 'far fewer brilliant boys' than at the established public schools.[68] This was corroborated by an internal inquiry into the state of Catholic education in 1871, when a subcommittee found that a 'higher average standard' was achieved at Catholic schools when compared to Eton and Rugby—but that the 'highest and cleverest boys' at the schools did not come close to the highest individual standard achieved at the public schools.[69] The emphasis on holistic education and a high general standard of learning was commendable, but prize-boys were what won headlines and greater notoriety in the educational market. Schools such as Stonyhurst and Downside would have to adapt or die.

The general impression of education at the English schools in the second half of the nineteenth century, academically at any rate, is one of stasis and frustration. Without degrees of accepted merit to aim for, the options for higher study were limited by the structure of the schools. This, in addition to their remote locations, tended to make Stonyhurst and Downside bottom-heavy schools, where only a small proportion of boys studied to the age of eighteen or nineteen. Fewer still remained in the college for further study, which meant that very many exited education at this stage. A later inspection, in 1903, found that the teaching of science, history, English and drawing all suffered as a result of the continued emphasis on the classics. More positively, the report concluded that this was the case at most public schools. In a section entitled 'General Remarks', the inspectors noted that the Jesuit system of constant surveillance ran counter-intuitively to the contemporary ideas of independence and character-building through student hierarchies and freedom of movement.[70]

Whatever their upward progression, it is reasonable to assume that those Irish boys attending English schools got exactly what they expected—a recognizably elite education, grounded in the classics. That the teaching of science at Stonyhurst was considered lax is something of a curiosity. The school had some unique selling points, such as the potential to teach advanced astronomy through its world-famous observatory, built in 1837–8. This seems to have been utilized only by the philosophers however, with demonstrations for the boys being somewhat

---

[68] Muir, *Stonyhurst*, 112.

[69] Quoted in W. J. Battersby, 'Secondary Education for Boys', in G. A. Beck (ed.), *The English Catholics, 1850–1950: Essays to Commemorate the Restoration of the Hierarchy of England and Wales* (London, 1950), 325–6.

[70] British National Archives, *Stonyhurst College Inspection 1903*, ED 109/2667, 16.

rare. Nevertheless, as Alban Hood has noted, it was a facility 'envied' by the Benedictine schools, and until Rugby school built their science facility in 1857 'no English school had anything comparable to it'.[71] In addition Stonyhurst had the capacity to teach science much earlier than most public schools, having built a chemical laboratory and mathematical room in 1808–10. Throughout the nineteenth century, and despite the emphasis on science in the revised *Ratio Studiorum* the subject did not feature as a major part of the education of the average student at the school.[72] The emphasis on classics at English schools was a rigid one and in some respects more limiting than the curriculum at Irish schools.

The 1880s ushered in an era of modernization and professionalization at the Catholic schools. Under the stewardship of Dom Aidan Gasquet Downside dispensed with the old class names such as Poetry and Rhetoric for the more recognizably public school titles of Sixth Form and Fifth Form. He bought in external expertise, recruiting talented laymen to teach the boys, and though the numbers at Downside had hitherto been comparatively small, under Gasquet they exceeded the one hundred barrier for the first time, rapidly rising in reputation to become the sixth most expensive school in Britain by 1919.[73] Amongst the men who were employed as lay masters in this period was Professor Davies, who went on to occupy the Latin Chair at Queen's College, Galway. Another external master was the QUB graduate and mathematician, C. V. Coates, who held a Foundation scholarship and MA degree from Trinity College, Cambridge and had several publications in the field.[74]

The emphasis on the correct level of training was not confined to externs however; Gasquet also insisted that the religious staff be allowed to upgrade their teaching abilities. In this period Downside priests were sent to study classics, with Professor Paley, and mathematics, with Professor John Casey of Dublin—who had also taught mathematics at Blackrock College and the Catholic University. In an article in the *Downside Review*, a member of the community argued that if Downside was to 'compete with the large Catholic colleges of England and Ireland, whose choice of masters is so great, a certain number of our monks...must be set apart specifically for the work, and must, in a sense and for a time, become professional schoolmasters'.[75] The reference to competing with Irish colleges is one of many in the article, showing perhaps that the academic success they enjoyed in the newly introduced intermediate examinations in Ireland was beginning to cause English colleges such as Downside, whose relatively low numbers were augmented by a significant Irish minority at the school, some serious concern.

[71] Alban Hood, 'From Repatriation to Revival: Continuity and Change in the English Benedictine Congregation, 1795–1850' (PhD, University of Liverpool, 2006), 225.
[72] For an extended discussion of the teaching of science at Stonyhurst see Michael J. Larkin, 'The Influence of External Examinations on Science Teaching in a Nineteenth-century Public School' (MEd, University of Manchester, 1980), 83–9.
[73] Birt, *Downside*, 238; Bamford, *Public School Data*, 43.
[74] C. V. Coates, 'Bessels Functions of the Second Order', *The Quarterly Journal of Pure and Applied Mathematics*, 21 (1886), 183–92.
[75] E. C. Butler, 'A Review of the Studies of the Past Five Years', *The Downside Review*, 3 (1884), 154.

Oscott, a major threat to Stonyhurst in the first half of the century, retained its classical emphasis right up until its closure in 1889. The Jesuit colleges were much more wary of conforming to the public school template than their Benedictine rivals and it was this reticence that cost them their place at the summit of Catholic education in Ireland and Britain. Throughout the nineteenth century the question of progression to university was perhaps the most frequently debated Catholic educational issue in the public sphere. The opening up of professional opportunities for middle-class families meant that Catholics more generally, thoroughly devoid of any real options at university level, were beginning to fall behind in a society that had given over fully to credentialism. Ostensibly, Irish Catholics were better off than their English counterparts in the nineteenth century with regard to university education. If they were willing to endure the disapproval of the hierarchy they could choose between Trinity College Dublin from 1793 and the Queen's Colleges from 1845. If they chose to conform to the wishes of the bishops the Royal University was a guilt-free option from 1879. These were all available to English Catholics as well, though the more delineated social structure meant that for most English Catholics it was a case of Oxbridge above all else. English Catholics also showed themselves to be more willing to obey their hierarchy on the issue of which university they might attend.

Roman Catholics were effectively prohibited from obtaining a degree at either Oxford or Cambridge until 1871, as they were required to sign oaths of allegiance and supremacy, and to declare themselves as members of the Church of England. Despite the removal of this restriction in 1871, the English bishops refused to grant permission to those wishing to attend either of the national universities until 1895–6, when the Pope was obliged to concede permission after a coalition of the Catholic bishops and the English laity presented a petition to the Congregation de Propaganda Fide in Rome demanding that they be allowed to take their place at the major universities. Almost immediately both the Jesuit and Benedictine orders set up private halls for their students and by doing so stated unequivocally that theirs were the schools of choice for the Catholic elite on both islands. Several Catholics *had* attended Oxbridge between 1871 and 1896, despite the 'ban'. One such example, an Irish old boy of Downside, Timothy Carew O'Brien, became the school's most famous athlete by winning an Oxford 'Blue' in cricket for 1884 and again in 1885.[76] His chief distinction, however, must be that he captained both Ireland and England at international level in the same sport. O'Brien performed better for Ireland, scoring a record 162 against England as captain. Somewhat fittingly for a man who bridged both Ireland and England, he made his home in the Isle of Man, and died there in 1948.[77]

For much of the nineteenth century the only recognized degree (approved of by the English Catholic hierarchy) was offered remotely by the University of London

[76] Timothy Carew O'Brien also served in the military, rising to the rank of captain in the Royal Irish Fusiliers and retiring as an honorary major. Jim Shanahan, 'Sir Timothy Carew O'Brien (1861–1948)', *DIB*.

[77] 'Sir Timothy O'Brien', *The Times*, 11 Dec. 1948.

external degree system—a qualification they could just as easily have procured in Ireland. That this was not a cause of concern for the type of Irish family that sent their boys to England is again reflective of the relatively privileged background from which they came. The main point of attending a university in the nineteenth century was after all, one of *necessity*. Most of these boys did not require a formal qualification in order to make ends meet, and therefore academic distinction at university education was only really desirable if one had the aptitude for further study, or was unfortunate enough to have precarious or finite financial resources.

The English Catholic colleges are conspicuous by their absence from the early lists of Newman's Catholic University in Dublin from 1854 to 1879. Out of 1,117 recorded entrants, just seven Stonyhurst boys attended in those twenty-five years, nine from Oscott, five from Downside, and a further four from Beaumont. In total, just forty-seven boys attended the Catholic University from England, about 4 per cent of the total.[78] Writing to the Rector of the Catholic University in 1871 John Henry Newman sought to explain why so few boys had attended the only dedicated Catholic university on either island by first admitting that he had founded the Oratory School in Birmingham with the hope of 'feeding' the Dublin university he had established five years earlier. This venture had failed, he argued, because of the poor uptake by Irish students, but also because in the experience of the English elite schools 'the opening of Oxford and Cambridge excited the minds both of parents and of sons and when they were forbidden this prospect, they abandoned the thought of university education altogether'.[79]

V OUTSIDE THE CLASSROOM, INSIDE THE WALLS: EXTRA-CURRICULAR EDUCATION AT ENGLISH SCHOOLS

As with the Irish schools, university progression and curriculum development were central features of the public face of education at the elite English schools, but the private or hidden curriculum was, arguably, equally significant. In this period organized sport had become more delineated along class lines than it had ever been before and boarding schools proved to be important hotbeds for its gradual development in the nineteenth century, housing as they did mostly young men with more time on their hands than most their age. These boys had little to distract them but schoolwork, and were effectively enclosed in acres of greenery. In retrospect, organized sport seems an obvious answer. High-level cricket dominated as the marker of elite status across the intermediate educational sector until it was replaced by rugby football in the early twentieth century. Association football,

---

[78] William J. Rigney, 'Bartholemew Woodlock and the Catholic University of Ireland 1861–1879', 2 vols. (PhD, UCD, 1995), Appendix.

[79] J. H. Newman to Bartholomew Woodlock, 12 Mar. 1871, Papers of Bartholomew Woodlock, Dublin Diocesan Archives.

or soccer, was also popular in the 1880s, before an excessive uptake amongst the urban poor resulted in widespread defection by the elite. This left plenty of room for expensive, and therefore exclusive, sports such as real tennis, hockey and polo to thrive amongst those who could afford them.

English public schools were self-contained, stratified communities in the nineteenth century. Special insignia developed to create an internal hierarchal division amongst the boys themselves, and this was very often connected to sport or academic achievement. At Thomas Arnold's school at Rugby exceptional athletes were denoted by special velvet caps with gold tassels and other paraphernalia. At Harrow, it was considered the 'very acme' of existence to get into the cricket XI, and those boys alone amongst the student body had the right to wear a black-and-white hat, brass buttons, and white flannel trousers.[80] Special favours were conferred on boys who were academically or athletically gifted. The Catholic public schools were not immune to this, and this informal stratification had an obvious effect. The importance of games was not doubted amongst the student body. An indication of how entrenched the cult of sports had become by the last decades of the nineteenth century is provided by an article in the first issue of *The Stonyhurst College Magazine*, in 1881. According to the author no boy with even a 'spark of boyish character' could fail to feel his 'heart moved and his pulse beat quick' at the mention of either sport.[81] Writing in 1898, W. Munster warned his classmates at Beaumont via the school journal that 'the boy who goes in for games will make many more friends and will get on much better than one who does not'.[82]

The fact that sports such as cricket and football were developing so rapidly at school level meant that the schools themselves began to populate the national sides, only then beginning to take on the prestige associated with international 'caps' today. Indeed, of the thirteen members of the Irish cricket squad that toured America in 1888, nine were educated at elite Catholic colleges, and six of those attended English schools.[83]

A regular 'Athletic Sports' day was held at all four schools, and was open to the public gaze. Such public displays of athleticism helped to nurture the image of the school as a sporting, healthy place where boys could develop as a person both in body and mind—something of a requirement for parents in an era that laid huge emphasis on the Juvenal-derived motto *mens sana in corpore sano*. Only certain sports were to be indulged in, however, and for every possibility for inclusion

---

[80] C. E. Pascoe (ed.), *Everyday Life at our Public Schools: Sketched by Head Scholars* (London, 1881), 187–230.

[81] Luceo Non Uro, 'Cricket and Football; Their Relative Merits and Advantages', *The Stonyhurst College Magazine*, 1 (May, 1881), 3–4.

[82] W. Munster, 'The Advantages of Games', *The Beaumont Review*, 3/17 (Oct. 1898), 27.

[83] The squad was as follows: J. W. Hynes (Clongowes Wood); Dominick Cronin (Beaumont); J. P. FitzGerald, E. E. FitzGerald (Oscott); J. P. Maxwell (Ushaw); J. M. Meldon (Clongowes Wood, Stonyhurst); T. Tobin (Tullabeg); D. F. Gilman (Blackrock); Walter Synnott (Stonyhurst); W. Johnston, Ralph Johnston (Foyle College, Londonderry); T. R. Lyle, F. Kennedy (unknown). See *Freeman's Journal*, 10 Aug. 1888.

in the developing Irish associational culture there was a possibility for exclusion. With clubs came rules.

A remarkable manifestation of such exclusion amongst the Irish boys was the creation of a football team in Dublin, Freebooters FC, based in the wealthy southern suburb of Sandymount in the 1890s. Freebooters FC was set up with a nakedly exclusive membership. It was to be a club for young Irish Catholic men that were educated in English Catholic colleges, and prevented all others from its membership.[84] This policy, in operation from the club's foundation, raised some progressive-nationalist hackles, D. P. Moran's in particular. His anger at the policy was made public in an editorial in which he drew attention to the 'exodus' of Irish Catholics to English schools and castigated the Freebooters for excluding boys educated in Ireland.[85] This editorial drew a remarkable response from 'a friend' of the club:

> No doubt the Freebooters are Irish by birth; some of them, I believe, are connected by family and other ties with Nationalist aspirations, and all of them, as you say, at the foundation of the clubs, were Roman Catholics. But, I confess, I cannot see in any, or all of these circumstances a reason why they should lay aside a preference which is the natural outcome of their English education. It was not their choice to be born in Ireland... There are, we know, disadvantages in being born an Irish Roman Catholic. Their parents did what was wisest and most effectual to minimise the evil, by procuring them some years' companionship with English gentlemen. Is it, then, surprising that they should refuse to associate on terms of equality with lads who are still under the full burden of social and religious disadvantage from which they have themselves, partially at least, been rescued?[86]

The idea that the members of Freebooters FC considered themselves to be minimizing evil by receiving their education is debatable, and it is conceivable that the letter was written ironically. Nevertheless, the fact that young professional men would insulate themselves in such a formal way on their return from an English education is interesting and poses significant questions about their life after school. The article states that, despite their education, the disadvantage of being Roman Catholic could only ever be partially reduced.

Freebooters who achieved Irish international football caps include Henry Mansfield (Stonyhurst: 1890), who was summoned to play centre forward against Scotland, England, and Wales in 1901.[87] His aptitude for the game was flagged in 1890 when writing home from Stonyhurst to his mother in Ireland, telling her that he liked the games at the College 'and football the best of them all'.[88] The sporting legacy of Stonyhurst mattered much in Ireland, and we can be certain that in a period when sport was becoming an important method of defining social class,

---

[84] The founders wrote that they were 'anxious to promote union and fellowship amongst the old boys of Stonyhurst, Downside and Beaumont'. 'Notes', *The Beaumont Review*, 3/18 (Dec. 1898), 55–6.
[85] *The Leader*, 11 Nov. 1900, 163.
[86] *The Leader*, 5 Jan. 1901, 298.
[87] NLI, Mansfield Papers, Reid to Mansfield 14 Mar. 1901, MS 38, 429/3.
[88] NLI, Mansfield Papers, Henry Mansfield to Alice Mansfield, 16 Nov. 1890, MS 38, 429/3.

their success in sports such as cricket, tennis, hockey, and billiards was a result of the careful cultivation of those sports at their school. It was not enough that the past pupils went on to achieve international honours and gain attention for the sporting tradition at Stonyhurst by doing so; the school also organized public matches with Irish teams such as Phoenix CC and Clongowes Wood in order to advertise the fact all the more clearly in Ireland.[89]

Sport was not the only extra-curricular activity. As we have seen in Downside, theatre and debating played a significant role in school life. The moral tone of the school was especially evident in its dramatic productions. It was common practice to censor female roles. Responding to a series of accusations of the staging of improper material in the press at the time of the Tichborne court case, an Irish-born past pupil, Hugh O'Beirne, wrote to *The Times* to defend the school's reputation. He recalled that the plays during his time at the school 'contained no loose matter whatever; that even the female parts were left out, and amorous passages tamed down to dullness'.[90] The traditional high-minded theatre of Shakespeare had dominated the programme until the 1880s (Figure 3.5 for a later *Macbeth*).[91] After that there was a willingness to incorporate modern English comic writers such as John Maddison Morton and F. C. Burnand. Periodically an Irish theme emerged, such as in 1878 with the staging of a farce entitled *An Irish Attorney, or Galway Practice*, by the American-born London writer William Bayle Bernard (1807–75).[92]

At Beaumont the tradition of Christmas and Shrovetide plays carried on from its sister foundation, as did the spontaneous productions throughout the year, such as a performance on Blandyke (a vacation day) or St Patrick's Day. One such example was the impromptu performance of a series of pieces by the Philharmonic society on St Patrick's Day in 1881.[93] A great deal of expense was accrued in the staging of these somewhat elaborate productions. For the staging of *Macbeth* in 1899 the scenic artistry was done by J. T. Bull and Sons, the costumes designed by C. and W. May, and the perruquier was W. Clarkson of London.[94] No expense was spared; the public nature of the performance meant that Beaumont would have to produce something worthy of its reputation, and usually did. A production of *Macbeth* in 1882 was rapturously received by the 200-strong audience, eulogized by *The Spectator*, and enthusiastically applauded by several Eton masters that had attended it.[95]

---

[89] These were reported often in the press, e.g. the game between Stoneyhurst (*sic*) College v Clongowes in the *Irish Times*, 26 Aug. 1870, 5.

[90] 'Stonyhurst College', *The Times*, 5 Aug. 1873, 10.

[91] Gruggen and Keating, *Stonyhurst*, 176.

[92] For a reasonably full listing of plays and farces staged at Stonyhurst see John Gerard, *Stonyhurst College: Its Life Beyond the Seas, 1592–1794 and on English Soil, 1794–1894* (Belfast, 1894), Appendix B, 305–7.

[93] The players were Cyril Russell, Charles Russell, Humphrey de Trafford, Charles Barry, John Morgan, Charles Evelyn O'Leary, Pio Benito, Philip Oddie, see ABPSJ, Beaumont College Archives, Plays and Academical Exhibitions, PG/2.

[94] ABPSJ, Beaumont College Archives, 5/3/3.

[95] 'Annals of the Beaumont Stage', in *The Beaumont Review*, 1/3 (Dec, 1895), 150.

Figure 3.5 Stonyhurst production of *Macbeth*, Shrovetide 1896

Debating and performing were both bound up with the idea of an ability to remain composed before large crowds and to project a particular image of refinement. In Victorian society an increase in mass literacy meant that speeches reached a larger readership than ever before, and the developments in the efficiency of public transport meant that large crowds were a more frequent phenomenon. The desire for correct pronunciation, emphasis, and accent is of course connected to the idea of elocution as central to an elite education. In 1884 an article in the *Raven* by a student who was a member of the Abingdon debating society at the school complained that elocution was seriously neglected by Catholics in the present age. This was a grievous error, particularly for Catholics who could 'with the power of skilful speaking do an enormous amount of good'.[96] The social pressure to speak correctly may well have impacted on Irish boys attending the schools. Professor Honey has highlighted a distinct advantage in having what is commonly referred to as a 'received pronunciation' (RP) accent in the late nineteenth and early twentieth centuries. Honey argues that by the later nineteenth century an RP accent signified that its user was 'either a genuine member of the new caste of public school men or he had gone to some trouble to adjust his accent elsewhere, thus advertising the fact that he identified with that caste and its values'.[97] In Ireland this had a rather more complex reception than in Britain and explains why the sobriquet 'Cawstle

[96] 'The Abingdon Society', *The Raven*, 2/12 (Nov. 1884), 4.
[97] John Honey, *Does Accent Matter? The Pygmalion Factor* (London, 1989), 28.

Catholic' which came into use in the last decades of the nineteenth century. The use of the phonetic 'caw' indicated the affectation of an English accent, the purest form of which could only have come from an extended immersion in an elite English school.

The 'values' of the caste were not left to chance by aspirational school authorities. Catholicism excluded their boys from most clubs in the uppermost echelon, but the creation of influential old boy associations was as vital to the leading Catholic schools, in terms of fundraising as well as status and continued engagement with the school, as it was to any established public school. School dinners and old boy associations were often thinly veiled excuses for some good press and formed part of each school's marketing strategy at a time when every school of distinction had already set one up or were about to. The St Gregory's Society at Downside was one of the earliest Catholic old boys clubs, founded in 1843. A list of its Irish members in 1907 revealed that some fifty-one Irish old boys remained paid-up members, and connected to their old school through the Society, out of 357 in total—about 14 per cent.[98] Though this figure is less than the percentage of the overall attendance from 1850 to 1900, we might well argue that the sheer geographical constraints in being an active member were prohibitive to an Irish adult. In 1844 the society met for what was intended to be the annual 'Irish' dinner, and again in 1853.[99] The society lapsed after several years and was revived in 1877, around the time that such associations became prevalent across the country. Its stated purpose was 'to form a centre of union for alumni and friends of St. Gregory's College', and to offer prizes to the current students to stimulate academic performance.[100] In this way students were turned into old boys by their secretaries and the importance of such a ready-made network of influential contacts at such a low price must surely have impressed itself on recent graduates. In 1896 an attempt was made to revive the Irish Gregorian dinner, which passed off as a success at the Shelbourne Hotel in Dublin on 22 August that year, 'a thoroughly enjoyable *réunion*', one commentator observed, 'the precursor of many similar gatherings, we hope'.[101] We must allow that the appeal of such gatherings was not merely social, but also afforded men of like status and mindset to remain in contact with one another, and form a support network of a kind.

The aims of the Beaumont Union, set up in 1876, were more direct. It sought 'to maintain and foster in old Beaumont boys loyalty and attachment' to their school, to aid 'studies' by incentivizing competition, and, in communion with the spirit of the age, the Union sought to 'encourage the out-door games and athletics'.[102] The Union thrived. Its annual dinners were held in prime London locations such as the Trocadero and the Savoy Hotel, where in 1893 both Cardinal Herbert

---

[98] 'St Gregory's Society Downside (List of Members and Rules for 1907)', Louth Papers, NLI, MS, 40, 102/6.
[99] 'The Gregorian Club', *The Downside Review*, 33 (Centenary Number, 1914), 199.
[100] DAA, 'Rules of St. Gregory's Society 1878', *St Gregory's Society Reports 1877–1900*, A/40/B.
[101] 'Odds and Ends', *The Downside Review*, 15 (Mar.–Dec. 1896), 325.
[102] Frank Devas, *The History of St. Stanislaus' College, Beaumont. A Record of Fifty Years, 1861–1911* (Old Windsor, 1911), 80–1.

Vaughan and the Lord Mayor of London Sir Stuart Knill were received as guests.[103] Such events naturally attracted widespread attention of the type that benefited both past and present pupil alike. Cardinal Vaughan had been installed as Cardinal Manning's successor to the position of Archbishop of Westminster just a year prior to the dinner, and was therefore the most important Catholic on the island. Stuart Knill occupied the most important civic position in the City of London. Being associated with such a prominent Catholic school ought not to have harmed the career prospects of those Irish boys attending Beaumont. The fundraising aspect was far from token. As the Catholic schools were not endowed they relied on exter-nal sources for major building works. The Stonyhurst Association was founded in 1879 with the vague intention 'of furthering the interests of the College'.[104] In its first ten years alone the Association paid out over £900 in prize money to students. It was this very 'corporate spirit' that made committed old boys of English public schools so desirable in the select job market and the civil service.[105]

The last great institution at the schools was undoubtedly the sodalities. As with schools such as Clongowes in Ireland, the sodality was taken very seriously at the English schools. The first sodality at Stonyhurst was the Sodality of Our Lady. At Stonyhurst membership of the main sodality was limited to the three upper classes in the college, and the philosophers. The other, created to include the lower classes in the college, was called the Sodality of Angels. Though these sodalities were really only simple prayer groups, their popularity amongst the boys was vital for the replenishment of the order, encouraging as they did a religious outlook and a vital preparation for the religious life. A healthy sodality meant an increase in likely vocations and so the Sodality of Our Lady at Stonyhurst was well resourced, with the provision of a specific chapel for their exclusive use from 1859 onwards.[106]

For the Irish boys, to become a prefect of Sodality, as in the case of William Campbell (Beaumont: 1878), was as important a boon to one's reputation as any distinction on the playing field.[107] The sodality at Beaumont was run in much the same way as that at Stonyhurst. Membership rarely exceeded twenty-five boys, and the sodality remained an important part of school life throughout the period. The rules of the society are explicit and detailed. A list of thirty-five rules was to be memorized and adhered to by the boys. Members were expected to provide exemplary conduct for their peers. Every Sodalist was expected to honour and reverence the Blessed Virgin Mary and to constantly endeavour to imitate her rare virtues by observing Christian behaviour on all occasions. In particular, the boys were expected to 'have an esteem for the virtue of chastity and preserve with all

---

[103] Knill was a past pupil of the school and the third-ever Roman Catholic to fill the office. Devas, *St Stanislaus College, Beaumont*, 84.

[104] *The Stonyhurst Magazine*, 1 (May 1881), 12.

[105] Robert Huessler, *Yesterday's Rulers: The Making of the British Colonial Service* (Syracuse, 1963), 89.

[106] The chapel was built in the Gothic style and designed by Charles Buckler. The remains of the boy-martyr of Rome, St Gordianus, are to be found there today.

[107] William Bernard Campbell (1865–1911), later a lawyer at the Irish and English Bar, see Beaumont Lists, *Stonyhurst College Magazine*, 31 (Oct. 1963), 469.

diligence true purity of body and mind'.[108] The sodalities were held in high regard by the boys attending. For an Irish boy from Queenstown such as Hugh Aloysius Ryan (Beaumont: 1892)—a member of the football, cricket, and boating team at Beaumont in the 1890s, and a prefect of the sodality—his Irish origin was never likely to have been a bar to popularity.

VI THE PRODUCT

Catholicism was a minor religion in the context of its position within the British and Irish state. To be a Catholic in Ireland or Britain meant sacrificing ease of social mobility or fluidity and the penalty was felt keenly by adherents on both islands. Therefore, the idea that Irish Catholics would attempt to close that gap by availing themselves of an exclusive and English education was one that was bound to stir controversy. The consistent flow of Irish boys to English Catholic colleges and seminaries did not pass without comment in the national press. Periodically, the letters column in the *Freeman's Journal* lit up with indignant parents responding to open accusations of a lack of patriotism. In the pre-intermediate era these accusations were more rare, but certainly noticeable. In 1871, an editorial marked 'Home Schools' in the *Freeman's Journal* poured scorn on those availing of an English education.[109] In such attacks attention was often drawn to the affectations of such boys educated abroad, and their disdain for all things Irish upon their return. They were vilified for their supposed lack of knowledge of Irish history, and their morality and purity was sometimes openly questioned. The 'Home Schools' editorial was no different; it also pointed out the popularly held perception that the majority of the boys sent to England were sons of those in the professions. This was not necessarily the case. As has been shown above, very often they were the sons of landowners and 'old Catholic families' also.

The public attacks were startlingly consistent in the methods employed to denigrate the English schools and those families that patronized them. Often, an overly ambitious mother was held to blame. This was a central theme in an editorial entitled 'Our Boys' in the *Freeman's Journal* of 31 August 1885. The article attacks first and foremost the figure of the priest of the English Catholic colleges himself, who it claims can be found in the Phoenix Park alongside scholastic agents of Oxford 'distributing prospectuses of his college to the youthful on-lookers during an interval in an exciting cricket match'. Not only does the invidious priest or agent work on the boy, but also on the mother. According to the editorial:

> The prospect of the 'accent' and the 'connection' decides the mother; the boy is secured by the visions of football and cricket; and so, unless the father be a man of practical turn and of some weight in the family councils, it is arranged that the boy shall join

---

[108] ABPSJ, Beaumont College Archives, Local Rules of Sodality of our Blessed Lady, Beaumont College, 5/2/5.
[109] 'Home Schools', *Freeman's Journal*, 29 May 1871, 6.

the batch of recruits which will travel to St. Hilda's with the scholastic agent when the holidays are over…Why should our boys be drafted to England for their education?[110]

The language is significant, and implies a measure of slavery and bondage—with words such as 'recruits' and 'drafted' used to full effect. If we were to read this as a colonial exchange then the Irish father is peripheral and is undone by a foreign 'scholastic agent' and an overly ambitious and snobbish wife. His equally blameless son is undone by his manly affinity for muscular sport.

'Our Boys' sparked a controversial exchange of letters that lasted for two full weeks until it was halted by the editor himself. The defence of those who sent their boys to England is perhaps more interesting than the attacks, and provide us with a pointer as to why an English education was coveted by many Irish Catholics. One father, signing himself as 'Paterfamilias', waded into the debate with a defence of the practice on free-trade principles:

> I must ask you to allow me space to claim for myself a right which I entrust no advance of Nationalism will deprive us of—the right to educate our children as we please. In common with other Liberal politicians, you are, I presume an advocate of Free Trade…A very large proportion of our wealthy merchants and successful professional men are educated in England. We may well believe that this would not be so if the advantages of education in England were no more than you represent them. Men of shrewdness and worldly sense do not pay for trifles the pensions paid at English schools.[111]

The Free Trade argument was a convincing one, and 'Paterfamilias' identified a pragmatic element of Irish Catholic thinking that can be taken as summative of this study of elite education in Ireland and England. In sending their boys to England for an expensive and elite education, Irish parents expected a return. In other words, they ought to be seen as informed consumers, seeking a product that would in all likelihood confer a real professional or social advantage on their sons upon their repatriation to Ireland. If many of the leading figures in business and social circles were educated abroad then such an education was all the more desirable. In this reading, the 'shrewdness' alluded to in Paterfamilias's letter must be given more respect than has thus far been the case.

This shrewdness in the matter of education ordinarily translated into an improved or maintained social position depending on the background of those who availed of it. For this increased dividend Irish families were willing to be separated from their sons for up to two years at a time, pay higher fees and travel a tremendous and costly distance. Disillusioned contemporaries, perhaps jealously, identified their reasons for doing so as self-interest and pretension. They alleged that their decision to send their children away was motivated by a desire that they should acquire an accent, fashionable affectation, or a network of influential peers. All of that would mark them out as different, and perhaps somewhat more refined. For those travelling to England, it is likely that such criticism could be cheerfully dismissed as an inevitable by-product of success and improved position.

---

[110] 'Our Boys', *Freeman's Journal*, 31 Aug. 1885, 5.
[111] Paterfamilias, 'Our Boys', *Freeman's Journal*, 1 Sep. 1885, 5.

4

Occupation, Career, and Afterlife
The Measurable Effect of an Elite Education

If Irishmen who achieve distinction were not so fond of that distinction syn-
chronising with Anglification we should be richer at home and more respected
abroad...Why should a Catholic merchant, or judge, or lawyer, or doctor
send his son to an English college, even though it be a Catholic college?

'Home Schools', *Freeman's Journal*, 29 May 1871, 6

Too many school histories ignore the main function of elite schooling—to produce graduates that perform well in society and in the process do credit to themselves, their parents, and their schools. The subsequent performance of students
will greatly affect the appeal and reputation of any elite school. Today, external
rankings have an effect on social cachet and catchment and the more competitive and elite a school is the more likely they are to keep track of past pupils and
to promote their success whenever possible. Statistics derived from such records
make useful advertisement literature for schools up to the present day. Accusations
of poor university progression rates, overcrowded classes, an over-reliance on rote
learning and a stunted learning experience arise periodically in every society, most
recently in Ireland in 2011 with the publication of the Hyland report.[1] Regulating
or student-assessing bodies such as Ofsted and PISA did not exist in Victorian
Britain and Ireland, though the obsession with the statistical measurement of performance metrics certainly dates to that era.[2]

The information presented here is drawn from a database of 1,303 boys
attending English public schools between the 1 January 1850 and 1 January
1900. This database was primarily based on school entrance ledgers from where
the basic information such as name, date of birth, next of kin, home address and
billing address was taken. This information was then fleshed out using a variety

---

[1] e.g. David Raffe et al., *Social-class Inequalities in Education in England and Scotland*, Special
CES Briefing No. 40 (May, 2006), 2; Alan Milburn, *Unleashing Aspiration: The Final Report of the
Panel on Fair Access to the Professions* (2009), 18; Christopher T. Whelan and Damian F. Hannan,
'Class Inequalities in Educational Attainment among the Adult Population in the Republic of Ireland',
The Economic and Social Review, 30/3 (Jul. 1999) 302–3; Aine Hyland, *Entry to Higher Education in
Ireland in the 21st Century* (Sep. 2011), <http://9thlevel.ie/wp-content/uploads/hyland.pdf>.

[2] Ofsted is the Office for Standards in Education, Children's Services and Skills, an impartial
inspecting body for educational institutions in the UK. PISA is Programme for International Student
Assessment, and tests 15-year-olds worldwide under the banner of the OECD.

of printed and online resources described in some detail in the appendix. Until relatively recently such an undertaking was next to impossible as it requires the compilation of a comprehensive life-summary which is then tabulated across several categories. The digitization of major reference texts has changed this landscape considerably, as has the easy availability of obituaries and news reports from 1800 to the present. These resources, often keyword searchable, have revolutionized and revitalized prosopographical research by allowing historians of particular groups to take a holistic approach rather than random sampling. This process has already increased our capacity to identify patterns of employment and recruitment within certain social classes and within preordained chronological limits. Table 4.1 indicates the professions pursued across the entire cohort.

The extent to which an English RC education can be compared to the non-Catholic public schools of England in terms of an elite-occupation outcome can be demonstrated in a rough way. In 1967 an occupational breakdown of boys at Winchester School was provided as part of a published doctoral thesis by T. J. H. Bishop. A summary of the top five occupations found by Bishop in a cohort of Winchester boys born 1840–90 will allow us to compare the outcome of a Catholic elite education with that of one of the leading schools in the Empire in the same period (Table 4.2).

We can see that there is a remarkable uniformity to the figures, except for the clear swing in military and the landowning class. It may also be mistakenly assumed that Winchester graduates entered at a higher level into the professions than their Catholic peers, even if the pattern was the same. Less than 25 per cent of Winchester boys ended up in truly lucrative or high-profile careers, and if we take the easiest to grade, those in the military, we can see that most of those that entered the officer corps ended up somewhere between lieutenant

Table 4.1 Occupation by category of all four English schools combined, 1850–99

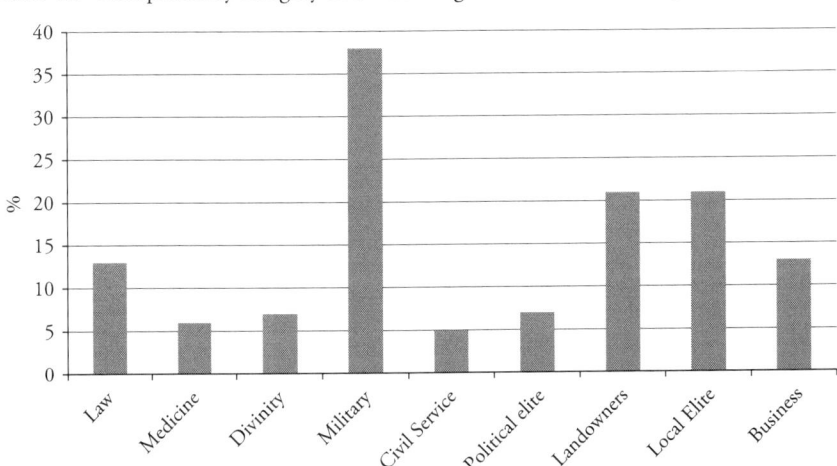

Table 4.2 Irish occupational categories compared to Winchester, 1840–90

Category	Winchester	Irish boys at English RC schools
Military service	19%	38%
Law	15%	13%
Business	15%	13%
Landowners/gentlemen	11%	21%
Government service/politics	8%	12%

colonel and captain, similar to the Irish cohort at English public schools.[3] There are many noticeable quirks: for example, with the exception of those who went on to teach in religious establishments as members of religious orders, very few Irish graduates of English Catholic schools ever taught at high-profile schools—a common career for Winchester graduates. Neither did many Catholic old boys become engineers or scientists either, though those professions were well represented at other public schools. Nevertheless, if Irish boys at schools like Stonyhurst and Downside entered the same professions and their lives followed similar paths, then it may be supposed that this type of schooling consistently yielded satisfactory remuneration, both in terms of finance and social status. The graduates of English Catholic schools could expect to compete on an almost equal footing with the graduates of the established public schools, and indeed, to gain a competitive advantage over those Irish Catholics who had remained at home. What separated the two cohorts, essentially, was the greater degree of wealth detectable in the English cohort which in turn led to a generally lower level of upward social mobility in that group as the base point for most of the families was a pre-existing elite status.

I THE ANCIENT LEARNED PROFESSIONS

The professionalization of Irish and British society was a gradual process that began to take its modern shape in the late eighteenth century. Analysing three separate county elites in England, Lawrence and Jeanne Fawtier Stone found that the Victorian elite had become something of a 'service aristocracy', so well-established was their connection to the professions. To take up a respectable profession cost the son of a landed family little or nothing in terms of status and often proved beneficial to the running of an estate in later life—not to mention giving him something to do while he waited to inherit.[4]

The 'ancient learned professions' are generally considered to be divinity, law, and medicine, to which is often added the military. Although we lack precise figures

[3] T. J. H. Bishop, *Winchester and the Public School Elite: A Statistical Analysis*, ed. Rupert Wilkinson (London, 1967), 65–7.

[4] Lawrence Stone and Jeanne C. Fawtier Stone, *An Open Elite? England, 1540–1880*, abridged edn (Oxford, 1986), 146.

for Ireland the estimates of Gregory King and others indicate that less than 3 per cent of the population of England and Wales were engaged in such occupations between 1688 and 1851, and the eventual expansion of this class to about 10 per cent of the overall population is a twentieth-century phenomenon.[5] The bridging period then, was the second half of the nineteenth century, when the percentage was creeping up past 3 per cent for the first time. This professional stratum has been seen, in particular by Toby Barnard, as an auxiliary or ancillary elite group respected as near-equals by the landed elite, and very often drawn from its ranks.[6] This ancillary elite provided a range of services that supported and reinforced the Protestant ascendancy throughout their period of dominance and so actively excluded Catholics until the late eighteenth century. Tactical conversion aside, the only one of these ancient professions open to Catholics until the relief acts was medicine. Law was off-limits and Catholics were automatically disqualified from the official religion of Ireland and Britain, meaning that any success in divinity could only be achieved in a parallel, penalized Church with very limited power.

All three ancient professions were open to Irish graduates of the English schools since the passing of the Relief Acts in the 1790s and all three represented a high-status professional option for elite families, and something just about achievable for the upper middle class. The liberal reforms of the 1830s had seen high-profile appointments of prominent Catholics to the bench, such as that of Stonyhurst graduate, Stephen Woulfe, to Baron of the Irish Exchequer in 1838. In the case of those opting for divinity, or the religious life, tuition fees were often subsidized by the Catholic hierarchy for those with small incomes, making it one of the most accessible elite groups in nineteenth-century Ireland, as Fergus Campbell has noted elsewhere.[7]

The Irish middle class were well provided for in terms of third-level institutions from which to gain the requisite degrees for the professions. The founding of three Queen's Colleges in Galway, Cork, and Belfast meant that, in addition to Trinity College and the markedly inferior Catholic University in Dublin, there was a multitude of options for those who wished to accumulate credentials. There was also the option to gain a remote degree through the external programme provided by the University of London. This remote alternative was pursued first by Carlow College in the 1840s and later by the elite Irish schools in the 1870s. The Catholic hierarchy's insistence that the Queen's Colleges and Trinity were off-limits for Catholics was certainly a potential barrier for Irish Catholics for much of the century, but only if they were inclined to obey them. Plenty chose not to. The registers of Trinity College Dublin for the years 1850 to 1875 indicate that of the 240 Catholics attending Trinity a total of 89 transferred from Clongowes Wood, and

    [5] See Marcus Ackroyd et al., *Advancing with the Army: Medicine, the Professions, and Social Mobility in the British Isles, 1790–1850* (Oxford, 2006), 10.
    [6] For more background information on the professions in Ireland see 'Professions', in Toby Barnard, *A New Anatomy of Ireland: The Irish Protestants 1649–1770* (New Haven, 2003).
    [7] Fergus Campbell, *The Irish Establishment 1879–1914* (Oxford, 2009), 291.

26 from Stonyhurst. Of the other English schools Oscott came third and Ushaw and Downside both featured in the top ten, alongside more solidly middle-class foundations such as Beaumont, Blackrock, and Carlow College. In Senia Pašeta's analysis of the registers from 1881–1901 the total number of Catholics attending Trinity almost doubled to 447, with Clongowes and Tullabeg together accounting for almost exactly a quarter of these (111) and the English colleges accounting for an increased number, 83 in total. Queen's College Belfast catered for an almost exclusively Protestant student body in the nineteenth century, though the other colleges at Galway and Cork attracted roughly even numbers of both Protestants and Catholics in the second half of the nineteenth century. Charging low fees and offering languages, applied science and professional qualifications (particularly medicine), the Queen's Colleges were aimed at the middle class but at no stage were socially exclusive or elite.[8] If they attended university at all, and most did not, the institution most patronized by elite Catholics was Trinity College, and it became more popular as the nineteenth century came to a close.

Law

A career in law refers to those who were called to the Bar in either England or in Ireland, as well as practicing barristers and solicitors—not just those who were proven to have practiced law for any significant duration. Thirteen per cent of the Irish boys at English schools either gained a legal qualification or are known to have practised. At Beaumont the figure exactly matches that at Stonyhurst: 13 per cent of the Irish boys went on to take a legal qualification. Fourteen per cent of those at Downside obtained a legal qualification and 11 per cent at Oscott. Such uniformity across the cohort shows that a legal career was a staple choice and was consistently high throughout the period examined. This is perhaps surprising, as it was often a difficult career in which to be exceptionally successful, though an established network of high-earning acquaintances certainly helped in this regard.

The mercurial early nineteenth-century careers of Stonyhurst graduates like Stephen Woulfe (Chief Baron of the Irish Exchequer, 1838) and Nicholas Ball (Judge of the Common Pleas 1839) can obscure a much more likely career path such as that of John Lewis More O'Ferrall. O'Ferrall was called to the Irish Bar in 1827, and later served as Deputy Lieutenant and Justice of the Peace for Co. Westmeath, where he had inherited land.[9] His legal career was therefore much more localized and, though important, was not a career of national significance.

Patrick Fagan has noted that the legal profession in Ireland was for a long time the 'special preserve' of Old English families, and that as a result of the English

[8] For a summary of recent work on the Queen's Colleges see Christopher Shepard, 'Cramming, Instrumentality and the Education of Irish Imperial Elites', in David Dickson, Justyna Pyz, and Christopher Shepard (eds), *Irish Classrooms and British Empire: Imperial Contexts in the Origins of Modern Education* (Dublin, 2012), 172–83.

[9] His sons would later attend both Clongowes and Stonyhurst. David Murphy, 'John Lewis More O'Ferrall (1800–1881)', *DIB*.

legal system in Ireland originating in the Pale, 'we find a preponderance of Old English names in the ranks of lawyers and judges, names such as Aylmer, Luttrell, White, Barnewall, Dillon, D'Arcy, Butler, Everard, Archer, Talbot, Verdon, Nugent, Fitzgerald, De Burgo'.[10] The ancient professions of 'physic' and 'barrister' were attractive as high-status and independent occupations with a reliable income if successful and well networked. They were highly regarded partly because they were based on remuneration by means of a discretionary honorarium, rather than a wage, and so did not compromise the definition of a 'gentleman'.[11] Although both were competitive professions which were controlled by metropolitan elite societies, only barristers enjoyed a self-regulating monopoly in their own field. The Irish Bar was regulated entirely by Benchers of the King's Inns in Dublin, and until 1829 Catholics were discriminated against within the profession and could not, for example, become a King's Counsel or a judge.[12] Catholics who chose a legal career most often studied at Trinity College Dublin or the Queen's Colleges as graduates of these institutions were called to the Bar three years from the date of their registration as law students, while non-graduates were inadmissible for such a call until the expiration of five years from such a date. The same formula applied to solicitors, who faced a preliminary examination if they did not graduate from either the Queen's Colleges or Trinity, and would have to wait an additional two years to gain parity.[13] These regulations meant that, as it did not have equal weight, graduates of the Catholic University's law faculty were severely disadvantaged.

A legal qualification was sometimes used merely as an adornment, a proof of higher education which conferred a degree of sophistication on its holder as well as some expertise that might be put to good use on a large landed estate. Of the total number of boys classed as legal professionals thirty-eight practised privately as a solicitor, mostly in Ireland, with twenty-seven becoming barristers.[14] At Downside, Stonyhurst, and Beaumont almost half as many boys became barristers as solicitors, though the pattern reversed for Oscott, where at least eleven boys became barristers but only five became solicitors. W. J. Reader has noted that to become a solicitor was to effectively limit one's career trajectory. Solicitors were 'utterly subservient' to judges and although officers of the court their social standing was

---

[10] Patrick Fagan, *Catholics in a Protestant Country: The Papist Constituency in Eighteenth-century Dublin* (Dublin, 1998), 104.

[11] Daniel Duman, 'Pathway to Professionalism: The English Bar in the Eighteenth and Nineteenth Centuries', *Journal of Social History*, 13/4 (1980), 616.

[12] See Colum Kenny, 'The Exclusion of Catholics from the Legal Profession in Ireland, 1537–1829', *Irish Historical Studies*, 25/100 (1987), 356.

[13] William J. Rigney, 'Bartholemew Woodlock and the Catholic University of Ireland 1861–1879', 2 vols. (PhD, UCD, 1995), 305.

[14] At Stonyhurst just two boys practised as a solicitor in England. One was Charles J. Guy (Stonyhurst: 1866), a boy from Newry, Co. Down. He was a member of the Liberal Party, lived in Hammersmith, and set up the People's Land and Dwelling Company. The other was Walter Joseph Synnott (Blackrock, 1870, Stonyhurst, 1871) of Monkstown in Dublin, who was called to the Bar in 1884 and later practised at Bellard, Coveney, Synnott and Figgis Solicitors, 13 Old Cavendish St, Cavendish Sq. in 1906. 'Charles Joseph Guy', *The Stonyhurst Magazine*, 1940; *The Belfast News-Letter*, 11 Nov. 1884; Hugh Montgomery-Massingberd (ed.), *Burke's Irish Family Records* (London: Burke's Peerage Ltd, 1976), 1094–6.

considerably lower than that of a barrister.[15] In the 1901 census of Ireland just 542 people identified themselves as a barrister, and 260 (48 per cent) of these were Catholic. A much higher figure of 2,169 identified themselves as 'solicitor' in 1901, 944 (44 per cent) of whom were Catholic. An Irish legal professional was therefore almost four times more likely to be a solicitor than a barrister, no matter where he worshipped on a Sunday, so the boys in this cohort were performing well above the average law graduate.

Of the Irish boys in the Stonyhurst cohort that became barristers some achieved national recognition. The barrister Nicholas J. Synnott, son of the Dublin corn merchant Thomas L. Synnott, was made director of the Bank of Ireland in 1918—underlining the extent of his varied business interests in the city.[16] Five of the boys went on to serve in a more local county-level capacity as a Justice of the Peace, Resident Magistrate, or Deputy Lieutenant of a county. At Beaumont, of the twenty-nine boys with a legal qualification, just seven were found to be practising as solicitors, while two became barristers. Seventeen had been called to the Bar in either England or Ireland and one went on to become a Bencher at King's Inns.

In contrast to the heights achieved by earlier Irish pupils at Stonyhurst such as Ball and Woulfe, just four of this cohort went on to high-profile roles such as Queen's Counsel or Solicitor General. The most prominent of the group was John Francis Moriarty, who entered Stonyhurst in 1870. He was at the school in the same period as Arthur Conan Doyle, the author of the Sherlock Holmes stories and, along with his brother Michael Augustus Moriarty, served as a real-life inspiration for the character of Professor James Moriarty, the most famous of the Holmes's fictional nemeses.[17] Back in the real world John Francis Moriarty enjoyed a successful legal career, significant enough for *The New York Times* to take note of his death. He attended TCD, became Solicitor General for Ireland in 1913, Attorney General for Ireland in 1914, and Lord Justice of Appeal 1913–15.[18] A significant number of the cohort had family connections to law—of the nineteen whose father's occupation is known, fourteen of them were legal professionals themselves or encountered law on a regular basis in their capacity as a Resident Magistrate, Justice of the Peace, or Deputy Lieutenant of a County.

At Downside, eleven boys practised for a time as solicitors, seven as barristers and one as a judge. A further nine boys were called to the Bar, many of whom acted as Justice of the Peace or Deputy Lieutenant in later life. One boy, Thomas David Sherlock (Downside: 1895), practised first on the Munster circuit, before moving

[15] W. J. Reader, *Professional Men: The Rise of the Professional Class in the Nineteenth Century* (London, 1966), 25.

[16] He had practised as a barrister in England for twenty years (1879–99), but was the only Irish boy in the cohort to do so. See Shaun Boylan, 'Nicholas Joseph Synnott (1856–1920)', *DIB*.

[17] Also in the school at that time was an Irish boy called Patrick Sherlock, quite probably the inspiration behind the name of the world's most famous fictional detective. Patrick Sherlock died aged twenty-six in 1884, having married in Chicago, and so did not live long enough to have seen his namesake solve so many fictional murders. Arian E. Collins, *The Sherlocks of Ireland and Wales* (San Diego, 2008), 54.

[18] 'Irish Lord Justice Dead; Rt. Hon. John Francis Moriarty was Former Attorney General', *The New York Times*, 3 May 1915, 11.

on to become Chief Justice of British North Borneo and Justice of Appeals, later Chief Justice of Jamaica (1943). He married Augusta Cruise (daughter of Sir Francis Cruise, the Dublin physician) who was a sister of his schoolmate Edward Cruise (Downside: 1889). Sherlock also served as a captain in the Royal Irish Regiment in World War I, and was eventually made an MBE.[19] Despite the fact that the percentage with legal qualifications at Downside was slightly higher than at either of the Jesuit schools, a similar pattern emerges with regard to their use of it. At both Stonyhurst and Beaumont it was clear that not all of those qualified went on to practise law, and that there was a prestige attached to a legal qualification that in itself was an attractive proposition in terms of social status. At Downside only roughly two-thirds of those who were called to the Bar were visible as practising solicitors or barristers for any length of time. One such instance of an 'invisible' law graduate is Martin Joseph Blake (Downside: 1864), a talented archaeologist, genealogist, and amateur historian—who went on to compile the Blake family records.[20] The Blakes were an 'Old English' family, with the most conspicuous branches living at Renvyle and Tower Hill, near Ballyglass in Co. Mayo. For Martin Joseph Blake, whose interests lay far away from the practice of law, a legal qualification could have been no more than an accessory.

Success on the law circuit was not confined to the provinces of Ireland. John Harvey Murphy, KC (Downside, 1877) served for many years as 'a conspicuous and beloved figure in the Probate and Divorce Division' in London, where he was notable for his geniality and his 'vast proportions'. Murphy was of a long line of legal figures, and both his father and his grandfather were famous 'silks' in their own right.[21] A more standard career, however, was that of William Frederick Kenny (Downside: 1871) who was called to the Irish Bar in 1879, was made a KC by 1904, and later a Crown Prosecutor and Revising Barrister for Co. Kerry.[22] Most of those Irish boys who went on to obtain a legal qualification attended the school in the 1860s and 1870s, with a sharp drop-off in the 1880s.

We have already mentioned the Tichborne trial in relation to Stonyhurst as a remarkable instance of a Catholic school being dragged through the courts in a rather uncomfortable manner. Oscott had its own legal travails in 1865 when a parent of an Irish boy, the Hon. Justice John David Fitzgerald decided to bring the president of Oscott, Dr James Spencer Northcote, before the courts for expelling his misbehaving son, David.[23] *Fitzgerald v Northcote* is chiefly remembered as

---

[19] See 'D. T. J. Sherlock, obituary', *Irish Times*, 3 Oct. 1964; 'D. T. J. Sherlock', Irish National Census 1911, NAI, <http://www.census.nationalarchives.ie/reels/nai000217107/>; Helen Andrews, 'Sir Francis R. Cruise', *DIB*; Dom Lucius Graham, *Downside and the War 1914–1919* (London, 1925), 30.

[20] Martin Joseph Blake, *Blake Family Records, 1300 to 1600; A Chronological Catalogue with Copious Notes and Genealogies of Many Branches of the Blake Family* (London, 1902).

[21] 'J. H. Murphy KC', *The Times*, 22 Dec. 1924, 12.

[22] He was also a Revising Barrister in Co. Tyrone for a time. 'Mr William Frederick Kenny', *Irish Times*, 28 Aug. 1929, 9.

[23] John David Fitzgerald had a spectacular legal career (during which he presided over the Fenian trial in 1865 and the Pigot libel case in 1868) and was later appointed HM Lord of Appeal and a life-peer in 1882. James Spencer Northcote was a formidable scholar and an early protégé of J. H.

the landmark case which established that teachers were legally responsible as the guardians of children *in loco parentis*—a very considerable consequence of a very petty trial. The final straw for Northcote appears to have been his pupil's formation of a secret society intent on persecuting less fortunate students. After a litany of misdemeanours, from firing pistols to smuggling spirits into his rooms and attempting to duplicate the school keys—David (who had been at the school from the age of eleven to the age of nineteen) began to form among the student body a group whose aim it was to bully the divinity students at the school. These divinity students were a minority, and typically studied at Oscott by virtue of a scholarship or subsidy. They were also generally of a lower social class than those who paid full fees. As a consequence of this bullying David was sent home immediately by the president, having offended the moral and democratic character of the school authorities. The jury, however, very quickly found in favour of Fitzgerald and his son and though *Fitzgerald v Northcote* may well be a landmark case in the history of law in relation to education, at its root there was a rather unpleasant demonstration of social hierarchy in mid-Victorian Britain and Ireland.[24] The subject of the case, David Fitzgerald, later became a barrister and was called to the Irish Bar in 1872 via a period of study at Cambridge.

Medicine

Just 6 per cent of Irish-born boarders either gained a medical qualification or practised in any of the branches of the profession. This number includes those that obtained a medical qualification, or practiced for any length of time as a physician, dentist, or surgeon. The lower-status 'pharmacist' or 'apothecary' does not figure in the cohort. With regard to qualification, prior to the recognition of degrees from the Royal University in the 1880s Catholics could qualify either in England, or at Trinity College, the Queen's Colleges, and the Catholic University. The Catholic University School of Medicine in Cecilia Street was generally considered the most successful wing of the ailing university, having received recognition for its teaching from the Royal College of Surgeons of Ireland and the Kings and Queens College of Physicians early in its existence. Its graduates were not placed at a disadvantage compared to other denominations, as was the case in law. F. O. C. Meenan estimates that, in addition to a high-quality intermediate education, it cost the average Cecilia Street student an additional £400–£500 to gain their medical qualification. In return for this investment they could expect a salary of at least £90–£120 per annum, and a little more than that if they entered the military.[25] This was quite a low figure when compared to other professions and though many of the boys in

---

Newman. He converted to Catholicism in 1846 following his wife's reception into the Church in 1845.

[24] See *Report of the Proceedings in the Case of Fitzgerald v Northcote and Another, Together with an Introductory Narrative and Documents* (Dublin and Birmingham, 1866)

[25] F. O. C. Meenan, 'The Catholic University School of Medicine 1860–1880', *Studies: An Irish Quarterly Review*, 66/262–3 (Summer/Autumn, 1977), 140.

the cohort established more wealthy practices, the potential for a parsimonious lifestyle was surely a significant deterrent for those from elite backgrounds.

Of the twenty-four boys (9 per cent) who qualified as doctors from Stonyhurst, fourteen also served in the military. Only fourteen Irish boys that attended Downside in the period went on to gain a medical qualification—just 7 per cent. Of those who obtained a medical qualification, the majority attended the school in the 1870s. Beaumont recorded only 5 per cent of their graduates as involved in medicine full-time, and at Oscott just four boys became medics, representing an atypical 2 per cent of the cohort.

Fagan notes that Catholics accounted for between one-third and a half of all medical practitioners in Dublin between 1861 and 1911.[26] Nevertheless, comparatively few of the boys educated in England chose this career route, and of those who chose it many ended up like George Digby (Stonyhurst: 1871), living an inoffensive provincial life in whatever part of rural Ireland they came from.[27] The Meldons, a landed Catholic family with property in Kildare and Dublin provide us with a good example of an elite family that concentrated on the professions. The family had a successful legal business Meldon & Co. Solicitors at 8 Merrion Square North, under the sole control of Aloysius Stanislaus Meldon (Stonyhurst: 1867). His sons George and Louis were also educated at Stonyhurst in this period, in 1896 and 1898 respectively. It was Louis who took over the running of Meldon & Co., while his older brother George contented himself with running a small medical practice in Stourbridge, Worcestershire, and in his spare time won caps for Ireland in both cricket and hockey.[28] The diversity of occupations in the male line of the Meldon family is striking. With land, medicine, and law covered the family was close to a self-sustaining unit.

Of the eleven medical professionals who graduated from Beaumont, nine were doctors, one was in the Royal Army Medical Corps, and one became a dental surgeon. A medical qualification differed from a legal qualification in that most boys practised as a general practitioner for the majority of their lives. It also offered the possibility of well-remunerated work abroad such as that taken up by Irish boys like Charles Renfric Chichester (Stonyhurst: 1877), whose work was praised in the yellow fever epidemic in Gambia in 1900.[29] Many career options opened up for those who could afford the qualification. Dr Anthony Roche MD (Downside: 1862) became a lecturer in Public Health at Maynooth, after a successful spell as Professor of Medical Jurisprudence and Public Hygiene at the Catholic University.[30] Another option was the Royal Army Medical Corps (RAMC) to which Charles Randolph Kilkelly (Downside: 1873) was attached. Kilkelly showed an early aptitude for leadership, acting as captain for the school in 1876. His career showed similar ambition

---

[26] Fagan, *Catholics in a Protestant Country*, 97–8.

[27] Digby was an MD in Roscommon in 1894. *Freeman's Journal*, 17 Jan. 1894.

[28] He also had the honour of playing in a cricket match against the legendary W. G. Grace, aged just 17. See 'George Meldon', *The Stonyhurst Magazine*, 1952.

[29] SCA, Stonyhurst College Register 1870–1921.

[30] F. C. Burnand (ed.), *The Catholic Who's Who and Yearbook 1908* (London: Burns & Oates, 1908), 344.

and drive, and he became Surgeon General of the Grenadier Guards at the end of a long and distinguished career that saw him on active service in both India and in South Africa and as governor of the Portland Hospital in Pretoria. His brother, Percy Kilkelly (Downside: 1878), a famous athlete, also served in the Indian Medical Service (IMS). In World War I, Percy was a surgeon lieutenant colonel, and at the outset of his career he had won the Gold Medal for Practical Surgery at Trinity College, Dublin.[31] Percy wrote a brief memoir of his time in India, entitled 'Buffalo Shooting in India', a breathless tale of hunting game with his Shikari, Hutti Singh. Remarkably, Percy does not once mention what it was that brought him to India at any stage during the three-page account, but ends with the promise of another article on tiger hunting, suggesting that the medical aspect of his life in India was at best somewhat peripheral.[32] His athletic endeavours, however, were lionized by the boys at Downside who followed him in their journal *The Raven*. 'Another brilliant success for Percy Kilkelly', it exclaimed on hearing of his achievement at the College Races in Dublin, where Kilkelly broke the world grass record (cycling) for 5 miles in 15 minutes 23 2/5 seconds.[33]

One Stonyhurst graduate, James Lewis Somers of Roscrea (Stonyhurst: 1877) had so traumatic a beginning to his medical career that it quite probably marked him for life. Aged just nineteen, Somers was the youngest in the Empire to graduate as a doctor in 1883. While a medical student in Dublin he was unfortunate enough to be called upon to identify the body of the Lord Lieutenant of Ireland, Lord Frederick Cavendish, who had just been murdered alongside the under-secretary Thomas Burke in the Phoenix Park.[34]

Divinity

The inclusion of Catholic priests and monks within the rubric of the ancient learned profession is something of a stretch, as it was not of equivalent status as the Anglican clerical career in terms of salary or social clout. Nevertheless, the fact that many of the Catholic elite chose this option shows us that within certain boundaries a religious vocation was not seen as a step down the social ladder, and it was considered a boon to the family to have a son or daughter in a socially desirable religious order. The second half of the nineteenth century saw an increasing bureaucratization and professionalization of the Catholic Church in Ireland. This 'devotional revolution' had been evident earlier in the century and was characterized by an increasing confidence and aggression. From this period the frequency of vocations began to climb steadily towards its mid-twentieth-century peak and it is not surprising that, on average, about 10 per cent of the boys being educated

---

[31] Graham, *Downside and the War*, 19; 'Medical News', *British Medical Journal*, 2/4840 (Oct. 1953), 839.

[32] P. P. Kilkelly, 'Buffalo Shooting in India', *The Downside Review*, 14 (Mar.–Dec. 1895), 114.

[33] 'Paragraphs', *The Raven*, 3/24 (Jul., 1890), 34.

[34] Somers later married his cousin, Mabel Usher, and moved to Ballarat, Australia. 'Dr James Lewis Somers', Obituaries, *Stonyhurst Magazine*, 1938.

at elite schools overseas took holy orders. The intensely religious atmosphere of the schools mirrored this general trend, and we can only imagine that boys of a young and impressionable age were affected by the devotion of the monks or priests who were mentoring and teaching them on a daily basis. It was these figures that they were taught to respect and revere. The ceremony, ritual, and apparent sanctity attached to religious practice in this micro-society was bound to make an impact on many of the boys, who were often far away from home and parental influence. Reflecting in a private memoir on his decision to enter the Benedictine order an Irish recruit, the Irish-born Abbot Edward Cuthbert Butler, was characteristically candid about his motivations (or lack of them) when joining the order. When he entered the Benedictine novitiate at Belmont in 1876 at just eighteen years of age he had no real idea of what the monastic life would entail. 'I acted on perfectly blind impulse', he admitted. 'I had no great attraction for Church services, or prayer; I was not drawn by affection for any of the monks; I was not flying from the dangers of the world—I knew nothing of them.'[35] Butler chose the most common route by joining the order he was most familiar with—the one which had educated him. This meant that those Irish boys who became, for want of a better term, professionally divine, the majority of them settled in England, in marked contrast to those who entered other professional contexts.

The uniformed and bureaucratic nature of religious service has often been commented on, as has the idea of priests acting as 'God's soldiers', particularly with regard to the Jesuit order. It is therefore not much of a stretch to regard a priest as a professional. That the religious life was competitive and divided according to social status, however, is an idea that is often elided. Certain orders specialized in helping the poor, or the indigent—others concentrated on targeting the wealthy and thus often attracted members of a higher social status. Some orders catered for both, but created a two- or three-tier hierarchy within the order, delegating manual labour to those of lower status. Another issue often ignored is the high level of domestic mobility that was available to the religious. Rather than spending a life in isolated and idle contemplation, the majority of those who opted for a religious vocation spent their career moving between parish posts, doing their share of the teaching duties, or engaging in foreign missions. Religious orders such as the Society of Jesus were transnational in character, split into missions along national borders, but with the potential to expand in most directions beyond them. Hence a Jesuit of the English 'province' may have easily crossed paths with one from a French or Irish 'province' whilst on entirely separate business somewhere in West Africa. Though all were theoretically answerable to the Superior General of the order in Rome, in effect individual provinces maintained control.

Seven per cent of Irish-born boarders (sixty-two) became either priests or monks after leaving school. Twenty-seven boys from Stonyhurst, ten from Beaumont, and twenty from Downside. If we leave aside seminarians at Oscott, who were often of

---

[35] DAA, Abbot E. C. Butler Papers, Dom Cuthbert Butler, 'Recollections of the Downside Movement 1880–1892' (unpublished MSS), B/1435/v.II.A.3.F.

a different social class, then just five of the boys not predetermined on that track opted to become priests. Because of the streaming that took place at Oscott it must be counted as an atypical case compared to the other schools.

Though the overall catch was less than 10 per cent at Stonyhurst, one in ten boys was a considerable success from a Jesuit point of view, considering that the lion's share went on to become Jesuits as well, though usually in the English province as opposed to the Irish. Upward mobility seems to have been fair within the orders. At Stonyhurst both Daniel Heffernan Considine (Stonyhurst: 1860) and Thomas White (Stonyhurst: 1881) held the position of Rector of Wimbledon College, William Joseph Bodkin (Stonyhurst: 1877) was Rector at Stonyhurst 1907–16 and George Gallagher (Stonyhurst: 1895) was Superior at Farm St in London. At Beaumont College Joseph Mary Woodlock (Beaumont: 1889) went on to become Prefect of Studies at his alma mater and his brother Francis Woodlock, SJ (Beaumont: 1880) (Figure 4.1) was a famous preacher in London. Of those boys that became religious outside of the Jesuit order, the Sheils enjoyed the most success in terms of the status of their subsequent positions. Justin Sheil (Beaumont: 1871) and Denis Sheil (Beaumont: 1878) went on to become a Trappist Sub-prior and Superior at the Oratory School in Birmingham respectively.

The religious life did not always mean a life of contemplation or stasis. The English province of the Jesuits also ran the Zambesi Mission in Rhodesia, to which Ignatius Gartlan (Stonyhurst: 1866) was attached.[36] Typically though, the

Figure 4.1 Francis Woodlock, SJ (Beaumont: 1880)

---

[36] Gartlan was born in Dundalk, Co. Louth. He attended Mount St Mary's before 'finishing' at Stonyhurst, where he later taught for several years. 'Fr Ignatius Gartlan', *Letters and Notices*, 42(1927).

Irish-born priest circulated between the major domestic projects in Britain, as was customary for members of the order. Not much is known of the individual Jesuits, outside of the full-length obituaries in the society's journal *Letters and Notices*. Daniel Heffernan Considine's obituarist noted that someone had once remarked of him that '[h]e was not much of an Irishman', but that he rose above the 'limitation of mere nationalism' to the point that one 'thought of him simply as a Jesuit'.[37] This was the preferred verdict of the Jesuits, that no member be overtly political. However, this outright assimilation was not always possible. An obituary for Matthew Aloysius Power, an Irish boy who had gone on to serve the order in Liverpool and Manchester stated that '[h]e was Irish by blood and temperament, a born fighter. He delighted in discussion, was cyclonic in controversy.' Likewise Michael Gavin, SJ (Stonyhurst: 1856) was seen to have been 'in immediate sympathy with any child of Erin whom he met'.[38] In this sense then the only true difference between those that opted for a life amongst the civilian population and those that opted to join the order that educated them was that the majority of the latter remained in England.

At Downside, the majority of those identified as priests or monks remained within the order. A total of fifteen were professed as Benedictine monks. Five joined the secular clergy, with Monsignor Canon Martin Howlett (Downside: 1875) perhaps the most successful of these, acting as private secretary to Cardinal Vaughan for a time and also becoming administrator of Westminster Cathedral in London. Career progression was not an issue within the Order of St Benedict either. One of the most important Benedictine thinkers and educationists in the nineteenth century, Edward Butler (Downside: 1869), was an Irish boy. Butler became Dom Cuthbert when he took his vows in 1877, aged twenty-one.[39] He later became second Abbot of Downside in 1906, and was an advocate of the Benedictine foundation at Oxford and a central character in what became known as the 'Downside Movement'—a theological debate within the Benedictine order in the late nineteenth century which centred on the question of whether the order should become fully enclosed.[40] Likewise, Dom Bernard Murphy was Prior of Downside 1870–8 and Dom Aidan Howlett was Headmaster of the school 1900–2 and was also Irish.

The record for Downside shows that a total of 114 boys entered the noviciate at Belmont between 1860 and 1908, with 30 leaving before professing.[41] If fifteen Irish boys professed as Benedictine monks, this means that the school was effectively replenishing the monastery at Downside from a base which was almost 20 per cent Irish, forming a significant internal Irish bloc in the staff as well as in the student body. It is curious that none of the boys at Downside in the 1890s went on to join the order—the last in this period to profess was John F. Sweetman

---

[37] 'Fr. Daniel Heffernan Considine', *Letters and Notices*, 37 (1922), 158.
[38] 'Fr. Matthew Aloysius Power', *Letters and Notices*, 41 (1926), 233; 'Fr Michael Gavin', *Letters and Notices*, 35 (1919–20), 124.
[39] ACA, Belmont Clothing Book, Saint Laurence Papers VI (Ampleforth Abbey: 2003), 12.
[40] See Aidan Bellenger, 'The English Benedictines: The Search for a Monastic Identity', in Judith Loades (ed.), *Monastic Studies: The Continuity of Tradition* (Bangor, 1991).
[41] ACA, Belmont Clothing Book, 57–8.

(Downside: 1889), later Dom Francis, who later founded the Irish Benedictine foundation, Mount St Benedict at Gorey, Co. Wexford in 1907–8. It is also of interest, however incidental, that five of the fifteen Irish monks were in the same class group in 1869, suggesting that peer-related dynamics may have been a factor in pursuing the religious life.

A common trajectory for an Irish boy who remained at Downside and professed as a monk was to spend most of his time on the mission, in parishes all around the country. For example, Dom Michael Caffrey (Downside: 1884) spent the academic year 1902–3 teaching theology at Downside, before moving to St Mary's, Liverpool in 1905. He then assisted the new Benedictine school at Enniscorthy, Co. Wexford in 1907 before returning to Liverpool in 1908, and from there to the missions at Hindley (1910), Coventry (1914), Redditch (1926), Whitehaven (1930), Downside (1933), Clayton (1935), and finally Ealing (1943).[42] He died in 1944, presumably somewhat exhausted.

Military

Nicholas Perry has recently argued that the Irish landed class was 'one of the most militarized social groups in the British Isles' in this period.[43] Although the large-scale wars in South Africa 1899–1902 and Europe 1914–18 certainly brought about an increase or 'spike' of Irish involvement in the British army, they did not radically alter the percentage of landed Irish families whose sons gained a commission. Perry's work shows that between 1830 and 1929 an average figure of 50 per cent of the males in the gentry (defined as Irish families with over 1,000 acres) were commissioned as officers.[44] The officer corps was mostly Protestant, as we might expect from the denominational distribution of landed estates. It is interesting to note, however, that a similar pattern of military service existed for Catholic and Anglican families with large estates, or elite status. In the nineteenth century that service was almost exclusively in the British army. The image of the 'wild geese' Catholic gentry serving as officers in Continental and Catholic armies in the seventeenth and eighteenth centuries has been a persistent one in Irish popular culture. This heroic image of Catholic affinity-in-arms is, however, at odds with the large-scale transition of Irish Catholics to the British army after the French Revolution. As Stephen Conway has recently noted, the main reason so many Irish Catholics fought for Continental armies was the denial of rank to Catholics in the British army until the passing of Catholic Relief Act of 1793.[45] As soon as it was possible to achieve rank domestically, the pattern of Continental service was disrupted, suggesting

---

[42] DAA, Dom Philip Jebb, 'John (Michael) Caffrey', Index of Benedictine Priests, D/Ref.

[43] Nicholas Perry, 'The Irish Landed Class and the British Army, 1850–1950', *War in History*, 18/3 (Jul. 2011), 314.

[44] Perry, 'The Irish Landed Class and the British Army', 310.

[45] Stephen Conway, *Britain, Ireland and Continental Europe in the Eighteenth Century* (Oxford, 2011), 172. See also See David Dickson, 'Jacobitism in Eighteenth-century Ireland: A Munster Perspective', *Eire-Ireland*, 39 (Fall/Winter, 2004), 77.

that status—rather than any transnational Catholic ties or even the furtherance of Irish separatist goals—was the motivation for it in the first place.

This career choice was to become an obvious and dominant one for Irish Catholics of all social classes as the Empire expanded in the nineteenth century, and altogether 38 per cent of the boys in our sample were involved in it at some point in their lives. At Stonyhurst, an impressive 36 per cent of those whose occupations are known were involved in some capacity in active service. The figure at Beaumont was even higher, with 47 per cent of those enrolled found to be on active service at some point. At Downside and Oscott the figure was 34 per cent— with many of the boys combining military careers with several other duties. Major Gerald Dease (Oscott: 1865) of the Royal Fusiliers is a good example of that, inheriting over 6,000 acres in counties Westmeath and Cavan where he served as Deputy Lieutenant, Justice of the Peace, and High Sheriff. He also acted as National Commissioner for Education.

The importance of the large-scale involvement of Irish and British boys and men in both the Boer War and World War I cannot be doubted as a significant reason for the predominance of military careers in this cohort, but, even prior to these conflicts, the Irish Catholic elite had a well-developed military tradition. Irish Catholic involvement in the army is generally held to have taken place predominantly at entry level, though the Stonyhurst sample goes some way towards proving that this fact might well be connected more to class than nationality. Of the ninety-nine boys with a military connection, eighty-one were in the regular British army, fourteen in the Army Medical Corps, three in the Royal Navy and one in the RAF. The rank achieved by these Catholic boys is in itself quite revealing. Below the ranks are displayed in order of importance (Tables 4.3 and 4.4), from Field Marshal down to the lowest of the commissioned officers, second lieutenant. The graph illustrates the specific number of Irish boys who attended Stonyhurst and Downside and what rank they obtained.

As these tables clearly show, the average Irish alumnus achieved a respectable commission in the British army, typically in the mid range between colonel and captain. Only one boy at Stonyhurst held a rank that was in the lower non-commissioned level.[46] The most successful boy of the period was Lt Col. Edward Stanislaus Bulfin, who entered the Yorkshire Regiment in 1884, was made captain the following year and eventually retired as honorary general in 1926, after forging an impressive reputation as an effective commander at brigade, divisional, and corps level.[47] Bulfin, however, was an exceptional case—the majority of his peers had fairly average military careers. To achieve rank in the British army nevertheless guaranteed a degree of respectability. For Irish Catholic boys such a feat cost a great deal of money, and continued to do so even when they emerged from

---

[46] Sergeant Victor Galwey-Foley (Stonyhurst: 1899), who enlisted at Liverpool and was posted as sergeant to the Royal Innsikilling Fusiliers and died 23 Oct. 1916, aged twenty-nine. Francis Irwin, SJ, *Stonyhurst War Record.*

[47] *The Times*, 22 Aug. 1939, 12. He was particularly noted for his actions at the first battle of Ypres in 1914.

Table 4.3 Irish-born boarders at Stonyhurst by rank attained in the military

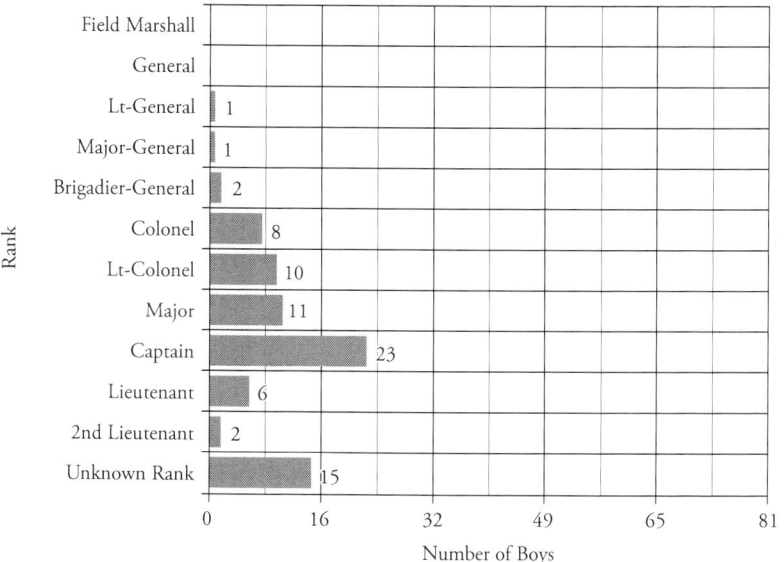

Table 4.4 Irish-born boarders at Downside by rank attained in the military

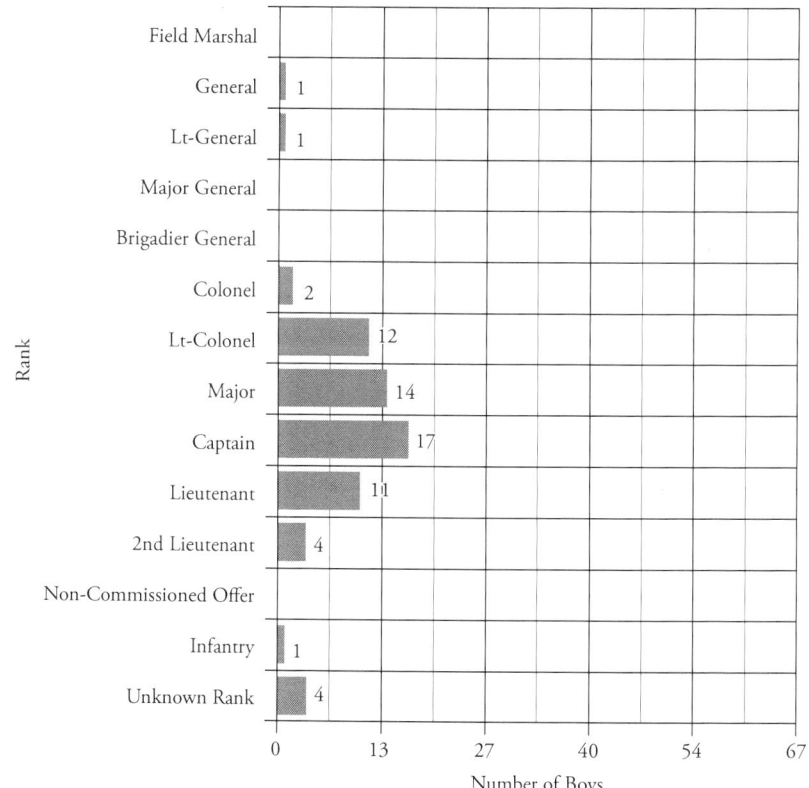

Sandhurst. Writing back from Sandhurst to his old schoolfellows at Castleknock College in Dublin in 1895, C. Lube Peart dispensed some fairly straightforward advice to those considering a military career:

> With regard to extravagance, or, rather, expense, £500 will see a young fellow well through Sandhurst, including an outfit for his regiment. If he joins an English regiment, he must have £70 a year, besides the pay he receives, for some years; if, however, he gets an Indian Staff Corps Commission (which means getting a higher place at the entrance examination), he can live comfortably on his pay alone, about £250 a year as lieutenant. A colonel, a position halfway up the ladder, in the Indian Staff Corps is worth about £1,300, and he retires on something like £900 a year. The fact that one is an Irishman and a Catholic seems to make little difference here. The Irish are quite as popular here as the English companions. As to your being a Catholic, it is sad but true, the average G.C cares too little about religion to trouble whether you are a R.C or not.[48]

Unless a boy had at least some continued financial support from his family, to become an officer in the British army was to risk a form of negative equity on his education and therefore points to the fact that most of the boys in the group came from existing wealth. In the early part of a career the family would have to subsidize his income, and the higher the status of the regiment the greater the subsidy would need to be.

In the 1870s, when an army career began to become a more common choice for Irish boarders, tuition at Beaumont College could be as high as £120 on average per year. If a boy was to spend five years at Beaumont, and then enter Sandhurst, the total outlay on education would be in the region of £1,100.[49] The average intermediate-level teacher earned either £82 per annum (if male) as late as 1905, or as little as £48 if female.[50] The sums expended by these families on an English education were enormous relative to regular income levels. As late as the 1890s the average income of a small farming household in Woodford, near Galway, was just over £38.[51]

It is also significant that Peart experienced little in the way of religious discrimination. For boys at Castleknock, often further down the chain of power and wealth than their contemporaries at Stonyhurst, that advice was most illuminating. Unless they rose above the rank of lieutenant it was probably less of a gamble to take a degree in medicine or law. For the boys at Stonyhurst, having typically had more financial clout, the privilege of the position was one worth aiming for. A military tradition was often evident in the family history of many of the largest landowners and this history of sterling service was sometimes invoked as a means of gaining advantage at selection stage. When the future 4th baronet Bellew,

---

[48] *The College Chronicle, Castleknock*, 1/10, Jun.1895, 31.

[49] The fees were sometimes much higher when extras such as music were taken into consideration. The playwright Edward Martyn boarded at a total cost of £175 between Sep. 1873 and Aug. 1874. ABPSJ, Beaumont College Archives, Beaumont College Accounts 1870–4, 5/2/9.

[50] John Coolahan, *Ireland's School Inspectorate, 1831–2008* (Dublin, 2009), 89.

[51] Fergus Campbell, *Land and Revolution: Nationalist Politics in the West of Ireland 1891–1921* (Oxford, 2005), 10.

Charles Christopher Grattan-Bellew, found his path blocked at entry level to the military colleges he simply appealed to the office of Secretary of State for War for preferential treatment on account of the military record of his forebears. Having outlined his father's service in the 5th Dragoons and the Connacht Rangers, his grandfather's military record, and the fact that his grand-uncle William died at the Battle of Alma in Crimea, young Christopher added with admirable optimism: 'I hope, therefore you will favourably consider my claims and grant me the favour which I now ask.'[52] His family possessed a 23,000 acre estate in east Galway in the late nineteenth century and were very proud of their military past, but also unafraid to use it as leverage. The Bellews also provide us with another telling example of the power of prevailing educational fashions amongst the Irish Catholic elite, and offer a useful instance of a lack of family loyalty to particular institutions. Christopher's father had been educated at Downside and Beaumont, he himself attended the Oratory school in Birmingham, and his own son (a famous horse-jumping broadcaster) was at Ampleforth in the 1940s.[53]

One obvious explanation for the high level of involvement by Irish boys from Stonyhurst in the military is, of course, increased demand. The outbreak of the World War I saw large-scale enlistment in Ireland, with some 50,000 Irishmen joining up in the first six months of war and a total aggregate figure of Irish male contribution to the wartime forces recently argued to have been as high as 210,000.[54] One of the first wave to sign up was Cyril Triscott (Stonyhurst: 1899), a qualified solicitor originally from Mullingar in Co. Westmeath, but with a relatively new practice in Thurles, Co. Tipperary. In December 1914 the *Irish Times* published one of his letters home from the front entitled 'Tipperary Officer in the Trenches'. Triscott had recently been made a lieutenant in the Sherwood Foresters. 'You ask me how I got my commission', he wrote. 'I did nothing out of the common; only did everything I was told and tried to be more useful than ever before, and I happened to have an officer that recognised the fact.'[55] It seems reasonable to suggest that Triscott's education at a prominent English public school might have marked him out as different from the average Irish soldier, and that this fact alone might have made him stand out as a man apart to his commanding officer. The school itself had much to do with the enthusiasm amongst the boys for all things military. The foundation of the Stonyhurst Officer Training Corps (OTC) in 1900 meant that the boys that entered in the late 1890s were being directly recruited into the officer corps in a process of streamlining that was common across all English public schools in that period, and one that to a certain extent still exists. In a sense there was an added pressure on Catholic public schools to prove that their

[52] He later won a Military Cross in 1918, and rose to the rank of lieutenant colonel. NLI, Mount Bellew Papers, Christopher Grattan-Bellew to Secretary of State for War, n.d. (most likely early 1907), MS, 27,292(2).
[53] 'Obituary: Lt.-Col. Sir C. C. Grattan-Bellew', *Irish Times*, 8 Nov. 1948; 'New Jumping Commentator this Year', *Irish Times*, 3 Aug. 1985.
[54] For a recent summary of the literature see Diarmuid Ferriter, *The Transformation of Ireland* (New York, 2005), 133–5.
[55] *Irish Times*, 21 Dec. 1914, 6.

values were compatible with those of the patriot, and the competition with schools such as Eton was a direct one.

The Catholic public schools certainly excelled in military service, that much is clear. The Irish influence is difficult to ignore—Stonyhurst can count seven recipients of the Victoria Cross, Britain's highest military honour, four of whom were Irish. The Stonyhurst OTC became one of the more efficient cadet forces in the country.[56] Stonyhurst would later become so trusted by the War Office as a source of committed young officers that the Rector of the school became one of very few headmasters in Britain to be granted the privilege of directly nominating boys to the Royal Military College at Sandhurst.[57]

The landed gentry dominated the officer corps of the British army in the late nineteenth and early twentieth centuries. It has been noted that by this time the landed gentry was a relatively open group which included 'newcomers, [who] having made their money in industry, commerce or speculation, moved on to the land'. For this *nouveau-riche* element, 'military service was one method by which an aspirant or his descendants might seek the approval of local society'.[58] This was a factor in the recruitment of Stonyhurst and Beaumont boys into the officer corps. The local elite factor can be verified in some cases: thirty-one of the ninety-nine boys with a military connection are known to have been either major landowners or served at some point as either a Justice of the Peace, Resident Magistrate, High Sheriff, or Deputy Lieutenant of their counties. Another and perhaps equally strong incentive was the desire to defend a set of principles cultivated quite deliberately by the English orders: a love of country and the desire to defend the Empire.

Those who attended in the 1890s were more than twice as likely to enlist in the armed forces as those who attended in the 1850s and 1860s, with a gradual rise in participation from the beginning of the 1870s as a result of the increasing army size, and involvement in the Boer War and World War I. In 1869 all six of the sons of the 3rd Baron de Freyne, Charles French (1790–1868) arrived at Downside. Four of them would go on to serve in the military. Their father had married Catherine Maree in an unrecognized ceremony in 1851, and again in 1854. This anomaly meant that the eldest three sons, Charles, John, and William, were all considered technically illegitimate and could not inherit his land (29,817 acres) or the peerage, all of which went instead to the fourth son, Arthur, a year before his arrival at Downside.[59] Of the four boys who served in the army, three climbed as high as lieutenant colonel, with one a captain. Such family involvement was not rare, and where a military tradition existed in a family, it was very likely to pass from one generation to the next, as with the legal and medical professions. English public

[56] T. E. Muir, *Stonyhurst College 1953–1993* (London, 1992), 156.

[57] 'Stonyhurst College', *The Catholic Encyclopedia*, New York, <http://www.catholic.org/encyclopedia/view.php?id=11108>.

[58] Spiers, quoted in Keith Jeffery, *Field Marshal Sir Henry Wilson: A Political Soldier* (Oxford, 2006), 11.

[59] While the French boys were at school in Downside the extensive Frenchpark estate was managed by their future brother-in-law Valentine Joseph Blake of Towerhill, who came from a major landowning family in the west with long ties to Stonyhurst College. *Irish Times*, 19 Apr. 1870.

schools enjoyed a near-monopoly on the officer corps of the British army through-out the nineteenth century. The formation of this army–public school nexus was a direct consequence of the decision to base the army entrance on the syllabus taught at those schools.[60]

Service in the Royal Army Medical Corps was rare, and the navy even more so.[61] Both Percy Kilkelly and Randolph Kilkelly served at the high rank of surgeon general in World War I, while Reginald Patrick FitzGerald (Downside: 1889) was a lieutenant commander in the Royal Navy.[62] The class of 1898 at Stonyhurst illustrates the variety of wartime service. Sixty-four boys entered the school that year, eleven of whom were Irish. At least seven of the boys served in some capacity during the war, and a brief description of their military career will give us some idea of the likely outcomes for this generation. Albert Roche, of 76 Merrion Square, Dublin, was a flight commander with the Royal Flying Corps. William Roche-Kelly was a flying instructor at the Beatty School during World War I before returning as a commissioned officer in the RAF in 1939. Owen O'Neill Cassidy had failed the navy examination in 1903 and became an actor in Paris. He served from 1914 in the Royal East Kent Yeomanry and Royal Irish Rifles. The cricketer Louis Meldon served in Flanders with the Army Service Corps (later Royal Army Service Corps), and Noel Nolan served in the Royal Army Medical Corps. Noel, a son of M. J. Nolan, Resident Medical Superintendent of the Downpatrick Asylum, was one of four Nolan cousins (all only sons) fighting in the war, a fact picked up on by the *Irish Times* in 1917.[63] Francis Power O'Reilly was flag lieutenant for Rear Admiral H. L. A. Hood, but died on board a vessel with the rather unfortunate name, the *Invincible*.

At least one Downside boy served in the Free State Army, the famous horse-breeder Frederick MacCabe (Downside: 1883)—who acted as medical colonel commandant in the Free State Army for a period, having originally seen active duty in the Boer War for the South Irish Horse. MacCabe was also the trainer of the first Irish winner at the Epsom Derby in 1907, a horse called Orby.[64] Nor was this the only case of an Irish boy serving in a different army. Leo Herbert Keegan (Stonyhurst: 1899), from Monkstown in south Dublin, became a lieutenant colonel in the Canadian army, having first served in the Connacht Rangers. He later graduated from the University of Toronto and worked in the Department of Agriculture.[65]

The majority of those serving in the military attended the school in the 1880s and 1890s, as a result of the greater enlistment for World War I—though those

---

[60] Ian Worthington, 'Antecedent Education and Officer Recruitment: The Origins and Early Development of the Public School–Army Relationship', *Military Affairs*, 41/4 (Dec. 1977), 185.

[61] The potential for more work to be done on Irish entrants to the Royal Navy is suggested by a recent article. See S. Karly Kehoe, 'Accessing Empire: Irish Surgeons and the Royal Navy, 1850–1880', *Social History of Medicine*, 26/2 (2013), 204–24.

[62] Graham, *Downside and the War*, 19; *The Times*, 29 Mar. 1945, 1.

[63] *Irish Times*, 2 Jun. 1917, 3.

[64] Desmond MacCabe, 'Frederick MacCabe', *DIB*.

[65] 'Leo Herbert Keegan', *The Stonyhurst Magazine*, 1938.

that entered the army in the 1850s and 1860s generally gained a higher rank as career officers. This was reflected in the recruitment at other English public schools. At Winchester recruitment into the army was less than 20 per cent amongst boys born 1840–70, but jumped to 45 per cent amongst those born in the 1890s.[66] This tallies with Perry's analysis, if we suppose that the constant military element in the high-profile schools was primarily from the landed gentry, with the other 'types' pitching in during wartime.

II LANDED GENTRY, PARISH GENTRY, AND LOCAL GOVERNMENT.

Lawrence Stone made a distinction between the aristocracy and parish gentry that has remained influential.[67] In general, the Irish Catholic landlord was more often in the latter category—but so too, of course, were the majority of the 6,500 land-owners in Ireland with more than 500 acres. That many of the boys at elite English schools came from a landed background is obvious from the information contained in the registers. As can be seen from the geographical distribution of the cohort, many came from rural areas in the south and west of Ireland, where often the only cash or asset-rich people were those with land. The system of local government in Ireland depended on the landlord class for its (mostly) voluntary operation until 1898, a situation that both reinforced their position as high status in the local community while effectively asking them to bear the brunt of the financial burden of county administration. This was cost-effective for the exchequer, and though the service was resented by the gentry the tradition of *noblesse civile* ensured that any protest was generally private.

The system of primogeniture usually dictated the inheritance of landed estates in Ireland. Nevertheless, where two or more sons were born into a family it is very difficult to ascertain to which the family property will pass. This difficulty is fur-ther compounded when both sons remained in the locality, and sometimes in the same house. The figures provided below are therefore no more than a conservative estimate. It is likely that the majority of graduates owned a considerable amount of land. Fergus Campbell has recently surveyed 291 of the largest landowners in Ireland in 1881, finding that just 7.5 per cent of them were Catholic, 0.5 per cent Presbyterian, and 92 per cent were Episcopalian—just 3 per cent were women.[68] This figure allows only for those with estates over 10,000 acres however, and the distribution of land at the lower end of the elite scale was much more even. After all, as W. E. Vaughan has shown, 43 per cent of large landowners in 1870 were Catholic, meaning that a very considerable portion of those that profited from the essentially feudal system of Irish landownership were Catholics.[69] It is therefore

---

[66] Bishop, *Winchester and the Public School Elite*, 66.
[67] Stone and Stone, *An Open Elite?*, 6.
[68] Campbell, *The Irish Establishment*, 20.
[69] W. E. Vaughan, *Landlords and Tenants in Mid-Victorian Ireland* (Oxford, 1994), 11.

difficult to argue for any section of the landowning class as representative of a coherent elite. Within each landed family, even, there were conflicting ideologies and loyalties. Convenient labels such as 'Catholic unionist', 'Anglo-Irish', 'castle Catholic' speak more to a general willingness of the historians of Ireland to categorize than anything else and have by now become largely meaningless terms of abuse. A Catholic with land was not necessarily more loyal, nor was he any less loyal, than any other member of society who collected a salary, wage, or endowment via the state. Nor should the owning of a large estate be supposed to have automatically translated into local and national political influence. As Hoppen has noted, Irish landlords could be as indifferent as anyone else to the social structure. When asked for help in procuring votes from his Tipperary estate in 1865 a Conservative candidate received a rather terse response: 'If you can get any votes among my people, you are perfectly welcome to do so', wrote the landlord. 'I have no feeling, one way or the other, and don't care one straw who are in.'[70]

Boys who would inherit landholdings of over 750 acres made up a significant 21 per cent of boys at English schools, though just as with a military career it was usually a role that took up just part of a life cycle (after inheritance) and usually landowners had at least one other occupation or social role alongside it. At Oscott many of the boys arrived as sons of major landowners and naturally inherited estates when older—some 28 per cent in total. At Stonyhurst the figure was 24 per cent, but at Downside (18 per cent) and Beaumont (15 per cent) the figure was significantly lower.

Some of the cohort had vast estates. Maurice Charles Blake (Stonyhurst: 1852) owned 11,888 acres between the counties of Galway and Mayo in 1882, and John Philip Nolan, MP, (Stonyhurst: 1851) had 7,666 acres in the same counties. The O'Conor Don inherited more than 12,000 acres from his father. A more typical amount of land to have inherited would be the amount held by George Patrick Lattin Mansfield in the same year, 5,639 acres.[71] G. P. L. Mansfield had been educated at Oscott, but sent his son George to Stonyhurst in 1864. His grandsons would later follow suit in the 1890s.[72] The family took a full part in county life in Kildare, corresponding with families such as the Thunders, Sweetmans, and the More-O'Ferralls who also had sons at Stonyhurst. This pattern of clustered strategic migration is general in the cohort, with the cost of conveyance shared between several families one principal reason, and the local reputation the other.[73]

---

[70] E. B. Purefroy, quoted in K. Theodore Hoppen, 'Landlords, Society and Electoral Politics in Mid-nineteenth-century Ireland', *Past and Present*, 75 (May, 1977), 84.

[71] Unless stated otherwise, figures for landholdings will be taken from both John Bateman, *The Great Landowners of Great Britain and Ireland* (Leicester, 1971); and U. H. Hussey de Burgh, *The Landowners of Ireland: An Alphabetical List of the Owners of Estates of 500 Acres or £500 Valuation and Upwards in Ireland* (Dublin, 1878), 1874.

[72] G. P. L. Mansfield had been educated at Oscott, as was his father Alexander, whose school diary of 1801 contains a historical note on the characters of both Oliver Cromwell and Walter Raleigh. NLI, Mansfield Papers, MS 38, 399/1 and MS 38, 399/2.

[73] Con Costello, *A Class Apart: The Gentry Families of County Kildare* (Dublin, 2005), 65–6.

Owning such an extraordinary amount of land separated these families from the majority of Irish Catholics and placed them in an uncomfortable position, straddling the mostly non-Catholic landed gentry and their own tenants and co-religionists. During the unrest caused by the Irish land war 1879–82, these Catholic landowners were in an unenviable position at a time when many were seeking to increase their holdings and to improve the land. The Stonyhurst boys were seldom of families that were absentee owners. Instead, typically they were resident on their land and their shared faith put them physically much closer to their tenants than was usually the case with their Protestant peers. Such proximity was potentially dangerous, as in the case of the Considine family of Derk, Pallas Green, Co. Limerick. The Considines were the owners of a relatively modest 2,074 acres, the majority of which was in Co. Tipperary. In the 1870s, that would have meant they were at about a median level for Irish landlords in general, though not quite at the same level as many of their fellow Stonyhurst alumni.[74] Heffernan Joseph Considine (Stonyhurst: 1859) was a prominent Resident Magistrate, later a District Inspector for the RIC 1900–11, and was knighted in 1908. The report below is of an event that took place during his time as High Sheriff of County Limerick during the land war in 1881:

> An extraordinary affair took place yesterday outside the chapel at Templebraden, county Limerick. Mr Heffernan Considine, of Derk, it is said, has recently taken action against some of his tenantry for non-payment of one year's rent. Mr H Considine, Jun; Mrs Considine, and the misses Considine attended as usual at Templebraden Chapel yesterday. Mud was flung at him and great shouting and bawling commenced... The people in great numbers collected... Mr Considine Jr now appeared and was made the occasion of a still wilder display of feeling... Appeals were in vain. He was pelted with mud and stones. Mrs Considine and her daughters were freely pelted at and their dresses all covered over with mud.[75]

The Considines were not the only Catholic landowners to feel the wrath of their tenantry, though most did not, it must be said, have the experience of being directly pelted by them. The consequences of status and wealth could be even more serious, however. The father of Thaddeus Michael Callaghan had been stoned to death by a tenant in 1856 in a land dispute, long before his son arrived at Stonyhurst aged sixteen in 1865. Influence was not always denoted by acreage, and neither was wealth. The Browne family of Kenmare (with over 118,000 acres and still insolvent) had assets that outstripped all others in the cohort, considerable political influence, and yet their finances were toxic. Most of the land held by Irish boys educated at the school was inherited, and, as was the case in England, there are few examples of Irish merchants buying large rural estates.[76]

Arthur French, first legitimate son of the 4th Baron de Freyne became heir to his father's lands after his death in 1868, a year before he entered Downside at

---

[74] Foster estimates that the typical Irish landlord had 2,000 acres in the 1870s. R. F. Foster, *Modern Ireland 1600–1972* (London, 1988), 375.

[75] 'An Extraordinary Affair', *Freeman's Journal*, 6 Dec. 1881.

[76] Stone and Stone, *An Open Elite?*, 128.

the age of fourteen. That inheritance amounted to 29,817 acres spread across Co. Roscommon, on the Frenchpark estate, and Counties Sligo, Galway, and Mayo, but the estate later expanded to 38,788 acres by the 1880s.[77] French was for a time considered a liberal unionist landlord and settled a five-year Land League dispute with his tenants over rent reduction reasonably amicably in 1889, though a series of evictions in 1893 did much to harm his reputation and he spent much of the period 1898 to 1904 in court because of excessive evictions from his land.[78] He served as Deputy Lieutenant for the county, and also found time to rise to the rank of lieutenant colonel in the Connacht Rangers.[79] Upon his death his estate passed to his son Arthur Reginald French, who became 5th Baron de Freyne. His life was no less colourful than his grandfather's, as he had spent the previous eight years 'missing'. Having fallen out with his father over a marriage to an innkeeper's daughter in 1902 Arthur Reginald had travelled to New York in January 1905, ostensibly to begin a life working for his uncle, William French (Downside: 1869), who had become a rancher in New Mexico. On arrival in New York he abandoned all of his material possessions (his unfortunate wife had long been abandoned) at his hotel and enlisted as a private in the US army, in which he served for some time in the Philippines. He somehow kept his identity secret from his fellow soldiers, only to return to claim his inheritance when his father died in 1913. That windfall was short-lived, however, and in the true romantic style he was killed in 1915 as a captain in the South Wales Borderers at the Battle of Aubers Ridge.[80]

A more modest landholding was that of Charles O'Conor (Downside: 1890), only son of Denis O'Conor, MP of Clonalis, Co. Roscommon, who held 2,776 acres with a rental value of £2,030.[81] Though some of the Irish families connected with Downside had less than O'Conor's acreage, such families tended to have a more diverse occupation range. Those with several offspring living in a gentlemanly manner from the proceeds of the land would need a more significant estate, such as that of Joseph O'Neill Power (Downside: 1853), who had extensive estates in Kilkenny and Waterford, totalling 8,319 acres in 1878, with an annual rental valuation of £6,930—more than enough to fund the lifestyles of several 'gentlemen'.[82]

The question of 'buying into' the Catholic elite is a complex one. Of the students with enormous estates awaiting them at home we can point to several cases of diversification of assets and wealth—made possible at the end of the eighteenth century as penal restrictions were relaxed. James Farrell, a Dublin brewer

---

[77] According to Bateman's, *Great Landowners*, 124.

[78] 'Lord de Freyne's Tenants', *Irish Times*, 7 Oct. 1885; 'The Frenchpark Eviction: Mr John Redmond and the Government and the Cardiff Resolution', *Irish Times*, 6 Nov. 1893; 'Sale of Lord de Freyne's County Sligo Estate', *Irish Times*, 3 Dec. 1904.

[79] 'Obituary', *The Times*, 11 Sep. 1913, 9.

[80] The Battle of Aubers Ridge was fought 9–10 May 1915, with disastrous losses for the British, who lost 11,000 men in just one day. For reports of the errant 5th Baron de Freyne see 'British Nobleman's Son Missing in New York', *The New York Times*, 18 Feb. 1905; 'Innkeeper's Daughter Is Now a Peeress', *The New York Times*, 30 Sep. 1913; 'Baron de Freyne Returns', *The New York Times*, 23 Dec. 1913.

[81] These valuations are for 1883, and taken from Bateman, *The Great Landowners*, 176.

[82] De Burgh, *The Landowners of Ireland*, 374.

and moneylender, was an early beneficiary of this, purchasing the entire village of Moynalty and the surrounding lands for £34,500 in 1790. His son constructed a planned settlement in the 1820s and 1830s, with Moynalty Lodge built in a Regency style. In the 1820s and early 1830s the remodelled village properties were built in the vernacular to provide a rather unsubtle contrast. The churches that book-ended the village (Catholic on the north side, Church of Ireland on the south) gave balance to a picturesque planned village which was rather a curiosity in Ireland as all of the properties were built on one side of the road. We can see a progression from these nouveau-riche origins, from estate improvement and consolidation in the first two generations to unionist and conservative sensibilities in the next head of family, John Arthur Farrell (1825–1904) who married Lucretia Pauline Preston, daughter of Viscount Gormanston. John Arthur was a Deputy Lieutenant and an anti-Home Rule landlord, publishing a long diatribe in the *Irish Times* after the Parnell split decrying the nationalist encroachment on local government and the civil service.[83] His eldest son, John Edward Farrell (Oscott: 1873) left Ireland for Tasmania, and upon his father's death in 1904 the estate was broken up and sold, though its legacy in the area is a lasting component of its topography and memory.

Local Government

Irish boys from the landed class often went on to become part of a more local elite. Quite a significant percentage in the cohort are known to have been involved in local civil administration, whether it was as a nominal Justice of the Peace (JP) in their own area, or as a paid post-holder in a different locality, such as a Resident Magistrate (RM). Any boy that went on to represent his area in a county council position, or serve in the more honorary capacity as Deputy Lieutenant (DL) or High Sheriff (HS) are also included here, as are members of 'County' clubs and presidents of local golf clubs, or masters of the hounds for example. The work of William Feingold identified a change in the pattern of local government from the 1870s onwards, when a parallel system of Local Government Boards began to further undermine the traditional rural power structure and in doing so furthered the work of the Poor Law Unions in this (limited) democratization of power. In general the boys attending schools in England continued to adhere to the older structure, despite its declining relevance as the century wore on, and very few of them engaged with the newer bodies as they emerged throughout the century.[84]

---

[83] J. A. Farrell, DL, 'Panaceas for Ireland', *Irish Times*, 21 Sep. 1891. For more information on the Farrell family and the architectural history of Moynalty see Valentine Farrell, *Not So Much To One Side* (Moynalty, 1984) and *Moynalty: Architectural Conservation Area Statement of Character* (Meath, 2009).

[84] There are, of course, some exceptions. Patrick Considine (Stonyhurst: 1874), of Pallas Green, Limerick, was an Auditor for the Local Government Board. William Bernard McCabe (Stonyhurst: 1877) was also briefly involved in the LGB, as an Inspector from 1879. For more on Poor Law Board composition see William L. Feingold, 'The Tenant's Movement to Capture the Irish Poor Law Boards, 1877–1886', *Albion: A Quarterly Journal Concerned with British Studies*, 7/3 (1975), 216–31.

Almost a quarter of the Stonyhurst boys served in a position of local elite power. The most common of these positions held was that of Justice of the Peace. JPs met at quarter sessions four times a year and tried offences of a summary nature, that is to say more or less everything except treason, murder, and felonies punishable by death or penal servitude for life. They were the first line of justice and conducted preliminary examinations of those who were to appear before Assizes, thus giving them considerable power in recommending cases to the Grand Jury.[85] JPs were expected to be men of sufficient social standing to gain the respect of their neighbours, and to exercise some calming influence over them. This definition fluctuated and though the majority of JPs came from stable landed backgrounds, a minority of merchants and small businessmen and so on began to appear in the role as the nineteenth century progressed. To become a JP, one had to apply to the Lord Chancellor, via the Lord Lieutenant of the county who sent forward a printed biography of the applicant indicating details about property held, family history, personal characteristics, previous applications, and anything else thought germane. This ensured a comprehensive filtering system, and the appointment itself was then usually made on the strength of that recommendation. Such roles had long roots— JP was a position which was begun in the fourteenth century under Edward III to augment the Norman system of sheriffs and constables as the population grew, and the Lord Lieutenant of the county was effectively chief of all such JPs.

Deputy Lieutenant was an office created by the Tudors and related mainly to an administrative role such as the raising of a national levy, the raising of armed forces in times of crisis, and the maintenance of order in a district which may have comprised (in England) of an area encompassing several counties or just one. However, the success of this role depended almost entirely on the cooperation of the local gentry, acting as Justices of the Peace and Sheriff, without which a DL could do very little, as the office brought with it no other form of support staff or structure.[86] By the nineteenth and early twentieth century these layers of local government were centuries out of date.

The Resident Magistrates were brought in over the heads of the JPs in 1836 by the Constabulary (Ireland) Act, in part as a response to the perceived failure of the JPs to have exerted enough control over their districts in the preceding decade. RMs were given a salary of just £400 a year in 1836, a stipend that was not increased until the late nineteenth century, and then only to £525—meaning that many of the men that held this prestigious but costly position were therefore necessarily of independent means.[87] The number of RMs was raised from

---

[85] A history of JPs in Ireland is required. See V. T. H. Delaney, *The Administration of Justice in Ireland*, ed. Charles Lysaght (Dublin, 1982), 26–8 for a basic description of their duties. For more detail see Constantine Molloy, *The Justice of the Peace for Ireland: A Treatise on the Powers and Duties of Magistrates in Ireland in Cases of Summary Jurisdiction in the Prosecution of Indictable Offenses and in Other Matters* (Dublin, 1890); W. E. Vaughan, *Murder Trials in Ireland 1836–1914* (Dublin, 2009), 69–116.

[86] Gladys Scott-Thompson, 'The Origin and Growth of the Office of Deputy-Lieutenant', *Transactions of the Royal Historical Society*, Fourth Series, 5 (1922), 150–66.

[87] Penny Bonsall, *The Irish RMs: The Resident Magistrates in the British Administration of Ireland* (Dublin, 1997), 13–15.

forty-six to seventy in 1850 and remained fairly stable at that figure for the rest of the century. Christopher Lynch-Robinson noted that the position was 'a job for mature people experienced in other walks of life', and that most of his fellow RMs were often 'lawyers, ex-police officers or retired soldiers'.[88] Likewise, the duties of the Deputy Lieutenants or High Sheriffs of a county were largely ceremonial, and one qualified for such a position in either Ireland or Great Britain simply by having enough land. Penny Bonsall notes that '[s]ocial class was more significant than religion in determining who became a resident magistrate' but that political patronage was also important.[89] Heffernan Considine (Stonyhurst: 1859) served as High Sheriff of his home county of Limerick in 1881, then as RM in Kilkenny from 1882–1900. His papers reveal the variety of functions that were expected of a magistrate, from receiving threatening notices from people who styled themselves 'Never Miss Fire' during the land war in 1883, to finding work for the daughter of a tenant named James O'Neill, who was a 'fine strong goodfaced girl' in 1900.[90] The RMs had a further use, however, such as calculating the harvest yields in their district and reporting on the general state of the locality to Dublin Castle at times of heightened tension. In this respect, quite apart from their liminal role somewhere between local judge and police detective, they were very much the eyes and ears of the Irish administration.

As highly prestigious posts that were mostly ceremonial and indeed costly, the preponderance of the initials DL and HS after the names of the Irish boys in the Stonyhurst cohort are testament to their commitment to the local power structure, and their place within it. It is also connected to their geographical position—a greater number of boys at Stonyhurst came from a landed background as compared to those at Beaumont. The fact that many were born in an urban setting accounts for the fact that boys attending Beaumont were less likely to be involved in local government, with just 12 per cent holding these types of positions. On average across all four schools 21 per cent of Irish boys held a position in local government, though that figure is conservative. At Downside fifty-three boys can be said to have fulfilled this criteria at some point of their lives, or 24 per cent of the total. This figure is exactly the same as the percentage at Stonyhurst (24 per cent) and close to that of Oscott (22 per cent), but twice that of those boys educated at Beaumont (12 per cent). The profile of the cohort that emerge as members of a local elite is predictable. Typically they are mid-range landowners, with a firm root in the local community and a family connection to positions of power and relatively high status. An example of one such boy would be Sir Valentine Grace, a Deputy Lieutenant and later High Sheriff (1908) of Queens County. His father, Sir Percy Grace, was a Baronet, who also served as a director of Hibernian Bank, a Commissioner of the National Education Board, and the Irish Lights Board.[91]

[88] Sir Christopher Lynch-Robinson, *The Last of the Irish R.M.s* (London, 1951), 96.
[89] Bonsall, *The Irish RMs*, 21.
[90] NLI, Considine Papers, 'Outrage Reports', MS 43,085/1; Rentbook 1900, MS 43, 074/2.
[91] 'Death of a Baronet', *New Zealand Tablet*, 8 Oct. 1903; 'Obituary', *The Times*, Friday, 4 May 1945.

Such families carried on a tradition of public service, and were consistently visible. That proximity to the power structure carried with it labels such as 'old Catholic family' which very often attached to them in press accounts.

The position of Justice of the Peace, in particular, has been a source of contention in Irish rural society. What was essentially an outmoded but popular system of local administration and law enforcement in English rural communities was never popular in Ireland, exposing as it did local sectarian or political difference that was generally absent elsewhere in the kingdom. The JP in the English system was based on the 'voluntary, part-time, unpaid service of the landed gentry in the shires and prominent citizens in the towns' and therefore depended on goodwill from both the gentry and the local population. In Ireland, where the gentry were, on the whole, less wealthy and less respected than their English counterparts, and consequently the effectiveness of the position depended much more on an individual JP's level of popularity. After 1829, Catholics began to be appointed JPs with much greater frequency, and the position was a sought-after one. It would be naïve to suggest that local politics did not impact upon the local judiciary—though it seems equally reasonable to suggest that many Catholic JPs were sympathetic to those involved in nationalist or agrarian protest. This power and influence ought not to be under-estimated. In the rural areas of south Munster many JPs and county officers were likely to be Catholic. As non-Catholics were in a minority the local system of government was administered by Catholics for Catholics—and boys from an educated and landed background were naturally to the fore. Many who became local Justices were retired military men such as George Taaffe in Co. Louth (Stonyhurst: 1876) or Constantine Maguire in Co. Down, who had been captain and lieutenant colonel in their respective regiments. There was often a direct link to either prestige of occupation, wealth, or simply having the biggest house in the area. For Taaffe, who had inherited Smarmore Castle near Ardee in Co. Louth, there was to be no real issue with legitimacy. The castle had been in the family for over 700 years, had walls that were 8-feet thick and was surrounded by an estate of 1,277 acres, and over 4,000 elsewhere in Ireland. The family had clearly done well within the current system and it was people such as the Taaffes that were the first line of support and defence for the union whether in times of peace or crisis.

III 'PUBLIC MEN'

Business

This category refers to those Irish boys at either school who went on to pursue a career in politics or finance, or as merchants or directors of commercial companies. In this area the more modern and metropolitan of the four schools, Beaumont College, surged ahead of the more rural and gentrified schools such as Stonyhurst or Oscott, as might be expected. The nineteenth century saw the creation of more varied and numerous super-rich magnates, to borrow a more recent term, or 'merchant-princes' to accord a contemporary designation. This expansion is now generally seen as part of the 'Second Industrial Revolution' in the second half of the nineteenth century when mass-production techniques saw the number of employees in the manufacturing sector boom after 1870. The Irish economy did not benefit evenly with the rest of the United Kingdom, though cities such as Belfast and Dublin certainly did. Irish Catholics, particularly those based in Dublin, were as likely as any to benefit from this.

In his O'Donnell lecture of 1979, 'The Catholic Middle Classes in Pre-famine Cork', Professor John B. O'Brien argued that the city had effectively delineated its business community along denominational lines over a long period of time. Catholics had control over the butter industry, for example, and operated their businesses in a networked and protectionist fashion by using Cork Corporation as an alternative chamber of commerce in the 1840s.[92] The Protestant community in the city simply used the other, official, chamber of commerce and also operated their network of businesses, whenever possible, to the near-exclusive benefit of their co-religionists. This picture of parallel business communities has been partially endorsed by Fergus Campbell, though he finds that at the upper end the major companies (those with capital of over £200,000) were almost always run in the Protestant interest, and that even the banking system was divided along unionist or nationalist lines.[93] Distribution was far from equal of course, and the Protestant community had enjoyed an early advantage, but the nineteenth century saw a slow but steady process of an improving market position for Irish Catholics. The feeling that this process was taking far too long was palpable by the late nineteenth century and appeared everywhere from newspaper columns to the fiction of the period. In May Laffan's *Hogan M.P.* (1876) we see the rising Catholic elite simultaneously excoriated for their vulgarity and pretensions to respectability in a novel one critic has recently characterized as 'an ambient satire of Dublin Catholic middle-class life'.[94] Characters referred to as 'whiskey people' represent new money and the important distinction between money made in retail or wholesale is noted. The protagonist of this very blunt novel, John Hogan, aspires to the position of MP and thus represents a more tolerable version of Catholic social mobility. In the novel Hogan attends Trinity College and is subsequently called to the English Bar, but nevertheless finds his path blocked by his religion. 'Dublin really is a perfect study…a drop of ditchwater under a microscope; everybody pushing upwards on the social ladder, kicking down those behind', he explains to an acquaintance. 'However the Protestants have pretty well laid down the line to our people now. "So far and no farther," ever since the passing of the Church Act.'[95] This tacit and accepted division of urban Ireland along religious lines has been noted elsewhere,

---

[92] John B. O'Brien, *The Catholic Middle Classes in Pre-famine Cork*, The O'Donnell Lecture, 1979 (Dublin, 1980), 19–20.

[93] Campbell, *The Irish Establishment*, 195.

[94] James H. Murphy, *Irish Novelists in the Victorian Age* (Oxford, 2011), 163.

[95] May Laffan (Lady Hartley), *Hogan M.P. A Novel* (London, 1876), 8, 153.

though O'Brien's work on Cork city is a rare examination of how it operated in practice in the business community.

Traditionally Catholic industries such as brewing and distilling are well represented in the cohort, with the Murphy family of Cork and the Smithwick family of Kilkenny all attending English Catholic schools, along with the various branches of Ryans and Powers associated with the whiskey giants John Power & Son distillers.[96] The sons of Michael J. Clery, proprietor of the landmark retail shop Clery & Co. on O'Connell Street in Dublin, attended Stonyhurst before becoming directors of the company later in life. In total 15 per cent of the boys at Beaumont led active careers in this area as compared to just 7 per cent at Stonyhurst. At Downside the percentage was the same as at Beaumont (15 per cent), with thirty-two boys entering the world of commerce. At Oscott the figure was reasonably high (13 per cent). This may be partly explained by the discrepancy in their geographical location, shown in Chapter 2. Almost half of all those attending Beaumont from 1861 to 1900 came from Co. Dublin. Within this definition are included those who speculated on property development or mining, such as Edward Fox (Beaumont: 1865) and Bertram Ossoli Kelly (Stonyhurst: 1878), who both had mining interests in Australia.

In keeping with O'Brien's identification of the pre-famine vigour of Catholic business in the city, many of those engaged in commerce in the cohort came from Cork city or its environs. Such families often intermarried, proving that social parity and proximity were as important to them as to anyone else. At Beaumont, for example, the son of a Cork butter merchant based in Queenstown (now Cobh), Dominic Cronin (Beaumont: 1874), married a sister of his schoolmate, Francis Lyons (Beaumont: 1877) of Montenotte, Cork. Lyons was heir to his family's wholesale textiles business T. Lyons & Co., through which over 200 people were 'engaged in the manufacture of ready-made clothing' in Cork.[97] Dominic's sister, Mary Cronin, married into the Morrogh family, of which Walter (her future husband) and Robert Morrogh (Beaumont: 1873) were also classmates of her brother.[98] They set up the successful stockbroking firm W. & R. Morrogh in Cork in 1901, one that remained in the family until 2001 when it was wound up as a result of being at the centre of Ireland's largest-ever proven fraud.[99] In Cork, families such as the Cronins, Lyons, and Morroghs converged on the Royal Yacht Club where ostentatious displays of wealth were common. As a result the social division of the city has been characterized in popular memory as 'the have-yachts and the have-nots', and the tradition of the merchant-princes schooling in England is believed by others to have contributed to the distinctive 'Montenotte' accent associated with suburban wealth, though this is admittedly speculative.[100]

---

[96] For a fascinating account of the sometimes denominational nature of brewing and distilling see Frank Shovlin, ' "Endless Stories About the Distillery": Joyce, Death, and Whiskey', *Joyce Studies Annual* (2007), 134–58.

[97] D. J. Coakley, *Cork, Its Trade & Commerce: Official Handbook of the Cork Incorporated Chamber of Commerce & Shipping: With Classified Trade Indices in English, French & Spanish* (Cork, 1919), p. 58.

[98] Another sister, Emily Cronin, married James Murphy of Ringmahon, Cork (Beaumont: 1883).

[99] See Michael Devane, 'W & R Morrogh Timeline', *The Sunday Business Post*, 16 Oct. 2005.

[100] Alison O'Connor, 'Have-yachts and the Have-nots', *Irish Times*, 27 May 1995.

Though words such as 'globalization' sit uneasily in a nineteenth-century context, there is sufficient evidence of transnational trade within the group to suggest it. The Harrington family of Lee View, Cork are a case in point of such trading practice. Stanley Joseph Harrington (Beaumont: 1870) founded the Shandon Chemical Factory with his brothers William and Ignatius, and was also involved in the Munster and Leinster Bank based in South Mall, Cork, where his position as a director was taken up by his son William Harrington on his death (Beaumont: 1895) in 1950.[101] Stanley's twin brother William was for a time director of the City of Cork Steam Packet Co., which was a (mostly) Catholic business running ferries between Ireland, England, and Wales. The Harrington family had opened a giant warehouse in Britain to aid international distribution of their chemical products. Francis Lyons (Beaumont: 1877) of Montenotte in Cork was director of T. Lyons & Co., a drapery wholesaler which had invested in Barbados, where another former student, Michael Barrett (Beaumont: 1883), also built a fortune through a separate shipping business. The harbour was the stimulus for much of the industry in Cork, with the Downside old boy and merchant Frank Daly eventually rising to the status of chairman of the Cork Harbour Board, as well as Lord Mayor of Cork (1930–1), and a Fianna Fáil TD late in life.[102]

The Jesuits themselves encouraged enterprising past pupils. A past pupil, Francis FitzGerald (Beaumont: 1866) found this out to his pleasure when in 1909 a joinery company in which he was a partner (T. & C. Martin, North Wall, Dublin) won the contract to furnish Stonyhurst. Todd Andrews noted in his autobiography that 'the Martins were different from the normal run of Dublin employers at the time', as they paid his uncle's wages while he was severely ill. The firm, a well-known building and joinery outfit, also appears in *Ulysses*, towards the end of the 'Cyclops' chapter.[103] English graduates were well represented across the commercial and financial sector. A future chairman of the Dublin Stock Exchange attended Beaumont in this period, and a son of the Lord Mayor of Dublin, the businessman Peter Paul MacSwiney, had attended Downside in the 1860s.[104] The MacSwiney family lived at 37 Upper Mount Street, a Georgian Terrace just off Merrion Square and therefore quite a typical residence for a well-to-do merchant at the time.

Five of the grandsons of J. J. Murphy, the famous Cork brewer, were educated at Downside, and most would serve as directors of the company in afterlife. One of the youngest sons, Albert St John Murphy, graduated an MD, became chairman of the Cork Golf Club, was a member of the local hunting party and lived first at Little Island, later Tivoli House, and finally at Rushbrooke in Cork, firmly ensconced in the local elite. Charles Murphy owned a sheep station at Broken Hill

---

[101] Full obituary published in *Irish Times*, 1 Aug. 1949.

[102] 'Funeral: Frank J. Daly', *Irish Times*, 22 Feb. 1950.

[103] C. S. Andrews, *Dublin Made Me* (Dublin, 2001, original 1974), 17; James Joyce, *Ulysses*, 2nd edn (Oxford, 1998), 329.

[104] These boys were John McCann (Beaumont: 1890) and Peter Paul McSwiney (Downside: 1867). MacSwiney's father had opened the largest department store in Dublin, 'The Palatial Mart' which was later bought out by Michael Clery and is better known to us now as Clery & Co.

in Australia, in addition to his role as a director of the brewery.[105] Two members of the Smithwick brewing family of Co. Kilkenny also attended Downside, George Joseph Smithwick (Downside: 1890) and Alfred Smithwick (Downside: 1892). Being born to a family of energetic industrialists did not always guarantee a work ethic in the next generation. When cited as a co-respondent in a rather ugly divorce case in London in 1921 George Smithwick would see his character and industriousness being extensively scrutinized. When the aggrieved husband, a Mr Fleming, was asked what Smithwick's occupation was he answered 'nothing in particular, I think that he was principally interested in horses'.[106] Indeed Smithwick had worked intermittently and managed a stud in Kildare for Lord Furness, which was later bought out by the Aga Khan, who, unconcerned with his infidelities of old, kept Smithwick on as manager. The trickle-down effect of the brewing industry can be seen in the business exploits of the Codd family of Mountmellick in Co. Laois—whose malting factory supplied Guinness until it folded in the 1940. The local effect of medium sized businesses can be gauged from this type of industry in a relatively remote midlands location. Francis Codd (Downside: 1864) was director of Francis Codd & Co. Maltmasters, along with his brother Eugene F. Codd (Downside: 1860). Their main local rival was a company founded by Charles Rochford Norton, a Stonyhurst old boy, in nearby Monasterevin, Co. Kildare. Norton eventually amalgamated into Minch Norton Maltmasters, the largest company of its type in Ireland, before his death in 1948.[107] Their common denominator was access to the canal network, which provided relatively frequent and cheap access for heavy goods destined for the Dublin market. Codd's Maltings, as it became known, was operational between 1880 and the 1940s at Mountmellick and its importance to that innocuous midlands town can be seen from the fact that the canal connection itself closed immediately after the company ceased to use it in the wake of the outbreak of World War II in 1939. Such businesses were vitally important for the creation and maintenance of jobs locally and further solidify the idea of the importance of enclaves of localized Catholic elites across much of Ireland—not just in the major urban centres.

Sir John Talbot Power had many and varied commitments as a landlord, MP, and Deputy Lieutenant of Co. Wexford, although his younger brothers James and Thomas had inherited control of the famous John Power & Son whiskey distillery from which the wealth had derived. Sir John, who inherited his father's baronetcy in 1877, had a total of 10,013 acres in Co. Wexford, originally bought from Lord Carew in 1833. The whiskey company set up in 1791 by his great grandfather, James Power of Dublin, remained in family hands until 1936. Considered one of the four great Dublin distilleries of the nineteenth century the Power operation

---

[105] 'Mr A. S. J. Murphy', *Irish Times*, 17 Dec. 1952, 5; *The Raven* (Downside, 1906); For more on the brewery see Diarmuid O Drisceoil and Donal O Drisceoil, *The Murphy's Story: The History of Lady's Well Brewery, Cork* (Cork, 1997).

[106] This was the *Fleming v Fleming* case. See 'Probate, Divorce, and Admiralty Division. Decree Granted to an Army Officer', *The Times*, 1 Jul. 1921.

[107] Norton left an estate of £32,791 on his death. *Irish Times*, 19 Mar. 1948, 5.

ran between their Wexford base in Enniscorthy, the nearby purpose-built village of Oylegate on their own estate, and the John's Lane distillery in Dublin. These premises were joined by addresses in 20 Harcourt Street and Roebuck House, giving the family a full range of high-status locations through which to channel their wealth. Their integration into political life and public service developed over the course of the century. John Power (1771–1855) was a personal friend of Daniel O'Connell and served as a magistrate, alderman, and guardian of the South Dublin Poor Law Union. His son James (1800–77) was an MP, a magistrate in both Dublin and Wexford, and Governor of the Bank of Ireland. Those who voted Sir John Talbot Power into the House of Commons in 1868 would have been fully aware of his reputation and that of his family. His education in England would have added to his aura as a gentleman and as somewhat 'different' from his Catholic tenantry. Though he was generally considered a reasonable landlord it ought to be pointed out that his insouciance towards the margin of profit from an already very valuable and viable estate was probably connected to the fact that whiskey was a popular drink in Ireland and the profits from John Power & Son were substantial. Other companies set up by Irish boys at Downside include L. & E. Egan, a bedding company based in Dublin and run by Laurence Egan (Downside: 1894) and Ernest Egan (Downside: 1899).[108] From the transnational to the local, and Barbados to Mountmellick, the Irish boys in business are perhaps the best example of the complex directions wealth and ambition could take.

Noblesse Civile: Foreign and Domestic State Service

Perhaps it was low remuneration, or low social status, but the prospect of sacrificing a son in the cause of *noblesse civile*, or in the service of the state, was uncommon among the wealthiest Irish Catholic families. Though the learned professions retained their appeal, as they do still, the civil service may have been one step too plebeian in the nineteenth century. Scholars have noted the large expansion of government bureaucracy in the mid nineteenth century, with open competition for places introduced in 1855 for the Indian Civil Service (ICS) and in 1870 for the domestic civil service. This realigning or reforming of a civil service Trevelyan thought 'indolent or incapable' was reasonably successful although as W. J. Reader has noted, mobility from the lower position to the top was restricted as very many of the top civil servants were 'parachuted into their position from the outside world'.[109] In the Irish context these places were sought after by those attending Irish schools such as Blackrock or St Columba's, the Queen's Colleges, and Trinity College in Dublin. Lawrence McBride's influential argument that the Irish civil service had become more 'green' (or Catholic-nationalist) in the last decades before Irish independence has recently been revised by Fergus Campbell who has argued that this greening has been overstated. Campbell's work indicates that

---

108 'Obituary', *Irish Times*, 11 Dec. 1958, 5.
109 Reader, *Professional Men*, 82.

those occupying elite positions in the civil service were generally not Catholic, and that a 'caste-system' was effectively in operation which frustrated Catholic upward mobility. He is perhaps guilty of overstatement himself, however, when he asserts that had this 'ethnic discrimination' not existed and had Catholics held the majority of positions within the administration, 'the British state in Ireland might have been maintained for a longer period'.[110]

In total just sixteen boys (6 per cent) at Stonyhurst were involved either in the Imperial project through the ICS or by becoming diplomats or mid-ranking domestic civil servants, and seven of the boys at both Beaumont (3 per cent) and Oscott (4 per cent). At Downside the figure was also low (5 per cent).

Valentine Irwin (Stonyhurst: 1852) demonstrated the benefits of the decision to open the ICS to competition in 1861 when his forty-fourth place in the ICS exams was enough to secure him a career in India, where he became Magistrate at Kuttack, Bengal.[111] Such a typical occupation was easily outshone by that of the prominent Rt Hon. Sir Nicholas Roderick O'Conor, PC, GCB, GCMG, KCB (Stonyhurst: 1856)—whose diplomatic career saw him move from Washington to Peking and eventually serve as an envoy to Russia and Constantinople.[112] The rarity of O'Conor's diplomatic status is confirmed by the fact that just two other high-level diplomats emerged from the Stonyhurst cohort. John Frederick Whyte (Stonyhurst: 1874) was consul to Persia, while Valentine O'Hara (Stonyhurst: 1890) published two books relating to his time as a diplomat in Estonia and Russia.[113] At Beaumont just seven of the cohort became either diplomats or foreign civil servants. Most successful amongst this group was Hugh O'Beirne (Beaumont: 1879) who progressed on to Balliol College in Oxford and from there to the diplomatic service. He was appointed Minister Plenipotentiary at Sofia in 1915, and died alongside Field Marshal Earl Kitchener on board *The Hampshire* in June 1916. The lack of Imperial careers is significant, and the fact that so many past pupils returned to Ireland may indicate that many saw themselves above Imperial exploration, or were more concerned with achieving Catholic equality at elite levels domestically.[114]

Just ten (5 per cent) of the boys at Downside went on to take positions in the Indian or domestic civil service—again challenging the orthodoxy that the ICS was a career path actively sought by a large proportion of those boys attending elite institutions. The first boy within the time period to take advantage of the ICS opportunity was John Nicholas Nugent (Downside: 1859), a son of Sir John

---

[110] F. Campbell, 'Who Ruled Ireland? The Irish Administration 1879–1914', *The Historical Journal*, 50, 3 (2007), 643.

[111] Indian Civil Service Examinations, *The Times*, 24 Aug. 1861.

[112] T. H. Sanderson, 'O'Conor, Sir Nicholas Roderick (1843–1908)', H. C. G. Matthew, *Oxford Dictionary of National Biography* (Oxford, 2004).

[113] Nicholas Makeev and Valentine O'Hara, *Russia* (London, 1925); Valentine O'Hara, *Esthonia: Past and Present* (Bournemouth, 1922).

[114] See Ciaran O'Neill, 'Education, Imperial Careers and the Irish Catholic Elite', in David Dickson, Justyna Pyz, and Christopher Shepard (eds), *Irish Classrooms and British Empire: Imperial Contexts in the Origins of Modern Education* (Dublin, 2012), 98–110.

Nugent, an unpopular Inspector of Lunatic Asylums in Ireland and one-time physician to Daniel O'Connell. Sir John's obituary noted that 'he was one of those
men in whom high and low tones are so intermingled as to produce a discord'.[115]
His son, John Nicholas, entered the ICS and was a member of the Council of
Governors of Bombay in 1896. John D. D. La Touche (Downside: 1873), born in
Tours but raised in Dublin and of an Irish family, became a successful ornithologist
for the Imperial Maritime Customs Service in China 1882–1922.

On the domestic front, Thomas J. P. Kelly (Downside: 1884) served
as consul for Chile in the Irish Free State in 1927 and Arthur and John Ross
(Downside: 1883) both worked on the Congested District Board.[116] The absence
of mid-ranked domestic civil servants is noticeable across all four schools. This
may be partly due to its unspectacular social status, but it is also due to the prevalent practice of debarring Irish Catholics from the inner circle at Dublin Castle.
Laurence McBride's influential monograph, *The Greening of Dublin Castle* (1991),
argues that in the thirty or so years before the Free State came into existence many
more Catholics were appointed to high positions in the civil service than had
previously been the case.[117] McBride's methodology has recently been criticized
by Fergus Campbell, who has concentrated on the social backgrounds of those
appointed at two critical junctures, 1891 and 1911. Campbell's analysis proves
that 11 per cent of the total number of senior Irish civil servants attended English
Catholic public schools, with more than a quarter attending Irish Catholic elite
schools such as Clongowes Wood. Catholics with any other type of education
were almost entirely unheard of in senior civil service posts, and they were in any
case under-represented at between 29 per cent and 41 per cent in 1891 and 1911
respectively.[118] It is apparent from this research that the wealthiest Irish Catholic
families did not embrace the domestic civil service. It seems likely, however, that
this was a combination of both active discrimination, and the reluctance of elite
Catholics to involve themselves in an administration that was uncomfortably visible, widely distrusted, and conferred limited social plaudits on those working
for it.

Politics

In total some fifteen boys (5 per cent) at Stonyhurst held public office in a position
of national importance, or served as a top-level domestic civil servant, and just
eight (3 per cent) of the boys at Beaumont. Of those Irish boys found at Downside

---

[115] 'Sir John Nugent', *British Journal of Psychiatry*, 45/189 (Apr. 1899), 431–2.
[116] 'New Consul for Chile', *Irish Times*, 27 Apr. 1928; 'Congested District Boards Proposed Offer
of 15 ½ Years', *Weekly Irish Times*, 31 Dec. 1904.
[117] Lawrence McBride, *The Greening of Dublin Castle: The Transformation of Bureaucratic and
Judicial Personnel in Ireland, 1892–1922* (Washington, 1991).
[118] Nevertheless, in the senior positions landed Catholics with a family history of loyalty to
public service were much more likely to be appointed to senior positions. Campbell, 'Who Ruled
Ireland?', 639.

twenty-three went on to take positions in this field, representing a considerable 11 per cent of the total. At Oscott the figure was fourteen (8 per cent).

The number of boys that went on to become either high-profile politicians or administrators from English schools was relatively low. The main political outlet for aspirant politicians was the Irish Parliamentary Party, and though several of the most prominent Home Rulers involved in the party were educated at prominent Irish schools, those attending English Catholic colleges never constituted a significant bloc in a party predominantly recruited from a lower social bracket, particularly from the mid 1880s onwards. James McConnel has written recently of the 'social distance' nationalist members typically experienced in a Parliament more accustomed to genteel members, their manners and even dress code clashing with accepted codes of behaviour.[119] In this respect boys educated at English public schools ought to have been a useful commodity for the IPP, and though Redmond in particular sought to recruit and utilize their expensively acquired oratorical skill and social capital he was often frustrated in the battle to have them nominated and then elected by an Irish constituency. At Stonyhurst six boys went on become MPs at Westminster.[120] Of the boys attending Beaumont just two Irish old boys were MPs, while three sat in the House of Lords.[121] William Munster, MP, along with his brother John, were the first Irish boys to enrol at Beaumont in 1861, having entered an address at Cashel, where his father (Henry Munster) had moved in an overt attempt to get elected to Parliament. Henry won two elections, one in Cashel and one in Mallow, but was stripped of his seat on both occasions for subscribing rather too enthusiastically to the Irish tradition of bribes-for-votes in a series of scandals so distasteful that it ultimately led to the disenfranchisement of the borough after 1869.[122] Though his father did not secure the seat he so coveted, his son, William Felix Munster, won a seat at Mallow in Co. Cork in 1872, at just twenty-three years of age. He was not re-elected, and died in tragic circumstances after a hotel fire at St Louis, Missouri, in 1877.[123]

Four sons of Sir Edward Bellew, 2nd Baron of Barmeath (Stonyhurst: 1840s) attended Beaumont at the same time. The first died young as a lieutenant in the 20th Regiment, leaving his younger brother Captain Charles Bertram Bellew (Beaumont: 1865) to succeed his father as 3rd Baron in 1895 and to take up

---

[119] James McConnel, *The Irish Parliamentary Party and the Third Home Rule Crisis* (Dublin, 2013), 184.

[120] Charles Henry Meldon (MP Kildare, 1875–85); John Philip Nolan (MP Galway, 1874–85; North Galway, 1885–95 and 1900–6); Rowland Blennerhassett (MP Galway, 1865–74); Richard O'Shaughnessy (MP Limerick City, 1874); Joseph Power (MP Waterford, 1884–1913); John Joseph Esmonde (MP North Tipperary, 1910–15).

[121] The MPs were William Munster (MP Mallow, 1872–4) and John Andrew Sweetman (MP East Wicklow, 1892–5).

[122] For more detail on the troubled borough see *Report of the Cashel Election Inquiry Commission 1869*.

[123] He lost his reason in the aftermath of a fire at a hotel in St Louis, Missouri, in which he and his wife were staying. Supposing his wife had perished, William took his own life at the home of a friend. It later emerged that his wife had survived. 'William Felix Munster Ex-MP', *New York Times*, 13 Apr. 1877.

his seat as a liberal unionist Irish representative peer. His brother, Major George Leopold Bellew, succeeded him in 1911. Perhaps the most interesting and varied political career at either school was that of Lt Col. Viscount Bernard Forbes (Oratory: 1884; Beaumont: 1889), the 8th Earl of Granard. His father, a convert and the main instigator of the ill-fated Catholic Union of Ireland, sent his son to both the Oratory School and Beaumont in preference to any Irish alternative, despite being heavily involved in domestic educational issues. That choice may have contributed to Bernard's subsequent high rank in society. He later became Vice Admiral of Connaught, Lord Lieutenant of Longford, a Liberal peer, a senator in the upper-house of the Irish Free State, 1922–34, and Master of the Horse for Ireland. He also served as chairman of Arsenal Football Club, 1922–34.

Of those Irish boys found at Downside twenty-three boys went on to take positions in this field, representing a considerable 11 per cent of the cohort. Hereditary peers are also taken into account here. In total six Downside boys served as MP in the House of Commons.[124] Perhaps the most celebrated of these was Charles Owen O'Conor (Downside: 1852), better known as the O'Conor Don, who was influential in the Intermediate Education Act of 1878, and a serving member on the Palles Commission in 1899. O'Conor was MP for Roscommon, 1860–80, as well as the president of the Royal Irish Academy and the Irish Language Society of Ireland.[125] The parliamentary tradition was a lively one at Downside. The school magazine even had the temerity to boast in 1899 that out of the hundred seats in the House of Commons available to their Irish pupils they had become accustomed to seeing a 'good half-dozen Downside men' sitting in them.[126]

This was largely true. Downside had many Irish voices in the House of Commons in the nineteenth century, though the only real pattern that can be detected is one of under-achievement. Matthew Kenny (Downside: 1874), later a judge, was elected as a Home Rule MP in 1882 for Ennis. His parliamentary record shows a dignified and progressive character, and though he served on several important committees with Irish relevance such as the Select Committee on Industries (Ireland) 1884 his was hardly a stellar political career.[127] Political representation was rarely the sole occupation of those who served as an MP. John A. Sweetman (Downside: 1858; Beaumont: 1863), an MP for Wicklow East in 1892, was a landowner primarily, with a colony in Minnesota as well as an estate in Drumbaragh, Co. Meath. In his politics he was a liberal Home Ruler and a committed land leaguer—proposing the setting up of the national land league committee in the 1870s. He eventually

---

[124] They were Charles Owen O'Conor (Downside: 1852; MP Roscommon, 1860–80); Denis O'Conor (Downside: 1852; MP Sligo, 1868–83); John Sweetman (Downside: 1858; MP Wicklow East, 1890–5) John Talbot Power (Downside: 1859; MP Wexford, 1868–74); Charles French (Downside: 1869; MP Roscommon, 1873–80); Matthew Kenny (Downside: 1874; MP Ennis, 1882–92).

[125] See Aidan Enright, 'The Political Life of Charles Owen O' Conor, 1860–1906' (PhD, Queens University Belfast, 2012).

[126] 'Odds and Ends', *The Downside Review*, 18 (1899), 208.

[127] Sir Eardley-Wilmot, Report from the Select Committee on Industries (Ireland), HC 1884 [1], ix, House of Commons Papers.

became more and more radicalized and in 1905 was one of the founders of Sinn Féin, and became its second president in 1908 (taking over from the Beaumont old boy Edward Martyn)—again demonstrating that the political convictions of those boys educated in England were often fluid or even diametrically opposed. The most notorious of the Oscott boys in Parliament was surely Captain William O'Shea, who by citing Charles Stewart Parnell as a co-respondent in a divorce case taken against his wife Katharine simultaneously made the only significant political intervention of his long career and brought down Ireland's greatest political figure since O'Connell. Sir Thomas Grattan Esmonde was another Oscott old boy to court controversy throughout a long political career. Born in the resort town of Pau in 1862, Esmonde attended Oscott for five years, 1874–81, graduating from the status of local magistrate to that of Parnellite politician in the 1885 election. A sometimes frustrating figure whom John Dillon once referred to as a 'wretched creature', Esmonde exasperated IPP colleagues in 1907–8 by converting briefly to Sinn Féin.[128] A political chameleon, his term as a Free State senator was marred in March 1923 when his ancestral home—the G. C. Ashlin-designed Ballynastragh House near Gorey, Co. Wexford—was reduced to ashes by the same campaign of targeted arson that had levelled Oliver St John Gogarty's Renvyle House and Lord Mayo's Palmerstown House.[129] Other, less divisive, political figures to go through Oscott were Dr John Joseph Esmonde (Oscott: 1876) who was national-ist MP for North Tipperary, 1910–15, and was replaced on his death by his son John Lymbrick Esmonde, who was elected aged twenty-one while serving with the Leinster Regiment during World War I. John Lymbrick had been educated at Clongowes and at schools in Germany and Belgium, qualified as a barrister in 1921, and was later elected as a TD for Fine Gael in Wexford, 1937–44 and 1948–51, where the *Irish Times* thought his contributions to debates on foreign policy were 'outstanding'.[130] Christopher Talbot Redington (Oscott: 1857) became MP for Galway having first attended Christ Church, Oxford and served as a JP locally.

Downside also produced civil servants worthy of inclusion within the term 'political elite'. Andrew Bonaparte-Wyse (Downside: 1880) was perhaps the most striking of these, rising to the position of permanent secretary to the Ministry of Education in the newly formed government of Northern Ireland, 1927–39—the only Catholic to be in charge of a civil service department for the duration of that administration. His career had begun with his appointment as National Commissioner of Education in Ireland and his reputation as an educationist was such that despite serving under what is now generally accepted to have been an anti-Catholic administration, it emerged unscathed.[131]

---

[128] Quoted in McConnel, *The Irish Parliamentary Party*, 129.

[129] In a curious turn of events Ballynastragh House was later rebuilt to a more modest plan by Dermot St, John Gogarty, son of Oliver St John Gogarty, in 1937 after a protracted compensation dispute. For more see Terence Dooley, 'The Burning of Ballynastragh', *Journal of the Wexford Historical Society*, 19 (2002–3).

[130] 'Fine Gael T.D. Leaves Party', *Irish Times*, 21 Sep. 1950; 'Obituary', *Irish Times*, 7 Jul. 1958.

[131] Bridget Hourican, 'Andrew Bonaparte Wyse', *DIB*.

John Mulhall (Downside: 1872) acted as private secretary to Lord Londonderry during his period as Lord Lieutenant of Ireland, before becoming vice-chairman of the Prisons Board, 1892–1912, a position previously held by another old Gregorian, William Patrick O'Brien (Downside: 1838). His appointment to the position of private secretary to Lord Londonderry in 1890 excited comment from John Dillon, a prominent Home Ruler, who memorably declared in Parliament that it was unacceptable that the Exchequer should pay '£829 a year to a young gentleman whose only duty, besides dining with the Lord Lieutenant, is to fill in printed cards of invitation, address the envelopes, and paste on the stamps'.[132] While Mulhall was serving as vice-chairman of the Prisons Board in 1905 his house in the fashionable Earlsfort Terrace in central Dublin was ransacked by burglars. The humour in the situation was not lost on the Dublin press, and the trial proceedings were laced with an understated ironic mirth. Their delight was multiplied further by a quite inaccurate report in the Chicago press that 'a Dublin gentleman' had lost property to the tune of £200,000 as a result of a 'daring raid', and that amongst the valuables taken was an 'ancient antique crown of the Irish Kings'.[133] The list of actual stolen items may give us some idea of how a senior civil servant such as Mulhall could afford to live. Amongst the items stolen, valued at a much more modest £200 were a gold and crystal box, a snuff box, a silver pocket-book, a gold medal (the Plunkett prize for oratory at TCD), two silver medals, a revolver, and a gold waist buckle.[134] On the death of his widow, Teresa, four-fifths of his estate was donated to Downside School, demonstrating an admirable loyalty to the education that had made him.[135]

Such a high government representation by Irish boys educated at Downside begs the question, why was the proportion larger than at the Jesuit schools? The answer can only be speculated upon, though it seems likely that the greater emphasis here on public speaking and debating might well have encouraged the boys in this regard. Mulhall had, after all, won his gold medal for his oratory. Overall, it is of wider interest that of the six MPs elected out of this particular cohort, only two could be said to have been committed Home Rulers, with none radically nationalist. Furthermore, only two of them were in Parliament through the radical 1880s, and only one of them can be considered to have had a dynamic and progressive political career: Matt Kenny was in his early twenties when he was elected in 1882, sweeping in with a host of young nationalists such as John Redmond and T. M. Healy who would later define the party.[136]

---

[132] This was paraphrased by the indignant editor of the school journal, see *The Downside Review*, 9 (Jul., 1890), 175; for the speech in full, HC Deb., 10 Jul. 1890, Vol. 346, cc.1340–3.

[133] The original article was published by Reuters in Chicago, 3 Oct. 1905; 'Tall Story from Chicago: How News Grows Crossing the Atlantic', *Weekly Irish Times*, 7 Oct. 1905.

[134] 'Burglaries in Dublin: Mr. Mulhall's Losses', *Irish Times*, 14 Sep. 1905.

[135] 'Wills and Bequests', *The Times*, 2 Dec. 1935.

[136] Kenny had one of the best attendance records in the House during his period of representation. See Alan O'Day, *The English Face of Irish Nationalism: Parnellite Involvement in British Politics* (Dublin, 1977), 108.

IV ROADS LESS TRAVELLED

Not all of the cohort can be so easily categorized in terms of career. Several of the group were artists, journalists, travel writers, and some were unemployed and leisured 'gentlemen'. Some died in prison; some were merely dull or idle.

An impressive roll-call of the Irish revivalist literati turn up in elite schools. Willard Potts has written perceptively of both the elite nature of the revival movement, and the denominational divisions within it. Underpinning the Catholic drive for the Irish revival was a desire for a greater market share in Irish society.[137] Many of those involved in the revival were Dublin- or London-based cosmopolitan Catholics, who were well educated rather than self-educated. It should not therefore be a surprise that so many of the leading Catholic lights were also elite educated. Oliver St John Gogarty, Edward Martyn, and Eimar O'Duffy all attended English Jesuit colleges—indeed O'Duffy's much-neglected first novel *The Wasted Island* (1920) was based mostly on his experiences of both Stonyhurst and UCD. The realist novelist George Augustus Moore attended Oscott, though his father suspected he was a 'dunce' while he was there. Some, like Gogarty, played up to their 'Cawstle Catholic' reputation, the name itself a parody of their Anglicized accent. Others, such as Martyn, took their Catholic-nationalist militancy to extremes and made it seem a reaction to their own backgrounds. Of the Irish boys at Downside only one can be considered a full-time artist, Roderic O'Conor (Downside: 1871), who also schooled at Ampleforth College between 1873 and 1878 and is now generally considered one of Ireland's finest Victorian artists. O'Conor was born to a junior branch of the O'Conor family and his impressionist style was influenced by Paul Gauguin. He spent most of his adult life in France, in particular Brittany, where his work focused on landscape and portraits of the peasantry. O'Conor was not successful in his lifetime, though he was well regarded by the Parisian circle of artists who nicknamed him 'le Père O'Conor'.[138]

Engineers and scientists are also rather under-represented in the cohort. Just four Irish boys at Downside, for example, can be said to have spent their lives working towards technological advancement as engineers, aviation experts, professional scientists, and so on. The most interesting of this group is perhaps Mervyn O'Gorman (Downside: 1885) (Figure 4.2), an expert and pioneer in aviation engineering. Educated at the Royal University in Dublin, O'Gorman rose to the rank of lieutenant colonel in the Royal Flying Corps, and is considered a major figure in British aviation as well as a noted photographer. On his death in 1958 *The Times* declared him to have been 'a man of agile mind and Hibernian eloquence'.[139]

O'Gorman headed up what was to become the Royal Aircraft Establishment and as such was at the forefront of the British attempt to utilize the developing aircraft industry for military purposes. At the outbreak of World War I in 1914,

---

[137] See his first chapter 'Sectarianism and the Irish Revival', Willard Potts, *Joyce and the Two Irelands* (Texas, 2000), 1–47.
[138] Bridget Hourican, 'Roderic Anthony O'Conor', *DIB*.
[139] 'Mervyn O'Gorman', *The Times*, 17 Mar. 1958.

Figure 4.2 Lt Col. Mervyn O'Gorman, 1871–1958

the army had four squadrons ready to fly to a base in Amiens, most of which had been designed under O'Gorman's supervision at Farnborough.[140] Other Irish boys, such as Joseph Musgrave Kearney (Downside: 1891) took advantage of the opportunities further afield by becoming engineers in mining centres. Kearney was a co-founder of the Cam & Motor gold mining company of Southern Rhodesia.[141] J. J. O'Reilly (Beaumont 1889) oversaw the construction and planning of Cochin Harbour (now called Kochi) in India as engineer-in-chief of what was then the largest port in India.[142] He was also a prominent member of the St Stephen's Green Club in Dublin, as well as a leading light in the Madras and Calcutta Racing Clubs. His brothers became, respectively, a lieutenant colonel in the army (Herbert); chairman of Power & Sons (Bertram)—a major distillery; and a colonel in the army (Charles). On the evidence of these brothers alone, it is obvious that an elite education could be put to a wide and varied use.

In the second half of the nineteenth century the cult of athleticism built gradually towards its Edwardian peak. The development of the concept of 'muscular Christianity' has long been acknowledged and Catholic schools were, as ever, scrupulously up to date in this regard. As a result, many of the cohort were sportsmen first and professionals second. For some, this was a useful way to broaden their social and professional networks. For others it was a guiding influence. Philip Meldon (Stonyhurst: 1887) won caps for Ireland in both football and cricket

[140] Theo Barker, 'O'Gorman, Mervyn Joseph Pius (1871–1958)', *Oxford Dictionary of National Biography*
[141] 'Kearney, Joseph Musgrave', *Transactions of the Institute of Mining Engineers*, 59 (1919–20).
[142] John Joseph O'Reilly (Beaumont: 1889), see obituary, *Irish Times*, 28 Dec. 1942, 3.

before moving to Canada where he became Professor of Artillery and Tactics at the Royal Military College in 1913. Many played golf and captained local clubs, more hunted, and several fished. They peopled the Irish cricket, rugby, and football teams at a time when internationals were becoming more commonplace. Cycling was a popular sport and, as we have seen, Percy Kilkelly was something of a star to his followers at Downside. Oliver St John Gogarty was an impressive athlete in his youth, winning many cycling races and even playing professional football for Preston North End while at Stonyhurst. A son of the Cork brewing family, Fitzjames Murphy (Downside: 1883) was on the Irish hockey XI, while Louis Meldon (Stonyhurst: 1898) represented Ireland six times in the Davis Cup in tennis and still cannot claim to be the most famous Irish tennis player. That distinction belongs instead to Vere Goold.

Vere Thomas St Leger Goold (Oscott: 1869) provides a fitting example of the folly of Victorian beliefs in the purifying effect of sport and its ability to produce muscular Christians and wholesome men. In his early twenties Vere Goold, youngest son of George Goold, JP of Tipperary, was the first ever Irish finalist at the Lawn Tennis championships at Wimbledon. A gifted stylist, but far from precise, Vere Goold lost the 1879 Wimbledon singles final to the Rev. John Hartley and thereafter his life proved something of a shambles. He emigrated to Montreal where he married Violet Girondin and disappeared from public view until arrested for murder in Monte Carlo in August of 1907. A heavy gambler, he had given his occupation as a milliner under interrogation and had also (incorrectly) claimed that he was the 5th Baronet Goold.[143] His crime, and that of his wife, had been discovered when a trunk they had sent to London from Monte Carlo was found to contain the remains of a Danish woman named Emma Liven. The crime was quickly dubbed the 'trunk murder' by the international press and it later transpired that the couple murdered the woman while she attempted to recover a gambling debt from them. Both were convicted of her murder and, while his wife was allowed to serve her sentence in France, Vere Goold was transported to the famous Devil's Island penal colony in French Guiana where he died, aged fifty-five, in September 1909.

Roads Not Travelled

The careers that were not pursued by the Irish boys at English schools are perhaps just as fruitful a line of enquiry in trying to identify the patterns of the Irish Catholic elite. It should be clear by now that manual labour was avoided across the cohort, with perhaps only the rare adventurous boys willing to get their hands dirty out in the world of mining or speculating. Boys attending these four schools almost never served even in the more lowly white-collar positions, such as clerk in a bank, nor were they inclined to make their careers in the more menial government jobs. They

---

[143] For the initial reaction to the case see 'Suspects Use Titles', *The Washington Post*, 9 Aug. 1907; for more on Vere St Leger Goold see Steven Lynch, 'The Extraordinary Lives of Players who Have Graced the Wimbledon Lawns', *Daily Telegraph*, 23 Jun. 2007.

did not engage in low-scale commerce, or own shops or pubs. They were not butch-
ers, salesmen, or tradesmen. James Francis Cronin (Beaumont: 1886) was one of
the few to so much as manage a bank—usually thought of as an upper-middle class
occupation of a respectable nature.

There were also lives not fully realized, or ended early by accident or suicide.
Charles Ambrose Morris, a boy whose glittering academic curve at the Oratory
School in Birmingham had won him a scholarship at Baliol College in Oxford
at the age of seventeen provides a terrible example of what can, inexplicably, go
wrong in a young person's life. Charles had many advantages. He was the youngest son of the famous Irish judge, Lord Killanin, and the *Irish Times* had noted his
'promising career' in December of 1897.[144] Less than eighteenth months later, in
April of 1899, he travelled alone to Dijon in France, where he committed suicide
and ended a life which had bristled with promise—shattering an already unhappy
family in the process.[145] Morris, a young man with everything to live for, shows us
that glib assumptions must not be made about lives of privilege and that unhappi-
ness and tragedy take no account of social status when they strike.

Accidents and deaths at school were also tragedies that were simply more frequent in the Victorian era, but accidents did not stop at the school gate. Francis
Hurley (Oscott: 1863) died in Bandon when he fell off a coach while reaching
for his hat in December 1873. The solicitor Thomas W. FitzGerald died in an
even more bizarre manner in May 1915, having left Killiney to post some letters at Kingstown. En route, he fell asleep and was carried past his destination.
The *Downside Review* noted that upon 'waking up he must have leaned out of
the window to ascertain his whereabouts, and while doing so was struck by an
arch which is very close to the line. The force of the impact dragged his body
through the opening, and he was found dead beside the arch some hours later.'[146]
Something similarly misfortunate happened to the son of the Lord Mayor of Cork,
Thomas Lyons Hackett (Oscott: 1864) when still a lowly probationary constable
at Belmore Park in Sydney. He died after falling from his horse and onto his sword
in September 1886.[147] Others met a more deliberate end—James Woulfe Flanagan
(Oscott: 1874) was assassinated in front of the Catholic cathedral in Newry (where
he was stationed as a Resident Magistrate) in June of 1922 at the height of the
civil war.

Marriage Strategies

Marriage strategy was vitally important to the life chances of not only the boys
themselves, but their families more generally. One of the most difficult things to
track in a prosopography is marriage patterns, in part because so many men had
more than one wife in a lifetime, but also because biographical detail on their

---

[144] 'Balliol College, Oxford', *Irish Times*, 3 Dec. 1897.
[145] Maud Wynne, *An Irishman and his Family: Lord Morris of Killanin* (London, 1937), 24.
[146] *Irish Times*, 13 Dec. 1873; *The Downside Review*, 34 (1915), 220.
[147] *The Sydney Morning Herald*, 7 Sep. 1886.

life partners are not always provided in extant sources. Details for family members do not feature, for instance, in school records, or in registers such as Bateman's *Great Landowners*. Nevertheless, something of the general background of wives may be extrapolated from other biographical sources. We have seen already how Cork's business elite intermarried, and the same practice is evidenced by landed families also. The landed elite of Co. Meath may serve as a convenient example of such intermarriage patterns.[148] Robert Ashurst Gradwell of Dowth Hall in Meath left the school at Oscott in 1877 and married Lady Henrietta Plunkett (daughter of the 10th Earl of Fingall, owner of close to 10,000 acres) in 1884 when she was twenty-three years of age. Gradwell's father, Richard, owned 4,000 acres in Co. Louth and had married a daughter (Maria Theresa) of another local landowner at Tobertynan in Co. Meath. Robert's marriage to Henrietta Plunkett was childless, however, and on his death he devised Dowth Hall to a cousin, Francis Gradwell.

At a slightly lower social scale Gerald More O'Ferrall (Stonyhurst: 1886) made just as advantageous a match as Gradwell when he married Mary FitzGerald, daughter of Lord Maurice FitzGerald and Lady Adelaide Forbes. Maurice was the third son of the 4th Duke of Leinster, and his wife was the daughter of the 7th Earl of Granard. The More O'Ferralls had land in the bordering counties of Longford and Kildare, making the match one that made sense locally. Late in life, Gerald, who lived at Lisard in Edgeworthstown, was shot in a raid in February 1935 by a party of men who were aggrieved by his role in sanctioning evictions for the nearby Sanderson (formerly Edgeworth) estate. Gerald survived, though his son, Richard, did not.[149] Other local families to have intermarried with the More-O'Ferralls include the O'Conors, Aylwards, Thunders, and Sweetmans—all notable landed families in nearby Co. Kildare.

Lastly, the Galway, Roscommon, and Mayo Catholic landed families were particularly fond of intermarriage. A web of families such as the Bellews, Burkes, Dillons, Nugents, Blakes, D'Arcys, and Bodkins all intermarried throughout the eighteenth and nineteenth centuries.[150] Sometimes estates traded names for lesser reasons, with the Cregg estate north of Galway city inherited by Arthur Francis Blake (Oscott: 1865) believed to have been won from the Kirwan family in a game of cards. Sir Henry Christopher Grattan-Bellew (Beaumont: 1871) broke the mould somewhat when he married Lady Sophia Forbes, remembered as the greatest beauty of the Dublin season of 1881 by his schoolmate George de Stacpoole (Beaumont: 1872). Their sons became best friends at Downside years later, before fighting in the Great War together.[151] Several other cases of marriage outside either the immediate locality, the country, or even the Catholic faith are evident, though

---

[148] For more on this see Terence A. M. Dooley, ' "A World Turned Upside Down": A Study of the Socio-economic Decline of the Meath Nobility, 1870–1935', *Ríocht na Midhe*, 12 (2001), 188–228.

[149] For reports on the raid see 'Father and Son Shot', *Irish Press*, 10 Feb. 1935. For the only account of this see Frank Columb, *The Shooting of More O'Ferrall* (Cambridge, 1997).

[150] The truth of this statement can be seen clearly enough in Blake, *Blake Family Records 1300 to 1600*.

[151] George de Stacpoole, *Irish and Other Memories* (London, 1922)

they are the exception to the rule. Nicholas Daniel Murphy (Oscott: 1864), for example, married an American Protestant, Helena Franklin.

It is this local marriage pattern that we see replicated among Irish Catholic landed families. There is a noticeable tendency to marry not only within the landed class but also into one of the families which are relatively close in proximity. There were also instances of Irish boys marrying the English sisters of their schoolmates, such as the 3rd Baron Bellew, Christopher Bellew (Beaumont: 1865), who married the truly aristocratic Mildred Mary Josephine de Trafford, daughter of Sir Humphrey de Trafford of Trafford Park, Manchester and his wife Lady Annette Mary Talbot, a sister of the 17th Earl of Shrewsbury. But these Irish-English formed a minority of the marriages recorded. This trend is unsurprising for a number of reasons—for one, the social scene is likely to have been somewhat localized, and the families would have been more likely to meet informally and frequently through, for example, social and sports clubs.[152] Important also, was the fact that, due to localized schooling preferences, the daughters of these families were as likely to be schooled alongside girls of neighbouring families, a process which increased the familiarity between elite sons and daughters of marriageable age as well as providing them all with a near-identical education and formation. Of paramount importance, nevertheless, was the notion that families who had successfully held estates through centuries of legal and military threat simply wanted to stick to the families they knew well and had relied upon as neighbours throughout that process. A wife or husband, after all, was only for one generation. Land was for as long as a family could hold on to it.

V CONCLUSION

There is a distinct pattern to the boys' careers, and it is one of caution, social conservativism, and high social status privileged over the accumulation of wealth. There are very few adventurous choices in the cohort and the few there are tend to be eccentrics, or exceptional cases such as Vere Goold. Marriage strategy conforms to career choice in its conservatism, with an emphasis on those professions and wives which would ensure the continuance or consolidation of elite status by accepted norms. Thus, when presented with the option of taking one's chances in the Empire as a scientist or speculator, Irish boys preferred to aim instead for a solid career such as practising at the Irish or English Bar, entering wholesale trade, or running the family estate. Everywhere we see careful consolidation and a preference for positions and professions with existing status in society ahead of anything involving speculation or adventure. The professions were attractive for this reason, as they guaranteed a degree of respectability while allowing someone either from a gentry family in decline or a middle-class family in ascent the same opportunity

---

[152] See Brian Griffin, 'The Big House at Play: Archery as an Elite Pursuit from the 1830s to the 1870s', in Ciaran O'Neill (ed.), *Irish Elites in the Nineteenth Century* (Dublin, 2013), 153–71.

to earn a steady salary without losing status. Similarly, a military career at high to mid rank would guarantee a solid income with concomitant high social status and irreproachably loyal credentials. This pattern would at least appear to confirm what historians such as Tom Bartlett and Kevin Whelan have identified as a conservative or cautious mentalité among middle-class and elite Irish Catholic families from the late seventeenth century onwards, inspired to that caution and tact by centuries of insecure tenure and the constant threat of the outright destruction of their pains-takingly constructed and maintained social status.

PART III

5

Fionnuala in France
Convent Education and the Irish Catholic Elite
1850–1900

When a girl leaves an English boarding school she is always fit for the duties of a drawing room.

> May Laffan, *Hogan M.P. A Novel* (1876), 93

A child with a home, a mother, a family, cast adrift on a grey winter's sea! Travelling from one land to another, like a valueless packet given to a stranger!

> Hannah Lynch, *Autobiography of a Child* (Edinburgh, 1899), 136

In 1958 the playwright Séamus de Búrca self-published his daughter's school diary and letters as *Fionnuala in France: Being the Diary of a Sixteen-year-old Girl in a French Convent School*. Fionnuala catalogued the trauma and intensity of a boarding school experience abroad in adolescent, excitable prose. 'Everyone cries in boarding school', she proclaimed, in between gushing capitalization and exclamation. Fionnuala attended the Dominican 'Institut Jehanne de France' convent school in Pithiviers, just south of Paris, making friends among French, English, and American girls alike.

As modish as it may have seemed by the 1950s, the tradition of Irish girls boarding on the Continent stretched back much further than Fionnuala de Búrca. Broadly speaking it became more common for elite families to send their daughters to a school from the early decades of the nineteenth century, though it remained a popular option to instruct young ladies at home, through a governess. The other options available were to attend an Irish convent school, or to spend several years at an English school for young ladies. These were the main choices available to girls in the nineteenth century and, as with the boys, the least prestigious of these choices was to school in Ireland. Female education aimed for very different ends in the nineteenth century than male education and the same parents had a different set of expectations and requirements from their educators for their sons and daughters. This subject has been mined with considerable merit by historians of French and English female education—most notably by Rebecca Rogers and Christina de Bellaigue—but the subject of the schooling of Irish Catholic girls of the elite class has yet to be considered extensively by historians.[1]

---

[1] Rebecca Rogers, *From the Salon to the Schoolroom: Educating Bourgeois Girls in Nineteenth Century France* (Pennsylvania, 2005); Christina de Bellaigue, *Educating Women: Schooling and Identity in*

The history of elite education for Irish girls in this period remains obscure, both in terms of its domestic provision and its availability overseas. In this short chapter we will not remedy this in any complete way, but rather aim to point out where the work lies and what might come out of more extensive investigation. The most pressing problem for anyone attempting a prosopographical history of girls educated in high-class convents is the question of reinforcing patriarchy by engaging in an unfairly gendered analysis. To use loaded terms such as wife, daughter, or sister is to fail this test even at the outset, but to attempt to analyse social mobility and marriage strategy without recourse to referencing the status and occupation of fathers, brothers, and husbands is a significant obstacle for any nineteenth-century historian to overcome. There are advantages too. Visibility is not an issue at this social level, for example, as most of the girls in the chapter that follows are relatively easy to track, drawn as they are from families that were well recorded in the first place.

I MARKET FORCES

Fiction is a good place to begin when trying to understand the landscape of Irish education for girls, its application, and its purpose. In *Hogan M.P.* (1876) May Laffan uses the object of Mr Hogan's affections, Miss Davoren, to exhort what one might suspect were her own deeply held convictions. Addressing the issue of whether Irish convents were really so inferior to English boarding schools she exclaims: 'I don't know much about gentlemen's tastes; but you know, of course, it is said that in every country women are educated up to the level of the men's requirements, not beyond.'[2] Laffan's criticism of the 'bread and butterism' of Irish convents in *Hogan M.P.* was consistent with an earlier attack in *Fraser's Magazine* in 1874 which was written in much the same tone.[3] That the variable 'tastes' of gentlemen were generally considered the arbiter of female education is a dangerous assumption to make; nevertheless, the marriage market was certainly one of the most relevant competitions for a young Irish girl in this period. There are countless examples in British and Irish fiction of young girls at school whiling away their leisure hours dreaming of a fantastical match. In novels of school life in England, Irish girls often play an incidental role as outsiders who will eventually be civilized by their predominantly English classmates. This trope runs through novels such as *Wild Kitty* (1897) and *The Rebel of the School* (1902) by L. T. Meade, the Cork-born creator of some of the earliest schoolgirl fiction.[4] A more balanced

---

England and France 1800–1867 (Oxford, 2007). For a recent synthesis on the subject of schooling wealthy young ladies in Britain and Ireland see Jane McDermid, *The Schooling of Girls in Britain and Ireland 1800–1900* (London, 2012), ch. 3.

  [2] Laffan, *Hogan M.P.*, 93.

  [3] May Laffan, 'Convent Boarding-schools for Young Ladies', *Fraser's Magazine*, 9/54 (Jun. 1874), 778–86.

  [4] I owe these insights to Whitney Standlee, '"The Irish Parent's Standing Terror": Convent Education and the Irish Catholic Elite in Memoir and Fiction, 1860–1900', a paper read before the Conference of the Society for the Study of Nineteenth-Century Ireland, at Liverpool, Jun. 2011.

approach is evident in Jessie Innes-Browne's twee debut novel *Three Daughters of the United Kingdom* (1897) in which an Irish girl, a Scottish girl, and an English girl strike up a real as well as symbolic friendship while attending a Benedictine abbey in the 'northern provinces of France'. Throughout the novel these three unified girls seem to eschew their lessons and are far more interested in their binary choice between either the religious life that has become so familiar to them or the attractions of each other's 'tall, stately' brothers. In Katharine Tynan's *A Daughter of the Fields* (1901) the heroine, Meg O'Donoghue, returns from an education above her station in the 'aristocratic' convent of St Cyprian in France. Her education makes reintegration into rural Ireland difficult, though an advantageous marriage provides her with a much-needed escape route.

The late nineteenth-century marriage market was mocked by George Moore in his proto-feminist novel *A Drama in Muslin* (1886), the early chapters of which were set at St Leonards-on-Sea, a prominent elite boarding school on the south coast of England mainly attended by Irish and English Catholics. Moore's cousins had attended the school, as had other girls of his acquaintance. His own sister, Nina, studied at the Sacré Coeur (Sacred Heart) Convent in Tours and sent her own daughters to the order's other French foundation at Lille, then run by her childhood friend Mother de Montelambert.[5] This multinational *smörgåsbord* of conventual education was complemented by the diversity of nationalities in the body of women circulating Irish townhouses and big houses plying their trade as governesses. The majority of the day and boarding schools in Ireland had a Continental tint as well, as many of the Catholic orders were in fact French in origin. In no way, then, was female education any less transnational or cosmopolitan in character than was male education in the period. Indeed, it was arguably more so.

The *Dictionary of Irish Biography* is useful here again, throwing up frequent examples of (often nationalist) Irish women who either spent their formative years abroad or whose families had imported foreign talent for private tuition. There seems to have been no real confessional pattern. Girls' educational choices were down to economics, fashion, and parental convictions in the same way that their brother's choices were. From their biographies we get a sense of the options that were available. The Protestant artist Rose Maynard Barton (1856–1929) was tutored by a German governess and never attended a regular school. Another unrelated artist, Molly Barton, was educated in schools at Southsea and Boulogne before returning home to become a governess to the gentry. From a Catholic gentry family came Mary Ellen Lambert Butler (1873–1920), energetic activist in the radical women's organization Inghinidhe na hÉireann (Daughters of Ireland) and the revival movement more generally, who was home-tutored by a governess and finished at the (mostly Protestant) Alexandra College in Dublin. Constance Gore-Booth (later Countess Markievicz) and her sister Eva

---

[5] Kenelm Gow, 'Nina Louisa Mary Moore', in Kevin Coyne, Kenelm Gow, and Art Ó Súilleabháin (eds), *Moores of Moore Hall: A Short History* (Carnacon, 1989).

were home-tutored by a governess who was Cambridge-educated and took them on a Grand Tour before their debut in high society.[6] The revivalist writer Mary Colum attended a German convent (in her previous life as Molly Maguire) after an initial immersion in French language and tradition made available to her at St Louis Convent more locally in Monaghan. In Colum's intriguing 'creative' autobiography, *Life and the Dream* (1947), she postulates that there was a European Catholic tradition that united the institutions she attended into one recognizable aristocratic ethos.[7] 'Step from a convent school in Ireland to a convent school in France, or Germany, or Belgium, or Italy' she wrote, 'and the difference was slight—same sort of discipline, same habits and customs, same uniform'.[8] This supposed uniformity of experience was, of course, exaggerated by Colum, but the essential point should not be lost. The experience of convent education was something that united the daughters of old aristocratic families with the bustling middle class merchants in the nineteenth century, even if they rarely attended the same one.

But what were all these girls being educated for? The creation of 'ladies' was a booming business in the late nineteenth century. The marriage market parodied so well by George Moore in *A Drama in Muslin* was an obvious destination. An epochal event in many young women's lives, it offered a brief window in which to make their match. The pressure on young women to make the most of their accomplishments, poise, and (more unfairly) the lottery of their looks, was famously intense. The well-known memoirs of the Countess of Fingall, *Seventy Years Young* (1937) perfectly capture this competitive drive, and the sometimes undignified race to marry the correct sort of husband. From the picture it paints of the jaded faux-grandeur of the Castle season, to the conspiracy of those attempting to auction off their daughters, the marriage market is not spared by one who made a successful, if apparently loveless, match from it herself.[9] The demographics of the period militated against the likelihood of marriage, especially at elite and upper middle-class levels where a woman was actually less likely to take a husband than at lower-income levels.[10] This was true all over Europe, with the question of how to train young women from a middle-class background for a vocational purpose without jeopardizing their chances of marriages occupying column inches across the Continent in the 1860s and 1870s.[11] Alongside this

[6] Frances Clarke, 'Molly Barton (1861–1949)', *DIB*.

[7] Too many accounts of female education take Colum's work literally. For a deconstruction of the creative elements in it see Taura Napier, 'The Mosaic "I": Mary Colum and Modern Irish Autobiography', *Irish University Review*, 28/1 (Spring–Summer 1998), 37–55.

[8] Mary Colum, *Life and the Dream,* 2nd edn (Dublin, 1966), 26–7.

[9] Elizabeth, Countess of Fingall, *Seventy Years Young: Memories of Elizabeth, Countess of Fingall Told to Pamela Hinkson*, 2nd edn (Dublin, 1991).

[10] For an extended and authoritative discussion of this see Timothy Guinnane, *The Vanishing Irish: Households, Migration, and the Rural Economy in Ireland 1850–1922* (Princeton, NJ, 2007), 193–241.

[11] James C. Albisetti, 'Philanthropy for the Middle Class: Vocational Education for Girls and Young Women in Mid-Victorian Europe', *History of Education*, 41/3 (May 2012), 287–301.

demographic tension was the age-old mission of taking girls and transforming them into 'young ladies'.

This transformative effect of an elite education is arguably even more difficult to prove for girls than it is for boys. The Irish writer Kate O'Brien remembered an atmosphere of *la pudeur et la politesse* at the Limerick convent of her childhood and the idea of a 'finish' that was somehow peculiar to female education. Her fifth novel, *The Land of Spices* (1941), is an unparalleled evocation of conventual life in Ireland and one of the few works of Irish fiction based on a girls' boarding school experience in Ireland. *The Land of Spices* has a complex narrative structure, split between a Reverend Mother, whose position is somewhat analogous to that of a headmistress, and a precocious student, Anna Murphy. Anna's path through school is charted from both perspectives. The story unfolds between 1904 and 1914 and much of it is based on O'Brien's attendance at a convent run by the Faithful Companions of Jesus at Laurel Hill in Limerick. The novel opens with Eileen O'Doherty, darling of the school, being accepted into the order of the *Compagnie de la Sainte Famille*. Eileen, we are told, had left three years earlier, and is seen to have entered the world on rather 'English' terms, having been 'presented at the English court, and admired, it was said, by the Queen herself…danced through a London season, and returned to decorate Irish society for a year'.[12] The local curate, Father Conroy, is shown to object to what he perceives as a colonial marriage market:

> 'Somehow it's a bit of a pity, it seems to me, Reverend Mother, to be training Irish girls as suitable wives for English majors and Colonial Governors!' He spoke angrily because he was afraid of his own audacity.
>
> 'We educate our children in the Christian virtues and graces. If these appeal to English majors, why, so much the better for those gentlemen!'
>
> 'Our young girls must be educated *nationally* now Reverend Mother—to be the wives of *Irishmen* and to meet the changing times!'[13]

Offered a prestigious scholarship the young Anna Murphy manages to elude her prescribed fate, 'liberated' in the end from domestic ignorance by a free-thinking and rational English authority figure at a French foundation in Limerick. This collision or marriage of Irish, French, and English traditions in female education continued to shape Irish girlhood throughout the twentieth century as it had throughout the nineteenth. For us to develop that history a greater emphasis will need to be placed on the gradual development of this fusion from the seventeenth century onwards. Quite what this 'finish' was for is something that remains obscure, though it is certain that the employment market for elite educated Irish girls was a much less diverse one than it was for their brothers. The next three sections will investigate the contours of elite education for Catholic girls between 1850 and 1900 in Ireland, England, and across the continent of Europe.

---

[12] Kate O'Brien, *The Land of Spices*, 2nd edn (London, 1949), 3.
[13] O'Brien, *Land of Spices*, 92.

II ELITE EDUCATION FOR GIRLS IN
IRELAND 1850–1900

High-status Irish convent schools suffered from the same crisis of confidence as their male equivalents; no matter how well they performed they were rarely first-choice for those who could afford to select whatever education they pleased. The market, as ever, reveals this stark truth. Jostling for space in the advertising columns of the *Freeman's Journal* were relatively small operations such as the convent run by the Soeurs de la Sainte Union des Sacrés-Cœurs in St Omer, which proclaimed that it could provide a 'high class English, French and German education' at a 'modest pension'.[14] For every girl lost to the Continental convents there was another threatened with temptation from English schools, considered a fashionable choice from the 1850s and 1860s as the collective schooling of girls began to become more commonplace at elite social levels. Domestically the convent schools were threatened by an expanding Protestant middle-class provision of high-performing and small-scale academy-style schools such as Alexandra College in Dublin (1866) and the Queen's Institute (1861) in Belfast.

The informal ad hoc economy of circulating governesses muddied the waters still further. Some work has been done on this unregulated but important sector, though much more ought to be.[15] The recently digitized 1901 and 1911 censuses reveal that the decline in that particular vocation was dramatic in Ireland as elsewhere, and had begun in the second half of the nineteenth century as schools for girls became more popular. There was a 25 per cent drop in the numbers registered as a governess in the ten years between 1901 and 1911, when 2,043 and 1,432 were recorded respectively. The governess had become an important figure not only in Victorian Britain and Ireland, but across Europe since the seventeenth century. Irene Hardach-Pinke has argued that these women, imported from the outside into aspirant and elite families, ought to be seen as important intercultural educators who passed on much more to their charges than a mere sprinkling of French, German, or English as needed. In an Irish context far too little is known of the inner lives of these freelance educational professionals. Of the 2,053 recorded in 1901 about 618 were Catholic women, though that does not necessarily follow that every Catholic child being home-tutored was tutored by a co-religionist. At least 527 of the 2,053 governesses were foreign born, with the greatest number of those coming from England (319), Germany (41), France (36), Scotland (29), and Switzerland (29). Where a Catholic family was concerned it was rare that they strayed from the template of English, French, or German-born governesses. Edmond de Poher de la Poer of Gurteen in Waterford was an exception in this regard, employing a governess named Louise von Arday who had been

---

[14] This order is now better known as the Holy Union Sisters. For the advertisement see 'Education', *Freeman's Journal*, 15 Aug. 1878.

[15] John Logan, 'Governesses, Tutors and Parents: Domestic Education in Ireland, 1700–1880', *Irish Educational Studies*, 7/2 (1988), 1–18; Deirdre Raftery, 'The Nineteenth Century Governess: Image and Reality', in Bernadette Whelan (ed.), *Women and Paid Work in Ireland, 1500–1930* (Dublin, 2000).

born an Austrian subject in Pisa, Italy. Von Arday had been employed to take care of the families' daughters, Elinor (sixteen), Ermyngarde (thirteen), and Yseult (twelve) while their brothers were at the Oratory School in Birmingham. Von Arday, then forty-one years old, had previously been employed in England, and, while we may only guess at her level of pay or proficiency, we ought not doubt her life experience and cosmopolitanism.[16]

In 1861 an estimated 141,000 Irish girls were receiving a primary education, with just 8,064 receiving an education in a superior school. The enumerators totalled the number of girls receiving a convent education at 2,430, out of a total female Roman Catholic population of 2.3 million.[17] By the 1870s and 1880s it seems that the most common route for a girl from a wealthy Irish background was either to have been exclusively home-tutored—a process that would often last into her late teens—or else to be schooled by a governess until about the age of eleven or twelve, at which stage she would have progressed either to a preparatory school or have been transferred straight to a high-class boarding school either at home or overseas. By 1911 the provision of basic education for girls was impressive. Girls had made up roughly half of the school-going population as early as the 1860s and 97.8 per cent of Irish women recorded by the 1911 census could read and write, as compared to 26.8 per cent in 1841.[18] Access to secondary education was still very much a middle-class affair, even more so than for boys in the nineteenth century. Very few girls were educated to an advanced level, and to be schooled into one's late teens was an indicator of financial comfort, if not outright wealth. For the ten years between 1889 and 1899 the number of girls presenting for intermediate examinations in Ireland was between 15 per cent and 25 per cent of the total number examined, or 1,500 to 2,500 in round numbers.[19] Almost all education provided in schools serving large numbers was the preserve of Catholic orders of nuns, but it was still rare to have a large school for girls at that stage. In the mid century even relatively successful convents such as the Ursulines in Thurles had enrollments of between just fifty to one hundred pupils and very few boarding schools exceeded that figure.

In her excellent 1986 essay 'Influences Affecting Girls' Secondary Education in Ireland, 1860–1910' Anne V. O'Connor argued that Irish girls' education was influenced on one side by a primarily religious French tradition and by a rational and utilitarian English tradition on the other.[20] A history teacher at Alexandra College, perhaps the most famous of all Dublin schools for girls, founded in 1866,

---

[16] Louise von Arday was in the employ of Adele C. Locke, Cornwall, England, at the time of the 1881 census. See '1881 British Census/Cornwall', digital database and images. Family Search, <www.familysearch.com>, Louise von Arday, 1881; Falmouth, Cornwall, England, RG11/28.

[17] Census of Ireland for the year 1861, Part IV: reports and tables relating to the religious professions, education, and occupations of the people, vol. I: religions and education, 6, 48.

[18] John Logan, 'The Dimensions of Gender in Nineteenth-century Schooling', in Margaret Kelleher and James H. Murphy (eds), *Gender Perspectives in Nineteenth-century Ireland* (Dublin, 1997), 37; Margaret Ó hÓgarthaigh, *Quiet Revolutionaries: Irish Women in Education, Medicine and Sport, 1861–1964* (Dublin, 2011),16.

[19] *Report of the Intermediate Education Board for Ireland for the year 1899*, HC 1900 [Cd. 172], viii.

[20] Anne V. O'Connor, 'Influences Affecting Girls' Secondary Education in Ireland, 1860–1910', *Archivium Hibernicum*, 41 (1986), 83–98.

O'Connor saw the story of modern female education as the product of progressive Protestant pioneers such as Isabella Tod, Margaret Byers, and her own predecessor at Alexandra, Anne Jellicoe. Indeed her equally influential chapter on intermediate education for girls in Mary Cullen's seminal collection of essays, *Girls Don't Do Honours* (1987), mapped out the contours of modern female education as if it essentially began with these secular pioneers and was then made concrete by the passing of the education legislation in 1878.[21] To a large extent, those historians who have succeeded O'Connor have retold or reworked this story.[22]

These are, however, hypotheses which are far too reductive, on both counts. The tendency of focusing on 'pioneers' was a marked feature of early scholarly work on nineteenth-century female educationalists—perhaps the result of locating a mirror image in those who marked out the territory of 'women's history' itself in the 1980s and early 1990s.[23] There has been little of substance since this work 'on pioneers, by pioneers' such as that of Susan M. Parkes and Anne V. O'Connor, though the work of Tom O'Donoghue, Deirdre Raftery, Jane McDermid, and Judith Harford promises to remedy this.[24] More straightforward histories of networks of institutions, of class hierarchy in girl's education, and more nuanced treatments of teacher and student experience are all required to augment the plethora of celebratory school histories and adoring biography through which we currently wade. This will involve a shift from the focus on the exemplar and the pioneer to the more mundane aspects of the schools themselves and the girls who emerged from them. It ought to also lead us to more advanced histories of convent education, which long preceded the 1860s revolution, and to a better understanding of that aloof Victorian figure—the governess. O'Connor also sees Irish education as simply absorbing influences from outside, as if it was merely a one-way flow. We might just as easily say English and French education was profoundly affected by Irish orders or Irish nuns, or that the Irish governess embedded in an elite Spanish or Russian family was as important as many a diplomat.[25] The Continental Catholic convents were in fact heavily influenced by the flow

---

[21] Anne V. O'Connor, 'The Revolution in Girls Secondary Education in Ireland 1860–1900', in Mary Cullen (ed.), *Girls Don't Do Honours: Irish Women in Education in the 19th and 20th Centuries* (Dublin, 1987), 31–54.

[22] Susan M. Parkes, 'Intermediate Education for Girls', in Deirdre Raftery and Susan M. Parkes (eds), *Female Education in Ireland 1700–1900: Minerva or Madonna?* (Dublin, 2007), 69–104.

[23] A classic manifesto for women's history in Ireland is Margaret MacCurtain, Mary O'Dowd, and Maria Luddy, 'An Agenda for Women's History in Ireland, 1500–1900', *Irish Historical Studies*, 28/109 (May 1992), 1–37. For a good overview of the main developments see Linda Connolly, *The Irish Women's Movement: From Revolution to Devolution* (Dublin, 2003), 17–26.

[24] Deirdre Raftery, Judith Harford, and Susan M. Parkes, 'Mapping the Terrain of Female Education in Ireland, 1830–1910', *Gender and Education*, 22/5 (Nov. 2010), 565–78; Judith Harford, 'The Movement for the Higher Education of Women in Ireland: Gender Equality or Denominational Rivalry?' in *History of Education*, 34/5 (Apr. 2005), 473–92; Tom O'Donoghue and Judith Harford, 'A Comparative History of Church–State Relations in Irish Education', *Comparative Education Review*, 55/3 (Aug. 2011), 315–41; Deirdre Raftery and Catherine Nowlan-Roebuck, 'Convent Schools and National Education in Nineteenth-century Ireland: Negotiating a Place within a Non-denominational System', *History of Education* 36/3 (May 2007): 353–65.

[25] An intriguing first-hand account of the Irish governess to the children of Nicholas II, Tsar of Russia, between 1898 and 1904 can be found in Margaret Eager, *Six Years at the Russian Court* (New York, 1906).

of Irish and British Catholic women throughout the penal era. Nevertheless, the idea that Irish female education was a ferment of outside ideas in the nineteenth century is accurate and worth preserving. It is also certain that this diversity was to the advantage of those girls lucky enough to remain in education for a considerable length of time. O'Connor was correct to identify that the French influence was a marked feature of Irish convent (and therefore Catholic) education, though as Christina de Bellaigue has demonstrated, this was the case across the various denominations in Britain also.[26] Nineteenth-century ideals of domestic femininity at all times informed educational practices although it is foolish to generalize or stereotype across different societies and schools. Imbibed notions of femininity will have differed from region to region, from school to school and from teacher to teacher.

The European model of convent education arrived directly in Ireland, from Paris, with the Ursulines in 1771. This French branch founded a school in Cork at the urging of the pioneering Irish nun Honora 'Nano' Nagle (1718–84), founder of the Presentation Sisters. The Ursulines, originally founded in Brescia, later set up schools at Thurles (1787), Waterford (1816), and Sligo (1826). The second influx of French orders began with the appearance of the Sacred Heart order in Roscrea in 1842.[27] From the 1840s to the 1870s the foundation of convents by 'foreign' orders hit a peak, with orders such as the Faithful Companions of Jesus, the Sisters of St Louis and St Joseph of Cluny all establishing Irish roots in this period. So great was the French influence that out of sixty-two convent boarding schools founded in Ireland in the nineteenth century, just six were run by Irish orders.[28] Ireland provided the promise of plentiful English-speaking postulants. Blackrock College, run by the French Holy Ghost Fathers, had originally been founded with a view to providing raw material for the society's missions in West Africa. So too did the female orders recognize that the English-speaking and largely Catholic Irish offered a concentration of potential postulants that would be of vital importance to them as they sought to expand into North America and Australia under the aegis of the British Empire. Madeleine Sophie Barat, foundress of the prestigious Society of the Sacred Heart, revealed as much in private correspondence in 1842. When weighing the merits of prospective sites in both Ireland and in England, Barat showed that the internalization of Irish Catholics as socially inferior but vocationally useful had travelled far. She thought the English location would be more acceptable 'as far as pupils are concerned. As for postulants, we would attract many more in Ireland!'[29] Just as important as the volume of postulants available was their willingness and predisposition to travel. The ambiguous position of Irish Catholics in relation to the British Empire can be easily seen in this situation. Though part of the British Empire and as likely as any to profit by it, Irish families could just as readily be called upon to assist in the Imperial mission of their

---

[26] De Bellaigue, *Educating Women*, 200–30.
[27] Mercedes Lillis, *Two Hundred Years Agrowing: The Story of the Ursulines in Thurles 1787–1987* (Thurles, 1987).
[28] O'Connor, 'Influences', 85.
[29] Phil Kilroy, *Madeleine Sophie Barat 1779–1865: A Life* (Cork, 2000), 343.

Church.[30] Nor was it simply the French orders that were expanding. The Loreto sisters had opened up a convent school in Ranchi in 1890, about which their Irish school magazines wrote rapturously.[31] The Brigidine sisters, originally a product of the diocese of Kildare and Leighlin, had travelled a great deal from Carlow and Laois by 1883 when they had set up the first of their several Antipodean convents at Coonamble in New South Wales.

For those who chose to stay at home in the nineteenth century the most prestigious schools were those of the Loreto, Ursuline, and Sacred Heart orders, with the Faithful Companions of Jesus at Laurel Hill in Limerick thought to be an acceptable alternative. Of the Irish convents that were considered high-profile educators at home in the nineteenth century the most in-depth work has been done by Máire M. Kealy, OP, who has researched the Dominicans between 1820 and 1930. In an important comparative analysis of the backgrounds of the girls at three separate schools (the Sacred Heart, Mount Anville; the Dominican Convent, Sion Hill, Dublin; and the Dominican Convent, Taylor's Hill, Galway) Kealy found that the distribution of the girls' father's occupations ranged from pawnbroker to Member of Parliament between 1850 and 1912.[32] This was a greater diversity of social background than was typical at schools such as Clongowes Wood or Castleknock, and Irish convent schools were in general considered to have been more déclassé than their high-profile male equivalents for that very reason. A rare outbreak of public debate on the matter in the *Freeman's Journal* saw a long-running series of letters to the editors under the banner 'Our Girls' early in 1883. The concern and sense of ownership implied in the title was justified. The main participants were parents and proprietors of convent schools who were stung by criticism of their work. Answering an initial charge early in 1883 that convents were not bearing in mind the need for 'their girls' to pay their own way in life, Sister M. Francis Clare from St Joseph's Convent in Knock went on the offensive. 'What inducement have they had…?', she asked, 'to induce people to work you must give them a motive or opportunity'.[33] The stress of the labour market, or lack thereof, meant that lower-status convents such as St Josephs retained their dual purpose of preparing for either domestic or public service.

Higher-class convents had even less scope for diversity, with inter-class mobility generally considered acceptable only if accompanied by an upward trajectory. When the Catholic schools were denounced again by the *Freeman's Journal* as 'deficient' in the wake of the intermediate education results in September of 1883 a

---

[30] For more on this relationship see recent work by Oliver P. Rafferty, 'The Catholic Church, Ireland and the British Empire, 1800–1921', *Historical Research*, 84 (2011), 288–309; Rosa McGinley, 'Irish Women Religious and their Convent High Schools in Nineteenth Century Australia', *Australasian Catholic Record*, 87/1 (Jan. 2010), 3–19.

[31] See 'Notes', *Loreto Magazine* (Midsummer 1896), 75. Available at the Loreto Central Archives, Dublin.

[32] Maire M. Kealy, OP, *Dominican Education in Ireland 1820–1930* (Dublin, 2007), 73.

[33] Sister M. Francis Clare 'The Training of Girls', *Freeman's Journal*, 10 Jan. 1883. This appears to have been Sister Mary Francis Clare (Margaret Cusack) better known as 'the Nun of Kenmare'—a convert, and prolific writer and historian who left Knock the following year, and eventually left the religious life.

flurry of correspondence followed, much of it from parents defending the decision to school their daughters in England by denigrating Irish schools. 'A girl is not turned out of the average Irish school, say at seventeen or eighteen, fit to take her place in modern society', one parent fumed, supporting their argument with caustic asides about a well-known Irish convent school in which 'a dish full of water is brought round after dinner into which each girl dips her knife and fork and dries them on the table napkin'. Such allegations of barbarity were both rejected and corroborated by subsequent correspondents, which included among them a professor in the Catholic university, James Kavanagh, and a host of former pupils, parents, and female religious. One lady who had spent eleven years in two of the most 'highly regarded' Irish convent schools recorded that she had often 'felt painfully conscious' of her own deficiencies when compared to those with a secular education.[34] Another thought the convents played a central role in making Irish girls 'the brightest, the truest, the holiest maidens on the face of God's earth'. The debate lasted for several weeks, and not before counter-allegations surfaced about the rather suspect motivations of some sending their girls to England. One correspondent pointed to a desire for an 'English accent or English "polish"' as the deciding factor.[35] Throughout the debate Continental education practices were invoked as an arbiter of either good or bad practice, though this issue never rose ire in the way that attendance at either English or secular schools could.

III ELITE IRISH GIRLS IN ENGLAND 1850–1900

Labouring under penal restriction, the history of English Catholic education for girls was necessarily Continental in the seventeenth and eighteenth centuries. The only British convent in continuous existence since the seventeenth century was one founded in York in 1686 by Mary Ward, foundress of the Institute of the Blessed Virgin Mary. The instability of the last decade of the eighteenth century meant that many of the Continental foundations drifted back to their spiritual home in Britain, renewing the dormant convent tradition. As the nineteenth century wore on the number of new foundations grew steadily, particularly from 1830 with the arrival of what are known as the 'modern orders', most of which were 'simple-vowed, active religious congregations'.[36] The acceleration of foundations was dramatic, as it was all over Catholic Europe. There were just 24 convents in England and Wales in 1801, but anything up to 596 convents by 1900.[37] The

---

[34] An Irish Parent, 'Our Girls', *Freeman's Journal*, 18 Sep. 1883; A. C., 'Our Girls', *Freeman's Journal*, 19 Sep. 1883.

[35] D. J. V., 'Our Girls', *Freeman's Journal*, 11 Oct. 1883; W. O'Malley, 'Our Girls', *Freeman's Journal*, 20 Sep. 1883.

[36] Carmen M. Mangion, *Contested Identities: Catholic Women Religious in Nineteenth-century England and Wales* (Manchester, 2008), 36.

[37] Mangion, *Contested Identities*, 36. This figure is a contested one, but the latest estimate is used here. Barbara Walsh previously estimated there were 469 convents by 1897. See Barbara Walsh, *Roman Catholic Nuns in England and Wales 1800–1937: A Social History* (Dublin, 2002), 177.

impact of Irish-born women in these congregations has been acknowledged by the major studies in the area. Carmen M. Mangion notes that almost as many Irish women as English joined these congregations between 1840 and 1900, with the percentage remaining between 35 and 50 per cent in that period.[38] The distribution of social status both within the hierarchy of female religious orders and within the convents themselves can be difficult to decipher. Barbara Walsh points out that many Irish women faced discrimination within various English and Welsh convents, and that it was commonplace for them to be relegated to low-status, non-leadership roles due to their ethnicity. This feature of conventual life was recently corroborated by S. Karly Kehoe in relation to Scottish convents in the same period.[39] This discrimination certainly reflected a general anti-Irish bias in mid- to late-Victorian Britain, now widely accepted, though it is important to note that if an Irish girl was from a wealthy enough background it seems that she was unlikely to face such discrimination—something that would reinforce the apparent lack of retardation in the careers of boys of the same class discussed earlier.

We lack precise figures or even estimates for the total number of Irish girls being schooled in England between 1850 and 1900. Convent schooling in England was a source of much concern to many Protestant groups, particularly as the availability of it increased in mid century. In a mirror image of the Catholic reaction to Protestant evangelism among the poor of Connacht, we can see Protestant opinion rallying to decry the provision of cheap Catholic education in English cities and its potential negative effect on the Protestant urban poor. The foundation of the Protestant Alliance in 1851 brought about a greater degree of organization to these protests, and the frequent (and frequently ridiculous) parliamentary outbursts of an anti-convent conservative MP, Charles Newdegate, lent them a great deal more publicity.[40] Newdegate was successful enough in his scaremongering to convince the Parliament to allow him to form an investigative committee in 1870 with which to investigate the murky truths behind convent walls, although he found little enough there to detain him.[41]

The bulk of this animosity was not aimed at elite boarding schools, but rather orders that were more likely to take in second-generation Irish or recent and dowry-less immigrant Irish. In the nineteenth century St Mary's Priory at Princethorpe, Warwickshire, was a popular choice for wealthy Catholics.[42] This was a community of Benedictine nuns whose school had endured a nomadic

[38]   Mangion, *Contested Identities*, 193.

[39]   Walsh, *Roman Catholic Nuns*, 142; S. Karly Kehoe, *Creating a Scottish Church: Catholicism, Gender and Ethnicity in Nineteenth-century Scotland* (Manchester, 2010), 97.

[40]   For more on the anti-convent movement see Rene M. Kollar, 'Foreign and Catholic: A Plea to Protestant Parents on the Dangers of Convent Education in Victorian England', *History Of Education*, 31/4 (Jul. 2002), 335–50.

[41]   For more on Newdegate see Walter L. Arnstein, *Protestant versus Catholic in Mid-Victorian Britain: Mr Newdegate and the Nuns* (Colombia, MO, 1982).

[42]   Jacinta Prunty noted that as 'citizens of substance' the Waterford-based parents of Margaret Aylward (1810–89), foundress of the Irish Sisters of Charity, chose to send one daughter to the Ursulines in Thurles and another to Princethorpe. Her brothers attended Stonyhurst and Clongowes respectively. Jacinta Prunty, *Margaret Aylward: Lady of Charity, Sister of Faith* (Dublin, 1999), 14.

existence beginning in Montmartre in 1630 and ending up in Warwickshire via extended stays at Wigan and London. Various English orders of nuns underwent similar transnational migration in the seventeenth and eighteenth century, with the Benedictine orders at Ghent, Cambrai, Paris, Dunkirk, and Brussels all transferring back to England as a result of the French 'terror' of 1794–5, and the repeal of the penal laws.[43] Irish nuns were to be found also at the various Augustinian communities at Leuven, Paris, and Bruges. Bridget Fitzherbert professed with the Carmelites at Antwerp in 1699, aged eighteen, and Eleanor and Cecily Dillon, two daughters of Sir Theobald Dillon, 1st Viscount Dillon of Costello-Gallen in Sligo, could be found with the English Poor Clares at Dunkirk in the 1620s.[44] They returned home to found the Poor Clares in Ireland, proving again that English and Irish orders of nuns owe much to one another and to their Continental period of coexistence and cooperation.

Convents such as Princethorpe had an international reach. In 1902 a Catholic convent school in Nainital, in the northern province of Uttrinchal in India, was addressed by a former Princethorpe pupil, Lady Henrietta MacDonnell, the Scottish-born wife of Sir Antony Patrick MacDonnell. Sir Antony was the Irish-born lieutenant governor of the United Provinces of Agra and Oudh at the time and had already filled some of the most important civil service positions in India with distinction before returning to the more lowly position of under-secretary for Ireland in 1902 at the request of Edward VII.[45] MacDonnell seemed a curiosity, a conservative choice despite being a Liberal, a Catholic and a nationalist, if not exactly a radical one. Just before taking up his Irish appointment MacDonnell's suitability was explained by Lord George Hamilton in a letter to the viceroy of India, George Curzon. Despite his being a 'Catholic and a nationalist', Hamilton explained, he was also a landlord who was 'known to have a very strong opinion as to the necessity of asserting authority and the law'.[46] As a Queen's College-educated Irish Catholic MacDonnell perfectly fitted the archetype of the successful middle-class Indian Civil Service Catholic of consequence in India, his relatively unassuming origins betrayed by the status of his secondary schooling at the diocesan foundation of Summerhill College in Athlone, a school largely ignored in Irish history which later migrated to Sligo in the 1880s.[47] His wife had schooled at an altogether higher level. Describing the beautiful red-brick Warwickian splendour of her own school, St Mary's in Princethorpe, Lady Henrietta reminded her

[43] Dom Denis Agius, 'Benedictines under the Terror 1794–95', English Benedictine Congregation History Commission (Symposium, 1982), <http://wwtn.history.qmul.ac.uk/>.

[44] For more on Eleanor see Judy Barry and Terry Clavin, 'Eleanor Mary Dillon (*c*.1601–1629)', *DIB*. Many more examples of Irish nuns on the Continent are now available through the database constructed by the 'Who Were the Nuns?' project at Queen Mary, University of London, <http://www.history.qmul.ac.uk/wwtn/index.html>.

[45] Barry Crosbie, *Irish Imperial Networks: Migration, Social Communication and Exchange in Nineteenth-century India* (Cambridge, 2012), 225.

[46] Quoted in M. L. Brillman, 'A Crucial Administrative Interlude: Sir Antony MacDonnell's Return to Ireland, 1902–04', *New Hibernia Review*, 9/2 (2005), 69.

[47] For more on Anthony MacDonnell see a discussion of his time in India in Crosbie, *Irish Imperial Networks*, 225–52; Patrick Maume, 'MacDonnell, Antony Patrick (1844–1925)', *DIB*.

listeners that hundreds of English girls had enjoyed a happy childhood or youth within those convent walls. 'These girls have grown up to be women and have been scattered all through our vast Empire', she continued, 'but wherever they have gone, they have carried with them the cherished memory of their convent home.'[48] This reinforcement of imperial legitimacy was as much the work of women such as Lady MacDonnell as it was their husbands.

Another big draw for Irish girls were the schools of the Sacred Heart order, a branch of which had opened in Ireland at Roscrea in 1842 and in Mount Anville in 1853. Most popular among the English foundations in this period was the school at Roehampton, near Richmond Park in south-west London, which had moved there from a former site at Berrymead in London in 1850. Irish girls were also to be found at the Sacred Heart School in Hove, Sussex, which opened in 1872, but Roehampton remained one of the most popular. Esther Grehan, née Chichester, daughter of Col. Charles Raleigh Chichester (Stonyhurst: 1845) attended the school in the 1870s and sent all four of her daughters there some thirty years later. Esther had married a wealthy Steven Grehan, son of George Grehan (a land-owner in Cork, with over 7,000 acres in Clonmeen, near Kanturk) who was a close friend of Abbot Cuthbert Butler of Downside Abbey. Their son Steven attended the Oratory School at Birmingham, and, completing this neat picture of elite insularity, the architect of their remodelled house in 1883 was George Ashlin, a Stonyhurst old boy.[49]

IV ST LEONARDS AND 'INTERNATIONAL' EDUCATION

Most notable of all the English options was the Holy Child Convent near Hastings on the south coast of England at St Leonards-on-Sea. Founded by a charismatic American convert, Cornelia Connelly, in 1846–8, this school was run by her order of nuns, the Society of the Holy Child Jesus (SHCJ). Holy Child later capital-ized on this Irish popularity in the same way the Benedictine monks had, by set-ting up an Irish house in the twentieth century in Killiney, south Co. Dublin. St Leonards was, in fact, comparable in every way to the English boys' schools examined earlier, and exhibited the same features of high-status education com-bined with a diverse international student body. Under Connolly the SHCJ was to acquire a lustre that it has not yet lost, and it became a high-status brand in much the same way (and at much the same time) as the Oratory School had under Cardinal Henry Newman. The popularity of SHCJ education in Ireland was firmly registered in 1929, when it was decided that the Irish old girls would set up an equivalent branch of the 'Holy Child Association', a group which involved

---

[48] 'An Excellent Maiden Speech', *The Irish Monthly*, 30/346 (Apr. 1902), 223–6.

[49] My thanks to Maeve O'Riordan for this information on Esther Grehan. For more see The Grehan Estate Collection, University College Cork Archives, 5.4/845.

Table 5.1 Number of Irish girls attending St Leonards, 1860–1900

	1860–9	1870–9	1880–9	1890–9
St Leonards (203)	21	64	68	50
Total in School (925)	169	208	282	266

itself in fundraising for various worthy causes. Seventy Irish old girls of the various Holy Child Schools were present, with the St Leonards past pupils the most prominent. St Leonards graduates such as Lady Chance, Mrs John Leonard, and Madeleine Maxwell were the controlling figures. The register at the school at St Leonards-on-Sea shows that throughout the nineteenth century this school was a considerable draw for Irish parents (Table 5.1), perhaps following the example of the future Countess of Kenmare who had attended the school in 1856 as sixteen-year-old Gertrude Harriet Thynne, daughter of Lord Charles Thynne, Canon of Canterbury. Whether or not the success of Gertrude Thynne's marriage match boosted attendance at St Leonards can only be guessed, though the schools' registers confirm that Irish enrolment increased substantially following her marriage in 1858. Furthermore she may have acted as a direct influence in some cases. The Ryans of Temple Mungret are believed to have sent their daughters to the school on her advice in 1868.[50]

The school itself had only begun to expand in 1856–7, the year in which Gertrude Thynne arrived. Cornelia Connelly (1809–79) had established it as a school for the upper classes in 1847 but her subsequent travails made her one of the most celebrated curiosities in the Catholic religious world during her lifetime. A convert, Connelly had dissolved her marriage (which had borne five children) to Pierce Connelly, formerly an Episcopal priest, in 1843 by petition to Pope Gregory XVI. Their dual conversion to Catholicism and consequent dissolution of their marriage and dissemination of their offspring was unusual enough until Pierce—a particularly volatile character—reneged on his conversion and sued his wife, who was a forty-year-old nun by this point, for restoration of conjugal rights in 1849. The sensational two-year trial ensured international press coverage and though the case was eventually dropped the stress and notoriety of these years appears to have only stunted the growth of her convent at St Leonards in the ten years between 1846 and 1856 as it thrived thereafter.[51] Emily Patmore—daughter of the poet Coventry Patmore—attended the school in the late 1860s and later became Sister Mary Christina, SHCJ. Her biographer alluded to the controversial, near-scandalous reputation of the foundress, which

[50] This intriguing detail is recorded in M. M. Xavier Gwynn, *From Hunting Field to Cloister* (Dublin, 1946), 11.

[51] See Judith Lancaster, SHCJ, *Cornelia Connelly and her Interpreters* (Oxford, 2004); Juliana Wadham, *The Case of Cornelia Connelly* (London, 1958); D. G. Paz, *The Priesthoods and Apostasies of Pierce Connelly: A Study of Victorian Conversion and Anticatholicism* (Lewiston, NY, 1986); Robert Ombres, OP, 'Connelly v Connelly (1851): The Trials of A Saint?', *Ecclesiastical Law Journal*, 8/36 (Jan. 2005), 21–31.

Figure 5.1 St Leonards pupils—winter recreation, *c.*1860s

nonetheless did nothing to detract from the growth of an order that had already by then become global in its reach, with ten convents up and running across Britain and the United States.[52]

The school at St Leonards-on-Sea (Figures 5.1 and 5.2) was immediately set apart from its competitors by its thorough education, based on a 'simple English spirit' of honour and trust rather than the surveillance culture at other Catholic institutions. It incorporated a teacher-training college as well, and the progressive education there has been the subject of several major works.[53] This more modern character put it in line with the leading Protestant schools, which was perhaps to be expected of an American convert with an Episcopalian background. The school day began at 6 a.m. and terminated around 8 p.m. Girls studied Latin, Italian, and French alongside the 'usual English subjects', and needlework, gymnastics, music, and drawing as standard. Extras included classes in ornamental printing, handwriting, and even paper-flower making. Their uniform consisted of a pale-blue tunic, with

[52] She attended the school against her stepmother's wishes and returned to join the order before dying at the age of twenty-nine. See *A Daughter of Coventry Patmore: Sister Mary Christina S.H.C.J* (London, 1924), 68.

[53] Roseanne McDougall, *Cornelia Connelly's Innovations in Female Education, 1846–1864: Revolutionizing the School Curriculum for Girls* (Lewistown, NY, 2008); John Marmion, 'Cornelia Connelly's Work in Education 1848–79', 2 vols. (PhD, University of Manchester, 1984).

Figure 5.2 Sodality of the Enfants des Anges, date unknown

a blue silk cord and tassels for waistband, worn over a white dress.[54] Daisy Burke, later Elizabeth, Countess of Fingall, remembered a warm and friendly school with an 'atmosphere' that she had loved. In her 1937 memoir she recalled entering the school in the early 1880s at the height of the land agitation and staying for over a year to be 'finished'.[55] She had spent much of the previous decade living in France at St Servan in Brittany with her mother, while her father tended to the 2,759-acre Burke estate at Danesfield in Co. Galway.

The precise breakdown at the school suggests a similar pattern of attendance as Irish boys at schools such as Stonyhurst, albeit with a more localized catchment area in Ireland. The percentage of students from outside the country in the period was equally pronounced, with nineteen different nationalities represented. Not all of these were ex-pat children of those working in the colonies, though this was certainly the case for those who hailed from more exotic locations such as South Africa, Demerara, India, and Mexico. A total of 925 girls attended the school between 1860 and 1899. Of these the greatest number of non-British or Irish students came from America (eighteen), India (twenty-three), France (twenty-three), the Caribbean (twenty-two), and Spain (fifteen). This 'foreign' contingent totalled 154, 17 per cent of girls, still less than the total number of Irish girls, which was

---

[54] See Anon., 'The Next Ten Years, 1850–1860—The School', *Old St Leonards Part 1*, unpublished MSS, Society of the Holy Child Jesus Archives, 53–60.
[55] Elizabeth, Countess of Fingall, *Seventy Years Young*, 43.

203 (22 per cent) and yet enough to dapple the demographics and prevent the school being divided into Irish and English blocs.

Most of the girls, therefore, were either English or Irish, with just two girls from Wales and one from Scotland. Marmion suggest that St Leonards was an example of a 'creative blend of the three sections of the Catholic community which was not to be found in the country at large', but this seems to ignore the fact that the girls came from near-identical backgrounds and social class and it is not clear what he means by three communities.[56] It can instead be suggested that this shared social class and socialization was the main reason for their easy cohabitation at St Leonards and that these Catholics are in no way comparable to the mixing of British and Irish Catholics in the tenement slums of Glasgow or Liverpool, for example. The registers at the school are quite detailed—with biographical information on almost exactly half of all girls that attended the school from 1856, so 570 out of 1,069.[57] Of those girls, 146 (26 per cent) joined religious orders and 374 (66 per cent) of them were recorded as having later married. Of the latter group at least thirty-five married men in the nobility. In this period, the future Ladies Dingle, Howard, Remington, O'Connell, Mostyn, and Young were all educated at the school, along with Marchioness de Stacpoole and the Countesses of Fingall, Granard, and Bantry. Such high-profile matches boosted the reputation of the school and the renown of its founder. It should not be imagined that these girls were marrying up the social scale. In fact such a trajectory was unlikely. The Countess of Granard, the second wife of the convert 7th Earl of Granard, was, after all, the daughter of the 12th Baron Petre and his wife, Mary Teresa Clifford, both prominent elite Catholic families in England.

The distribution of religious devotion is equally interesting. The initial statistic is that more than double the number of girls joined religious orders when we compare the St Leonards group to a school such as Downside or Stonyhurst. Unlike the boys' schools, however, it would appear that the girls attending St Leonards were more adventurous in their subsequent choices and often departed from the order that had educated them. Nevertheless the largest proportion with a vocation chose to pursue it with the SHCJ, though at 45 per cent (sixty-six) this was far from the only order considered. The other major draws were the Poor Clares (nine), the Sisters of Mercy (seven), the Sisters of Charity (ten) and the Sacred Heart (eleven). In all, over twenty-five different orders were represented in the options taken by graduates of St Leonards, and it appears to be beyond doubt that more Irish female religious returned home than did Irish male religious. Their motivation for choosing the religious life may only be guessed at, but it seems likely that the financial strain of dowries may have stunted marriage rates among the upper middle class and gentry, and in general women from this class were less likely to marry in this period than women from lower socio-economic categories.[58] Something of the religious culture or character of the school can be gleaned from a poem submitted

---

[56] Marmion, 'Cornelia Connelly's Work in Education 1848–79', I, 400.

[57] For the purposes of the Irish attendance the figure of 1,069 has been reduced to the 925 between 1860 and 1900.

[58] Timothy Guinnane, *The Vanishing Irish*, 204.

to *The Irish Monthly* by a past pupil in 1888, signed by Katherine M. Grey—presumably a pseudonym as she does not appear in the register. The author, who has surely rejoined the real world and has perhaps married, rhapsodizes St Leonards as the 'stately convent by the sea', but it is the final stanza that captures something of the religious devotionalism of the day, and of the school:

> Oh, stately convent, standing by the sea
> In dreamland I revisit each fair scene,
> And sadly think of all that might have been,
> And to thy saints of sweet and gracious mien,
> In heartfelt pleading, murmur 'Pray for me'.[59]

The girls who entered the order appear to have had the same chances and opportunities as any other. Sisters Eugénie and Bertha Ryan of Limerick, subjects of a biography by M. M. Xavier Gwynn, offer a gripping example of the type of choices that were possible, if not always probable. Before joining her sister Eugénie as a member of the SHCJ, Bertha had accompanied her sister Rosetta on a three-year trip around the world. Rosetta had been advised to spend three years in Australia on medical grounds and set off in January 1882 at just twenty-one years of age chaperoned by a sister two years her junior. While away on convalescence Rosetta fell in love and became engaged to a young gold-miner, Kenneth Hutchinson, in Queensland before ill-health necessitated another move, this time to California where her condition worsened. She returned to Queensland where she died in October 1884. Having managed to corral both herself and an invalid sister on a two-year trip around the world Bertha then had to circumvent a late proposal of marriage from Rosetta's bereft fiancé.[60] She returned home and entered the SHCJ in 1885–6, by which time if she was fleeing from the world it was at least one which she had seen plenty of.

The Irish girls in attendance were of a consistently high social level. The rate of attendance peaked in the 1870s, with 31 per cent of the girls attending in that period Irish-born. Thereafter the percentage declines to 24 per cent in the 1880s and 19 per cent in the last decade. This may reflect the increased competitiveness of the Irish convent schools, whose participation in the intermediate examinations began in earnest towards the end of the century. The geographical background reflects regional clusters, but largely conforms to the pattern of elite boys' education. With an address given for 94 per cent (191) of the Irish girls this pattern is clear (Map 5.1). The majority of girls gave home addresses in either Munster or Leinster, with the largest concentration in Dublin, seventy-eight girls (41 per cent) in total. Again we see Ulster close to absent from the rolls with just five girls attending the school from that province between 1860 and 1900.

The Dublin addresses closely match those of boys attending schools such as Stonyhurst or Downside. Before joining the SHJC Mother Mary Delores (Maria

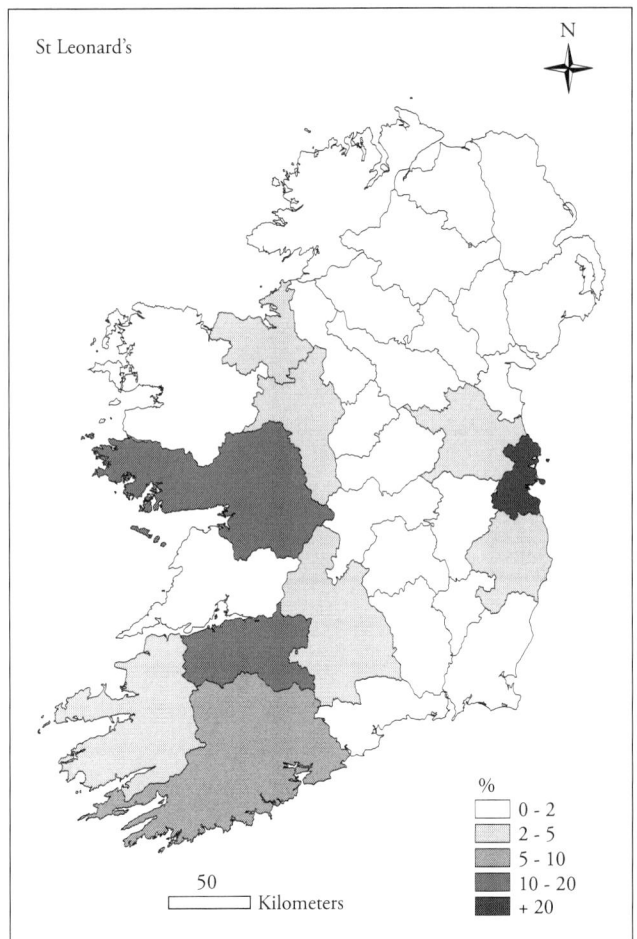

Map 5.1 Irish girls at St Leonards 1860–99 by county of origin, 1860–99

Kirwan) grew up on one of Ireland's most exclusive streets, at 29 Ailesbury Road, Dublin. Her classmate in 1886, Barbara Netterville, grew up in a Georgian townhouse at 12 Herbert St, off Baggot St Lower in what is now Dublin 4. Barbara had prepped for St Leonards at an Irish-founded French convent called the Institute of the Assumption, in Cannes, and was a daughter of Captain Joshua McEvoy Netterville and Mary Netterville.[61] While Maria could, through the selection of a socially exclusive order, look forward to a life led in the company of women of her own class Barbara made her way on the marriage market. Here her education

---

[61] For more on the Irish co-foundress of the Institute see Virginia M. Crawford, 'The Institute of the Assumption: Its Centenary and Its Co-foundress Catherine O'Neill', *Studies: An Irish Quarterly Review*, 28/110 (Jun. 1939), 303–13. For more on the Nettervilles see David Synnott, 'Marcella Gerrard's Estate', *Journal of the Galway Archaeological and Historical Society*, 57 (2005), 38–64.

Figure 5.3 St Leonards group, *c.*1888

and breeding proved an asset and she married a young Dublin barrister from Glenageary, Nicholas Joseph Synnott, in 1891. Synnott was a future Governor of the Bank of Ireland, High Sheriff of Kildare (1906), director of the Great Southern Railway, and president of the Stonyhurst Association, where he had schooled in the late 1860s.[62] The transnational carousel of Irish education had resulted, on this occasion, in desirable lives spent within the correct social circle. Both choices had kept these classmates in the comfort akin to that in which they were reared.

Figure 5.3 shows a St Leonards group *c.*1888, along with several young boys in the front rows, of whom there is no record of attendance at the school. The photograph is of a confirmation group, most of whom arrived at the school between 1885 and 1886 and are displaying their medals proudly. It shows the uniforms worn on special occasions by the girls, and the habit of the Holy Child community. There are forty-seven students identified as St Leonards girls, along with three members of the community—Mother St Stephen, Mother Mary Theresa, and Mother Mary Paul. Of the girls, thirteen (28 per cent) can positively be identified as Irish, and without proof we can only suppose that Nora Fitzgerald and Teresita Cannon are also Irish.

---

[62] See also 'Obituary: Mr Nicholas J. Synnott', *Irish Times*, 16 Aug. 1920.

Table 5.2 Irish girls at St Leonards by age on entry, 1860–1900

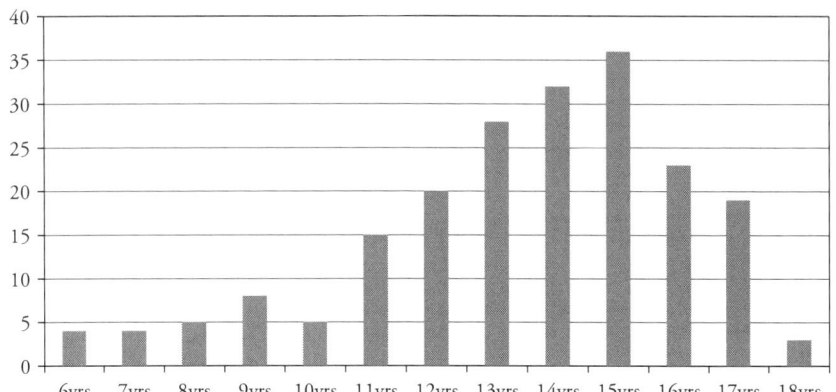

With over 200 Irish girls at St Leonards alone, and with some evidence there to suggest that there were considerable numbers of wealthy Irish girls attending convents at Roehampton and Princethorpe, the picture that emerges is of a strategic migration of girls from Irish Catholic elite families in numbers close to or matching the estimated number of Irish boys travelling to England for an education during the same period.

Table 5.2 shows that most Irish girls entered St Leonards between the ages of twelve and sixteen. The youngest Irish girls on record were just six years old on entry. Many had prepped elsewhere, or had been educated at home by governesses before attending the school. Since the average length of attendance was about two and a half years it would seem that the majority of girls were sent here to be 'finished' in their early to mid teens. Transfers from other convents were more common than home schooling, but as a general rule those from the wealthiest backgrounds were those most likely to have been educated through their early years by a governess. Sisters Alice and Katie Balfe, daughters of Patrick Balfe, a landowner in and former High Sheriff of Roscommon, were home-schooled before arriving at St Leonards at the age of thirteen and fourteen respectively. Their father, with an estate of over 6,000 acres, could presumably afford to educate his daughters as he pleased. Kate Power (St Leonards: 1880) was also home-tutored in salubrious surroundings. A daughter of Lady Olivia Nugent and Patrick Joseph Power, she was born at Woodlands but grew up at Faithlegg House in Waterford after the death of Nicholas Mahon Power in 1873 meant her father inherited that estate. Patrick Power had, at that time, in excess of 5,000 acres and he had commissioned Samuel Ussher Roberts to add another storey and wings to the family seat in a confident display of their permanence at the property.[63] The Faithlegg property

---

[63] Joe Falvey, 'The Story of Faithlegg House', *The Munster Express*, 17 Sep. 2010; 'Samuel Ussher Roberts (1821–1900)', *Dictionary of Irish Architects 1720–1940*, Irish Architectural Archive, <www.dia.ie>.

Figure 5.4 The hounds at Faithlegg House, County Waterford, 1902

had been bought by the Power family in 1819, thereby returning it to Catholic hands after a hiatus of nearly 200 years. The former Catholic occupants were the Cambro-Norman Aylward family who resided there before their Cromwellian resettlement in Leitrim in the mid seventeenth century. Figure 5.4 shows a hunt at Faithlegg House in 1902.

The registers at St Leonards show girls, many of whom were Irish, transferring from convent schools both in Ireland and across Europe. The Irish schools with the most transfers were Sacred Heart Convent at Mount Anville, the Faithful Companions of Jesus Convent at Laurel Hill in Limerick, and the Ursuline Convents in Waterford and Thurles. St Leonards also operated a number of feeder schools in Blackpool and nearby Mayfield, but the most frequent transfers from other schools were usually from the Sacred Heart Convent at Roehampton. Another popular route was to attend New Hall—a particularly beautiful convent at the Palace of Beaulieu in Chelmsford, run by an English community of the Canonesses Regular of the Holy Sepulchre from 1799.[64] Among the most popular Continental schools were the Sacré Coeur, Paris (now the Rodin Museum on Rue de Varenne, Paris), the Ursuline convents at Boulogne and Nice, or the society's

---

[64] The Palace of Beaulieu was once the property of Thomas Boleyn, later 1st Earl of Wiltshire who sold it to Henry VIII *c*.1516.

own schools at Neuilly and in Blumenthal in Germany. This network of schools circulated not only Irish girls, but also the female lines of much of the European Catholic elite.

V IRISH GIRLS AT SCHOOL ON THE CONTINENT 1850–1900

> Would that more Fionnualas come to France and more French Fathers visit Ireland to quicken and strengthen the missionary spirit that is the common heritage of the land of St. Patrick and that of Joan of Arc.[65]
>
> Abbé George Leguay, 1956

A real challenge for historians of nineteenth-century female education will be tracking the sheer variety of Continental convents patronized by Irish Catholic families from the seventeenth century to the middle of the twentieth century. Irish girls were typically schooled in Central and Western Europe, with a particular concentration in the towns of north-eastern France, Belgium, the Netherlands, and across Germany. The story of the most notable and renowned of the Irish establishments on the Continent will never now be told as much of their archival material was destroyed in a fire in 1959. The community of Irish Benedictine nuns at Ypres had a continuous existence in Flanders from their foundation in 1665 until World War I finally forced them out in 1914. Known for most of their existence as *De Iersche Damen* or 'Irish dames of Ypres', the community eventually settled at Kylemore Abbey in Connemara in December 1920, via a short stay at Macmine House in Wexford.[66] These 'Irish dames' educated Irish girls throughout the eighteenth century, and Nano Nagle is believed to have attended the school in her childhood in the late 1720s.[67] Irish girls were by no means restricted to Irish foundations however, and the most prestigious convent schools across Europe were to feel the benefit of their patronage in the nineteenth century. The problem, for most, must have been narrowing down the options.

With their sons at Stonyhurst, James and Anne MacCarthy-Morrogh, mid-sized landowners in Co. Cork, chose a Continental education for their daughters in the 1890s. It is not easy to identify from family correspondence which parent decided to send the girls to the continent. Whoever it was, they seem to have chosen a

---

[65] Fionnuala de Búrca, *Fionnuala in France: Being the Diary of a Sixteen-year-old Girl in a French Convent School* (Dublin, 1956), preface.

[66] Kylemore was originally built by Mitchell Henry, a Manchester-based financier and politician. For more on the Benedictine nuns at Ypres see Patrick Nolan, *The Irish Dames of Ypres: Being a History of the Royal Irish Abbey of Ypres… and Some Account of Irish Jacobitism, with a Portrait of James II and Stuart Letters Hitherto Unpublished* (Dublin, 1908); D.M.C., *The Irish Nuns at Ypres: An Episode of War*, ed. R. B. O'Brien (London, 1915); Kathleen Villiers-Tuthill, 'The Irish Benedictine Nuns from Ypres to Kylemore', in Martin Browne and Colmán Ó Clábaigh (eds), *The Irish Benedictines: A History* (Dublin, 2005), 122–39.

[67] Noreen Gifney, 'Honora "Nano" Nagle (1718–84)', *DIB*.

relatively popular convent school in Brussels in the first instance, sending three of her daughters—Daisy, Annie, and Rita—to the Soeurs de Sainte-Marie in Rue de Constantinople, Brussels in the early 1890s. By 1892, however, Daisy was writing from a different school, this time a boarding school for young ladies at Vallendar, about an hour from Koblenz in western Germany. This German school issued a prospectus in the English language that indicated a basic cost of about £50 per annum 'including all subjects and as special subjects: music and drawing, besides books, stationery, baths and boarding for the vacation'.[68] Daisy's letters to her sisters in Brussels were censored by the nuns for some rather loose references to her roaming the city of Koblenz freely and chatting to officers. Sr Victoria O'Kearny, very probably an Irish nun who had joined the Souers de Sainte-Marie, wrote back to Monsieur MacCarthy-Morrogh on the matter in a gently scolding and rather worried manner:

> You know Daisy was always too fond of plenty of liberty . . . I am so particular for them not to get into these ideas. Notice also what she says about officers talking so to such a young child. In fact, dear Mr MacCarthy Morrogh, you a devoted father shall understand better than anyone else what I mean. I hope Daisy will get sensible, but I fear for her . . . please advise her . . . to write and act as a Miss Morrogh, consequently no more like Daisy. Excuse me dear Mr MacCarthy Morrogh annoying you, but I think it my duty to let you know every thing concerning your dear girls. I even dread the vacation on account of dear Annie and Rita mixing once more with Daisy as I see she has no good influence over them.[69]

The letter reveals both a monitoring of correspondence and a desire to control behaviour that was frequently resented by girls attending such schools. This surveillance culture, objected to by modernizers such as Cornelia Connelly at St Leonards in England, continued to be a feature of older foundations and was something that was read as both a positive and negative feature of convent education by those who went through it. In Mary O'Leary's history of the Sacred Heart order, *Education with a Tradition* (1936), this surveillance and socialization was cast in a positive light as a 'tradition' and reinforced with positive memories from former pupils of the schools at Blumenthal and Rue de Varenne in Paris. For Hannah Lynch memories of having been stripped naked, beaten, and having her letters home censored were all unsettling memories from her time at a convent school.[70] For O'Leary this enforced docility was desirable: she remarked that a 'quietness of speech' distinguished those who had been educated at the Sacré Coeur Convent from other young ladies of the same class.[71]

[68] My thanks to Dr Mike MacCarthy-Morrogh for alerting me to this family correspondence. The originals are retained privately. Anna Wolter to Christine MacCarthy-Morrogh, 12 Sep. 1892, Papers of James MacCarthy Morrogh of Inisbeg, Co. Cork.

[69] Sr Victoria O'Kearny to James MacCarthy Morrogh, 27 Sep. 1892, Papers of James MacCarthy Morrogh of Inisbeg, Co. Cork.

[70] Lynch may well have added to these memories, and seems to have transplanted the French education of her youth to a fictional school called 'Lysterby' near Birmingham. See Lynch, *Autobiography of a Child*, 154, 157, 174.

[71] Mary Florence Margaret O'Leary, *Education with a Tradition: An Account of the Educational Work of the Society of the Sacred Heart* (London, 1936), 184.

The spiritual centre of the Society of the Sacred Heart was at Paris in the convent on Rue de Varenne. The order had been founded by Madeleine Sophie Barat in 1800 and catered for the poor in free parochial schools, but more deliberately made their mission 'the Christian education of young women from the elite' with their high-quality boarding schools.[72] The school at Paris, which competed with the Abbaye aux Bois for local patronage, was later run by an Irish member of the community, Mother Marie-Therese D'Arcy. One historian noted that D'Arcy was brought up in a 'cultured Irish home' and combined 'a deep appreciation of The French tradition in education, sublimated, if one may so put it, by her Irish sense of humour'.[73] With a presence in management and in the student body the Sacred Heart schools accounted for a formidable cross section of the Catholic elite. By far the greatest number of students who transferred to St Leonards in England came from Sacred Heart schools. In addition to the school at Rue de Varenne, several girls had transferred from Sacred Heart schools at Blumenthal, Madrid, Brussels, and Vienna. Emily Cavanagh, of 18 Earlsfort Terrace in Dublin, had attended the Sacré Coeur in Paris in the 1880s before finishing at St Leonards.

We are fortunate to have at least one written account of an Irish girl's time at this Parisian school. The memoir of Countess de la Boissiere, née Matilda O'Kelly of Newtown House, near Abbeyknockmoy in Galway, reveals the path a privileged Irish girl might take through life. Born in 1865 at her father's Dublin residence at 34 Fitzwilliam Square, Matilda O'Kelly spent most of her childhood socializing with Galway's wealthiest Catholic families, most of whom are carefully name-checked in her memoir.[74] Closest to the family were the Redingtons of Kilcronan, the Dalys of Raford, the Bodkin family of Annagh, and the Roches of Rye Hill—all landholding families with extensive estates, many of whom sent their boys to English schools. As a young girl Matilda was taught by four different governesses, two English, one Irish, and one German. Even the chambermaid at Newtown was exotic: a Spanish 'beauty' who sang the Basque song *Gastibelza* around the house as she worked. The second governess, a Miss Collins, was a former pupil of St Leonards and taught Matilda and her sister Alice to draw and to play piano, along with the more mundane lessons on geography, history, and composition. The girls did not, however, take to their 'peevish and ugly' German governess, or her 'stupid strictness'.[75] Following their home schooling the sisters were sent to Sacré Coeur, Rue de Varenne in 1880–1, where one of the nuns recognized Matilda's name, her aunt having attended the same school in 1840. Returning to Dublin aged sixteen in the winter of 1881 Matilda completed her education by

---

[72] Rogers, *From the Salon to the Schoolroom*, 57.

[73] O'Leary, *Education with a Tradition*, 243.

[74] Her father was Charles Kelly (as with many Catholic families, the 'O' may have been dropped at some point for reasons of expedience or fashion), owner of more than 2,000 acres in east Galway and a member of the Kildare Street, St Stephen's Green, and University clubs in the 1870s. He was also a QC, having been called to the bar in 1839, and had an MA from the University of Dublin.

[75] A copy of this remarkable memoir is available in the libraries of both NUI Galway and Trinity College Dublin. See Jacques Dumont de Montroy (ed.), *Memoirs of the Countess Turquet de la Boissiere (née Matilda O'Kelly of Newtown), 1865–1956* (Paris, 1969), 2–3, 11–19.

attending some lectures by Dr Carmichael at Alexandra College.[76] She was still in Dublin when the Phoenix Park murders took place in May 1882, an event which particularly affected her family as Thomas Burke, the permanent under-secretary of Ireland who was assassinated in the park alongside Lord Frederick Cavendish, was a relative. The winter of 1883 was spent at the resort town of Pau, on the northern edge of the Pyrenees in France, where she socialized with the Princesses of Schleswig-Holstein and Ourusoff and many others at the salon of Mlle de Castelbajac. Pau had long been popular with British and Irish tourists and while there Matilda met prominent Irish gentry such as Lord Howth, Sir Robert and Lady Shaw, Lady Kilmaine, and her sister-in-law Isabella, Lady Beaumont.

Throughout the memoir a careful record is kept of the marriages and lives made by her female companions throughout her childhood and early adulthood. Frequent reference is made to the physical characteristics and social etiquette of her peers, reinforcing our perception that the marriage market provided much entertainment to those who found themselves outside of it by accident, their own marriage, or design. Social hierarchy was seldom threatened and usually the exceptional marriage proved the rule. In one particularly caustic aside about 'the daughter of a magistrate', who later converted to Protestantism and became Countess of Limerick, Matilda recalled that though the woman in question was beautiful she also had 'a rich Irish brogue'. The Countess herself had been 'presented' aged nineteen in the winter of 1884. The occasion was marked at Dublin Castle (as had happened to Daisy Burke, later Countess of Fingall) by the awkward, bearded kiss of Lord Spencer, then Lord Lieutenant of Ireland. She recalled that she acquitted herself well at the ceremony, and that the training she had received in deportment at the Sacré Coeur Convent in Paris had helped her in her hour of need.[77] Apparently a beauty herself, she remembered being accosted in her eligible phase by Johnny Mahon of Ballydonnelan Castle after he had downed a carafe of wine, by Captain Joyce who had propositioned her in similar circumstances while she visited friends at Monivea Castle, and also recalled Lord Emly running near-naked from his bath every morning of her stay at Tervoe. Her many formal suitors included the educationalist and founder of the Olympics, Baron Pierre de Coubertin.[78]

Though important, the Sacré Coeur Convent at Paris was far from the only draw for Irish girls. The Ursulines at Boulogne and Nice were also attractive to Irish families familiar with their style of education from their eighteenth-century foundations in Ireland. The reasons for schooling a daughter so far away were not always straightforward. In the 1740s George Anne Bellamy—the illegitimate daughter of the 2nd Baron Tyrawley, James O'Hara by a Miss Seal—was educated with the Ursulines at Boulogne at her father's expense. She later became an actress in London, her life the subject of the most entertaining scandal to which

---

[76] Dr Frederick Falkiner Carmichael LLD (1830–1919), Canon of Christchurch Cathedral and a prominent supporter of women's right to vote.

[77] *Memoirs of the Countess Turquet de la Boissiere*, 42.

[78] *Memoirs of the Countess Turquet de la Boissiere*, 31–9. Pierre de Coubertin was educated at the famous Jesuit school at Rue de Madrid in Paris.

she liberally added lustre in her celebrated memoir *An Apology for the Life of George Anne Bellamy*. Remembering the '[d]ear, happy, much-regretted mansion' of her school at Boulogne, perhaps the only real nod to her expensive education was in the impressive prose style she utilized while scandalizing theatrical Dublin and London with her memories of the 5th Baron Byron and Thomas Sheridan.[79]

French education was considered especially attractive for girls, the language and the style adding apparently unquantifiable lustre to the young Irish maidens exposed to it. Irish newspapers often noted the profession of an Irish girl at various Continental establishments. In 1876 the *Freeman's Journal* noted one such profession; that of Mary Frances Downing of Killarney at the English College in Bruges.[80] The hierarchy of status in the Catholic female orders meant that there were opportunities, too, for those from a relatively humble background to access a religious life outside of Britain and her former or current dependencies. De Bellaigue notes that though they shared ideas of feminine domesticity, the institutional models of French and English education for girls were remarkably different in the nineteenth century, with English boarding houses typically much smaller and modelled on the home.[81] For Catholics this difference was less marked, with conventual education enjoying a universality and uniformity that Protestant or secular schooling did not. 'This uniformity of experience leads us to believe that, as with Irish Catholic boys attending English schools, it was the exoticism of schooling elsewhere that led Irish girls to attend Continental colleges. The writer Hannah Lynch, herself a product of a similar education, noted the social hierarchy of convents in *French Life in Town and Country* (1901). Commenting on social distinction within the French convent system she wrote 'there are no greater worshippers at the shrine of birth and fortune than nuns'. This, she maintained, more fairly, was at the behest of the parents. 'The nobles would cry foul if assurance were withheld of perfect social exclusiveness for their offspring', she continued, 'and more angry still would be the sham nobles, the purse-proud snobs, whose selection of a convent for their daughters depends solely upon its fashionable reputation.'[82] Lynch wrote as a critic, but we can detect something of the motivation for Irish girls attending Continental convents in her tirade, however biased and negative it may have been. The acquisition of a better French accent and of a more varied group of friends across many countries made the overseas option more attractive, and French education was seen as the very acme of bourgeois and elite education for not only Irish girls, but

---

[79] George Anne Bellamy, *An Apology for the Life of George Anne Bellamy. Late of Covent Garden Theatre. Written by Herself. To which is annexed her original letter to John Calcraft, Esq. Advertised to be published in Oct. 1767, but which was then violently suppressed*, 5 vols. (1786), I, Letter III, 29. The memoir ran to four editions within a year of publication. For more see Francesca Sagginni, 'Memories Beyond the Pale: The Eighteenth-century Actress Between Stage and Closet', *Restoration and Eighteenth-Century Theatre Research*, 19/1 (Summer 2004), 43–63; Frances Clarke, 'George Anne Bellamy (*c.*1731–1788)', *DIB*; Caroline Breashears, 'The Female Appeal Memoir: Genre and Female Literary Tradition in Eighteenth-Century England', *Modern Philology*, 107/4 (2010), 607–31.

[80] *Freeman's Journal*, 3 Feb. 1876.

[81] Christina de Bellaigue, *Educating Women: Schooling and Identity in England and France 1800–1867* (Oxford, 2007), 232–3.

[82] Hannah Lynch, *French Life in Town and Country*, 2nd edn (New York, 1906), p. 142.

British girls as well. For girls such as Matilda O'Kelly such expensively acquired extras would gild the lily, help to attract a viable match, and perhaps lead to the type of life worth recording in a memoir.

VI CONCLUSION

The impression gained from this brief overview of elite Catholic education for girls is that it was less static than has been previously imagined. Far from simply receiving external ideas from the Continent and from England Irish conventual education had progressive, international origins. The process of developing female education in the nineteenth century was a model of transnational flows, and Irish girls, no strangers to movement, were at the forefront of the greater reach enjoyed by women of means in this period. The abundance of English-speaking raw material helped to attract French orders into Ireland throughout the nineteenth century, ensuring that the debate over women's proper place in the social order were aired in Ireland as elsewhere. It is clear, too, that the importation of governesses into Irish homes, however difficult for a historian to measure, mirrors the flow of wealthy Irish girls to boarding schools and houses in England and on the Continent and forces us to think outside the ternary of Franco-Irish Catholic education and English secular education. Since all three 'systems' were aware of developments within and without, greater attention must be paid to Ireland's place in a European-wide embourgeoisement of female education in the nineteenth century.

6

The Fatted Geese?
Irish Boys at Continental Colleges 1850–1900

The Parish of St Peter in Drogheda is preparing for the annual St Oliver Plunkett Festival of Prayer, which is expected to draw record visitors to the town from all over Ireland, as well as a large group from Lambspringe in Germany. They will be led by the Dean of Alfeld in Lower Saxony, who will give the homily.

The Drogheda Independent, 15 June 2011

The earthly remains of Ireland's most recent saint, Oliver Plunkett (1625–81), lie in two parts at present, inconveniently separated by the Irish Sea. The man was hung, drawn, and quartered in Tyburn in London in 1681, an act which greatly facilitated his eventual bilocation and his head is now regularly on display at St Peter's Church in Drogheda, Co. Louth. It came over from Rome, having been smuggled into the country in a grandfather clock (according to legend) by Hugh MacMahon, later Archbishop of Armagh.[1] The rest of his remains are kept in calm and remote isolation by the Benedictine monks at Downside College, near Bath. The monks at Downside have, perhaps, a greater claim to his head than the Dominican nuns at Drogheda, though there is little enough chance that he will be united any time soon. The remains of the Saint provide us with a telling metaphor for the trans-continental trafficking of Irish and British learning. His body had in fact lain in Lambspringe in central Germany for many years, interred in a remote Benedictine monastery of English foundation in Lower Saxony. Between 1681 and 1881 his quartered remains had been interred in the crypt of this German Abbey, before the Downside monks had him reinterred in their own. He is remembered in Lambspringe at the annual 'OliverPlunkettFest', held on the last Saturday of August, and, less explicably, in the name of the local Kindergarten—Kindertagesstätte St Oliver, Lambspringe.

This chapter seeks to update our present understanding of Irish legacies on the Continent and in particular to investigate the extent to which the celebrated phenomenon of Irish Catholic Continental education had survived into the nineteenth

---

[1] For more on his head see Siobhán Kilfeather, 'Oliver Plunkett's Head', *Textual Practice* 16/2 (2002), 229–48. The head has since been the subject of one major novel, Colin Bateman's *Bring Me the Head of Oliver Plunkett* (2005) and a short film *The Holy Ghost of Oliver* (2011).

century. Providers of Irish Catholic education, like their English and Scottish equivalents, had originally migrated to Europe in order to facilitate the training of priests for an outlawed religion. Many of these colleges that subsequently emerged developed their own hybrid culture over the two centuries of their existence and though few survived the last tumultuous decades of the eighteenth century their role as keepers of the flame for Catholic Ireland has long been acknowledged in Irish historiography and very often conflated with the more mercenary tradition of Irish soldiering on the Continent.

The classic image in Irish historiography and popular culture of the post-1691 mercenary soldiers—'the wild geese'—is an entrenched one. The image of a Jacobite army, 14,000 or so in number, boarding ships at Limerick to go and fight for the highest bidder is a seductive one for those who would mourn the demise of the Jacobite claimant, James II and his descendants. For the next one hundred years or so the Irish enlisted in French, Spanish, and Italian armies, but also fought for Swedish, Polish, and Austrian concerns.[2] This narrative appeals for many reasons, not least for its potential to reinvigorate age-old nationalist themes of exile, suppression, and entitlement. This tradition of Continental service predated 1691, however, and it continued to be a viable option for Irish Catholics until such a time as higher-ranking positions became available in the British army in the late eighteenth century. As a result, the scholarship on the transnational movement of people and ideas has generally focused on the seventeenth and eighteenth centuries, as if it were somehow discontinued after the Act of Union was passed.

We ought to rank alongside this military connection to Catholic Europe both the tradition of trade and the tradition of learning. The cultural implications of extensive trade networks between Ireland and port towns such as Cadiz, Bordeaux, and Nantes have been recently noted by Irish scholars, though these await a thorough exploration.[3] Scholars have been more active in researching the tradition of learning and remembering fostered by the various 'Irish colleges' across Europe, the most famous of which is probably at Leuven in Flanders. The preservation of the Irish language in printed form at Leuven contributed even more to the idea of a Continental 'keeping of the flame' of Gaelic Ireland. The recent work of Jeroen Nilis in researching a prosopogaphy of 1,173 Irish students at Leuven between 1548 and 1797 shows the importance of the Continental *bourse* or *pensionne* to

---

[2] Much work has been done on this phenomenon. For some of the most recent publications connected to *The Irish in Europe Project* at NUI, Maynooth, see Mary Ann Lyons and Thomas O'Connor, *Strangers to Citizens: The Irish in Europe, 1600–1800* (Dublin, 2008); Thomas O'Connor, *The Irish in Europe, 1580–1815* (Dublin, 2001); Mary Ann Lyons and Thomas O'Connor, *Irish Communities in Early-modern Europe* (Dublin, 2006). See also Andrea Knox, '"Women of the Wild Geese": Irish Women, Exile and Identity in Spain, 1750–1775', *Immigrants & Minorities*, 23/2–3 (Jul.-Nov. 2005), 143–59; Nathalie Genet-Rouffiac, *Le Grand Exil: les Jacobites en France, 1688–1715* (Paris, Service Historique de la Défense, 2007). See also David Murphy, *The Irish Brigades 1685–2006* (Dublin, 2007); Charles Ivar McGrath, *Ireland and Empire 1692–1770*, Empires in Perspective (London, 2012).

[3] Ian McBride, *Eighteenth Century Ireland: The Isle of Slaves* (Dublin, 2009), 226; James Livesey, *Civil Society and Empire: Ireland and Scotland in the Eighteenth-century Atlantic World* (New Haven, CT, 2009); Samuel Fannin 'The Irish Community in Eighteenth-century Cadiz', in Mary Ann Lyons and Thomas O'Connor (eds), *Irish Migrants in Europe after Kinsale, 1602–1820* (Dublin, 2003).

Irish Catholic families who could not otherwise have afforded to educate their sons to such a high standard.[4] Such pensions were common at the other Irish colleges and generally worked as fee reductions, or sometimes a very adequate stipend for Irish boys far from home, and were generally distributed according to the historic ecclesiastical divisions in Ireland.[5] This was not the case at Leuven, where 'students were recruited on an all-Ireland basis'. In addition to pursuing theological studies, many of the boys attending Leuven studied medicine and law, and several of them remained on in Spanish Flanders to practice their professions. Such students, Nilis argues, tended to come from families who were connected to the founders of the bursary, and they used the stipend to train as medical and legal professionals as well as becoming highly trained religious prepared to minister to the domestic faithful.[6] In addition to the work of Nilis on Leuven we are fortunate to have detailed lists of those boys attending the Dominican Colleges at Lisbon and Leuven, the Protestant universities in Spanish Flanders 1650–1750, and the many Irish who attended the University of Paris and Toulouse 1573–1792.[7] It seems certain that the nineteenth-century attendance at Continental colleges had become much less pervasive, and for a variety of reasons. Such detailed prosopography on the Irish networks of learning would seem to indicate that just as the Continent had become less welcoming or palatable by then, so too had the global reputation of English education altered Irish educational patterns.

As many as twenty-nine schools were set up specifically for Irish needs on the Continent as early as the late sixteenth century. The Irish colleges were mainly based in Spain, France, and Belgium, with minor foundations at Prague, Lisbon, and elsewhere. Patricia O Connell has contributed three recent institutional histories of the Iberian Irish colleges at Lisbon, Alcalá de Henares and Santiago de Compostela. Her work complements the influential survey of the Irish colleges based in France by T. J. Walsh in the 1970s.[8] These institutional surveys offer little by way of information on the education received at these Continental colleges, which were usually set aside for the education of priests rather than lay Catholics.

---

[4] Jeroen Nilis, 'Irish Students at Leuven University, 1548–1797 (with index)', *Archivium Hibernicum*, 60 (2006–7), 1–304.

[5] For an example of one such subsidized student see the story of James Lyons, who attended the prestigious Collegio Urbano of the Propaganda Fide in Rome in the middle of the eighteenth century. Hugh Fenning, OP, 'The Journey of James Lyons from Rome to Sligo, 1763–65', *Collectanea Hibernica*, 11 (1968), 91–110.

[6] Nilis, 'Irish Students at Leuven University', 11.

[7] The work of Hugh Fenning, in particular, ought to be consulted by anyone with an interest in the Irish on the Continent. Hugh Fenning, OP, 'Irish Dominicans at Louvain before 1700: A Biographical Register', *Collectanea Hibernica*, 43 (2001), 112–60; Hugh Fenning, OP, 'Irish Dominicans at Lisbon before 1700: A Biographical Register', *Collectanea Hibernica*, 42 (2000), 27–65; Esther Mijers, 'Irish Students in the Netherlands, 1650–1750', *Archivium Hibernicum*, 59 (2005), 66–78; L. W. B. Brockliss and Patrick Ferté, 'Prosopography of Irish Clerics in the Universities of Paris and Toulouse, 1573–1792', *Archivium Hibernicum*, 58 (2004), 7–166.

[8] Patricia O'Connell, *The Irish College at Alcalá de Henares, 1649–1785* (Dublin, 1997); Patricia O'Connell, *The Irish College at Lisbon, 1590–1834* (Dublin, 2001); Patricia O'Connell, *The Irish College at Santiago de Compostela, 1605–1769* (Dublin, 2007); T. J. Walsh, *The Irish Continental College Movement: The Colleges at Bordeaux, Toulouse, and Lille* (Dublin, 1973). See also John J. Silke,

It has been estimated that as many as a quarter of all Irish priests were educated in France as late as the first half of the nineteenth century and therefore their importance ought not to be downplayed. Such Irish Continental establishments were usually poor and very often educated no more than ten priests at any one time, the majority of whom were typically at least twenty years old on arrival. By the nineteenth century the already limited impact of much of these institutions had lapsed to the point of near irrelevance. The Collège des Irlandais, or 'Irish College' at Rue des Irlandais and the College Des Lombards remained live concerns, while the continuing relevance of the Irish College in Rome in the nineteenth century is well-documented. In addition to these foundations Irish boys might be found at various schools in the traditionally Catholic areas of northern France and present-day Belgium. There were English colleges at Douai, Rome, Valladolid, and Liège, as well as the Scots College in Paris.[9] These, in addition to the various colleges of the regular orders such as the Jesuits, Dominicans, and Franciscans were the likeliest destinations for Irish boys. The two Parisian colleges, and the Benedictine school at Douai will form the basis for this discussion of the continued Continental tradition.

I IRISH BOYS AT CONTINENTAL COLLEGES

The decline in the numbers of Irish boys schooled in Continental colleges and boarding schools coincided with the French revolutionary period and the related relaxation of the penal laws in Ireland and Britain. The great impact of the revolution and subsequent 'French terror' in the 1790s on Irish students is well documented thanks, in the main, to the prominence of one such boy, Daniel O'Connell. His supposed exposure to violence and bloodshed while studying in Saint Omer and Douai forms an important part of the mythology surrounding his pacifism. It is a measure of his eminence that, writing in 1875, the president of one of those foundations to have educated O'Connell during his time in northern France thought that it might be 'pardonable' for him to point out the formative influence exerted on the Liberator by 'English Catholics on French soil'.[10]

William Martin Murphy, the Jesuit-educated owner of the *Irish Independent* sent his son to the Jesuit college at Stella Matutina in Feldkirch, Austria, in 1893 to finish an intermediate education which had begun in Belvedere and then Clongowes Wood. He later studied medicine at Cambridge.[11] A period spent at preparatory school in France was often a precursor to finishing one's education

---

'The Irish College, Seville', *Archivium Hibernicum*, 24 (1961), 103–47; Jeroen Nilis, 'The Irish College Antwerp', *Clogher Record*, 15/3 (1996), 7–86.

[9] Peter Phillips, 'Replanting Douai in the North of England 1794–1808', *Recusant History*, 29/3 (May 2009), 367–79; Julian Russell, 'The Last Students at the Scots College, Douai', *The Innes Review*, 58/2 (Autumn 2007), 222–5. College Des Lombards was amalgamated with College des Irlandais in 1805.

[10] *Freeman's Journal*, 17 Aug. 1875.

[11] Marie Coleman, 'Murphy, William Lombard (1876–1943)', *DIB*.

in the English public schools. Beaumont graduates Francis Philip Lynch and his brother Edmund Ambrose (Beaumont: 1882) both spent time at school in Tours. The botanist Lionel Bonaparte-Wyse (Downside: 1887) was educated in Belgium and France before finishing in England. Day-schools in Paris seem to have been popular too. Maurice MacCarthy O'Leary of Coomlegane in Cork attended one before progressing to Beaumont, as did Edmund Hale, one of two brothers from Sligo at Beaumont in the late 1870s.[12]

II ST EDMUND'S COLLEGE, DOUAI

Of the very few English Catholic foundations that remained in France after the 'French Terror' of 1794–5, the Benedictine community of St Edmund's continued to educate Irish and British boys throughout the nineteenth century in Paris and then Douai before finally returning to English soil early in the twentieth century.[13] Douai School, as it was known in the twentieth century, has its roots in the foundation of St Edmund's, Paris (dioc. Paris) in 1615, from where it migrated to Douai in 1820, and to its present site in Woolhampton, near Reading, in 1903. Two noteworthy occurrences were retained in the institutional memory of the community from their time in Paris. First, it was apparently believed that Benjamin Franklin had lodged with the community during his stay at Paris in 1776, and that the American Constitution bears some comparison with the rule of St Benedict as a result of his sojourn there. Secondly, it was believed that the body of James II was interred on the property, but was removed after the tomb was desecrated.[14]

The school left for Woolhampton in 1903, having been caught up in one of the last waves of anti-clerical legislation in French history. The controversial expulsion of the Benedictines from their French base by the French government was bitterly resented.[15] The Irish Parliamentary Party were lobbied via John Redmond by both former pupils and current staff of the school to have the matter raised in Parliament, though it was English Catholics such as Lord Edmund Talbot who took up the matter in earnest in the House of Commons.[16]

---

[12] Probably sons of Richard Hale, a landowner with an address at Easky, Co. Sligo. Edmund served in the British army in Uganda having progressed through the entrance examination to Woolwich. He died young, in 1899.

[13] The boys attending the Benedictine St Edmund's College in Douai 1850–1900 ought not to be confused with those attending another college of the same name which moved back to Old Hall, near Ware in Hertfordshire *c*.1793. Nor should they be mixed up with the Irish College at Douai, which had also wound up in 1793 after a spell of two centuries spent in exile.

[14] See Louis G. Redmond-Howard, 'The Romance of Douai', unpublished typescript, n.d., Douai Abbey Archives, VII.A.2/1, 3.

[15] For more see Peter Guilday, *The English Catholic Refugees on the Continent 1558–1795* (London, 1914); Geoffrey Scott, *Gothic Rage Undone: English Monks in the Age of Enlightenment* (Bath, 1992).

[16] Marmaduke Constable-Maxwell, 11th Baron Herries, raised the matter in the House of Lords, though the issue was immediately buried. HL Deb., 31 Jul. 1903, vol. 126, cc. 1041–46. For the

While at Paris the school, which eventually settled near Rue St Jacques on the Left Bank, had extensive links with the nearby Irish College on Rue des Irlandais.[17] Irish influence continued in reduced form when it had moved to Douai. Indeed the community itself was in reduced circumstances, almost skeletal, with just three members remaining in 1818.[18] At Douai it replaced the Benedictine community of St Gregory's, who had left the town six years earlier in 1814 before moving back to Downside. For the rest of the nineteenth century, then, St Edmund's would occupy the former buildings of the Downside community.[19] The exact number of Irish boys who attended Douai in the nineteenth century remains somewhat unclear. Though the school has published the lists they are regrettably scant in information, whether on pupil origins or future destinations.[20] The archival material held at the school does not substantially improve this situation, though it seems likely that the percentage of Irish at the school did not at any time come close to that at schools such as Downside, Oscott, or Stonyhurst. The school had begun as a tiny enterprise in 1820 and had never quite recovered the reputation it had enjoyed while at Paris. The number of students there ranged between seventy and one hundred or so throughout the nineteenth century, following the classic model of educating seminarians alongside a variable number of lay students. Perhaps the most famous Irish connection in the Douai community 1850–1900 was that the person on whom G. K. Chesterton is reputed to have based his 'Father Brown' character, Monsignor John O'Connor, was educated there. O'Connor was born in Kilmacomma, Co. Waterford, in 1870 and had received his early education with the Christian Brothers and the Irish Franciscans before training as a priest in St Edmund's in Douai in the 1890s.[21] O'Connor seems to typify the Irish student attending St Edmund's, being from an altogether more modest background than his contemporaries at Stonyhurst or Oscott.

The school appears to have survived largely due to a series of *bourses* connected to the various English dioceses and from the periodic appearance of an Irish trainee or lay student. We can see from the various ledgers that diocesan money was crucial. In the 1880s the diocese of Birmingham was sending seven boys through school at £24 each per annum—worth £340 to St Edmund's for the year. This fee, even when combined with travelling costs, was much less than half what most boys were costing at English schools at the same time. Of course, the division here

Redmond correspondence see Abbot H. L. Larkin to John Redmond, 10 Jul. 1903, John Redmond Papers, NLI, MS 15,242/8.

[17] Indeed the Irish College inherited some of the community's art collection, library books, and choir stalls when they left Paris under duress. See Geoffrey Scott, 'Paris 1677–1818', in Geoffrey Scott (ed.), *Douai 1903–2003 Woolhampton: A Centenary History* (Worcester, 2003), 39–40.

[18] Alban Hood, 'Douai 1818–1903', in Geoffrey Scott (ed.), *Douai 1903–2003 Woolhampton: A Centenary History* (Worcester, 2003), 61.

[19] For a general account of this see Aidan Bellenger, 'The English Foundations in France and the Low Countries and the Impact of the French Revolution', *English Benedictine Congregation History Commission 1993* (Downside, 1994), <http://www.plantata.org.uk/pdf1977-1996/1993bellenger.htm>.

[20] The full list of the pupils and monks of the school is available on the Douai website. See <http://www.douaiabbey.org.uk/HistBook.htm>.

[21] See Aideen Foley and Lawrence William White, 'O'Connor, John (1870–1952)', *DIB*.

between what constitutes an Irish and English Catholic may at times be a facile one. Through the 1890s the diocese of Leeds was absorbing the cost of as many as eleven boys at Douai in any one year and most of those had surnames that, at nothing more than an impressionistic level, would lead us to believe that they were drawn from the second-generation Irish population.[22] Most boys arriving from England on a diocesan *bourse* were aged somewhere between sixteen and nineteen and often returned home to become a secular priest in that diocese.

Not all Irish boys at St Edmund's arrived via English diocesan funds. One of the few registers to give detail of origins (regrettably uneven) between 1891 and 1898 shows Henry McKenna from Donegal entering in 1891 and returning in 1896, before becoming a secular priest. Gerald McNally, from Kingstown in Dublin was attending the school from 1893 to 1902 at a cost to his parents of £30 plus extras. The same price was paid by Patrick Burke, of Cork, who arrived in 1896 aged four-teen, paid for by a local priest. The fees paid by students attending St Edmunds varied somewhat, with the majority heavily subsidized. Nevertheless, in the 1870s it was possible to pay £20 per half-term, which meant an annual bill of almost £70 in some cases, even before travel costs were calculated. This put St Edmund's out of the reach of all but the relatively strong farming class and above, and was certainly not an option for the working classes. The average Irish boy (sent directly from Ireland) was likely then to have been from a family that might well have been able to have afforded the fees at Stonyhurst, with the acquisition of better French a possible attraction.

Much work remains to be done on the social origins of those second-generation Irish recruited in English dioceses throughout the nineteenth century though one would imagine that the recipients of such generosity were drawn from families that were considered 'respectable' by the relevant parish priest and his superiors. It seems fair to suggest that the social status of those boys attending St Edmund's was clearly less than that of those boys attending the elite English schools, despite the historical importance of the community and the high regard in which the Benedictine order was held in England and Ireland.

III THE IRISH COLLEGE, PARIS

The Irish College in Paris (ICP) has been fortunate to have received more attention than most of the Continental colleges, and its reputation is now faithfully pre-served by the *Centre Culturel Irlandais*, which stands as a reminder of centuries of precarious existence at the heart of an often hostile polity. Located within shouting distance of the centre of reconstituted French civic nationalism at the Panthéon, it can count as its near neighbours the illustrious elite schools of France, the Lycée Henri-IV and Lycée Louis-Le-Grand which have educated generations of French

---

[22] 'Accounts Boys Journal 1896–1900', Douai Abbey Archives, VII.A.2/12. This was also true of other, more glamorous destinations: e.g. Daniel Stephen O'Connor came to the school in 1897 from Mauritius.

writers, intellectuals, and politicians such as Voltaire, Victor Hugo, Deleuze, Sartre, Foucault, and Jacques Chirac. The level of learning may not have reached a similar pitch at the ICP, but the numbers attending remained consistently high throughout the second half of the nineteenth century and thus of interest to us in this study. This tentative analysis of those attending the school 1850–1900 draws from a database created Dr Liam Chambers, whose extraordinarily detailed work will add considerably to the store of knowledge generated by Liam Swords, Timothy Walsh, Patrick Boyle, and others.[23]

Chambers has already shown the extent to which the ICP, much like St Edmund's in Douai, floated on money from Ireland in the form of *pensionnes* or *bourses*. During the eighteenth century these bursaries were utilized to circumvent penal restrictions on the training of Catholic priests, but also to facilitate legal and medical study. Liam Swords cited several examples of scholarship money being employed by relatives of the founders to pursue medical or legal studies at the University of Paris in the eighteenth century.[24] Such an opportunity would add considerable value to the scholarship and, if widely known, must surely have heightened their allure to any aspiring Irish family with reasonable means. Even those who did become priests often chose to stay abroad, where a living could more easily be made in the warmer and more welcoming surrounds of an archdiocese like Bordeaux—a particular favourite for Irish clerics.[25] In the eighteenth century then, it is clear that in some cases the ICP (and the Irish colleges in general) were being used by some of their patrons for their potential to improve social mobility, whether inside or outside the religious life.

By the mid nineteenth century the ICP was in a curious position. The tumult of the revolutionary period in Paris had seen the College first threatened with extinction, then lumped together with the remaining Scottish, Irish, and English colleges to form a generic 'British establishment' in the Napoleonic period.[26] Since 1824 the superior of the OCP had been appointed by agreement of the four archbishops of Ireland with the consent of the French authorities. This situation also pertained to the priests who taught at the school. Access to the University of Paris was no longer possible in the way that it had been in the eighteenth century, meaning that the studies at the ICP were of an altogether reduced quality in the nineteenth century. In 1858 the management of the ICP was given over to the Vincentian Fathers, whose instincts in advanced education had been honed by

[23] For the history of the college see, in particular, Liam Chambers, 'Irish Fondations and Boursiers in Early Modern Paris, 1682–1793', *Irish Economic and Social History*, 35 (2008), 1–22; Liam Chambers, '"Une Seconde Patrie": The Irish College, Paris, in the Eighteenth and Nineteenth Centuries', in Susanne Lachenicht and Kirsten Heinsohn (eds), *Diaspora Identities: Exile, Nationalism and Cosmopolitanism in Past and Present* (Frankfurt, 2009), 16–30; Walsh, *The Irish Continental College Movement*; Cardinal Tomás Ó Fiaich, *The Irish Colleges in France* (Dublin, 1990); Patrick Boyle, CM, *The Irish College in Paris from 1578 to 1901* (London, 1901).

[24] Liam Swords, 'College des Lombards', in Liam Swords (ed.), *The Irish-French Connection, 1578–1978* (Paris, 1978), 44.

[25] See a discussion of this phenomenon in Emmet Larkin, *The Pastoral Role of the Roman Catholic Church in Pre-Famine Ireland* (Dublin, 2006), 33–6.

[26] Liam Chambers, '"Une Seconde Patrie"', 24.

their experiences at Castleknock. This did not result, however, in a greater gen-
trification of either the College or its clientele. The handover was the result of a
bitter wrangle between the superior of the College, John Miley, and his staff and
students. The ICP had a reputation for factionalism, and this reputation had been
given greater credence by the rowdy behaviour of the students in response to the
1848 rising in Paris when they were recorded as having chanted the Marseillaise,
planted a tree of liberty, and attacked soldiers 'from the window of the college'.[27]
With the College becoming increasingly unruly and disputatious the need for a
change of management became clear and the Vincentian rector, James Lynch, was
handed something of a poisoned chalice when he took over in 1858. The story of
the ICP under Vincentian management is one of gradual decline, with the College
limping along on a falling income, offering an alternative route to the priesthood
in an exotic location, but receiving no additional investment from Ireland. This
sense of suspended animation is captured well in an annual report for 1883–4
written by Thomas MacNamara, Rector of the ICP 1868–9. He began his report
thus: 'My Lords, In presenting to your Lordships our Annual Report for the past
year we have very little to convey. The year has passed without notable incident.'[28]

A total of 1,233 boys entered the ICP between 1850 and 1900. What became
of most of those is something that can be surmised with reasonable accuracy—the
large majority of them became secular priests back home in Ireland. The register is reasonably detailed—with some sort of additional information on 73 per
cent (903) of the boys who entered the College (Table 6.1). Out of these boys
the register records 629 ordinations, along with three boys who had *sous-diacre*
(sub-deacon) noted beside their name. The majority of these ordinations took
place upon returning to Ireland, thus respecting one of the original purposes of the
Irish colleges on the Continent—to replenish and restock the secular clergy from
afar. Where a boy joined one of the regular orders or the American mission such
an event is often recorded adjacent to their name.

That so many were willing to go to at least some expense or effort to train for the
priesthood in Paris after 1850 is impressive indeed. After all, the controversial trebling
of the annual government grant at Maynooth in 1845 from *c.*£9,000 per annum to
c.£26,000 per annum had led to a much larger domestic provision of places for
would-be-priests. Irish options were plentiful. The more domestically minded might

Table 6.1 Irish boys at the Irish College, Paris, 1850–99

	1850–9	1860–9	1870–9	1880–9	1890–9
The Irish College, Paris	394	246	239	218	136

[27] Gerard Moran, 'John Miley and the Crisis at the Irish College, Paris, in the 1850s', *Archivium
Hibernicum*, 50 (1996), 113. See also Fearghas Ó Fearghail, 'A Stormy Decade in the Irish College,
Paris, 1849–59', in Liam Swords (ed.), *The Irish-French Connection, 1578–1978* (Paris, 1978), 108–18.
[28] Thomas MacNamara, 'The Annual Report of the Irish College for the Year 1883–84', Archives
of the Irish College, Paris, A2.b122, <http://archives.centreculturelirlandais.com/>, 1.

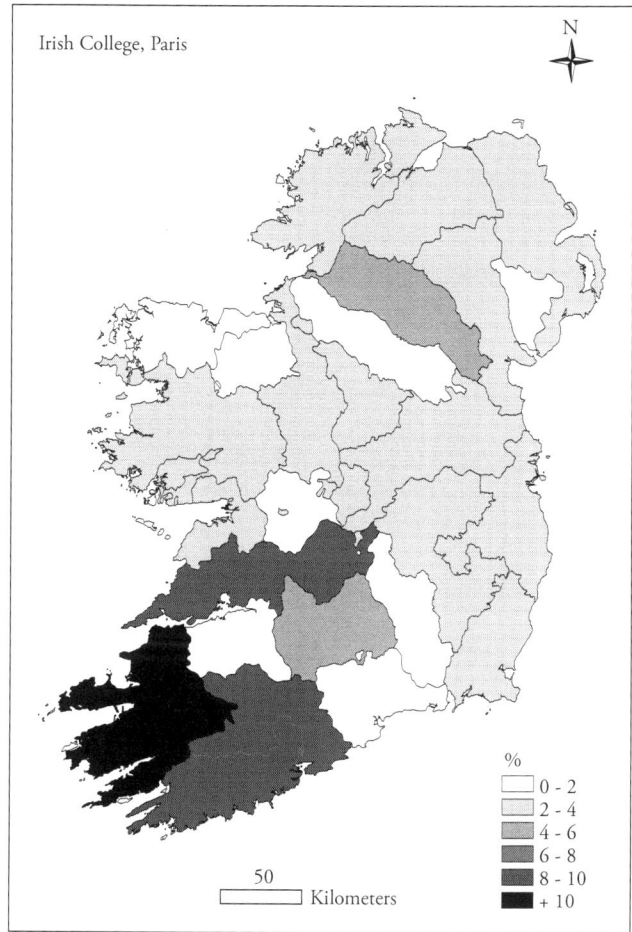

Map 6.1 Irish boys at the Irish College, Paris, by diocese of origin, 1849–92

also choose to pursue the ecclesiastical course until its natural end at Carlow College, to join the missionaries at All Hallows in Dublin from 1842, or to sign up to the Cullenite army at Holy Cross College, Clonliffe, from 1854. The crisis surrounding Miley and the transfer of the College to Vincentian custodians, combined with this explosion in places for priests at home, saw the number of Irish at Rue des Irlandais decline gradually in this fifty-year period, with attendance dropping by over a third in the 1860s. By the 1890s the size of the student body was just over a third of what it was in the 1840s (409) and 1850s (394). Map 6.1 shows how the distribution of diocesan subsidies meant a much more even spread of recruits are visible at the ICP when compared to the English schools discussed earlier.

Of the 23 per cent (330) with little or no additional information recorded in the register we must unfortunately resign ourselves to ignorance. A further thirty-eight boys died at a young age, usually after travelling home when sick or in 'delicate' health. Some, however, died while in College.[29] Thirty-five boys were expelled for various reasons (drink, disorder, immorality, imbecility, being 'very odd') and another forty-nine left citing ill-health. Some left for reasons which will now, presumably, remain obscure. This leaves us with a total of 271 boys from which we can extrapolate some pattern.

Pathways through life, as we have seen in Chapter 3, are not always predictable. Some of those that left Paris changed their mind when they returned home and were ordained there. Thomas Vaughan is an example of one such case, recorded as leaving the religious life early at Paris, but turning up as a parish priest in Co. Clare in the 1901 census despite being recorded in the College register as 'very odd and hippish'. Others, such as Michael Floyd, left on the advice of their confessor. Some left of their own accord, or at least that is what the register records. Bartholomew Horgan, of Kerry, spent four years at the college before returning home. He seems to have ended up living on Spike Island off the Cork coast where he was recorded as a 'boatman' in the employ of the Department of War in 1911. Richard Liston, from the diocese of Limerick, left the ICP in the 1860s and went on to become a Relieving Officer living at Ballingarry, Limerick, according to his 1901 and 1911 census returns. Liston had married quite late—*c.*1877 (Honora)—and had a son and daughter who lived at home. The family's social rank would also seem to indicate that a year or two spent at the ICP ought not to be compared with a year or two spent at Stonyhurst or Downside. Those that exited the preordained path to priesthood and returned to Ireland did so on reduced or at best equal terms, and to lives of lower middle-class respectability comparable to that of their parents. Larkin, and more recently Campbell, have discussed the social origins of much of the priesthood in the nineteenth century and nothing found in the Paris registers would appear to conflict with the current picture of priests being drawn from the shopkeeper and strong farmer classes.

The Paris registers are nonetheless full of incident. Intriguing references to insanity (loosely defined) can be found here and there. William Cleary (1884) was apparently declared insane while at college, an event recorded in the registers simply as: 'Lost his mind; died in the Asylum at Villejuif 16 September '89'. The asylum at Villejuif, on the outskirts of Paris, is now famous for its utilization as a foundation myth for the *Art Brut* movement. It was the supposed site of the first display of the art of the insane in 1905 and thus considered the forerunner to the phenomenon of *La Musée de la folie*—literally the 'Museum of Madness'— the basis of the 'outsider art' of the *Art Brut* movement.[30] When William Cleary entered it Villejuif had only been open five years since 1884, under the stewardship

[29] Ten died at the college itself, and from a variety of complaints. Peter McKeon, Thomas Brady (meningitis); Michael Walsh (typhoid); Patrick Conway, Andrew O'Hanlon (inflammation of the lungs); Edward Kelly (smallpox); John FitzGerald (consumption); Thomas Slattery (1858), Patrick FitzGerald (1885), and Thomas Healy (1890) all died from unknown or unrecorded causes.

[30] The extent to which we should take this claim at face value has recently been contested. See Alison Moorehead, 'The Musée de la Folie: Collecting and Exhibiting Chez les Fous', *Journal of the History of* Collections, 23/1 (2011), 101–26.

of Dr August Marie who—like Sigmund Freud—was a student of the celebrated neurologist Jean-Martin Charcot at the Salpêtrière Hospital in Paris, just a stone's throw from the ICP at Rue des Irlandais. That their son was in such eminent care would presumably have been scant consolation for the parents of William Cleary back in the diocese of Cashel and in any case it did not seem to help him in any discernible way.

Some sense of the daily life of the ICP during this Vincentian period can be gleaned from the annual reports submitted to the secular hierarchy in Ireland by Thomas MacNamara, Superior of the College through the turbulent period of the Franco-Prussian War. MacNamara noted that in 1869 five of their 103 students had 'retired of their own accord to embrace another state of life having arrived at the conviction that they were not called to the Ecclesiastical state'. Another three of this cohort were removed for behavioural reasons, and another three had died of either consumption or smallpox, despite the vaccination of the whole College that year. MacNamara appended a very basic income and expenditure sheet which put the total income for the ICP at just under £3,200, with expenditure at about £3,367. With the wages for the rector, medical consultation, seven professeurs, and eighteen servants accounting for just £588 it seems the bulk of the money was spent on sustenance—the food and wine bill amounting to an impressive £2,150.[31]

By 1890 the ICP was charging 800 francs, or £32, per annum, making it roughly one half to a quarter as expensive as the English schools discussed earlier. Most of the students were heavily subsidized, of course, so few ever paid the full amount. The burses were distributed nationally, with a strong southern bias. Since an Irish ecclesiastical commission had reorganized them by ecclesiastical province in 1849 the eighty-three burses had not altered, and were divided as per Table 6.2.

This remained the distribution until 1892 when the Bureau Gratuit—the (mostly French) governing hierarchy of the ICP—decided to limit the number of free places

Table 6.2 Distribution of burses at the Irish College, Paris, 1889–90*

Armagh		Dublin		Cashel		Tuam	
Armagh	2	Dublin	3	Cashel	4	Tuam	3
Ardagh	1	Kildare	2	Cloyne	9	Achonry	2
Clogher	4	Ferns	2	Cork	4	Clonfert	1
Derry	1	Ossory	1	Kerry	13	Elphin	3
Down & Connor	3			Killaloe	6	Galway-Kilmacduagh	2
Dromore	2			Limerick	2	Kilfenora	1
Kilmore	1			Ross	3	Killala	2
Meath	2			Waterford	2		
Raphoe	2						
Total	18	Total	8	Total	43	Total	14

* Figures taken from Patrick Boyle, CM, 'The Annual Report of the Irish College for the Year 1889–90', Archives of the Irish College, Paris, A2.b138.

[31] Thomas MacNamara, 'The Annual Report of the Irish College for the Year 1869–70', Archives of the Irish College, Paris, A2.b26, <http://archives.centreculturelirlandais.com/>, 1–3.

to just fifty rather than over eighty as before.[32] This target had been achieved by 1893, with the number of subsidized students at just forty-nine by June 1893. As the burses became vacant the rector transferred the responsibility of distributing them equitably to the Irish bishops, whose role in the government of the ICP had become more and more distant as the century wore on. By 1894 there were only forty-six students enrolled at the College, almost half the number that had been enrolled just five years earlier in 1889 and a far cry from the heyday of the ICP in the eighteenth century.[33] Calls from the Rector for direct investment or support from Ireland fell on deaf ears despite repeated exhortation.

As a result of this consistency between 1849 and 1892 the distribution of addresses at the ICP differs substantially to that at the English public schools. There is a much more even distribution of boys across Ireland, with each diocese represented at the ICP as a direct result of the geographical spread of the burses. Nevertheless, we can still detect a distinct regional bias, with the south-west of Ireland clearly over-represented. The diocese of Kerry, which barely featured at all at the English schools, provided the most boys to the ICP in this period, 155 in total, and the dioceses of Cork, Ross, Cloyne, and Killaloe all sent large numbers of recruits. The diocese of Dublin, by contrast, sent very few, as might be expected given the wealth of places available for those wishing to study for the priesthood in that area. The archdiocese of Tuam was also poorly represented, although the relatively high number of students from the northern diocese of Armagh marks the ICP as the only educational establishment identified in this research that engaged with northern Irish Catholics with any regularity.

IV CONCLUSION

The ICP never attracted boys of similar social cache to those attendng the English congregations that eventually migrated back to England in the late eighteenth and early nineteenth century. It did, however, play an important role as one of many satellites in Irish transnational education, and referenced by its very existence a much larger and stronger network of schools across Europe that catered for Irish students, clerical and lay. Signing off on another century at the ICP, the Rector Patrick Boyle ended his June 1900 report with a phrase that is worthy of the position of Irish education on the Continent in the nineteenth century:

> In the century now closing the College has continued its work amid various vicissitudes. It has passed through three revolutions, and two sieges. But like the city in which it stands, it may claim the device, *Fluctuat nec mergitur*.

---

[32] The Bureau Gratuit was a seven-person board which was created in the aftermath of the 1848 riots at the ICP and was appointed by the Minister of Public Instruction. Five of the board were laymen, and two were ecclesiastics—the Superior/Rector of the ICP and a representative of the Archbishop of Paris. This had effectively removed the absolute control of the ICP from the Irish bishops and from the Rector himself and placed into lay control, however sympathetic they might have been.

[33] Patrick Boyle, CM, 'The Annual Report of the Irish College for the Year 1894–95', Archives of the Irish College, Paris, A2.b138, <http://archives.centreculturelirlandais.com/>, 43.

Boyle's use of the Latin motto of the city of Paris *Fluctuat nec mergitur*, 'he who rises with the wave is not swallowed by it', was surely anachronistic. The slow decline of the ICP, proud though its history may have been, belied it. The waves of successive revolts, revolutions, and sieges had entirely changed the College's character and swallowed whatever relevance it had. In the late nineteenth century the tradition of Continental education for boys faded just as it became even more fashionable for girls. The carrot of a Continental education was no longer sufficient to bring young men of rank to Paris or Douai in the numbers both towns had become accustomed to. Greater spoils were to be had, for a higher price, in leafy walled estates across England.

Conclusion

> No one should suppose that the history of a school will make exciting reading.
> Maurice J. Wigham, *Newtown School Waterford 1798–1998:*
> *A History* (Waterford, 1998), preface

Maurice Wigham's pithy remark carries with it some truth, but only because so many school histories are written so badly or so narrowly. They are rarely interesting for those whose exploits and achievements are not recalled in its pages. Yet, as one of the few social institutions through which nearly all of us pass they offer a historian an unparalleled opportunity to investigate social formation. This book has attempted to contribute to that process for the history of Irish elite education by addressing educational choice, social stratification and elitism in relation to a network of Catholic institutions across Ireland, Britain, and the Continent.

Why did most of the wealthiest Catholic families in Ireland prefer an English education to an Irish education? After all, there was little difference between the curriculum delivered at Clongowes in Kildare and that of Stonyhurst in England. It was the goal of both Parts II and III to answer this question. The prosopographical analysis of the Irish-born cohort at Stonyhurst, Beaumont, Oscott, and Downside proved that a high-status education in England appealed to a broad range of relatively wealthy Irish Catholics, 1850–1900. It also demonstrated that the typical outcome of such an education was a prestigious or well-remunerated occupation in later life. In Part III we followed the greatly diminished migration of Irish boys to Continental Catholic schools. More intriguing, and more comprehensive was the trail of Irish girls to France, Belgium, and Germany in the same period. One of the main conclusions must be that a movement within Catholic society for equality of professional and social status was a motivating factor for these families, and that sending their children to an English school was one way of establishing domestic difference by procuring an expensive, exotic, transnational education in preference to a lower-status domestic one. This served another goal, which was to identify and connect with the wider international elite practice of procuring a transnational education by attending leading English schools in the period of their greatest global reputation.

I EQUALITY OF OPPORTUNITY

This movement for equality of opportunity also influenced the Irish schools, and manifested itself in ways that jar retrospectively. These middle-class and elite

Catholics strove rather to replicate the dominance enjoyed by the Protestant 'Ascendancy' over their co-religionists. In that sense 'equality of opportunity' was understood by them literally, that is to say the opposite of an equal and fair society but rather one in which those with the greatest abilities, talents, and hereditary advantage would triumph. This was social Darwinism, not simply Catholics attempting to rise together—though that was considered by many to be a happy and desirable by-product. The Anglocentrism of the Irish schools has been misunderstood for generations in Ireland as a straightforward mimicry or imitation of the established English elite. It was the goal of Part I to prove this theory to have been reductive and simplistic. By pandering to a clientele that was anxious for social betterment, schools such as Clongowes and Castleknock certainly imitated the trends and mores of English public schools, all the more so as the nineteenth century came to a close. The real emphasis at the schools and the orders behind them, however, was on Catholic advancement and the delivery of a quality education. The finery, the pomp, and the social clout mattered, of course, but not more than a Catholic education. Though the draw of the English schools remained strong, a large portion of the Catholic elite and the upper middle class attended schools such as Clongowes Wood and Castleknock. To a certain extent the families sending boys there were even more ambitious and even more in tune with the trends and fashions of elite education in England—in much the same way that more middle-class schools in England insisted on house systems and fagging from the 1860s onwards. The demands of the Catholic laity at home, then, forced the Catholic colleges to cater for this demand for an Anglocentric education. Their primary goal, proven through their actions, was to improve funding in Catholic education in general, and at the same time to remain in pole position to educate the Catholic elite. They hoped to form this elite into a dominant replacement-elite upon independence in whatever guise, and an effective rival elite until that came about.

In the context of the second half of the nineteenth century, it is reasonable to assume that Catholics in Ireland could envisage a situation in which a version of Home Rule would be restored to Ireland—and that they could expect to be in control of it.[1] As Conor Cruise O'Brien noted, when his grandmother approved of the Clongowes-educated Tom Kettle as a prospective husband for her daughter, Mary Sheehy, she did so in the expectation that someone of his profile, if not Tom himself, would one day take a leading role in Irish politics and state-building.[2] Central to Cruise O'Brien's argument was the idea that a ready-made Catholic political elite was robbed of its natural progression to control of a Home Rule Ireland by the events of 1916–22. This view has much currency in Irish history, and is a central premise of both Senia Pašeta's *Before the Revolution* and Tom Garvin's *Nationalist Revolutionaries in Ireland 1858–1928*. The idea that the Irish Parliamentary Party was one that represented the claims of the Irish Catholic elite is problematic, as has been demonstrated by the analysis of the Irish-born cohort at English Catholic

[1] See Ciaran O'Neill, *Irish Elites in the Nineteenth Century* (Dublin, 2013), 'Introduction'.
[2] Conor Cruise O'Brien, *States of Ireland* (London, 1972), 63.

colleges. If this cohort was representative of the wealthiest Catholic families then the lack of political mobilization or ambition is striking.

For the most part, the Irish Catholic elite steered clear of politics, and did not come to dominate either the Irish Parliamentary Party or the Free-State government. Instead, they preferred to remain in the private sector, the professions, military service, or local government—secure occupations that relied on political allegiance only to a certain degree. This has led to a curious and almost unique under-representation of the Irish Catholic elite in politics, and to a political system and electoral pattern that is notable amongst European nations for its relatively weak relationship to class structure. The Gonzaga-educated writer Ronan Sheehan could argue by the 1990s that Ireland was one of the few countries where holding a Cabinet position did not mean that one was necessarily 'a great draw at a dinner party'.[3] This absence of the Irish Catholic elite from visible high-ranking positions in politics should not, however, be taken to mean that there was no continuity of wealth and influence for the class of people described in the book. The occupational analysis of boys attending English Catholic schools proves that this privelege was retained by families that had long enjoyed it and offers a challenge to any attempt to characterize blocked mobility to Irish Catholics en masse.

The questions raised in this book undermine the received image of total Catholic poverty in nineteenth-century Ireland by highlighting that a tried and trusted route to success was available to Irish people of moderate to wealthy means. The geographical data emerging from the schools reinforces the idea of a 'Catholic core' in south Munster for those interested in the socio-economic history of Catholic Ireland, and shows us that by the mid nineteenth century the Dublin address of choice for Catholics with money was already in the south suburbs, or in the Georgian residential areas south of the Liffey in Dublin city centre. It is obvious from the maps produced that the provinces of Ulster and Connacht must be largely absent from any discussion of the Irish Catholic elite in the nineteenth century and that the greatest concentration of Catholic wealth was undoubtedly based in rural south Munster, or distributed amongst the urban centres of Cork, south Dublin, Waterford, Limerick, and other major towns. The proliferation of local-government positions amongst the cohort in England must also point to a widespread tradition of public service amongst the landed Catholic class, and to a comparatively small amount of emigration from within this group. This distribution of power amongst respectable and wealthy Catholics must have had an effect on their less-wealthy co-religionists in areas with few Protestant families and requires further attention.

Irish historians have generally accepted the 'blocked mobility' thesis in relation to the emerging Irish Catholic elite. John Hutchinson and Tom Garvin have both argued that an educated group of lower middle-class educated Catholics experienced professional discrimination and in consequence turned towards cultural

---

[3] Ronan Sheehan, quoted in Fintan O'Toole, 'A Middle Class Losing Its Confidence', *Irish Times*, 6 Apr. 1990.

and then revolutionary nationalism between 1890 and 1914. This blocked mobility contributed to the cataclysmic events of 1916–23. Senia Pašeta's work on the university-educated Catholic middle class concludes that this group were more likely to have been Home Rulers (politically) and experienced less discrimination than the group immediately below them in social status. Pašeta's influential thesis then draws on an argument originally made by Conor Cruise O'Brien that a university-educated elite was denied its rightful position as the natural governors of Home Rule Ireland by the events of 1916–23 and the political collapse of the Irish Parliamentary Party in the elections of 1918. It has been the work of this thesis to suggest that elite Catholic identity has been inadequately examined, and its general conclusions show that none of the arguments above fully capture the complexity and diversity of the wealthiest Catholic families in Ireland.

Fergus Campbell has recently completed a prosopographical analysis of the Irish establishment between 1879 and 1914. In his analysis of 1,200 people whom he considers to have controlled the main networks of power and influence (land, business, civil service, policing, and religion) Campbell concludes that there was less Catholic penetration into these elites than has been previously believed by Irish historians. The Irish establishment was, he argues, 'like a head without a body', and overwhelmingly dominated by British and Irish Protestants.[4] Campbell's study is a valuable one, and he acknowledges that beneath this top tier of Irish society, the super-rich and the old ascendancy, there lies a relatively unexplored Catholic upper middle class and elite. This section of society held sway over local government and local power structures, and had traction at national level also. In areas where Catholic population was high, these were the people who upheld law and order. They were the most immediate civic post-holders and acted as a social reference point for many of their co-religionists, especially in rural Ireland. It is a section of Irish society that has received no real critical attention, most likely because it is so difficult to define. Their access to social capital and personal wealth was achieved much more in the private sphere, and they were for the most part politically and socially conservative. It is this group, along with the large landed magnates that we ought to identify as the Catholic elite. That definition ought to be a soft one, and elastic—at no point in the nineteenth century did Catholics enjoy enough power as a bloc to be considered a dominant elite in the classic sense. Rather it was their gradual infiltration of the professions, of land ownership, of shipping, and of banking and commerce that we ought to take as evidence of their encroachment.

Isolating the wealthiest Irish Catholic families at school, a most important stage in socialization, has allowed us to identify this social strata with an accuracy that has eluded so many Irish historians. Campbell's study aimed above it, revealing a super-rich section of Irish society that had little day-to-day contact with the general population. The work of Pašeta, Garvin, and Hutchinson all reveals much about an aspirant middle class with limited social mobility immediately below

---

[4] Fergus Campbell, *The Irish Establishment 1870–1914* (Oxford, 2009), 304.

it. Those identified in this study were amongst the most successful in Ireland, and were in constant contact with a wide array of social groups in Ireland. They had identified and then pursued one obvious route to power and influence, a high-status education. It has been argued that these families chose either to send their sons and daughters abroad to high-status Catholic schools in England or to the most prestigious boarding schools in Ireland for a specific goal: to further and enhance their career prospects, and by doing so to place them within an established network of influential and well-connected peers. These schools had developed a recognizably elite educational product which incorporated many of the surface aspects of an English public school experience but retained an overriding emphasis on Catholicism. The boys educated there joined a tiny minority of the Irish population by virtue of this expensive and holistic education, and for the most part went on to occupy positions in life that were either financially or socially desirable.

As we pointed out in the beginning of this book, R. V. Comerford has argued that the great constant of history has been the 'manoeuvring for survival and advancement of self and family through access to material resources and socio-political advantage'.[5] It is a very human trait to be mindful of providing a better life for one's children, and education remains a key element in social mobility in both Britain and Ireland today. The Irish children attending English, Irish, and Continental elite schools between 1850 and 1900 understood the value of an elite education and took full advantage of it.

---

[5] R. V. Comerford, *Ireland* (London, 2003), 266.

APPENDIX

Methodology and Sources Used to Compile Biographical Data

Much of this book is based on prosopographical analysis of 1,303 Irish-born boys at Stonyhurst, Beaumont, Downside, and Oscott 1850–1900, and 203 Irish girls attending the Holy Child convent at St Leonards-on-Sea. To this original work is added an analysis of a database compiled by Dr Liam Chambers at Mary Immaculate College, University of Limerick, on 1,233 Irish boys at the Irish College, Paris. Prosopography is an inexact technique and one that is subject to variables. A 'James Murphy' from Cork will always be more difficult to track than a 'Rowland Blennerhassett' from Kerry due to the sheer number of people who share the name of the former. Likewise, the absence of a date of birth or address in the source documents will complicate matters immensely when it comes to proving a life story beyond reasonable doubt. Nevertheless, it is easier now to find information on relatively obscure people in modern society, and the range and depth of sources grows by the week. So much of our historiography has concentrated on the political and the landed precisely because of the availability of detail on the rich and the powerful. At the other end of the spectrum the work done on the lives of the working class, what little we have, has tended to be statistical and quantitative precisely because we lack real access to the lived experience of those working in the factories and the fields. In Irish historiography this absence of anything in between is particularly marked.

The source material for the occupational breakdown of Irish boys has come from a variety of printed, online, and archival resources. The first, and most useful, is that information compiled by members of the schools themselves on their past pupils. At Stonyhurst only some of this information is in the public domain through its publication in *The Stonyhurst Magazine* in two forms: the 'Stonyhurst Biographical Dictionary' (tracking past pupils from 1794 to the early twentieth century, beginning in the October issue 1930) and the obituaries section of past pupils, which is a constant feature of the publication. The biographical information is in short-entry format and taken from a much larger card file in the school archives, and typically contains information on their family, their years of attendance, future careers, and county of origin.[1] At Beaumont College a similar project was carried out in the 1960s at the time of the closure of the schools. This took the form of 'The Beaumont Lists 1861–1961' and was published in *The Beaumont Review*, beginning in October 1963, and ordered alphabetically. This short-entry format information was then compared to the information in the school registers and the 'obituary' and 'notes' sections in the school publications. These typically provide a date of birth and address for most pupils and allow us to successfully identify the lives led by the bulk of those students that were proven to have been Irish. At Stonyhurst we have reliable biographical details for 277 (60 per cent) of a total cohort of 462, and considerably more at Beaumont—230 (78 per cent) of the 294 boys in total. Taken together, this provides a clear indication of the material and social benefits that could be derived from an elite English education.

[1] Stonyhurst College Archives, Card file, 'Past pupils'.

The occupational breakdown of Irish boys at Downside has been obtained from a variety of online, archival, and printed resources. The source data for the names of the boys that attended Downside between 1 January 1850 and 31 December 1899 is the *List of Boys at St Gregory's*, printed privately and held at the Downside Abbey Archives.[2] This list, in addition to fees' registers and handwritten admission registers in the archives provide, for the most part, a full list of names, date of birth, date of entrance, and date of departure for each boy at the school in the period—except for the period 1850–55 where the date of birth is not always available. This register does not indicate nationality, or where a boy may or may not be related to another in the school. This list may be considered as the base document for the information then gathered on individual boys and combined with the handwritten register covering 1856–86.[3]

The school archives also contain otherwise unavailable student magazines, some of which turn up information on Irish-born boarders. The widely circulated *Raven* and *Downside Review* include obituaries of past pupils in addition to contemporary entries on the whereabouts or achievements of past pupils, all of which was added to the database on discovery. *The Downside Review* has an index for volumes I–XXV, sorted by topic and authors, allowing for a retrospective identification of the articles written by Irish old boys. Another vital source of information is *Downside and the War 1914–1919*, compiled by Dom Lucius Graham, which lists old boys that were known combatants in World War I, and gathered regimental and biographical information on as many as possible.[4] Graham published memoirs on 109 of the Downside dead, twenty-six of whom were Irish, five of whom attended in this period. He included much more basic information on a total of 496 old boys that served in the war. An additional privately printed source of information, only useful for identifying old boys that remained within the order, is *The Belmont Clothing Book*, a record of all English Benedictine novices between 1860 and 1920.

Of the 309 boys discovered at Downside to have been Irish-born, ten of them died at a young age (twenty-five or under) and therefore their careers (if they had one at all) are not considered in the analysis. A further eighty-two Irish boys are considered to have insufficient biographical data to be included in this occupational breakdown, meaning that the total number considered within the following section is 217, or 70 per cent of the overall cohort. This will allow general conclusions to be made in relation to the boys as a body. Where a figure is quoted as a percentage of the Irish-born cohort, it therefore refers to the figure of 217 considered to have verifiable evidence of occupation. Equally, and to accommodate the fact that several boys have overlapping or simultaneous careers (for example, a local landowner who served as an MP and a local Justice of the Peace) the percentage of boys quoted will refer to the number of boys *involved* for a period in the relative occupation, or qualified for it.

Oscott have published their pupil lists both in printed form and now online. The lists provided do not automatically indicate nationality by way of birthplace of parental address but, despite this, biographical information has been acquired for 71 per cent of the boys attending that were identified as Irish and who lived long enough to pursue a livelihood. This means we have detailed career information on 169 boys in total, out of 238 Irish boys in total at Oscott. A further nineteen boys died young and without time to develop any sort of career. The sample size is smaller than the rest, primarily because the school ceased

[2] *List of Boys at St Gregory's: Together with a List of Professed Monks of St Gregory's* (Downside Abbey, 1972).

[3] DAA, 'Register of Students at Downside', C/52/H.

[4] Dom Lucius Graham, *Downside and the War 1914–1919* (London, 1925).

to be a going concern in the mid 1880s and at all times had a mixed social intake of very wealthy boys alongside subsidized seminarians, leading to periodic friction between the two strands. Altogether the figure of Irish boys with known careers is 893 out of 1,303, so 69 per cent.

This original information has been tested, where possible, with alternative sources, a process which assures that every finding is likely to be more convincing and accurate.[5] For the Irish landed gentry, there are several comprehensive reference books.[6] Online sources such as the Census of Ireland 1901 and 1911, the *Irish Times*, and the *Freeman's Journal* have been most useful in identifying past pupils using date of birth and address as a base for identifying obituary notices. For the medical and legal professions, a directory such as *Thom's Who's Who in Ireland* and newspaper advertisements are useful. Both schools have publications that commemorate those that fought in World War I, which along with newspaper records have helped to identify the rank achieved by Irish boys at the Jesuit colleges.[7] The *Stonyhurst War Record* was even compiled by an Irish boy that had joined the Jesuits and taught at Stonyhurst, Francis Irwin, SJ. Other external sources used include local history society publications, the archives of the *Dictionary of Irish Biography* and private family archives located in the Irish National Archives, National Library of Ireland, and the British Library. Such auxiliary information has augmented the basic information found in the school registers, and allows us to build a reasonably reliable database that incorporates career and family information, along with county of origin. Such an undertaking is not without its gaps, and a substantial number of the boys' occupations could not be satisfactorily proven—particularly those at Stonyhurst. This systematic process has naturally lessened the overall number of boys that are considered. Where a significant doubt has arisen over a boy his information has been omitted for the sake of accuracy. Specific information relating to individuals was noted in the main text; many of the newspapers quoted have been accessed online, beginning September 2007.

For the girls a slightly different methodology was pursued. The bulk of the information garnered on the 203 girls attending St Leonards was taken from the registers of the school, now held at the Archives of the Society of the Holy Child Jesus at 14 Norham Gardens, Oxford. The ledgers there provide a very complete record of girls attending St Leonards-on-Sea from about 1857. The record of entrants begins in 1850 and ends in 1976 on entry No. 4,609. In the analysis I dispensed with the years 1850–7 as there was no reliable indication of place of birth, parents, or origin for most of the girls attending. The ledgers often contained information such as the order entered, or man married, as well as some occasional observations. These were cross-checked and proved using the same methodology, and often the same source material as on the boys above.

Lastly, I owe the use of the Irish College, Paris database to the generosity of Liam Chambers. According to his database, which was in preparation at the time of use, a total of 1,233 boys entered the Irish College, Paris between 1850 and 1900. The register is

---

[5] See Robert K. Yin, *Case Study Research: Design and Methods*, 3rd edn (London, 2003).

[6] In addition to the very well-known *Burke's Peerage, Burke's Irish Family Record* (London, 1976) is the most useful. The main reference books for the Irish Catholic gentry are John Bateman's, *Great Landowners of Great Britain and Ireland*, 4th edn (Leicester, 1971); Edward Walford, *County Families of the United Kingdom; or, Royal Manual of the Titled and Untitled Aristocracy of England, Wales, Scotland, and Ireland* (1860, 1899, 1910); U. H. Hussey De Burgh's *The Landowners of Ireland: An Alphabetical List of the Owners of Estates of 500 Acres or £500 Valuation and Upwards in Ireland* (Dublin, 1876).

[7] Stephen Baybut, *Pro Patria, Beaumont War Dead* (London, 2005); Francis Irwin, SJ, *Stonyhurst War Record* (Derby, 1927).

reasonably detailed, with some sort of additional information on 73 per cent (903) of the boys who entered the college. Out of these boys the register records 629 ordinations, along with three boys who had *sous-diacre* (sub-deacon) noted beside their name.

The database compiled during this research will be made available to any bona fide researcher, upon request to the author.

Bibliography

PRIMARY SOURCES

School Archives

Archives of the British Province of the Society of Jesus
PO/3   Athletic Sports at Beaumont
PG/2   Plays and Academical Exhibitions
PE/5   Prospectus File
5/1/4   Diary of the Prefect of Studies 1866–
5/2/8   Beaumont College Accounts 1861–74
5/2/9   Beaumont College Accounts 1874–93
5/2/10   Beaumont College Accounts 1894–1901
5/1/17   Beaumont Consultation Book 1883–93
5/2/20   List of Boys at Beaumont 1861–76

Irish Jesuit Archives
J/456   Fr Delany Papers
FM/TULL   Tullabeg College Archives
SC/CLON   Clongowes Wood College Papers

Unpublished MSS
L.   McKenna SJ, 'Fr William Delany and his Work for Irish Education'

Downside Abbey Archives
C/59/C   Examination Lists
C/58/D   Course of Studies
C/52/H   Register of Students at Downside

Uncatalogued Material
Cardinal Gasquet Papers   Downside College Archives
Abbot E. C. Butler Papers   Abbot Snow Papers

Ampleforth College Archives
JX/22   Student Register 1866–95
NX/87   Student Accounts 1883–9
EX/39   Prospectus Files 1814–60

Belvedere College Archives
ATT/RBK/1–60   Roll Books
ATT/ABS/1–34   Absentee Books
REG/1   School Registers 1839–89
REG/3   Belvedere College SJ Prefect of Studies Book

Blackrock College Archives

Uncatalogued Material
Ledger of Student Accounts 1867–72
Grand Livre, Section Professeurs, n.d.
Fr Reffe Papers
Blackrock Prospectus File 1905–6
Student Accounts at Blackrock College 1867–1903 (C–K)

Stonyhurst College Archives
E/I/II   School Societies
F/II/7/7   Prospectus Files
F/VI/22   Private Diary of Tom Ullathorne 1847–51
G/2/7/10   Customs and Traditions

Uncatalogued Material
Stonyhurst Biographical Dictionary (Card File)
Rector's Book for Matters Connected with the Interests of the College 1869–93
Stonyhurst College Register 1841–70
Stonyhurst College Register 1870–1927

Clongowes Wood College Archives

Uncatalogued Material
School Rules of Tullabeg
Diary of the Prefect of Studies 1885–7

Oratory School Archives

Uncatalogued Material
School Accounts Ledger 1859–60
School Accounts Ledger 1873–93
Oratory School Society, Members Name Book *c.*1890–1910
Oratory School Society Annual Report 1920

Westminster Diocesan Archives
19/3/93   Conference of Roman Catholic Headmasters 1897
19/4   Printed Reports of the Conferences of Roman Catholic Headmasters 1896–1918

Uncatalogued Material
St Edmund's College Archives

Archives of the Society of the Holy Child Jesus, Oxford

Uncatalogued Material
St Leonards-on-Sea Entrance Ledgers
Unpublished MS of Eugenie Ryan's Life
The St Leonards Chronicler

Manuscripts

National Library of Ireland, Manuscripts (with list number)
33	Bellews of Mountbellew Papers
119	Bonaparte-Wyse Papers
125	Considine Papers
132	Gormanston Papers
90	Louth Papers
77	Mansfield Papers
118	Redmond Papers
156	Sweetman, John A., Papers

Dublin Diocesan Archives (partially catalogued)
DDA/319	Cullen Papers
DDA/2803	Bartholomew Woodlock Papers
DDA/337	MacCabe Papers
DDA/364	Walsh Papers

National Archives of Ireland (with accession number)
1155	Bodkin Papers
1125	Talbot Press/Educational Co. of Ireland Papers
1189	Woulfe-Flanagan Papers

University College Dublin Archives
P150	De Valera Papers
LA 34	Kettle Papers
P/102	O'Rahilly Papers

The National Archives of the UK
HO 73 58/1/21	Clarendon Commission Papers
ED 109	School Inspections 1900–27

Trinity College Dublin Archives
MUN/V/23/6	TCD Entrance Ledger 1847–76
MUN/V/23/7	TCD Entrance Ledger 1877–1910

Printed Primary

Reference Works

Anon., *St. Vincent's College Castleknock: Centenary Record 1835–1935* (Dublin, 1935).

Bateman, John, *The Great Landowners of Great Britain and Ireland* (Leicester, 1971).

Baybut, Stephen, *Pro Patria, Beaumont War Dead* (London, 2005).

Burnand, F. C., *The Catholic Who's Who & Year-Book 1908* (London, 1908).

Constable, C. C. and Francis J. Irwin (eds), *Stonyhurst War Record* (Stonyhurst, 1927).

Corcoran, SJ, Rev. Timothy, *The Clongowes Record 1814–1932* (Dublin, 1936).

De Burgh, U. H. Hussey, *The Landowners of Ireland: An Alphabetical List of the Owners of Estates of 500 Acres or £500 Valuation and Upwards in Ireland* (Dublin, 1874).

Graham, Dom Lucius, *Downside and the War 1914–1919* (London, 1925).

McGuire, James and Quinn, James. *Dictionary of Irish Biography: From the Earliest Times to the Year 2002* (Cambridge: Cambridge University Press, 2009).

Montgomery-Massingberd, Hugh (ed.), *Burke's Irish Family Records* (London, 1976).

Walford, Edward, *County Families of the United Kingdom; or, Royal Manual of the Titled and Untitled Aristocracy of England, Wales, Scotland, and Ireland* (London, 1860, 1899, 1910).

Parliamentary Papers and Reports (chronological order)

Cashel election. Index to the minutes of the evidence taken at the trial of the Cashel election petitions, HC 1868–9 (121), XLIX, 129.

Powis, Earl Edward James Herbert, *Royal Commission of Inquiry into Primary Education* (Ireland), Vol. I., Part II. Containing appendix to the report and also special reports by Royal Commissioners on Model Schools (district and minor), the Central Training Institution, etc., Dublin, and on agricultural schools, HC 1870 [C.6a], XXVIII, Pt II.1.

Intermediate Education (Ireland). [HL] A bill [as amended in committee] intituled an act to promote intermediate education in Ireland. HC 1878, (275), III.

Report of the Intermediate Education Board for Ireland for the Year 1880, HC 1881 [C.29190], XXXIV.19.

Report of the Intermediate Education Board for Ireland for the Year 1886, HC 1887 [C.5032], XXXI.13.

Report of the Intermediate Education Board for Ireland for the Year 1889, HC 1890 [C.6001], XXIX.13.

Palles, Chief Baron Christopher, Intermediate Education (Ireland) Commission, First Report of the Commissioners, HC 1899 [C.9116] [C.9117].

—— Intermediate Education (Ireland) Commission, Final Report of the Commissioners, HC 1899 [C.9511] [C.9512] [C.9513].

Dale, F. H. and T. A. Stephens, Report of His Majesty's Inspectors, Board of Education, on Intermediate Education in Ireland, HC 1905 [2546], XXVIII.

Eardley-Wilmot, Sir John Eardley, Report from the Select Committee on Industries (Ireland), IX.1, House of Commons Papers. H.C. (288) IX. 1.

Newspapers and Popular Journals

Belfast Newsletter
Daily Telegraph
Freeman's Journal (Dublin)
Irish Book-Lover
Irish Independent (Dublin)
Irish Times (Dublin)
Letters and Notices
New Zealand Tablet
The Bristol Mercury and Daily Post
The Irish Catholic (Dublin)
The Leader (Dublin)
The Liverpool Mercury
The Manchester Guardian
The New York Times
The Preston Guardian
The Times (London)
The Wexford Echo

Contemporary Books, Pamphlets, and Memoirs

Ahn, Franz, *Dr. Ahn's First French Reading-book. New edition* (London: 1874).

Almond, Dom Leo, *The History of Ampleforth Abbey from the Foundation of St. Lawrence's at Dieulouard to the Present Time* (London, 1903).

—— *Downside Abbey and School, 1814–1914: Illustrated in Photogravure: With a Short Historical Introduction* (Exeter, 1914).

Anon., *Letters on the Selection of a College for the Education of Irish Boys* (Dublin, 1883).

—— 'Medical News', *British Medical Journal*, 2/4840 (Oct. 1953), 837–9.

—— 'Sir John Nugent', *British Journal of Psychiatry*, 45/189 (Apr. 1899), 431–2.

Arthur, Sir George (ed.), *The Letters of Lord and Lady Wolseley, 1870–1911* (London, 1922).

Austin, Alfred, *The Autobiography of Alfred Austin, Poet Laureate, 1835–1910*, 2 vols. (London, 1911).

Birt, Henry Norbert, Dom, *Downside: The History of St. Gregory's School from its Commencement at Douay to the Present Time* (London, 1902).

Blake, Martin Joseph, *Blake Family Records, 1300 to 1600 (1600–1700)* (London, 1902).

Bodkin, Matthias MacDonnell, *Recollections of an Irish Judge: Press, Bar and Parliament* (London, 1914).

Boyd-Barrett, Edward, *Ex-Jesuit* (Edinburgh, 1931).

Brown, Carleton F. (ed.), *The Stonyhurst Pageants* (Baltimore, 1920).

Browne, Jessie Elizabeth Innes, *Three Daughters of the United Kingdom* (London, 1897).

Butler, Sir William Francis, *Why Not As We Once Were?* (Dublin, 1910).

Butt, Isaac, *The Problem of Irish Education: An Attempt at its Solution* (London, 1875).

Casey, James, *An Essay on Education, Catholic and Mixed. A Poem in Two Parts. By a Catholic Priest* (Dublin, 1867).

Clancarty, Earl, *Ireland: Her Present Condition and What It Might Be* (Dublin, 1864).

Clery, Arthur E., 'Accents: Dublin and Otherwise', *Studies: An Irish Quarterly Review*, 10/40 (Dec. 1921), 545–52.

Coates, C. V., 'Bessels Functions of the Second Order', *The Quarterly Journal of Pure and Applied Mathematics*, 21 (1886), 183–92.

Colum, Mary, *Life and the Dream*, 2nd edn (Dublin, 1966).

Committee of Irish Catholics, *Intermediate and University Education in Ireland* (Dublin, 1872).

Contanseau, Leon, *Guide to French Translation; Being a Selection of Instructive and Entertaining Pieces; with Notes* (London, 1847).

Cullen, Cardinal Paul, *Catholic Education: Report of a Meeting of the Catholics of the Diocese of Dublin, Held at the Cathedral, Marlborough-Street, January 17th, 1872* (Dublin, 1872).

De Stacpoole, Duke, *Irish and Other Memories* (London, 1922).

Devas, Frank, *The History of St. Stanislaus' College, Beaumont: A Record of Fifty Years, 1861–1911* (Old Windsor, 1911).

Devitt, SJ, Fr Michael, 'The Rampart of the Pale', *Journal of the Archaeological Society of County Kildare and Surrounding Districts*, 3 (1899–1902), 284–9.

Doyle, James Warren, *Letters on the State of Education in Ireland; and on Bible Societies. Addressed to a Friend in England* (Dublin, 1824).

Eager, Margaret, *Six Years at the Russian Court* (New York, 1906).

Emly, William Monsell, Lord, 'Intermediate Education in Ireland: An Address', *The Irish Monthly*, 6 (1878), 108–16.

Falkiner, Frederick, 'The Irish Schoolboy Exodus', *The Dublin University Review*, 2 (Dec. 1885), 328–38.

Ffrench, Gregory, 'The Sodality of Our Lady', *The Furrow*, 5/9 (Sep. 1954), 539–48.

FitzGibbon, Gerald, Master in Chancery, *Roman Catholic Priests and National Schools* (Dublin, 1872).

Foster, R. D., 'Promotion by Merit in the Army', *The RUSI Journal*, 70/480 (Feb. 1925).

Gavin, Michael,. *Memoirs of Father P. Gallwey, S.J.* (London, 1913).

Gerard, John, *Oliver Cromwell and his Table, or, Protector versus Rector. An Historical Harmony* (Belfast, 1894).

—— *Stonyhurst College: Its Life Beyond the Seas, 1592–1794 and on English Soil, 1794–1894* (Belfast, 1894).

Godkin, James, *A Hand-book of the Education Question. Education in Ireland: Its History, Institutions, Systems, Statistics, and Progress from the Earliest Times to the Present* (Dublin, 1862).

Gogarty, Oliver St John, *It Isn't this Time of Year at All! An Unpremeditated Autobiography* (London, 1954).

Gruggen, George and Joseph Keating, *Stonyhurst: Its Past History and Life in the Present* (London, 1901).

Gullan, Marjorie, *Speech Training in the School* (London, n.d.).

Heffernan, Patrick, *An Irish Doctor's Memories* (Dublin, 1958).

Hime, Maurice Charles, *Home Education, or Irish versus English Grammar Schools for Irish Boys* (London, 1887).

—— *Intermediate Schools in Ireland* (London, 1887).

—— *Efficiency of Irish Schools and their Superiority to English Schools, as Places of Education for Irish Boys, Proved and Explained* (London, 1889).

Horgan, John J., *Parnell to Pearse, Some Recollections and Reflections* (Dublin, 1948).

Hughes, Thomas, *Tom Brown's Schooldays* (London, 1971).

Ignotus (pseud.), *Beaumont v. Oratory, 1867–1925* (Windsor, 1926).

Inglis, Brian, *Downstart: The Autobiography of Brian Inglis* (London, 1990).

Joyce, James, *A Portrait of the Artist as a Young Man* (Dover, 1994 [1916]).

—— *Ulysses* (Oxford, 1998 [1922]).

Kettle, Thomas M., *The Open Secret of Ireland* (London, 1912).

Laffan, May, 'Convent Boarding-Schools for Young Ladies', *Fraser's Magazine*, 9/54 (Jun. 1874), 778–86.

—— *Hogan M.P. A Novel* (London, 1876).

Lynch, Hannah, *Autobiography of a Child* (Edinburgh, 1899).

—— *French Life in Town and Country*, 2nd edn (New York, 1906).

Meagher, Thomas Francis, Brigadier General, US, *Meagher of the Sword. Speeches of T. F. Meagher in Ireland, 1846–1848*. Ed. Arthur Griffith (Dublin, 1916).

Molloy, Constantine, *The Justice of the Peace for Ireland: A Treatise on the Powers and Duties of Magistrates in Ireland in Cases of Summary Jurisdiction in the Prosecution of Indictable Offenses and in Other Matters* (Dublin, 1890).

O'Brien, Hon. Georgina, *The Reminiscences of the Right Hon. Lord O'Brien of Kilfenora* (London, 1916).

O'Dwyer, Michael Francis. *India as I Knew It, 1885–1925* (London,1925).

—— *The O'Dwyers of Kilnamanagh: The History of an Irish Sept* (Limerick, 2000 [1933]).

O'Faoláin, Sean, 'The Spurious Fenian Tale', *Folklore*, 41/2 (30 Jun. 1930), 154–68.

—— *Vive Moi! An Autobiography* (London, 1965).

O'Malley, Ernie, *On Another Man's Wound* (Dublin, 1979 [1936]).

Pascoe, C. E. (ed.), *Everyday Life at our Public Schools: Sketched by Head Scholars* (London, 1881).

Paul-Dubois, Louis, *Contemporary Ireland... with an introduction by T. M. Kettle*. Ed. Tom Kettle (Dublin, 1908).

Pearse, P. H., *The Murder Machine and Other Essays* (Cork, 1976).

Peter, R. M., *The Origins and Development of Football in Ireland, 1880, with an Introduction by Neal Garnham* (Belfast, 1999 [1880]).

Power, Arthur, *From The Old Waterford House* (Dublin, 1940).

Power, Frank, *Letters From Khartoum* (London, 1885).

Regan, John M., *The Memoirs of John M. Regan: A Catholic Officer in the RIC and RUC, 1909–1948*. Ed. Joost Augusteijn (Dublin, 2007).

Samuels, Arthur, *Early Cricket in Ireland* (Dublin, 1888).

Sheehy, Eugene, *May it Please the Court* (Dublin, 1951).

Sherlock, Rev. Canon, 'The Lattin and Mansfield Families in the Co. Kildare', *Journal of the Archaeological Society of County Kildare and Surrounding Districts*, 3 (1899–1902), 186–90.

Stacpoole, OSB, Alberic, 'The Return of the Roman Catholics to Oxford', *New Blackfriars*, 67/791 (Jul. 2007), 221–32.

Stonyhurst College, *Our Tercentenary... Stonyhurst College* (Clitheroe, 1892).

—— *Souvenir of the Centenary Celebration, Stonyhurst College 1592–1894* (Belfast, 1894).

—— *A Stonyhurst Handbook for Visitors and Others* (Stonyhurst, 1927).

Toksvig, Signe, *Eve's Doctor* (New York, 1937).

Tynan, Katharine, 'Recent Irish Novels', *Studies: An Irish Quarterly*, 32/8 (Dec. 1919), 521–33.

Walsh, William Joseph, Archbishop of Dublin, *Statement of the Chief Grievances of Irish Catholics in the Matter of Education, Primary, Intermediate and University* (Dublin, 1890).

—— *The Irish University Question* (Dublin, 1897).

Whittle, James Lowry, *On Freedom of Education* (Dublin, 1867).

Wynne, Maud, *An Irishman and his Family: Lord Morris of Killanin* (London, 1937).

Wyse, Sir Thomas, *Historical Sketch of the Late Catholic Association of Ireland* (London, 1829).

Yarr, Sir Michael Thomas, *Manual of Military Ophthalmology for the Use of Medical Officers of the Home, Indian, and Colonial Services* (London, 1902).

School Journals

The Ampleforth Journal
The Beaumont Review
The Belvederian
The Blackrock College Annual
The Clongownian
The College Chronicle, Castleknock
The Collegian (St. Malachy's College, Belfast)
The Downside Review
The Oscotian (Oscott)
The Raven (Downside)
The Stonyhurst Magazine

Irish Schoolboy Novels

Bodkin, Matthias MacDonnell, *When Youth Meets Youth* (Dublin, 1920).

Bodkin, SJ, Matthias, *Floodtide: A Story of Cluan College* (Dublin, 1927).

Bullock, Shan F., *The Cubs: The Story of a Friendship* (London, 1920).

Elrington, Helen, *Schoolboy Outlaws* (London, 1904).

FitzGerald, M. J., *The Making of Jim O'Neill: A Story of Seminary Life* (Dublin, 1910).

FitzGerald, Percy Hetherington, *Schooldays at Saxonhurst* (Edinburgh, 1867).

—— *Stonyhurst Memories; or, Six Years at School* (London, 1895).

Gaffney, Michael Henry, *The Boys of Ben Eadar: A School Story of 1950* (Dublin, 1930).

Hackett, Francis, *The Green Lion* (New York, 1936).

Kelly, William Patrick, *Schoolboys Three: Life at a Catholic School*. 4th edn (Dublin, 1923).

McGrath, Fergal, *The Last Lap* (New York, 1925).

O'Brien, Willam, *When We Were Boys. A Novel* (London, 1890).

O'Duffy, Eimar Ultan, *The Wasted Island* (Dublin, 1920).

Pawle, Kathleen, *We in Captivity. A Novel* (New York, 1936).

Sheehan, Patrick Augustine, *Geoffrey Austin: Student. A Tale* (Dublin, 1895).

—— *The Triumph of Failure* (New York, 1976).

ONLINE RESOURCES

1911 Census (Ireland)

Archives of the Pontifical Irish College Rome

Dictionary of Irish Biography

NUI Galway Database of Landed Estates

Oxford Dictionary of National Biography

SECONDARY READING

Ackroyd, Marcus et al. (eds), *Advancing with the Army: Medicine, the Professions, and Social Mobility in the British Isles, 1790–1850* (Oxford, 2006).

Airasian, Peter W. et al., 'Payment by Results: An Analysis of a Nineteenth Century Performance-Contracting Programme', *The Irish Journal of Education/Iris Eireannach an Oideachais*, 21/2 (Winter 1987), 80–91.

Akenson, Donald Harman, *The Irish Education Experiment: The National System of Education in the Nineteenth Century* (London, 1970).

—— *Education and Enmity: The Control of Schooling in Northern Ireland, 1920–50* (Newton Abbot, 1973).

—— *A Mirror to Kathleen's Face: Education in Independent Ireland, 1922–1960* (London, 1975).

Albisetti, James C., 'Philanthropy for the Middle Class: Vocational Education for Girls and Young Women in Mid-Victorian Europe', *History of Education*, 41/3 (May 2012), 287–301.

Allanson, Athanasius, *Biography of the English Benedictines*. Saint Laurence Papers 4 (Ampleforth Abbey, 1999).

Anderson, R. D., 'Secondary Education in Mid Nineteenth-century France: Some Social Aspects', *Past & Present*, 53/1 (1971), 121–46.

—— *Education and Opportunity in Victorian Scotland: Schools & Universities* (Edinburgh, 1989).

—— 'The Idea of the Secondary School in Nineteenth-century Europe', *Paedagogica Historica*, 40/1–2 (2004), 93–106.

Andrews, C. S., *Dublin Made Me* (Dublin, 2001 [1979]).

Archer, Margaret Scott and Michalina Vaughan, *Social Conflict and Educational Change in England and France 1789–1848* (Cambridge, 1971).

Arnstein, Walter L., *Protestant versus Catholic in Mid-Victorian Britain: Mr Newdegate and the Nuns* (Colombia, 1982).

Atkinson, Norman, *Irish Education: A History of Educational Institutions* (Dublin, 1969).

Auchmuty James Johnston, *Irish Education: A Historical Survey* (Dublin, 1937).

—— *Sir Thomas Wyse, 1791–1862* (London, 1939).

Bamford, Thomas W., *Public School Data: A Compilation of Data on Public and Related Schools (Boys) Mainly from 1866*. Aids to Research in Education No. 2 (Hull, 1974).

Barnard, Toby, *A New Anatomy of Ireland: The Irish Protestants 1649–1770* (New Haven, CT., 2003).

Barnes, A. S., *The Catholic Schools of England* (London, 1926).

Basset, SJ, Bernard, *The English Jesuits: From Campion to Martindale* (London, 1967).

Bayly, C. A. et al., 'AHR Conversation: On Transnational History', *The American Historical Review*, 111/5 (Dec. 2006), 1441–64.

Beck, Archbishop George Andrew, *The English Catholics, 1850–1950: Essays to Commemorate the Centenary of the Restoration of the Hierarchy of England and Wales* (Glasgow, 1950).

Bell, Pat, *Long Shies and Slow Twisters, 150 Years of Cricket in Kildare* (Kildare, 1993).

Bellenger, Dom Aidan, 'The English Benedictines: The Search for a Monastic Identity', Judith Loades (ed.), *Monastic Studies: The Continuity of Tradition* (Bangor: Headstart, 1991).

Bence-Jones, Mark, *The Remarkable Irish* (New York, 1966).

Bergin, John, 'The Irish Catholic Interest at the London Inns of Court, 1674–1800', *Eighteenth-Century Ireland: Iris an dá chultúr*, 24 (2009), 36–61.

Bernard, Agnes et al., *L'enseignement des elites en Europe centrale: 19–20e siècles* (Krakow, 1999).

Bew, Paul, *Ireland: The Politics of Enmity 1789–2006* (Oxford, 2007).

Bhreathnach, Edel, Joseph MacMahon, and John McCafferty, *The Irish Franciscans, 1534–1990* (Dublin, 2009).

Birch, Rev. Peter. *St. Kieran's College Kilkenny* (Dublin: MH Gill and Son, 1951).

Birmingham, George A. *An Irishman Looks at his World* (London: Hodder and Stoughton, 1919).

Bishop, Erin (ed.), *My Darling Danny: Letters from Mary O'Connell to her Son Daniel, 1830–1832* (Cork, 1999).

Bishop, Thomas James Henderson, *Winchester and the Public School Elite: A Statistical Analysis*. Ed. Rupert Wilkinson (London, 1967).

Bonsall, Penny, *The Irish RMs: The Resident Magistrates in the British Administration of Ireland* (Dublin, 1997).

Bossy, John, *The English Catholic Community, 1570–1850* (London, 1975).

Bourdieu, Pierre, *Language and Symbolic Power*. Ed. John Brookshire Thompson (Cambridge, 1991).

—— *The State Nobility: Elite Schools in the Field of Power* (Stanford, CA, 1996).

Bowman, John and Ronan O'Donoghue, *Portraits: Belvedere College, Dublin, 1832–1982* (Dublin, 1982).

Boyd, Kelly, *Manliness and the Boys' Story Paper in Britain: A Cultural History, 1855–1940* (Basingstoke, 2003).

Bradley, SJ, Bruce, *James Joyce's Schooldays* (Dublin, 1982).

Bradley, Ian and Brian Simon (eds), *The Victorian Public School: Studies in the Development of an Educational Institution* (Dublin, 1975).

Bratton, Jacqueline Susan, *The Impact of Victorian Children's Fiction* (London, 1981).

Breashears, Caroline, 'The Female Appeal Memoir: Genre and Female Literary Tradition in Eighteenth-century England', *Modern Philology*, 107/4 (2010), 607–31.

Breen, Richard, *Social Mobility and Social Class in Ireland*. Ed. Christopher T. Whelan (Dublin, 1996).

Breen, Richard and Christopher T. Whelan, 'Social Class, Class Origins and Political Partisanship in the Republic of Ireland', *European Journal of Political Research*, 26/2 (Sep. 1994), 117–33.

Brenan, Martin, *Schools of Kildare and Leighlin A.D. 1775–1835* (Dublin, 1935).

Brillman, M. L., 'A Crucial Administrative Interlude: Sir Antony MacDonnell's Return to Ireland, 1902–04', *New Hibernia Review*, 9/2 (2005), 65–83.

Broadley, Martin John (ed.), *Bishop Herbert Vaughan and the Jesuits: Education and Authority*. Catholic Records Society Series 82 (Woodbridge, 2010).

Brockliss, L. W. B. and Patrick Ferté, 'Prosopography of Irish Clerics in the Universities of Paris and Toulouse, 1573–1792', *Archivium Hibernicum*, 58 (2004), 7–166.

Brooke, P. F., *Daly's Club and the Kildare St Club, Dublin* (Dublin, 1930).

Browne, Martin and Colmán N. Ó Clabaigh, *The Irish Benedictines: A History*. Ed. Martin Browne, OSB and Colmán N. Ó Clabaigh (Blackrock, Dublin, 2005).

Buckley, Jerome Hamilton, *Season of Youth: The Bildungsroman from Dickens to Golding* (Cambridge, MA, 1974).

Bush, M. L., *Social Orders & Social Classes in Europe since 1500: Studies in Social Stratification* (London, 1992).

Butler, Sir William Francis, *Sir William Butler: An Autobiography* (London, 1911).

Byrne, John Francis, *Silent Years* (New York, 1953).

Cadogan, Mary, *You're a Brick, Angela!: A New Look at Girls' Fiction from 1839 to 1975*. Ed. Patricia Craig (London, 1976).

Cadogan, Tim and Jeremiah Falvey, *A Biographical Dictionary of Cork* (Dublin, 2006).

Campbell, Fergus, *Land and Revolution: Nationalist Politics in the West of Ireland 1891–1921* (Oxford, 2005).

—— 'Who Ruled Ireland? The Irish Administration 1879–1914', *The Historical Journal*, 50/3 (2007), 623–44.

—— *The Irish Establishment 1879–1914* (Oxford, 2009).

Candy, Catherine, *Priestly Fictions: Popular Irish Novelists of the Early 20th Century* (Dublin, 1995).

Capparini, Bernardo Rodriguez, 'A Catholic Public School in the Making: Beaumont College during the Rectorate of the Reverend Joseph M. Bampton, S.J. (1901–1908)', *Paedagogica Historica*, 39/6 (Dec. 2003), 737–57.

—— 'Alumnos Españoles en el Internado Jesuita de Beaumont (Old Windsor, Inglaterra), 1861–1868', *Archivum Historicum Societatis Iesu*, 76/151 (Jan.–Jun. 2007), 3–38.

Castle, Gregory, *Reading the Modernist Bildungsroman* (Gainesville, FL, 2006).

Chadwick, Hubert, *St. Omers to Stonyhurst: A History of Two Centuries* (London, 1962).

Chamberlain, OSB, Leo, 'A Catholic Eton? Newman's Oratory School, Paul Shrimpton's Book and Catholic Education Then and Now', *Logos: A Journal of Catholic Thought and Culture*, 11/3 (Summer 2008), 68–85.

Chambers, Liam, 'Irish Fondations and Boursiers in Early Modern Paris, 1682–1793', *Irish Economic and Social History*, 35 (2008), 1–22.

—— '"Une Seconde Patrie": The Irish College, Paris, in the Eighteenth and Nineteenth Centuries', in Susanne Lachenicht and Kirsten Heinsohn (eds), *Diaspora Identities: Exile, Nationalism and Cosmopolitanism in Past and Present* (Frankfurt, 2009).

Champ, Judith F. (ed.), *Oscott College, 1838–1988: A Volume of Commemorative Essays* (Oscott, 1988).

Charle, Christophe, 'Elite Formation in Late Nineteenth Century: France Compared to Britain and Germany', *Historical Social Research*, 33/2 (2008), 249–61.

Clarke, Joe, *Christopher Dillon Bellew and his Galway Estates, 1763–1826* (Dublin, 2003).

Coakley, D. J., *Cork, Its Trade & Commerce: Official Handbook of the Cork Incorporated Chamber of Commerce & Shipping: With Classified Trade Indices in English, French & Spanish* (Cork, 1919).

Cohan, A. S., *The Irish Political Elite* (Dublin, 1972).

Coldrey, Barry M., *Faith and Fatherland: The Christian Brothers and the Development of Irish Nationalism, 1838–1921* (Dublin, 1988).

Coleman, Michael C., *American Indians, the Irish, and Government Schooling* (Lincoln, US, 2007).

Collins, Arian E., *The Sherlocks of Ireland and Wales* (San Diego, 2008).

Columb, Frank, *The Shooting of More O'Ferrall* (Cambridge, 1997).

Comyn, Sir James, *Irish at Law: A Selection of Famous and Unusual Cases* (London, 1981).

—— *Summing It Up: Memoirs of an Irishman at the English Bar* (Dublin, 1991).

Condon, Jeanette, 'The Patriotic Children's Treat: Irish Nationalism and Children's Culture at the Twilight of Empire', *Irish Studies Review*, 8/2 (Aug. 2000), 167–78.

Conway, Stephen, *Britain, Ireland and Continental Europe in the Eighteenth Century* (Oxford, 2011).

Cook, Scott B., 'The Irish Raj: Social Origins and Careers of Irishmen in the Indian Civil Service, 1855–1914', *Journal of Social History*, 20/3 (Spring 1987), 507–29.

—— *Imperial Affinities: Nineteenth Century Analogies and Exchanges between India and Ireland* (London, 1993).

Coolahan, John, *Irish Education: Its History and Structure* (Dublin, 1981).

—— 'The Daring First Decade of the National Board of Education 1831–1841', *Irish Journal of Education*, 17/1 (Summer 1983), 33–54.

—— *Ireland's School Inspectorate, 1831–2008* (Dublin, 2009).

Cooper, Bryan, *The Tenth Irish Division in Gallipoli* (Blackrock, 1993).

Costello, Con, *A Class Apart: The Gentry Families of County Kildare* (Dublin, 2005).

Costello, Peter, *Clongowes Wood: The History of Clongowes Wood College, 1814–1989* (Dublin, 1989).

Coyne, Kevin, Kenelm Gow, Art Ó Súilleabháin (eds), *Moores of Moore Hall* (Carnacon, 1989).

Cramer, Anselm, *Ampleforth: The Story of St Laurence's Abbey and College*. Saint Laurence Papers 5 (York, 2001).

Cramer, Anselm (ed.), *The Belmont Clothing Book: English Benedictine Novices, 1860–1920*. Saint Laurence Papers 6 (York, 2003).

Crosbie, Barry, *Irish Imperial Networks: Migration, Social Communication and Exchange in Nineteenth-century India* (Cambridge, 2012)

Cullen, Bob, *Thomas L. Synott: The Career of a Dublin Catholic*. Maynooth Studies in Local History Series, 14 (Dublin, 1997).

Cullen, Louis M., 'Catholic Social Classes under the Penal Laws', in T. P. Power and Kevin Whelan (eds), *Endurance and Emergence: Catholics in Ireland in the Eighteenth Century* (Dublin, 1990).

—— 'Merriman in a World of Schoolmasters', *Eighteenth-century Ireland*, 26 (2011), 80–94.

Curtis, Stephan, 'Swedish in Name Only: The International Education of Nineteenth-century Swedish Medical Students and Practitioners', *History of Science*, 50/3 (Sep. 2012), 257–88.

D'Alton, Ian, 'Educating for Ireland? The Urban Protestant Elite and the Early Years of Cork Grammar School, 1880–1914', *Éire-Ireland*, 46/3–4, (Fall/Winter 2011), 201–66.

D'Arcy, Fergus A., *Terenure College 1860–1910* (Dublin, 2009).

Dawson, Carrie, ' "The Slaughterman of Wagga Wagga": Imposture, National Identity, and the Tichborne Affair', *Australian Literary Studies*, 21/4 (Oct. 2004), 1–13.

De Bellaigue, Christina, *Educating Women: Schooling and Identity in England and France 1800–1867* (Oxford, 2007).

Delaney, Enda, 'Our Island Story? Towards a Transnational History of Late Modern Ireland', *Irish Historical Studies*, 37/148 (Nov. 2011), 599–621.

Delaney, V. T. H., *The Administration of Justice in Ireland*. Ed. Charles Lysaght (Dublin: Institute of Public Administration, 1982).

Dickson, David, 'Jacobitism in Eighteenth-century Ireland: A Munster Perspective', *Eire-Ireland*, 39 (Fall/Winter 2004), 38–99.

—— *Old World Colony: Cork and South Munster 1630–1830* (Cork, 2005).

Dickson, David, Justyna Pyz, and Christopher Shepard (eds), *Irish Classrooms and the British Empire: Imperial Contexts in the Origins of Modern Education* (Dublin, 2012).

Donnelly, James S., *The Land and the People of Nineteenth-century Cork: The Rural Economy and Land Question* (London, 1975).

Dooley, Terence, *The Decline of the Big House in Ireland: A Study of Irish Landed Families 1860–1960* (Dublin, 2001).

—— *Iniskeen, 1912–1918: The Political Conversion of Bernard O'Rourke*. Maynooth Studies in Local History Series, 56 (Dublin, 2004).

—— '*The Land for the People*': Politics and the Land Question in Independent Ireland, 1923–73 (Dublin, 2004).

Dowling, P. J., *A History of Irish Education: A Study in Conflicting Loyalties* (Cork, 1971).

Doyle, Sir Arthur Conan, *Memories and Adventures* (Oxford, 1989 [1924]).

Duff, Patrick and Gerard Moran, *To and from Ireland: Planned Migration Schemes c.1600–2000* (Dublin, 2004).

Duman, Daniel, 'Pathway to Professionalism: The English Bar in the Eighteenth and Nineteenth Centuries', *Journal of Social History*, 13/4 (Summer 1980), 615–28.

Elliott, Marianne, *The Catholics of Ulster: A History* (London, 2000).

—— *When God Took Sides: Religion and Identity in Ireland—Unfinished History* (Oxford, 2009).

Elwes, Columba Cary and Abbot Justin McCann, *Ampleforth and Its Origins* (London, 1952).

Enright, Aidan, 'Catholic Elites and the Irish University Question, 1860–80: European Solutions for an Irish Dilemma', in Brian Heffernan (ed.), *Life on the Fringe: Ireland and Europe 1800–1922* (Dublin, 2012).

Evennett, Henry Outram, *The Catholic Schools of England and Wales* (Cambridge, 1944).

Fagan, Patrick, *Catholics in a Protestant Country: The Papist Constituency in Eighteenth-century Dublin* (Dublin, 1998).

Farmar, Tony, *Privileged Lives: A Social History of Middle-class Ireland, 1882–1989* (Dublin, 2010).

Farragher, Sean P., *Père Leman 1826–1880: Educator and Missionary Founder of Blackrock College* (Dublin, 1988).

Farragher, Sean P. and Annraoi Wyer (eds), *Blackrock College 1860–1995* (Dublin, 1995).

Farrell, Valentine, *Not So Much To One Side* (Moynalty, 1984).

Farren, Sean, *The Politics of Irish Education 1920–65* (Belfast, 1995).

Feheney, J. M., *Catholic Education in Trinidad in the Nineteenth Century* (Dublin, 2001).

Feingold, William L., 'The Tenant's Movement to Capture the Irish Poor Law Boards, 1877–1886', *Albion: A Quarterly Journal Concerned with British Studies*, 7/3 (1975), 216–31.

Fenning, OP, Hugh, 'The Journey of James Lyons from Rome to Sligo, 1763–65', *Collectanea Hibernica*, 11 (1968), 91–110.

—— 'The Parish Clergy of Tuam', *Collectanea Hibernica*, 39/40 (1998), 155–75.

—— 'Irish Dominicans at Lisbon before 1700: A Biographical Register', *Collectanea Hibernica*, 42, (2000), 27–65.

—— 'Irish Dominicans at Louvain before 1700: A Biographical Register', *Collectanea Hibernica*, 43, (2001), 112–60.

Ferriter, Diarmaid, *The Transformation of Ireland 1900–2000* (London, 2004).

Fielding, Steven J., *Class and Ethnicity: Irish Catholics in England, 1880–1939* (Buckingham, 1993).

Fingall, Countess Elizabeth Mary, *Seventy Years Young: Memories of Countess Fingall as Told to Pamela Hinkson*. 2nd edn (Dublin: 1991).

Finnegan, Frances, *Poverty and Prejudice: A Study of Irish Immigrants in York, 1840–1875* (Cork, 1982).

Fitzpatrick, David, *Irish Emigration, 1801–1921* (Dublin, 1984).

Flanagan, Kieran, 'The Shaping of Irish Anglican Secondary Schools, 1854–1878', *History of Education*, 13/1 (1984), 27–43.

Fleming, John and Seán O'Grady, *St Munchin's College Limerick 1796–1996* (Limerick, 1996).

Flower, Raymond, *Oundle and the English Public School* (London, 1989).

Fogarty, L., *James Fintan Lalor, Patriot & Political Essayist 1807–1849* (Dublin, 1919).

Foster, John Wilson, 'Natural History in Modern Irish Culture', in Peter J. Bowler and Nicholas Whyte (eds), *Science and Society in Ireland: The Social Context of Science and Technology, 1800–1950* (Belfast, 1997).

—— *Irish Novels, 1890–1940: New Bearings in Culture and Fiction* (Oxford, 2008).

Foster, R. F., 'To the Northern Counties Station: Lord Randolph Churchill and the Prelude to the Orange Card', in F. S. L. Lyons and R. A. J. Hawkins (eds), *Ireland Under the Union: Varieties of Tension: Essays in Honour of T. W. Moody* (Oxford, 1980).

—— *Modern Ireland 1600–1972* (London, 1989).

Gallagher, Frank, *The Indivisible Island: The History of the Partition of Ireland* (Westport, CT, 1974 [1957]).

Garnham, Neal, *Association Football in Pre-partition Ireland* (Belfast, 2004).

Garvin, Tom, *1922: The Birth of Irish Democracy* (Dublin, 2005).

—— *The Evolution of Irish Nationalist Politics* (Dublin, 2005).

—— *Nationalist Revolutionaries in Ireland 1858–1928* (Dublin, 2005).

Genet-Rouffiac, Nathalie, *Le Grand Exil: les Jacobites en France, 1688–1715* (Paris, 2007).

Giddens, Anthony, *Modernity and Self-Identity: Self and Society in the Late Modern Age* (Cambridge, 1991).

Gilley, Sheridan (ed.), *Victorian Churches and Churchmen: Essays Presented to Vincent Alan McClelland* (Suffolk, 2005).

Glickman, Gabriel, *The English Catholic Community, 1688–1745: Politics, Culture and Ideology* (Suffolk, 2009).

Gough, General Sir Hubert, *Soldiering On: Being the Memoirs of General Sir Hubert Gough* (London, 1954).

Greaney, Vincent and Thomas Kellaghan, *Equality of Opportunity in Irish School: A Longitudinal Study of 500 Students* (Dublin, 1984).

Green, Bernard, *The English Benedictine Congregation: A Short History* (London, 1980).

Green, Roger Lancelyn, *Kipling and the Children* (London, 1965).

Grogan, Geraldine, 'O'Connell and German Catholicism during the Kulturkampf', *Studies: An Irish Quarterly Review*, 91/362 (Summer 2002), 167–73.

Guilday, Peter, *The English Catholic Refugees on the Continent 1558–1795* (London, 1914).

Guinnane, Timothy, *The Vanishing Irish: Households, Migration and the Rural Economy in Ireland 1850–1922* (Princeton, NJ, 2007).

Gulay, Erol N., 'The Gülen Phenomenon: A Neo-Sufi Challenge to Turkey's Rival Elite?', *Middle East Critique*, 16/1 (Spring 2007), 37–61.

Hannon, Damien F. and Christopher T. Whelan, 'Class Inequalities in Educational Attainment among the Adult Population in the Republic of Ireland', *The Economic and Social Review*, 30/3 (Jul. 1999), 285–307.

Harford, Judith and Tom O'Donoghue, 'The Movement for the Higher Education of Women in Ireland: Gender Equality or Denominational Rivalry?', in *History of Education*, 34/5 (Apr. 2005), 473–92.

—— 'A Comparative History of Church–State Relations in Irish Education', *Comparative Education Review*, 55/3 (Aug. 2011), 315–41.

Harford, Judith, Deirdre Raftery, and Susan M. Parkes, 'Mapping the Terrain of Female Education in Ireland, 1830–1910', *Gender and Education*, 22/5 (Nov. 2010), 565–78.

Harrigan, Patrick J., *Mobility, Elites, and Education in French Society of the Second Empire* (Ontario, 1980).

Henderson, Andrew, *The Stone Phoenix: Stonyhurst College, 1794–1894* (Worthing, 1986).

Hewitson, Anthony, *Stonyhurst College, Present and Past* (Preston, 1878).

Hibbert, Christopher, *No Ordinary Place: Radley College and the Public School System 1847–1997* (London, 1997).

Hickman, Mary J., 'Integration or Separation? The Education of the Irish in Britain in Roman Catholic Voluntary-Aided Schools', *British Journal of Sociology of Education*, 14/3 (1993), 285–300.

Hodgetts, M. and Vincent Alan McClelland (eds), *From Without the Flaminian Gate: 150 Years of Roman Catholicism in England and Wales 1850–2000* (London, 1999).

Honey, John Raymond de Symons, *Tom Brown's Universe: The Development of the Victorian Public School* (London, 1977).

—— *Does Accent Matter? The Pygmalion Factor*. 2nd edn (London, 1991).

Hoppen, K. Theodore, 'Landlords, Society and Electoral Politics in Mid-nineteenth-century Ireland', *Past and Present*, 75 (May 1977), 62–93.

—— *Elections, Politics and Society in Ireland, 1832–1885* (Oxford, 1984).

Hout, Michael, *Following in Father's Footsteps: Social Mobility in Ireland* (Cambridge, MA, 1989).

Howe, Stephen, *Ireland and Empire: Colonial Legacies in Irish History and Culture* (Oxford, 2000).

Huessler, Robert, *Yesterday's Rulers: The Making of the British Colonial Service* (Syracuse, 1963).

Hutchinson, John, *The Dynamics of Cultural Nationalism: The Gaelic Revival and the Creation of the Irish Nation State* (London, 1987).

Hyland, Áine, 'The Treasury and Irish Education: 1850–1922: The Myth and the Reality', *Irish Educational Studies*, 3/2 (1983), 57–82.

—— *Entry to Higher Education in Ireland in the 21st Century* (Dublin, 2011).

Iriye, Akira and Pierre-Yves Saunier (eds), *The Palgrave Dictionary of Transnational History* (Basingstoke, 2009).

Jackson, Patrick Wyse and Ninian Faulkner, *A Portrait of St Columba's College 1843–1993* (Dublin, 1993).

Jæger, Mads Meier, 'Equal Access but Unequal Outcomes: Cultural Capital and Educational Choice in a Meritocratic Society', *Social Forces*, 87/4 (2009), 1943–71.

James, Lawrence, *The Middle Class: A History* (London, 2006).

Jeffery, Keith, *Ireland and the Great War* (Cambridge, 2000).

—— *Field Marshal Sir Henry Wilson: An Irish Soldier* (Oxford, 2006).

Jonas, Raymond, *France and the Cult of the Sacred Heart: An Epic Tale for Modern Times* (Berkeley, CA, 2000).

Karabel, Jerome, *The Chosen: The Hidden History of Admission and Exclusion at Harvard, Yale, and Princeton* (New York, 2006).

Kealy, OP, Maire M., *Dominican Education in Ireland 1820–1930* (Dublin, 2007).

Kehoe, S. Karly, *Creating a Scottish Church: Catholicism, Gender and Ethnicity in Nineteenth-century Scotland* (Manchester, 2010).

Keogh, Dáire, *Edmund Rice and the First Christian Brothers* (Dublin, 2008).

Kenny, Kevin (ed.), *Ireland and the British Empire* (Oxford, 2004).

Kerr, Donal A., *Peel, Priests and Politics: Sir Robert Peel's Administration and the Roman Catholic Church in Ireland, 1841–1846* (Oxford, 1982).

Kiberd, Declan, *Inventing Ireland* (London, 1995).

Kidd, Colin, 'Sentiment, Race, and Revival: Scottish Identities After the Enlightenment', in L. Brockliss and D. Eastwood (eds) *A Union of Multiple Identities: The British Isles, c.1750–c.1850* (Manchester, 1997).

Kilfeather, Siobhán, 'Oliver Plunkett's Head', *Textual Practice*, 16/2 (2002), 229–48.

Kirby, Henry L., *The Seven V.C.s of Stonyhurst* (Blackburn, 1987).

Kirby, Peadar, 'Civil Society, Social Movements and the Irish State', *Irish Journal of Sociology*, 18/2 (2010), 1–21.

Knowles, David, *The Benedictines* (London, 1929).

Knowles, David (ed.), *Great Historical Enterprises: Problems in Monastic History* (Londons, 1963).

Knox, Andrea, ' "Women of the Wild Geese": Irish Women, Exile and Identity in Spain, 1750–1775', *Immigrants & Minorities*, 23/2–3 (Jul.–Nov. 2005), 143–59.

Kollar, Rene M., 'Foreign and Catholic: A Plea to Protestant Parents on the Dangers of Convent Education in Victorian England', *History Of Education*, 31/4 (Jul. 2002), 335–50.

Laheen, Kevin A., 'Further Letters of Robert Haly, S. J., 1810–29, in the Irish Jesuit Archives', *Collectanea Hibernica*, 44/45 (2002/2003), 173–213.

—— *The Jesuits in Tullabeg: The Early Years from Mission 1810 to Province 1860* (Limerick, 2007).

—— *The Jesuits in Tullabeg: A Century of Service, 1814–1914* (Limerick, 2009).

—— *The Jesuits in Tullabeg, 1817–1991: The Final Curtain 1991* (Limerick, 2010).

Lane, Fintan (ed.), *Politics, Society and the Middle Class in Modern Ireland* (Basingstoke, 2010).

Larkin, Emmet, *The Roman Catholic Church and the Emergence of the Modern Irish Political System 1874–1878* (Dublin, 1996).

Lehman, Joseph, *The Model Major-General: A Biography of Field-Marshal Lord Wolseley* (Boston, 1964).

Lennon, Colm (ed.), *Confraternities and Sodalities in Ireland: Charity, Devotion, and Sociability* (Blackrock, 2012).

Levi, Peter, *Beaumont 1861–1961* (London, 1961).

Lillis, Mercedes, *Two Hundred Years Agrowing: The Story of the Ursulines in Thurles 1787–1987* (Thurles, 1987).

Livesey, James, *Civil Society and Empire: Ireland and Scotland in the Eighteenth-century Atlantic World* (New Haven, CT, 2009).

Logan, John, 'Governesses, Tutors and Parents: Domestic Education in Ireland, 1700–1880', *Irish Educational Studies*, 7/2 (1988), 1–18.

—— 'The Dimensions of Gender in Nineteenth-century Schooling', in Margaret Kelleher and James H. Murphy (eds), *Gender Perspectives in Nineteenth-century Ireland* (Dublin, 1997).

Loughlin, James, *The British Monarchy and Ireland, 1800 to the Present* (Cambridge, 2007).

Lynch-Robinson, Sir Christopher, *The Last of the Irish R.M.s.* (London, 1951).

Lyons, J. B., *The Enigma of Tom Kettle: Irish Patriot, Essayist, Poet, British Soldier 1880–1916* (Dublin, 1983).

Lyons, Francis Stewart Leland, *Culture and Anarchy in Ireland, 1890–1939* (Oxford, 1979).

—— *Ireland Since the Famine*, 11th edn (London, 1989).

—— *Charles Stewart Parnell* (Dublin, 2005).

Mary Ann Lyons and Thomas O'Connor (eds), *Irish Communities in Early-modern Europe* (Dublin, 2006).

—— *Strangers to Citizens: The Irish in Europe, 1600–1800* (Dublin, 2008).

Maas, Ineke and Marco H. D. van Leeuwen, 'Social Mobility in a Dutch Province, Utrecht 1850–1940', *Journal of Social History*, 30/3 (Spring 1997), 619–44.

MacAulay, Thomas Babington, *The Life and Letters of Lord Macaulay*. Ed. George Trevelyan. 10 vols. 3rd edn (New York, 1878), vol. I.

McBride, Ian, *Eighteenth Century Ireland: Isle of Slaves*. New Gill History of Ireland 4 (Dublin, 2009).

McBride, Lawrence W., *The Greening of Dublin Castle: The Transformation of Bureaucratic and Judicial Personnel in Ireland, 1892–1922* (Washington, DC, 1991).

McClelland, Vincent Alan, *English Roman Catholics and Higher Education, 1830–1903* (Oxford, 1973).

—— 'School or Cloister? An Educational Dilemma 1794–1880', *English Benedictine History Commission* (1997).

McClelland, Vincent Alan and Michael Hodgetts (eds), *From Without the Flaminian Gate: 150 Years of Roman Catholicism in England and Wales 1850–2000* (Dublin, 1999).

McConnel, James, *The Irish Parliamentary Party and the Third Home Rule Crisis* (Dublin, 2013).

McDermid, Jane, *The Schooling of Girls in Britain and Ireland 1800–1900* (London, 2012).

McDougall, Roseanne, *Cornelia Connelly's Innovations in Female Education, 1846–1864: Revolutionizing the School Curriculum for Girls* (Lewistown, NY, 2008).

McDowell, R. B., *Ireland in the Age of Imperialism and Revolution 1760–1801* (Oxford, 1979).

—— *Land & Learning, Two Irish Clubs* (Dublin, 1993).

—— *Crisis and Decline: The Fate of the Southern Unionists* (Dublin, 1997).

McElligott, T. J., 'Some Thoughts on Our Educational Discontents', *University Review*, 1/5 (Summer 1955), 27–36.

—— *Secondary Education in Ireland: 1870–1921* (Blackrock, 1981).

McGinley, Rosa, 'Irish Women Religious and their Convent High Schools in Nineteenth Century Australia', *Australasian Catholic Record*, 87/1 (Jan. 2010), 3–19.

McGrath, Charles Ivar, *Ireland and Empire 1692–1770*. Empires in Perspective (London, 2012).

Mack, Edward Clarence, *Public Schools and British Opinion since 1860: The Relationship between Contemporary Ideas and the Evolution of an English Institution* (London, 2003).

McLaughlin, Eugene, 'Ireland: Catholic Corporatism', in A. Cochrane and J. Clarke (eds), *Comparing Welfare States: Britain in International Context* (London, 1993).

McManus, Antonia, *The Irish Hedge School and Its Books, 1695–1831* (Dublin, 2002).

McMillan, James, '"Priest Hits Girl": On the Front Line in the 'War of the Two Frances', in Christopher Clark and Wolfram Kaiser (eds), *Culture Wars: Secular–Catholic Conflict in Nineteenth-century Europe* (Cambridge, 2003).

McRedmond, Louis, *To the Greater Glory: A History of the Irish* (Dublin, 1991).

Mair, Peter, 'Explaining the Absence of Class Politics in Ireland', in J. H. Goldthorpe and C. T. Whelan (eds), *The Development of Industrial Society in Ireland* (Oxford, 1992).

Mangan, J. A., *Athleticism in the Victorian and Edwardian Public School: The Emergence and Consolidation of the Educational Ideology* (Cambridge, 1981).

Mangion, Carmen M., *Contested Identities: Catholic Women Religious in Nineteenth-century England and Wales* (Manchester, 2008).

Marett-Crosby, Anthony, *A School of the Lord's Service: A History of Ampleforth* (London, 2002).

Maume, Patrick, 'Nationalism and Partition: The Political Thought of Arthur Clery', *Irish Historical Studies*, 31/122 (Nov. 1998), 222–40.

—— *The Long Gestation: Irish Nationalist Life 1891–1918* (New York, 1999).

Memmi, Albert, *The Colonizer and the Colonized* (New York, 1965).

Menton, William A., *The Clongowes Union Centenary Chronicle* (Clongowes, 1997).

Mescal, John, *Religion in the Irish System of Education* (Dublin, 1957).

Milburn, Alan, *Unleashing Aspiration: The Final Report of the Panel on Fair Access to the Professions* (London, 2009).

—— *Fair Access to Professional Careers: A Progress Report* (London, 2012).

Miles, Andrew, *Social Mobility in Nineteenth- and Early Twentieth-century England* (London, 1999).

Miller, David W., 'Irish Christianity and Revolution', in Jim Smyth (ed.), *Revolution, Counter-revolution and Union: Ireland in the 1790s* (Cambridge, 2000).

Mitchell, B. R., *European Historical Statistics 1750–1975*. 2nd edn (London, 1981).

Mokyr, Joel, *Why Ireland Starved: A Quantitative and Analytical History of the Irish Economy 1800–1850* (London, 1983).

Money, Tony, *Manly & Muscular Diversions: Public Schools and the Nineteenth-century Sporting Revival* (London, 1997).

Moorehead, Alison, 'The Musée de la Folie: Collecting and Exhibiting Chez les Fous', *Journal of the History of Collections*, 23/1 (2011), 101–26.

Moran, Gerard, 'John Miley and the Crisis at the Irish College, Paris, in the 1850s', *Archivium Hibernicum*, 50 (1996), 113–26.

Moretti, Franco, *The Way of the World: The Bildungsroman in European Culture* (London, 1987).

Morrissey, Thomas J., *Towards a National University: William Delany, 1835–1924: An Era of Initiative in Irish Education* (Dublin, 1983).

—— *As One Sent: Peter Kenney SJ, 1779–1841: His Mission in Ireland and North America* (Dublin, 1996).

—— *Thomas A. Finlay SJ, 1848–1940: Educationalist, Editor, Social Reformer* (Dublin, 2004).

Mugglestone, Lynda, *Talking Proper: The Rise of Accent as Social Symbol*. 2nd edn (Oxford, 2003).

Muir, T. E., *Stonyhurst College 1953–1993* (London, 1992).

Murphy, David, *The Irish Brigades 1685–2006* (Dublin, 2007).

Murphy, James H., *Catholic Fiction and Social Reality in Ireland 1873–1922* (Westport CT, 1997).

—— *Abject Loyalty: Nationalism and Monarchy in Ireland during the Reign of Queen Victoria* (Cork, 2001).

—— 'The Irish Catholics in Science Debate: John Tyndall, Cardinal Cullen and the Uses of Science at Castleknock College in the Nineteenth Century', in Juliana Adelman and Eadaoin Agnew (eds), *Science and Technology in Nineteenth-century Ireland* (Dublin, 2011).

Murphy, James H. (ed.), *Nos Autem: Castleknock College and its Contribution* (Dublin, 1996).

—— *Evangelicals and Catholics in Nineteenth-century Ireland* (Dublin, 2005).

Murphy, Martin, *Saint Oliver Plunkett and Downside* (Stratton on the Fosse (Bath), 1975).

Musgrove, F., 'Middle-class Education and Employment in the Nineteenth Century', *The Economic History Review*, New Series, 12/1 (1959), 99–111.

Napier, Taura, 'The Mosaic "I": Mary Colum and Modern Irish Autobiography', *Irish University Review*, 28/1 (Spring/Summer 1998), 37–55.

Newsome, David, *Godliness & Good Learning: Four Studies on a Victorian Ideal* (London, 1961).

Nic Congáil, Ríona, ' "Fiction, Amusement, Instruction": The Irish Fireside Club and the Educational Ideology of the Gaelic League', *Eire-Ireland*, 44/1–2, (Spring/Summer 2009).

Nilis, Jeroen, 'The Irish College Antwerp', *Clogher Record*, 15/3 (1996), 7–86.

—— 'Irish Students at Leuven University, 1548–1797 (with index)', *Archivium Hibernicum*, 60 (2006–7), 1–304.

Nolan, Patrick, *The Irish Dames of Ypres: Being a History of the Royal Irish Abbey of Ypres. . . and Some Account of Irish Jacobitism, with a Portrait of James II and Stuart Letters Hitherto Unpublished* (Dublin, 1908).

Norman, E. R., *The English Catholic Church in the Nineteenth Century* (Oxford, 1984).

O'Boyle, Lenore, 'The Problem of an Excess of Educated Men in Western Europe, 1800–1850', *The Journal of Modern History*, 42/4 (Dec. 1970), 471–95.

O'Brien, Conor Cruise, *States of Ireland* (London, 1972).

—— *Ancestral Voices: Religion and Nationalism in Ireland* (Dublin, 1994).

O'Brien, John B., *The Catholic Middle Classes in Pre-famine Cork*. The O'Donnell Lecture, 1979 (Dublin, 1980).

O'Brien, Kate. *The Land of Spices*, 2nd edn (London, 1949).

O'Buachalla, Seamas, *Education Policy in Twentieth-century Ireland* (Dublin, 1988).

Ó Catháin, Seán, *Secondary Education in Ireland* (Dublin, 1958).

O'Connell, Patricia, *The Irish College at Alcala de Henares 1649–1785* (Dublin, 1997).

—— *The Irish College at Lisbon, 1590–1834* (Dublin, 2001).

—— *The Irish College at Santiago de Compostela, 1605–1769* (Dublin, 2007).

O'Connell, Philip J, Selina McCoy, and David Clancy, 'Who Went to College? Socio-Economic Inequality in Entry to Higher Education in the Republic of Ireland in 2004', *Higher Education Quarterly*, 60/4 (Oct. 2006).

O'Connor, Anne V., 'Influences Affecting Girls' Secondary Education in Ireland, 1860–1910', *Archivium Hibernicum*, 41 (1986), 83–98.

—— 'The Revolution in Girls Secondary Education in Ireland 1860–1900', in Mary Cullen (ed.), *Girls Don't Do Honours: Irish Women in Education in the 19th and 20th Centuries* (Dublin, 1987), 31–54.

O'Day, Alan, *The English Face of Irish Nationalism: Parnellite Involvement in British Politics, 1880–86* (Dublin, 1977).

O'Donoghue, Tom A., *The Catholic Church and the Secondary School Curriculum in Ireland, 1922–1962* (New York, 1999).

O Drisceoil, Diarmuid and Donal O Drisceoil, *The Murphy's Story: The History of Lady's Well Brewery, Cork* (Cork, 1997).

O'Dwyer, Michael Francis, *India as I Knew It, 1885–1925* (London, 1925).

—— *The O'Dwyers of Kilnamanagh: The History of an Irish Sept* (Limerick, 2000 [1933]).

O'Dwyer, Peter, *The Irish Carmelites (of the Ancient Observance)* (Dublin, 1988).

Ogilvie, Vivian, *The English Public School* (London, 1957).

O'Hara, Valentine, *Esthonia: Past and Present* (Bournemouth, 1922).

O'Hara, Valentine and Nicholas Makeev, *Russia* (London, 1925).

Ohlmeyer, Jane, *Making Ireland English: The Irish Aristocracy in the Seventeenth Century* (New Haven, CT, 2012).

Ó hÓgartaigh, Margaret, *Quiet Revolutionaries: Irish Women in Education, Medicine and Sport, 1861–1964* (Dublin, 2011).

O'Leary, Don, *Catholics and Science: From 'Godless Colleges' to the Celtic Tiger* (Cork, 2012).

O'Leary, Mary Florence Margaret, *Education with a Tradition: An Account of the Educational Work of the Society of the Sacred Heart* (London, 1936).

O'Malley, Ernie, *On Another Man's Wound* (Dublin, 1979 [1936]).

Ombres, OP, Robert, 'Connelly v Connelly (1851): The Trials of A Saint?', *Ecclesiastical Law Journal*, 8/36 (Jan. 2005), 21–31.

O'Neill, Ciaran (ed.), 'The Irish Schoolboy Novel', *Eire-Ireland*, 44/1–2 (2009), 147–68.

—— *Irish Elites in the Nineteenth Century* (Dublin, 2013).

Parkes, Susan M. and Deirdre Raftery, *Female Education in Ireland 1700–1900: Minerva or Madonna?* (Dublin, 2007).

Pašeta, Senia, *Before the Revolution: Nationalism, Social Change and Ireland's Catholic Elite, 1879–1922* (Cork, 1999).

—— 'The Catholic Hierarchy and the Irish University Question, 1880–1908', *History*, 85/278 (Dec. 2002), 268–84.

Paz, Denis G., *The Priesthoods and Apostasies of Pierce Connelly: A Study of Victorian Conversion and Anticatholicism* (Lewiston, NY, 1986).

Percival, Alicia C., *The Origins of the Headmasters' Conference* (London, 1969).

Perry, Nicholas, 'The Irish Landed Class and the British Army, 1850–1950', *War in History* 18/3 (Jul. 2011), 304–32.

Phillips, Peter, 'Replanting Douai in the North of England 1794–1808', *Recusant History*, 29/3 (May 2009), 367–79.

Po-Chia Hsia, R., *The World of Catholic Renewal, 1540–1770*. 2nd edn (Cambridge, 2005).

Prunty, Jacinta, *Margaret Aylward: Lady of Charity, Sister of Faith* (Dublin, 1999).

Quigly, Isabel, *The Heirs of Tom Brown: The English School Story* (London, 1981).

Quinn, Dermot A., *Patronage and Piety: The Politics of English Roman Catholicism* (Basingstoke, 1993).

Raffe, David et al., *Social-class Inequalities in Education in England and Scotland*. Special CES Briefing No. 40 (Edinburgh, 2006).

Rafferty, Oliver P., 'The Jesuit College in Manchester, 1875', *Recusant History*, 20/2 (1990), 291–304.

—— *Catholicism in Ulster 1603–1983: An Interpretative History* (London, 1994).

—— *The Catholic Church and the Protestant State: Nineteenth-century Irish Realities* (Dublin, 2008).

Raftery, Deirdre, 'The Nineteenth-century Governess: Image and Reality', in Bernadette Whelan (ed.), *Women and Paid Work in Ireland, 1500–1930* (Dublin, 2000).

Raftery, Deirdre and Catherine Nowlan-Roebuck. 'Convent Schools and National Education in Nineteenth-century Ireland: Negotiating a Place within a Non-denominational System', *History of Education*, 36/3 (May 2007), 353–65.

Randall, Don, *Kipling's Imperial Boy: Adolescence and Cultural Hybridity* (Basingstoke, 2000).

Reader, W. J., *Professional Men: The Rise of the Professional Class in the Nineteenth Century* (London, 1966).

Resnik, Julia (ed.), *The Production of Educational Knowledge in the Global Era* (Rotterdam, 2008).

Rich, P. J., *Elixir of Empire: The English Public Schools, Ritualism, Freemasonry, and Imperialism* (London, 1989).

Richards, Jeffrey, *Imperialism and Juvenile Literature* (Manchester, 1989).

Ringer, Fritz K., 'The Education of Elites in Modern Europe', *History of Education Quarterly*, 18/2 (Summer 1978), 159–72.

Roach, John, *A History of Secondary Education in England, 1800–1870* (London, 1986).

Roberts, Ian D., *A Harvest of Hope: Jesuit Collegiate Education in England, 1794–1914* (St Louis, MO, 1996).

Robinson, C. N., 'Promotion by Merit in the Navy', *The RUSI Journal*, 71/481 (Feb. 1926), 42–51.

Rogers, Rebecca, *From the Salon to the Schoolroom: Educating Bourgeois Girls in Nineteenth-century France* (Pennsylvania, 2005).

Rothblatt, Sheldon, *The Revolution of the Dons: Cambridge and Society in Victorian England* (London, 1968).

—— *Tradition and Change in English Liberal Education: An Essay in History and Culture* (London, 1976).

Russell, Julian, 'The Last Students at the Scots College, Douai', *The Innes Review*, 58/2 (Autumn 2007), 222–5.

Sagginni, Francesca, 'Memories Beyond the Pale: The Eighteenth-century Actress between Stage and Closet', in *Restoration and Eighteenth-Century Theatre Research*, 19/1 (Summer 2004), 43–63;

Sandgren, Petter, 'The Etons of the Swedish Welfare State: The Transnational Spread of the British "Elite-boarding School" Ideology', Paper Read before the 5th Annual Graduate Conference in European History (GRACEH 2011)—Transfers and Demarcations (Florence, 2011).

Saunders, Peter R., *Social Class and Stratification* (London, 1990).

Saveth, Edward N, 'Education of an Elite', *History of Education Quarterly*, 28/3 (Autumn 1988), 367–86.

Schwarze, Tracy Teets, 'Silencing Stephen: Colonial Pathologies in Victorian Dublin', in *Twentieth Century Literature*, 43/3 (Autumn 1997), 243–63.

Scott, Geoffrey, *Gothic Rage Undone: English Monks in the Age of Enlightenment* (Bath, 1992).

Scott, Geoffrey (ed.), *Douai 1903–2003 Woolhampton: A Centenary History* (Worcester, 2003)

Scott, George, *The R.Cs: A Report on Roman Catholics in Britain Today* (London, 1967).

Scott-Thompson, Gladys, 'The Origin and Growth of the Office of Deputy-Lieutenant' *Transactions of the Royal Historical Society*. Fourth Series, 5 (1922), 150–66.

Seaborne, Malcolm, *The English School: Its Architecture and Organization*. Ed. Roy Lowe (Londo, 1971).

Silvestri, Michael, '"The Sinn Fein of India": Irish Nationalism and the Policing of Revolutionary Terrorism in Bengal', *The Journal of British Studies*, 39/4 (Oct. 2000), 454–86.

Sire, H. J. A., *Gentlemen-Philosophers: Catholic Higher Education at Liège and Stonyhurst 1774–1916* (London, 1988).

Shannon, James P., *Catholic Colonization on the Western Frontier* (New Haven, 1957).

Sheils, William J., *The Churches, Ireland and the Irish* (Oxford, 1989).

Shovlin, Frank, '"Endless Stories about the Distillery": Joyce, Death, and Whiskey', *Joyce Studies Annual* (2007), 134–58.

Shrimpton, Paul, *A Catholic Eton? Newman's Oratory School* (Leominster, 2005).

Silvestri, Michael, *Ireland and India: Nationalism, Empire and Memory.* Cambridge Imperial and Post-Colonial Studies Series (Basingstoke, 2009).

Sisson, Elaine, *Pearse's Patriots: St Enda's and the Cult of Boyhood* (Cork, 2004).

Skyrme, Sir Thomas, *History of the Justices of the Peace* (Chichester, 1991).

Smith, Anthony D., 'The Resurgence of Nationalism? Myth and Memory in the Renewal of Nations'. LSE Centennial Lecture. *The British Journal of Sociology*, 47/4 (Dec 1996), 575–98.

Spacks, Patricia Meyer, *The Adolescent Idea: Myths of Youth and the Adult Imagination* (London, 1982).

Stacpoole, Alberic, 'The Return of the Roman Catholics to Oxford', *New Blackfriars*, 67/791 (Jul. 2007), 221–32.

Stone, Lawrence and Jeanne C. Fawtier Stone, *An Open Elite? England 1540–1880* (Oxford, 1984).

Stray, Christopher, *Classics Transformed: Schools, Universities and Society in England 1830–1960* (Oxford, 1998).

Swords, Liam (ed.), *The Irish-French Connection, 1578–1978* (Paris, 1978).

Taussig, Michael T., *Mimesis and Alterity: A Particular History of the Senses* (London, 1993).

Thompson, Francis Michael Longstreth, *The Rise of Respectable Society: A Social History of Victorian Britain, 1830–1900* (London, 1988).

Tinkel, Tony, *Cardinal Newman's School: 150 Years of the Oratory School Reading* (London, 2009).

Trgovčević-Mitrović, Ljubinka, 'Les Boursiers serbes en France de 1878–1914', *Revue d'Europe Centrale*, 7/1 (1999), 45–57.

Tyrell, Ian, 'Making Nations/Making States: American Historians in the Context of Empire', *The Journal of American History*, 86/3 (Dec. 1999), 1015–44.

Vaughan, W. E., *Landlords and Tenants in Mid-Victorian Ireland* (Oxford, 1994).

—— *Murder Trials in Ireland 1836–1914* (Dublin, 2009).

Wadham, Juliana, *The Case of Cornelia Connelly* (London, 1958).

Wagner, Anne-Catherine, 'L'Internationalisation de la formation des élites: vers une recomposition des classes dirigeantes?', in M. D. Gheorghiu (ed.), *La Mobilité des élites: Reconversions et circulation internationale* (Iasi, 2012).

Walker, Brian Mercer, *Parliamentary Election Results in Ireland, 1801–1922* (Dublin, 1978).

Wallace, Justin, 'Science Teaching in Irish Schools 1860–70', *The Irish Journal of Education*, 6/1 (Summer 1972), 50–64.

Wallace, W. J. R., *Faithful to our Trust: A History of the Erasmus Smith Trust and The High School, Dublin* (Dublin, 2004).

Walsh, Barbara, *Roman Catholic Nuns in England and Wales 1800–1937: A Social History* (Dublin, 2002).

Walsh, Brendan, *The Pedagogy of Protest: The Educational Thought of Patrick H. Pearse* (New York, 2007).

Walsh, Oonagh, *Ireland Abroad: Politics and Professions in the Nineteenth Century* (Dublin, 2003).

Walsh, T. J., *The Irish Continental College Movement: The Colleges at Bordeaux, Toulouse and Lille* (Dublin, 1973).

Walshe, Éibhear, *Ordinary People Dancing: Essays on Kate O'Brien* (Cork, 1993).

—— *Kate O'Brien: A Writing Life* (Dublin, 2004).

Ward, Wilfrid, *The Life and Times of Cardinal Wiseman in Two Volumes* (New York, 1900).

Whelan, Kevin, 'Catholic Mobilisation 1750–1850', in Louis Bergeron and L. M. Cullen (eds), *Culture et pratiques politiques en France et en Irlande XVIe–XVIIIe siècle* (Paris, 1991).

—— *The Tree of Liberty: Radicalism, Catholicism and the Construction of Irish Identity, 1760–1830* (Cork, 1996).

Whelan, Kevin and Daire Keogh (eds), *United Irishmen: Republicanism, Radicalism and Rebellion* (Dublin, 1998).

Whitehead, Maurice, 'A View from the Bridge: The Catholic School', in V. A. McClelland and M. Hodgetts (eds), *From Without the Flaminian Gate: 150 Years of Roman Catholicism in England and Wales 1850–2000* (London, 1999).

—— 'Randal Lythgoe and the Work of the Society of Jesus in Early Victorian England and Wales', in Sheridan Gilley (ed.), *Victorian Churches and Churchmen: Essays Presented to Vincent Alan McClelland* (Suffolk, 2005).

Whyte, J. H., *Church & State in Modern Ireland 1923–1970* (Dublin, 1971).

Whyte, William, 'Building a Public School Community', in *History of Education*, 32/6 (Nov. 2003), 601–26.

Winkle-Wagner, Rachelle. 'Foundations of Educational Inequality: Cultural Capital and Social Reproduction', *ASHE Higher Education Report*, 36/1, (May 2010), 1–17.

Wood, Frederick Thomas, *The Schoolboy in Fiction* (London, 1949).

Worthington, Ian, 'Antecedent Education and Officer Recruitment: The Origins and Early Development of the Public School–Army Relationship', *Military Affairs*, 41/4 (Dec. 1977), 183–9.

Yin, Robert K., *Case Study Research: Design and Methods*. Applied Social Research Methods Series 5 (London, 2003).

Zipes, Jack David, *Fairy Tales and the Art of Subversion: The Classical Genre for Children and the Process of Civilization* (New York, 1991).

Zuckerman, Alan, 'The Concept "Political Elite": Lessons from Mosca and Pareto', *The Journal of Politics*, 39/2 (May 1977), 324–44.

UNPUBLISHED PhD THESES/ARTICLES

Bradley, SJ, Fr Bruce. 'Tullabeg 1818–1860: Towards Maturity'. Unpublished MSS.

Champ, Judith F., 'Assimilation and Separation: The Catholic Revival in Birmingham, *c.*1650–1850'. DPhil, University of Birmingham (1984).

Davis, Marguerite Constance Mary, 'The Upbringing of Children in Ireland 1700–1831 from Visual and Historical Sources'. 2 vols. MLitt, Trinity College Dublin (1992).

Flanagan, Kieran, 'The Rise and Fall of the Celtic Ineligible: Competitive Examinations for the Irish and Indian Civil Services in Relation to the Educational and Occupational and Occupational Structure of Ireland 1853–1921'. Unpublished DPhil, University of Sussex (1978).

Fontana, Velmo F., 'Some Aspects of Roman Catholic Service in the Land Forces of the British Crown, *c.*1750 to *c.*1820'. DPhil, University of Portsmouth (2003).

Galliver, Peter, 'Development of Ampleforth College as an English Public School 1802–1954'. Unpublished DEd, University of Leeds (1999).

Gooch, Leopold, 'From Jacobite to Radical: The Catholics of North East England, 1688–1850'. DPhil, University of Durham (1989).

Hickman, Mary J., 'A Study of the Incorporation of the Irish in Britain with Special Reference to Catholic State Education: Involving a Comparison of the Attitudes of Pupils and Teachers in Selected Secondary Schools in London and Liverpool'. DPhil, University of London (1989).

Hood, Alban, 'From Repatriation to Revival: Continuity and Change in the English Benedictine Congregation, 1795–1850'. PhD, University of Liverpool (2006).

Jordan, Sally Anne, 'Catholic Identity, Ideology and Culture: The Thames Valley Catholic Gentry, from the Restoration to the Relief Acts'. PhD, University of Reading (2002).

Kelly, Mary J., 'Selection and Transmission Processes within the Irish National System of Education: 1831–1900'. DPhil, University of Cambridge (1968).

Lannon, David, 'Catholic Education in the Salford Diocese, 1870–1944'. PhD, University of Hull (2003).

Larkin, Michael L., 'The Influence of External Examinations on Science Teaching in a Nineteenth-century Public School'. Unpublished MEd thesis, University of Manchester (1980).

McCormack, Christopher F., 'The Endowed Schools Commissions 1791–1894, as Mediators of Superior Schooling in Ireland'. PhD, UCD (2010).

Marmion, John P., 'Cornelia Connelly's Work in Education 1848–79'. PhD, University of Manchester (1984).

Morrissey, Thomas J., 'Some Jesuit Contributions to Irish Education: A Study of the Work of Irish Members of the Society of Jesus in Connection with the Irish College at Salamanca (1592 to 1610); Mungret College, Limerick (1881 to 1889); St Stanislaus College, Tullabeg (1818 to 1886); and University College Dublin (1883 to 1909)'. 2 vols. Unpublished PhD, NUI (1973).

Murphy, Richard T., 'Minor Formations: The Irish Bildungsroman, Modernity and Canonical Aesthetics'. Unpublished DPhil, Boston College (2006).

Power, Sean Bernard, 'The Development of Roman Catholic Education in the Nineteenth Century, with Some Reference to the Diocese of Hexham and Newcastle'. Master's thesis, University of Durham (2003).

Quinn, Dermot A., 'English Roman Catholics and Politics in the Second Half of the Nineteenth Century'. DPhil, University of Oxford (1986).

Ridden, Jennifer, 'Making Good Citizens': National Identity, Religion, and Liberalism among the Irish Elite, c.1800–1850'. DPhil, University of London (1998).

Rigney, William J., 'Bartholemew Woodlock and the Catholic University of Ireland 1861–1879'. 2 vols. Unpublished PhD, University College Dublin (1995).

Shrimpton, Paul, 'John Henry Newman and the Oratory School, 1857–72: The Establishment of an English Catholic Public School by Converts from the Oxford Movement'. PhD, University of London (2000).

Whitehead, Maurice, 'The Contribution of the Society of Jesus to Secondary Education in Liverpool: The History of the Development of St. Francis Xavier's College c.1840–1902'. PhD, University of Hull (1984).

Index

Note: Page numbers in *italics* refer to Figures; those in **bold** to Tables.

Printed and bound by CPI Group (UK) Ltd, Croydon, CR0 4YY